Friedrich Max Müller

Chips from a German workshop

Friedrich Max Müller

Chips from a German workshop

ISBN/EAN: 9783742808011

Manufactured in Europe, USA, Canada, Australia, Japa

Cover: Foto ©Andreas Hilbeck / pixelio.de

Manufactured and distributed by brebook publishing software (www.brebook.com)

Friedrich Max Müller

Chips from a German workshop

CHIPS

FROM

A GERMAN WORKSHOP.

BY
F. MAX MÜLLER, M. A.,
FOREIGN MEMBER OF THE FRENCH INSTITUTE, ETC.

VOLUME III.

ESSAYS ON LITERATURE, BIOGRAPHY, AND ANTIQUITIES.

NEW YORK:
CHARLES SCRIBNER AND COMPANY.
1871.

TO

FRANCIS TURNER PALGRAVE,

IN GRATEFUL REMEMBRANCE OF KIND HELP

GIVEN TO ME

IN MY FIRST ATTEMPTS AT WRITING IN ENGLISH,

AND AS A MEMORIAL

OF MANY YEARS OF FAITHFUL FRIENDSHIP.

CONTENTS OF THIRD VOLUME.

I.	German Literature, 1858	1
II.	Old German Love-Songs, 1858	61
III.	Ye Schyppe of Fooles, 1858	62
IV.	Life of Schiller, 1859	74
V.	Wilhelm Müller, 1858	100
VI.	On the Language and Poetry of Schleswig-Holstein, 1864	116
VII.	Joinville, 1858	151
VIII.	The Journal des Savants and the Journal de Trévoux, 1866	192
IX.	Chasot, 1856	200
X.	Shakespeare, 1864	214
XI.	Bacon in Germany, 1857	217
XII.	A German Traveller in England A. D. 1598, 1857 .	232
XIII.	Cornish Antiquities, 1867	238
XIV.	Are there Jews in Cornwall? 1867	287
XV.	The Insulation of St. Michael's Mount, 1867 .	316
XVI.	Bunsen, 1868	342
	Letters from Bunsen to Max Müller in the Years 1848 to 1859	391

L

GERMAN LITERATURE.[1]

There is no country where so much interest is taken in the literature of Germany as in England, and there is no country where the literature of England is so much appreciated as in Germany. Some of our modern classics, whether poets or philosophers, are read by Englishmen with the same attention as their own; and the historians, the novel-writers, and the poets of England have exercised, and continue to exercise, a most powerful and beneficial influence on the people of Germany. In recent times, the literature of the two countries has almost grown into one. Lord Macaulay's History has not only been translated into German, but reprinted at Leipzig in the original; and it is said to have had a larger sale in Germany than the work of any German historian. Baron Humboldt and Baron Bunsen address their writings to the English as much as to the German public. The novels of Dickens and Thackeray are expected with the same

---

[1] This article formed the preface to a collection of extracts published in 1858, under the title of *German Classics*. The extracts are arranged chronologically, and extend from the fourth to the nineteenth century. They are given in the original Gothic, Old High-German, and Middle High-German with translations, while in the more modern portions the difficult words only are explained in notes. A list of the principal works from which the extracts are taken will be found at the end of the article, p. 44.

impatience at Leipzig and Berlin as in London. The two great German classics, Schiller and Goethe, have found their most successful biographers in Carlyle and Lowes; and several works of German scholarship have met with more attentive and thoughtful readers in the colleges of England than in the universities of Germany. Goethe's idea of a world-literature has, to a certain extent, been realized; and the strong feeling of sympathy between the best classes in both countries holds out a hope that, for many years to come, the supremacy of the Teutonic race, not only in Europe, but over all the world, will be maintained in common by the two champions of political freedom and of the liberty of thought, — Protestant England and Protestant Germany.

The interest, however, which Englishmen take in German literature has hitherto been confined almost exclusively to the literature of the last fifty years, and very little is known of those fourteen centuries during which the German language had been growing up and gathering strength for the great triumphs which were achieved by Lessing, Schiller, and Goethe. Nor is this to be wondered at. The number of people in England, who take any interest in the early history of their own literature, is extremely small, and there is as yet no history of English literature worthy of that name. It cannot be expected, therefore, that in England many people will care to read in the original the ancient epic poems of the "Nibelunge" or "Gudrun," or acquire a grammatical knowledge of the Gothic of Ulfilas and the Old High-German of Otfried. Gothic, Old High-German, and Middle High-German are three distinct languages, each possessing its own grammar, each differing from the others and from Modern

German more materially than the Greek of Homer differs from the Greek of Demosthenes. Even in Germany these languages are studied only by professional antiquarians and scholars, and they do not form part of the general system of instruction in public schools and universities. The study of Gothic grammar alone (where we still find a dual in addition to the singular and plural, and where some tenses of the passive are still formed, as in Greek and Latin, without auxiliary verbs), would require as much time as the study of Greek grammar, though it would not offer the key to a literature like that of Greece. Old High-German, again, is as difficult a language to a German as Anglo-Saxon is to an Englishman; and the Middle High-German of the "Nibelunge," of Wolfram, and Walther, nay even of Eckhart and Tauler, is more remote from the language of Goethe than Chaucer is from Tennyson.

But, without acquiring a grammatical knowledge of these ancient languages, there are, I believe, not a few people who wish to know something of the history of German literature. Nor is this, if properly taught, a subject of narrow or merely antiquarian interest. The history of literature reflects and helps us to interpret the political history of a country. It contains, as it were, the confession which every generation, before it passed away, has made to posterity. "Without Literary History," as Lord Bacon says, "the History of the World seemeth to be as the Statue of Polyphemus with his eye out; that part being wanting which doth most shew the spirit and life of the person." From this point of view the historian of literature learns to value what to the critic would seem unmeaning and tedious, and he is loath to miss the works even of mediocre poets, where they throw light on the times in which they lived, and serve to connect the otherwise disjointed productions of men of the highest genius, separated, as these necessarily are, by long intervals in the annals of every country.

Although there exists no literature to reward the student of Gothic, yet every one who cares for the history of Germany and of German thought should know something of Ulfilas, the great Bishop of the Goths, who anticipated the work of Luther by more than a thousand years, and who, at a time when Greek and Latin were the only two respectable and orthodox languages of Europe, dared for the first time to translate the Bible into the vulgar tongue of Barbarians, as if foreseeing with a prophetic eye the destiny of these Teutonic tribes, whose language, after Greek and Latin had died away, was to become the life-spring of the Gospel over the whole civilized world. He ought to know something of those early missionaries and martyrs, most of them sent from Ireland and England to preach the Gospel in the dark forests of Germany, — men like St. Gall (died 638), St. Kilian (died 689), and St. Boniface (died 755), who were not content with felling the sacred oak-trees and baptizing unconverted multitudes, but founded missionary stations, and schools, and monasteries; working hard themselves in order to acquire a knowledge of the language and the character of the people, and drawing up those curious lists of barbarous words, with their no less barbarous equivalents in Latin, which we still possess, though copied by a later hand. He ought to know the gradual progress of Christianity and civilization in Germany, previous to the time of Charlemagne; for we see from the German translations of the Rules of the Ben-

edictine monks, of ancient Latin hymns, the Creeds, the
Lord's Prayer, and portions of the New Testament,
that the good sense of the national clergy had led
them to do what Charlemagne had afterwards to en-
join by repeated Capitularia.[1] It is in the history of
German literature that we learn what Charlemagne
really was. Though claimed as a saint by the Church
of Rome, and styled *Empereur Français* by modern
French historians, Karl was really and truly a German king, proud, no doubt, of his Roman subjects, and
of his title of Emperor, and anxious to give to his uncouth Germans the benefit of Italian and English
teachers, but fondly attached in his heart to his own
mother tongue, to the lays and laws of his fatherland:
feelings displayed in his own attempt to compose a
German grammar, and in his collection of old national
songs, fragments of which may have been preserved to
us in the ballads of Hildebrand and Hadubrand.

After the death of Charlemagne, and under the
reign of the good but weak King Ludwig, the prospects of a national literature in Germany became dark-
ened. In one instance, indeed, the king was the
patron of a German poet; for he encouraged the author of the "Heliand" to write that poem for the benefit of his newly converted countrymen. But he
would hardly have approved of the thoroughly German and almost heathen spirit which pervades that
Saxon epic of the New Testament, and he expressed
his disgust at the old German poems which his great
father had taught him in his youth. The seed, however, which Charlemagne had sown had fallen on

[1] " Ut eamdam homiliam quisque (episcopus) aperte transferre studeat in
rusticam romanam linguam aut theodiscam, quo facilius cuncti possint intel-
ligere quæ dicantur." — Conc. Tur. can. 17. Wackernagel, *Geschichte
der Deutschen Literatur*, § 28.

healthy soil, and grew up even without the sunshine of royal favor. The monastery of Fulda, under Hrabanus Maurus, the pupil of Alcuin, became the seminary of a truly national clergy. Here it was that Otfried, the author of the rhymed "Gospel-book" was brought up. In the mean time, the heterogeneous elements of the Carlovingian Empire broke asunder. Germany, by losing its French and Italian provinces, became Germany once more. Ludwig the German was King of Germany, Hrabanus Maurus Archbishop of Mayence; and the spirit of Charlemagne, Alcuin, and Eginhard was revived at Aachen, Fulda, and many other places, such as St. Gall, Weissenburg, and Corvey, where schools were founded on the model of that of Tours. The translation of the "Harmony of the Gospels," gives us a specimen of the quiet studies of those monasteries, whereas the lay on the victory of Louis III. over the Normans, in 881, reminds us of the dangers that threatened Germany from the West at the same time that the Hungarians began their inroads from the East. The Saxon Emperors had hard battles to fight against these invaders, and there were few places in Germany where the peaceful pursuits of the monasteries and schools could be carried on without interruption. St. Gall is the one bright star in the approaching gloom of the next centuries. Not only was the Bible read, and translated, and commented upon in German at St. Gall, as formerly at Fulda, but Greek and Roman classics were copied and studied for educational purposes. Notker Teutonicus is the great representative of that school, which continued to maintain its reputation for theological and classical learning, and for a careful cultivation of the national language, nearly to the close of the eleventh century. At the court of the Saxon Emperors, though their policy was thoroughly German, there was little taste for German poetry. The Queen of Otto I. was a Lombard, the Queen of Otto II. a Greek lady; and their influence was not favorable to the rude poetry of national bards. If some traces of their work have been preserved to us, we owe it again to the more national taste of the monks of St. Gall and Passau. They translate some of the German epics into Latin verse, such as the poem of the "Nibelunge," of "Walther of Aquitain," and of "Ruodlieb." The first is lost; but the other two have been preserved and published.[1] The stories of the Fox and the Bear, and the other animals, — a branch of poetry so peculiar to Germany, and epic rather than didactic in its origin, — attracted the attention of the monks; and it is owing again to their Latin translations that the existence of this curious style of poetry can be traced back so far as the tenth century.[2] As these poems are written in Latin, they could not find a place in a German reading-book; but they, as well as the unduly suspected Latin plays of the nun Hrosvitha, throw much light on the state of German civilization during the tenth and eleventh centuries.

The eleventh century presents almost an entire blank in the history of literature. Under the Frankish or Salic dynasty, Germany had either to defend herself against the inroads of Hungarian and Slavonic armies, or it was the battle-field of violent feuds between the Emperors and their vassals. The second half of that century was filled with the struggles be-

[1] *Lateinische Gedichte des X. und XI. Jahrhunderts*, von J. Grimm und A. Schmeller. Göttingen, 1838.
[2] *Reinhard Fuchs*, von Jacob Grimm. Berlin, 1834. *Sendschreiben*, an Karl Lachmann. Leipzig, 1840.

tween Henry IV. and Pope Gregory VII. The clergy, hitherto the chief support of German literature, became estranged from the German people; and the insecurity of the times was unfavorable to literary pursuits. Williram's German had lost the classical correctness of Notker's language, and the "Merigarto," and similar works, are written in a hybrid style, which is neither prose nor poetry. The Old High-German had become a literary language chiefly through the efforts of the clergy, and the character of the whole Old High-German literature is preëminently clerical. The Crusades put an end to the preponderance of the clerical element in the literature of Germany. They were, no doubt, the work of the clergy. By using to the utmost the influence which they had gradually gained and carefully fomented, the priests were able to rouse a whole nation to a pitch of religious enthusiasm never known before or after. But the Crusades were the last triumph of the clergy; and with their failure the predominant influence of the clerical element in German society is checked and extinguished.

From the first beginning of the Crusades the interest of the people was with the knight, — no longer with the priest. The chivalrous Emperors of the Hohenstaufen dynasty formed a new rallying point for all national sympathies. Their courts, and the castles of their vassals, offered a new and more genial home to the poets of Germany than the monasteries of Fulda and St. Gall. Poetry changed hands. The poets took their inspirations from real life, though they borrowed their models from the romantic cycles of Brittany and Provence. Middle High-German, the language of the Swabian court, became the language of poetry. The

earliest compositions in that language continue for a
while to bear the stamp of the clerical poetry of a former age. The first Middle High-German poems are
written by a nun; and the poetical translation of the
Books of Moses, the poem on Anno, Bishop of Cologne,
and the " Chronicle of the Roman Emperors," all continue to breathe the spirit of cloisters and cathedral
towns. And when a new taste for chivalrous romances
was awakened in Germany; when the stories of
Arthur and his knights, of Charlemagne and his champions, of Achilles, Æneas, and Alexander, in their
modern dress, were imported by French and Provençal
knights, who, on their way to Jerusalem, came to stay
at the castles of their German allies, the first poets
who ventured to imitate these motley compositions
were priests, not laymen. A few short extracts from
Konrad's " Roland " and Lamprecht's " Alexander "
are sufficient to mark this period of transition. Like
Charlemagne, who had been changed into a legendary
hero by French poets before he became again the subject of German poetry, another German worthy returned at the same time to his native home, though
but slightly changed by his foreign travels, " Reinhard
the Fox." The influence of Provence and of Flanders is seen in every branch of German poetry at that
time; and yet nothing can be more different than the
same subject, as treated by French and German poets.
The German Minnesänger in particular were far from
being imitators of the Trouvères or Troubadours.
There are a few solitary instances of lyric poems translated from Provençal into German;[1] as there is, on the
other hand, one poem translated from German into

[1] *Poems of Grave Rudolf von Fenis, Her Berager von Horheim;* see
Des Minnesangs Frühling, by Lachmann and Haupt. Leipzig, 1857.

Italian,¹ early in the thirteenth century. But the great mass of German lyrics are of purely German growth. Neither the Romans, nor the lineal descendants of the Romans, the Italians, the Provençals, the Spaniards, can claim that poetry as their own. It is Teutonic, purely Teutonic in its heart and soul, though its utterance, its rhyme and metre, its grace and imagery, have been touched by the more genial rays of the brilliant sun of a more southern sky. The same applies to the great romantic poems of that period. The first impulse came from abroad. The subjects were borrowed from a foreign source, and the earlier poems, such as Heinrich von Veldecke's "Æneid," might occasionally paraphrase the sentiments of French poets. But in the works of Hartmann von Aue, Wolfram von Eschenbach, and Gottfried von Strassburg, we breathe again the pure German air; and we cannot but regret that these men should have taken the subjects of their poems, with their unpronounceable names, extravagant conceits, and licentious manners, from foreign sources, while they had at home their grand mythology, their heroic traditions, their kings and saints, which would have been more worthy subjects than Tristan and Isold, Schionatulander and Sigune. There were new thoughts stirring in the hearts and minds of those men of the twelfth and thirteenth centuries. A hundred years before Dante, the German poets had gazed with their eyes wide open into that infinite reality which underlies our short existence on earth. To Wolfram, and to many a poet of his time, the human tragedy of this world presented the same unreal, transitory, and transparent aspect which we find again in Dante's "Divine Comedy." Every-

¹ Poem of the *Kürenberger;* see *Des Minnesangs Frühling,* pp. 8 and 230.

thing points to another world. Beauty, love, virtue, happiness, — everything, in fact, that moves the heart of the poet, — has a hidden reference to something higher than this life; and the highest object of the highest poetry seems to be to transfer the mind to those regions where men feel the presence of a Divine power and a Divine love, and are lost in blissful adoration. The beginning of the thirteenth century is as great an era in the history of German literature as the beginning of the nineteenth. The German mind was completely regenerated. Old words, old thoughts, old metres, old fashions, were swept away, and a new spring dawned over Germany. The various branches of the Teutonic race which, after their inroads into the seats of Roman civilization, had for a time become separated, were beginning to assume a national independence, — when suddenly a new age of migration threatened to set in. The knights of France and Flanders, of England, Lombardy, and Sicily, left their brilliant castles. They marched to the East, carrying along with them the less polished, but equally enthusiastic, nobility of Germany. From the very first the spirit of the Roman towns in Italy and Gaul had exercised a more civilizing influence on the Barbarians who had crossed the Alps and the Rhine, whereas the Germans of Germany proper had been left to their own resources, assisted only by the lessons of the Roman clergy. Now, at the beginning of the Crusades, the various divisions of the German race met again, but they met as strangers; no longer with the impetuosity of Franks and Goths, but with the polished reserve of a Godefroy of Bouillon and the chivalrous bearing of a Frederick Barbarossa. The German Emperors and nobles opened their courts to receive their guests with brilliant hospitality. Their festivals, the splendor and beauty of their tournaments, attracted crowds from great distances, and foremost among them poets and singers. It was at such festivals as Heinrich von Veldecke describes at Mayence, in 1184, under Frederick I., that French and German poetry were brought face to face. It was here that high-born German poets learnt from French poets the subjects of their own romantic compositions. German ladies became the patrons of German poets; and the etiquette of French chivalry was imitated at the castles of German knights. Poets made bold for the first time to express their own feelings, their joys and sufferings, and epic poetry had to share its honors with lyric songs. Not only France and Germany, but England and Northern Italy were drawn into this gay society. Henry II. married Eleanor of Poitou, and her grace and beauty found eloquent admirers in the army of the Crusaders. Their daughter Mathilde was married to Henry the Lion, of Saxony, and one of the Provençal poets has celebrated her loveliness. Frenchmen became the tutors of the sons of the German nobility. French manners, dresses, dishes, and dances were the fashion everywhere. The poetry which flourished at the castles was soon adopted by the lower ranks. Travelling poets and jesters are frequently mentioned, and the poems of the "Nibelungo" and "Gudrun," such as we now possess them, were composed at that time by poets who took their subjects, their best thoughts and expressions, from the people, but imitated the language, the metre, and the manners of the court poets. The most famous courts to which the German poets resorted, and where they were entertained with generous hospitality, were the court of Leopold, Duke of

Austria (1198–1230), and of his son Frederick II.; of
Hermann, Landgrave of Thuringia, who resided at the
Wartburg, near Eisenach (1190–1215); of Berthold,
Duke of Zähringen (1186–1218); and of the Swabian
Emperors in general. At the present day, when not
only the language, but even the thoughts of these
poets have become to most of us unintelligible and
strange, we cannot claim for their poetry more than
an historical interest. But if we wish to know the
men who took a leading part in the Crusades, who
fought with the Emperors against the Pope, or with
the Pope against the Emperors, who lived in magnificent castles like that of the Wartburg, and founded
cathedrals like that of Cologne (1248), we must read
the poetry which they admired, which they composed
or patronized. The subjects of their Romances cannot
gain our sympathy. They are artificial, unreal, with
little of humanity, and still less of nationality in them.
But the mind of a poet like Wolfram von Eschenbach
rises above all these difficulties. He has thoughts of his
own, truly human, deeply religious, and thoroughly
national; and there are expressions and comparisons
in his poetry which had never been used before. His
style, however, is lengthy, his descriptions tiresome,
and his characters somewhat vague and unearthly.
As critics, we should have to bestow on Wolfram von
Eschenbach, on Gottfried von Strassburg, even on
Hartman von Aue and Walther von der Vogelweide,
as much of blame as of praise. But as historians, we
cannot value them too highly. If we measure them
with the poets that preceded and those that followed
them, they tower above all like giants. From the deep
marks which they left behind, we discover that they
were men of creative genius, men who had looked at

life with their own eyes, and were able to express
what they had seen and thought and felt in a language
which fascinated their contemporaries, and which even
now holds its charm over all who can bring themselves to study their works in the same spirit in which
they read the tragedies of Æschylus, or the " Divina
Commedia " of Dante.

But the heyday of German chivalry and chivalrous
poetry was of short duration. Toward the end of the
thirteenth century we begin to feel that the age is no
longer aspiring, and hoping, and growing. The world
assumes a different aspect. Its youth and vigor seem
spent; and the children of a new generation begin to
be wiser and sadder than their fathers. The Crusades
languish. Their object, like the object of many a
youthful hope, has proved unattainable. The Knights
no longer take the Cross " because God wills it;" but
because the Pope commands a Crusade, bargains for
subsidies, and the Emperor cannot decline his commands. Walther von der Vogelweide already is most
bitter in his attacks on Rome. Walther was the
friend of Frederick II. (1215–50), an Emperor who
reminds us, in several respects, of his namesake of
Prussia. He was a sovereign of literary tastes, — himself a poet and a philosopher. Harassed by the Pope,
he retaliated most fiercely, and was at last accused of
a design to extirpate the Christian religion. The ban
was published against him, and his own son rose in rebellion. Germany remained faithful to her Emperor,
and the Emperor was successful against his son. But
he soon died in disappointment and despair. With
him the star of the Swabian dynasty had set, and the
sweet sounds of the Swabian lyre died away with the
last breath of Corradino, the last of the Hohenstaufen,

on the scaffold at Naples, in 1268. Germany was
breaking down under heavy burdens. It was visited
by the papal interdict, by famine, by pestilence.
Sometimes there was no Emperor, sometimes there
were two or three. Rebellion could not be kept under, nor could crime be punished. The only law was
the "Law of the Fist." The Church was deeply
demoralized. Who was to listen to romantic poetry?
There was no lack of poets or of poetry. Rudolf von
Ems, a poet called Der Stricker, and Konrad von
Würzburg, all of them living in the middle of the
thirteenth century, were more fertile than Hartmann
von Aue and Gottfried von Strassburg. They complain, however, that no one took notice of them, and
they are evidently conscious themselves of their inferi-
ority. Lyric poetry continued to flourish for a time,
but it degenerated into an unworthy idolatry of ladies,
and affected sentimentality. There is but one branch
of poetry in which we find a certain originality, the
didactic and satiric. The first beginnings of this new
kind of poetry carry us back to the age of Walther
von der Vogelweide. Many of his verses are satirical,
political, and didactic; and it is supposed, on very good
authority, that Walther was the author of an anonymous didactic poem, "Freidank's Bescheidenheit." By
Thomasin von Zerclar, or Tommasino di Circlaria, we
have a metrical composition on manners, the "Italian
Guest," which likewise belongs to the beginning of
the thirteenth century.[1] Somewhat later we meet, in
the works of the Stricker, with the broader satire of
the middle classes; and toward the close of the cen-

[1] See an account of the *Italian Guest* of Thomasin von Zerclaria by Eugene Oswald, in *Queene Elizabethe's Achademy*, edited by F. J. Furnivall.
London, 1869. This thoughtful essay contains some important information on Thomasin.

tury, Hugo von Trimberg, in his "Renner," addresses himself to the lower ranks of German society, and no longer to princes, knights, and ladies.

How is this to be accounted for? Poetry was evidently changing hands again. The Crusades had made the princes and knights the representatives and leaders of the whole nation; and during the contest between the imperial and the papal powers, the destinies of Germany were chiefly in the hands of the hereditary nobility. The literature, which before that time was entirely clerical, had then become worldly and chivalrous. But now, when the power of the emperors began to decline, when the clergy was driven into taking a decidedly anti-national position, when the unity of the empire was well-nigh destroyed, and princes and prelates were asserting their independence by plunder and by warfare, a new element of society rose to the surface, — the middle classes, — the burghers of the free towns of Germany. They were forced to hold together, in order to protect themselves against their former protectors. They fortified their cities, formed corporations, watched over law and morality, and founded those powerful leagues, the first of which, the Hansa, dates from 1241. Poetry also took refuge behind the walls of free towns; and at the fireside of the worthy citizen had to exchange her gay, chivalrous, and romantic strains, for themes more subdued, practical, and homely. This accounts for such works as Hugo von Trimberg's "Renner," as well as for the general character of the poetry of the fourteenth and fifteenth centuries. Poetry became a trade like any other. Guilds were formed, consisting of master-singers and their apprentices. Heinrich Frauenlob is called the first Meistersänger; and during the fourteenth, the fifteenth, and even the sixteenth centuries, new guilds or schools sprang up in all the principal towns of Germany. After order had been restored by the first Hapsburg dynasty, the intellectual and literary activity of Germany retained its centre of gravitation in the middle classes. Rudolf von Hapsburg was not gifted with a poetical nature, and contemporaneous poets complain of his want of liberality. Attempts were made to revive the chivalrous poetry of the Crusades by Hugo von Montfort and Oswald von Wolkenstein in the beginning of the fifteenth century, and again at the end of the same century by the "Last of the German Knights," the Emperor Maximilian. But these attempts could not but fail. The age of chivalry was gone, and there was nothing great or inspiring in the wars which the Emperors had to wage during the fourteenth and fifteenth centuries against their vassals, against the Pope, against the precursors of the Reformation, the Hussites, and against the Turks. In Fritsche Closener's "Chronicle" there is a description of the citizens of Strassburg defending themselves against their bishop in 1312; in Twinger's "Chronicle" a picture of the processions of the Flagellants and the religious enthusiasm of that time (1349). The poems of Suchenwirt and Halbsuter represent the wars of Austria against Switzerland (1386), and Niclas von Weyl's translation gives us a glimpse into the Council of Constance (1414) and the Hussite wars, which were soon to follow. The poetry of those two centuries, which was written by and for the people, is interesting historically, but, with few exceptions, without any further worth. The poets wish to amuse or to instruct their humble patrons, and they do this, either by giving them the dry bones of the romantic poetry of former ages, or by telling them fables and the quaint stories of the "Seven Wise Masters." What beauty there was in a Meistergesang may be fairly seen from the poem of Michael Beheim; and the Easter play by no means shows the lowest ebb of good taste in the popular literature of that time.

It might seem, indeed, as if all the high and noble aspirations of the twelfth and thirteenth centuries had been lost and forgotten during the fourteenth and fifteenth. And yet it was not quite so. There was one class of men on whom the spirit of true nobility had descended, and whose works form a connecting chain between the great era of the Crusades and the still greater era of the Reformation. These are the so-called Mystics, — true Crusaders, true knights of the Spirit, many of whom sacrificed their lives for the cause of truth, and who at last conquered from the hands of the infidels that Holy Sepulchre in which the true Christian faith had been lying buried for centuries. The name of Mystics, which has been given to these men, is apt to mislead. Their writings are not dark or unintelligible, and those who call them so must find Christianity itself unintelligible and dark. There is more broad daylight in Eckhart and Tauler than in the works of all the Thomists and Scotists. Eckhart was not a dreamer. He had been a pupil of Thomas Aquinas, and his own style is sometimes painfully scholastic. But there is a fresh breeze of thought in his works, and in the works of his disciples. They knew that whenever the problems of man's relation to God, the creation of the world, the origin of evil, and the hope of salvation come to be discussed, the sharpest edge of logical reasoning will turn, and the best defined terms of metaphysics die away into mere mu-

sic. They knew that the hard and narrow categories
of the schoolmen do greater violence to the highest
truths of religion than the soft, and vague, and vanish-
ing tones with which they tried to shadow forth in the
vulgar language of the people the distant objects which
transcend the horizon of human understanding. They
did not handle the truths of Christianity as if they
should or could be proved by the syllogisms of our
human reasoning. Nevertheless these Mystics were
hard and honest thinkers, and never played with words
and phrases. Their faith is to them as clear and as
real as sunshine; and instead of throwing scholastic
dust into the eyes of the people, they boldly told them
to open their eyes and to look at the mysteries all
around them, and to feel the presence of God within
and without, which the priests had veiled by the very
revelation which they had preached. For a true appreciation of the times in which they lived, the works
of these Reformers of the Faith are invaluable. Without them we should try in vain to explain how a nation which, to judge from its literature, seemed to have
lost all vigor and virtue, could suddenly rise and dare
the work of a reformation of the Church. With them
we learn how that same nation, after groaning for centuries under the yoke of superstition and hypocrisy,
found in its very prostration the source of an irresistible strength. The higher clergy contributed hardly
anything to the literature of these two centuries; and
what they wrote would better have remained unwritten.
At St. Gall, toward the end of the thirteenth century,
the monks, the successors of Notker, were unable to
sign their names. The Abbot was a nobleman who
composed love-songs, a branch of poetry at all events
out of place in the monastery founded by St. Gall.

It is only among the lower clergy that we find the traces of genuine Christian piety and intellectual activity, though frequently branded by obese prelates and obtuse magistrates with the names of mysticism and heresy. The orders of the Franciscans and Dominicans, founded in 1208 and 1215, and intended to act as clerical spies and confessors, began to fraternize in many parts of Germany with the people against the higher clergy. The people were hungry and thirsty after religious teaching. They had been systematically starved, or fed with stones. Part of the Bible had been translated for the people, but what Ulfilas was free to do in the fourth century, was condemned by the prelates assembled at the Synod of Trier in 1231. Nor were the sermons of the itinerant friars in towns and villages always to the taste of bishops and abbots. We possess collections of these discourses, preached by Franciscans and Dominicans under the trees of cemeteries, and from the church-towers of the villages. Brother Berthold, who died in 1272, was a Franciscan. He travelled about the country, and was revered by the poor like a saint and prophet. The doctrine he preached, though it was the old teaching of the Apostles, was as new to the peasants who came to hear him, as it had been to the citizens of Athens who came to hear St. Paul. The saying of St Chrysostom that Christianity had turned many a peasant into a philosopher, came true again in the time of Eckhart and Tauler. Men who called themselves Christians had been taught, and had brought themselves to believe, that to read the writings of the Apostles was a deadly sin. Yet in secret they were yearning after that forbidden Bible. They knew that there were translations, and though these translations had

been condemned by popes and synods, the people
could not resist the temptation of reading them. In
1373, we find the first complete version of the Bible
into German, by Matthias of Beheim. Several are
mentioned after this. The new religious fervor that
had been kindled among the inferior clergy, and among
the lower and middle classes of the laity, became
stronger; and, though it sometimes degenerated into
wild fanaticism, the sacred spark was kept in safe
hands by such men as Eckhart (died 1329), Tauler
(died 1361), and the author of the German Theology.
Men like these are sure to conquer; they are persecuted justly or unjustly; they suffer and die, and all
they thought and said and did seems for a time to have
been in vain. But suddenly their work, long marked
as dangerous in the smooth current of society, rises
above the surface like the coral reefs in the Pacific,
and it remains for centuries the firm foundation of a
new world of thought and faith. Without the labors
of these Reformers of the Faith, the Reformers of the
Church would never have found a whole nation waiting to receive, and ready to support them.

There are two other events which prepared the
way of the German Reformers of the sixteenth century: the foundation of universities, and the invention
of printing. Their importance is the same in the
literary and in the political history of Germany. The
intellectual and moral character of a nation is formed
in schools and universities; and those who educate a
people have always been its real masters, though they
may go by a more modest name. Under the Roman
Empire public schools had been supported by the government, both at Rome and in the chief towns of the
Provinces. We know of their existence in Gaul and

parts of Germany. With the decline of the central authority, the salaries of the grammarians and rhetors in the Provinces ceased to be paid, and the pagan gymnasia were succeeded by Christian schools, attached to episcopal sees and monasteries. Whilst the clergy retained their vigor and efficiency, their schools were powerful engines for spreading a half clerical and half classical culture in Germany. During the Crusades, when ecclesiastical activity and learning declined very rapidly, we hear of French tutors at the castles of the nobility, and classical learning gave way to the superficial polish of a chivalrous age. And when the nobility likewise relapsed into a state of savage barbarism, new schools were wanted, and they were founded by the towns, the only places where, during the fourteenth and fifteenth centuries, we see any evidence of a healthy political life. The first town schools are mentioned in the beginning of the fourteenth century, and they were soon followed by the high schools and universities. The University of Prague was founded in 1348; Vienna, 1366; Heidelberg, 1386; Erfurt, 1392; Leipzig, 1408; Basle, 1460; Tübingen, 1477; Mainz, 1482. These universities are a novel feature in the history of German and of European civilization. They are not ecclesiastical seminaries, not restricted to any particular class of society; they are national institutions, open to the rich and the poor, to the knight, the clerk, the citizen. They are real universities of learning: they profess to teach all branches of knowledge, — theology and law, medicine and philosophy. They contain the first practical acknowledgment of the right of every subject to the highest education, and through it to the highest offices in Church and State. Neither Greece nor Rome had known such institutions: neither the Church nor the nobility, during the days of their political supremacy, were sufficiently impressed with the duty which they owed to the nation at large to provide such places of liberal education. It was the nation itself, when forsaken by its clergy and harassed by its nobility, which called these schools into life; and it is in these schools and universities that the great men who inaugurate the next period of literature — the champions of political liberty and religious freedom — were fostered and formed.

The invention of printing was in itself a reformation, and its benefits were chiefly felt by the great masses of the people. The clergy possessed their libraries, where they might read and study if they chose; the castles contained collections of MSS., sacred and profane, illuminated with the most exquisite taste; while the citizen, the poor layman, though he might be able to read and to write, was debarred from the use of books, and had to satisfy his literary tastes with the sermons of travelling Franciscans, or the songs of blind beggars and peddlers. The art of printing admitted that large class to the same privileges which had hitherto been enjoyed almost exclusively by clergy and nobility: it placed in the hands of the third estate arms more powerful than the swords of the knights, and the thunderbolts of the priests: it was a revolution in the history of literature more eventful than any in the history of mankind. Poets and philosophers addressed themselves no longer to emperors and noblemen, to knights and ladies, but to the people at large, and especially to the middle classes, in which henceforth the chief strength of the nation resides.

The years from 1450 to 1500 form a period of preparation for the great struggle that was to inaugurate the beginning of the sixteenth century. It was an age "rich in scholars, copious in pedants, but poor in genius, and barren of strong thinkers." One of the few interesting men in whose life and writings the history of that preliminary age may be studied, is Sebastian Brant, the famous author of the famous "Ship of Fools."

With the sixteenth century, we enter upon the modern history and the modern literature of Germany. We shall here pass on more rapidly, dwelling only on the men in whose writings the political and social changes of Germany can best be studied.

With Luther, the literary language of Germany became New High-German. A change of language invariably betokens a change in the social constitution of a country. In Germany, at the time of the Reformation, the change of language marks the rise of a new aristocracy, which is henceforth to reside in the universities. Literature leaves its former homes. It speaks no longer the language of the towns. It addresses itself no longer to a few citizens, nor to imperial patrons, such as Maximilian I. It indulges no longer in moral saws, didactic verses, and prose novels, nor is it content with mystic philosophy and the secret outpourings of religious fervor. For a time, though but for a short time, German literature becomes national. Poets and writers wish to be heard beyond the walls of their monasteries and cities. They speak to the whole nation; nay, they desire to be heard beyond the frontiers of their country. Luther and the Reformers belonged to no class, — they belonged to the people. The voice of the people, which during the preceding periods of literature could only be heard like the rolling of distant thunder, had now become articulate and distinct, and for a time one thought seemed to unite all classes, — emperors, kings, nobles, and citizens, clergy and laity, high and low, old and young. This is a novel sight in the history of Germany. We have seen in the first period the gradual growth of the clergy, from the time when the first missionaries were massacred in the marshes of Friesland to the time when the Emperor stood penitent before the gates of Canossa. We have seen the rise of the nobility, from the time when the barbarian chiefs preferred living outside the walls of cities to the time when they rivaled the French cavaliers in courtly bearing and chivalrous bravery. Nor were the representatives of these two orders, the Pope and the Emperor, less powerful at the beginning of the sixteenth century than they had been before. Charles V. was the most powerful sovereign whom Europe had seen since the days of Charlemagne, and the papal see had recovered by diplomatic intrigue much of the influence which it had lost by moral depravity. Let us think, then, of these two ancient powers: the Emperor with his armies, recruited in Austria, Spain, Naples, Sicily, and Burgundy, and with his treasures brought from Mexico and Peru; and the Pope with his armies of priests and monks, recruited from all parts of the Christian world, and armed with the weapons of the Inquisition and the thunderbolts of excommunication: let us think of their former victories, their confidence in their own strength, their belief in their divine right: and let us then turn our eyes to the small University of Wittenberg, and into the bleak study of a poor Augustine monk, and see that monk step out of his study with no weapon in his hand but the Bible, — with no armies and no treasures, — and yet defying with his clear and manly voice both Pope and Emperor, both clergy and nobility: there is no grander sight in history; and the longer we allow our eyes to dwell on it, the more we feel that history is not without God, and that at every decisive battle the divine right of truth asserts its supremacy over the divine right of Popes and Emperors, and overthrows with one breath both empires and hierarchies. We call the Reformation the work of Luther; but Luther stood not alone, and no really great man ever stood alone. The secret of their greatness lies in their understanding the spirit of the age in which they live, and in giving expression with the full power of faith and conviction to the secret thoughts of millions. Luther was but lending words to the silent soul of suffering Germany, and no one should call himself a Protestant who is not a Lutheran with Luther at the Diet of Worms, and able to say with him in the face of princes and prelates, "Here I stand; I can do otherwise; God help me; Amen."

As the Emperor was the representative of the nobility, as the Pope was the representative of the clergy, Luther was the head and leader of the people, which through him and through his fellow-workers claimed now, for the first time, an equality with the two old estates of the realm. If this national struggle took at first an aspect chiefly religious, it was because the German nation had freedom of thought and of belief more at heart than political freedom. But political rights also were soon demanded, and demanded with such violence, that during his own life-time Luther had to repress the excesses of enthusiastic theorists and of a violent peasantry. Luther's great influence on the lit-

erature of Germany, and the gradual adoption of his
dialect as the literary language, were owing in a great
measure to this, that whatever there was of literature
during the sixteenth century, was chiefly in the hands
of one class of men. After the Reformation, nearly
all eminent men in Germany — poets, philosophers,
and historians — belonged to the Protestant party, and
resided chiefly in the universities.

The universities were what the monasteries had
been under Charlemagne, the castles under Frederick
Barbarossa, — the centres of gravitation for the intellectual and political life of the country. The true nobility of Germany was no longer to be found among
the priests, — Alcuin, Hrabanus Maurus, Notker Teutonicus ; nor among the knights, — Walther von der
Vogelweide, Wolfram von Eschenbach, and their patrons, Frederick II., Hermann von Thüringen, and
Leopold of Austria. The intellectual sceptre of Germany was wielded by a new nobility, — a nobility that
had risen from the ranks, like the priests and the
knights, but which, for a time at least, kept itself from
becoming a caste, and from cutting away those roots
through which it imbibed its vigor and sustained its
strength. It had its castles in the universities, its
tournaments in the diets of Worms and Augsburg,
and it counted among its members, dukes and peasants, divines and soldiers, lawyers and artists. This
was not, indeed, an hereditary nobility, but on that
very ground it is a nobility which can never become
extinct. The danger, however, which threatens all
aristocracies, whether martial, clerical, or municipal,
was not averted from the intellectual aristocracy of
Germany. The rising spirit of caste deprived the second generation of that power which men like Luther

had gained at the beginning of the Reformation. The moral influence of the universities in Germany was great, and it is great at the present day. But it would have been greater and more beneficial if the conceit of caste had not separated the leaders of the nation from the ranks whence they themselves had arisen, and to which alone they owed their position and their influence. It was the same with the priests, who would rather form a hierarchy than be merged in the laity. It was the same with the knights, who would rather form a select society than live among the gentry. Both cut away the ground under their feet; and the Reformers of the sixteenth century fell into the same snare before they were aware of it. We wonder at the eccentricities of the priesthood, at the conceit of the hereditary nobility, at the affectation of majestic stateliness inherent in royalty. But the pedantic display of learning, the disregard of the real wants of the people, the contempt of all knowledge which does not wear the academic garb, show the same foible, the same conceit, the same spirit of caste among those who, from the sixteenth century to the present day, have occupied the most prominent rank in the society of Germany. Professorial knight-errantry still waits for its Cervantes. Nowhere have the objects of learning been so completely sacrificed to the means of learning, nowhere has that Dulcinea, — knowledge for its own sake, — with her dark veil and her barren heart, numbered so many admirers; nowhere have so many windmills been fought, and so many real enemies been left unhurt, as in Germany, particularly during the last two centuries. New universities have been founded: Marburg, in 1527; Königsberg, in 1547; Jena, in 1558; Helmstädt, in 1575; Giessen, in 1607.

And the more the number and the power of the professors increased, the more they forgot that they and their learning, their universities and their libraries, were for the benefit of the people; that a professor might be very learned, and very accurate, and very laborious, yet worse than useless as a member of our toiling society. It was considered more learned and respectable to teach in Latin, and all lectures at the universities were given in that language. Luther was sneered at because of his little German tracts which " any village clerk might have written." Some of the best poets in the sixteenth century were men such as Eoban Hessius (1540), who composed their poetry in Latin. National poems, for instance, Brant's "Ship of Fools," were translated into Latin in order to induce the German professors to read them. The learned doctors were ashamed of their honest native names. Schwarzerd must needs call himself Melancthon; Meissel Celtes, Schnitter Agricola; Hausschein, Œcolampadius! All this might look very learned, and professorial, and imposing; but it separated the professors from the people at large; it retarded the progress of national education, and blighted the prospects of a national policy in Germany. Everything promised well at the time of the Reformation; and a new Germany might have risen before a new France, if, like Luther, the leaders of the nation had remained true to their calling. But when to speak Latin was considered more learned than to speak German, when to amass vast information was considered more creditable than to digest and to use it, when popularity became the same bugbear to the professors which profanity had been to the clergy, and vulgarity to the knights, Luther's work was undone; and two more centuries had to be spent in pedantic controversies, theological disputes, sectarian squabbles, and political prostration, before a new national spirit could rise again in men like Lessing, and Schiller, and Fichte, and Stein. Ambitious princes and quarrelsome divines continued the rulers of Germany, and, towards the end of the sixteenth century, everything seemed drifting back into the Middle Ages. Then came the Thirty Years' War, a most disastrous war for Germany, which is felt in its results to the present day. If, as a civil and religious contest, it had been fought out between the two parties, — the Protestants and Roman Catholics of Germany, — it would have left, as in England, one side victorious; it would have been brought to an end before both were utterly exhausted. But the Protestants, weakened by their own dissensions, had to call in foreign aid. First Denmark, then Sweden, poured their armies into Germany, and even France — Roman Catholic France — gave her support to Gustavus Adolphus and the Protestant cause. England, the true ally of Germany, was too weak at home to make her influence felt abroad. At the close of the war, the Protestants received indeed the same rights as the Roman Catholics; but the nation was so completely demoralized that it hardly cared for the liberties guaranteed by the treaty of Westphalia. The physical and moral vigor of the nation was broken. The population of Germany is said to have been reduced by one half. Thousands of villages and towns had been burnt to the ground. The schools, the churches, the universities, were deserted. A whole generation had grown up during the war, particularly among the lower classes, with no education at all. The merchants of Germany, who formerly, as Æneas Sylvius said, lived more hand-

somely than the Kings of Scotland, were reduced to
small traders. The Hansa was broken up. Holland,
England, and Sweden had taken the wind out of her
sails. In the Eastern provinces, commerce was suspended by the inroads of the Turks; whilst the discovery of America, and of the new passage to the East
Indies, had reduced the importance of the mercantile
navy of Germany and Italy in the Mediterranean.
Where there was any national feeling left, it was a
feeling of shame and despair, and the Emperor and the
small princes of Germany might have governed even
more selfishly than they did, without rousing opposition among the people.

What can we expect of the literature of such
times? Popular poetry preserved some of its inde-
structible charms. The Meistersänger went on composing according to the rules of their guilds, but we
look in vain for the raciness and honest simplicity of
Hans Sachs. Some of the professors wrote plays in
the style of Terence, or after English models, and
fables became fashionable in the style of Phædrus.
But there was no trace anywhere of originality, truth,
taste, or feeling, except in that branch which, like the
palm-tree, thrives best in the desert, — sacred poetry.
Paul Gerhard is still without an equal as a poet of
sacred songs; and many of the best hymns which are
heard in the Protestant churches of Germany date
from the seventeenth century. Soon, however, this
class of poetry also degenerated on one side into dry
theological phraseology, on the other into sentimental
and almost erotic affectation.

There was no hope of a regeneration in German
literature, unless either great political and social
events should rouse the national mind from its lan-

guor, or the classical models of pure taste and true art should be studied again in a different spirit from that of professorial pedantry. Now, after the Thirty Years' War, there was no war in Germany in which the nation took any warm interest. The policy pursued in France during the long reign of Louis XIV. (1643–1708) had its chief aim in weakening the house of Hapsburg. When the Protestants would no longer fight his battles, Louis roused the Turks. Vienna was nearly taken, and Austria owed its delivery to Johann Sobiesky. By the treaty of Ryswick (1697), all the country on the left side of the Rhine was ceded to France, and German soldiers fought under the banners of the Great Monarch. The only German prince who dared to uphold the honor of the empire, and to withstand the encroachments of Louis, was Frederick William, the great Elector of Prussia (1670–88). He checked the arrogance of the Swedish court, opened his towns to French Protestant refugees, and raised the house of Brandenburg to a European importance. In the same year in which his successor, Frederick III., assumed the royal title as Frederick I., the King of Spain, Charles I., died; and Louis XIV., whilst trying to add the Spanish crown to his monarchy, was at last checked in his grasping policy by an alliance between England and Germany. Prince Eugene and Marlborough restored the peace and the political equilibrium of Europe. In England, the different parties in Parliament, the frequenters of the clubs and coffee-houses, were then watching every move on the political chess-board of Europe, and criticising the victories of their generals and the treaties of their ambassadors. In Germany, the nation took but a passive part. It was excluded from all real share in the great questions of the day; and, if it showed any sympathies, they were confined to the simple admiration of a great general, such as Prince Eugene.

While the policy of Louis XIV. was undermining the political independence of Germany, the literature of his court exercised an influence hardly less detrimental on the literature of Germany. No doubt, the literature of France stood far higher at that time than that of Germany. "Poet" was amongst us a term of abuse, while in France the Great Monarch himself did homage to his great poets. But the professorial poets who had failed to learn the lessons of good taste from the Greek and Roman classics, were not likely to profit by an imitation of the spurious classicality of French literature. They heard the great stars of the court of Louis XIV. praised by their royal and princely patrons, as they returned from their travels in France and Italy, full of admiration for everything that was not German. They were delighted to hear that in France, in Holland, and in Italy, it was respectable to write poetry in the modern vernacular, and set to work in good earnest. After the model of the literary academies in Italy, academies were founded at the small courts of Germany. Men like Opitz would hardly have thought it dignified to write verses in their native tongue had it not been for the moral support which they received from these academies and their princely patrons. His first poems were written in Latin, but he afterwards devoted himself completely to German poetry. He became a member of the "Order of the Palm-tree," and the founder of what is called the *First Silesian School*. Opitz is the true representative of the classical poetry of the seventeenth century. He was a scholar and a gentleman; most correct in his language and versification; never venturing on ground that had not been trodden before by some classical poet, whether of Greece, Rome, France, Holland, or Italy. In him we also see the first traces of that baneful alliance between princes and poets which has deprived the German nation of so many of her best sons. But the charge of mean motives has been unjustly brought against Opitz by many historians. Poets require an audience, and at his time there was no class of people willing to listen to poetry, except the inmates of the small German courts. After the Thirty Years' War the power of these princes was greater than ever. They divided the spoil, and there was neither a nobility, nor a clergy, nor a national party to control or resist them. In England, the royal power had, at that time, been brought back to its proper limits, and it has thus been able to hold ever since, with but short interruptions, its dignified position, supported by the self-respect of a free and powerful nation. In France it assumed the most enormous proportions during the long reign of Louis XIV., but its appalling rise was followed, after a century, by a fall equally appalling, and it has not yet regained its proper position in the political system of that country. In Germany the royal power was less imposing, its prerogatives being divided between the Emperor and a number of small but almost independent vassals, remnants of that feudal system of the Middle Ages which in France and England had been absorbed by the rise of national monarchies. These small principalities explain the weakness of Germany in her relation with foreign powers, and the instability of her political constitution. Continental wars gave an excuse for keeping up large standing armies, and these standing armies stood between the nation and her sovereigns, and made any moral pressure of the one upon the other impossible. The third estate could never gain that share in the government which it had obtained, by its united action, in other countries; and no form of government can be stable which is deprived of the support and the active coöperation of the middle classes. Constitutions have been granted by enlightened sovereigns, such as Joseph II. and Frederick William IV., and barricades have been raised by the people at Vienna and at Berlin; but both have failed to restore the political health of the country. There is no longer a German nobility in the usual sense of the word. Its vigor was exhausted when the powerful vassals of the empire became powerless sovereigns with the titles of king or duke, while what remained of the landed nobility became more reduced with every generation, owing to the absence of the system of primogeniture. There is no longer a clergy as a powerful body in the state. This was broken up at the time of the Reformation; and it hardly had time to recover and to constitute itself on a new basis, when the Thirty Years' War deprived it of all social influence, and left it no alternative but to become a salaried class of servants of the crown. No third estate exists powerful enough to defend the interests of the commonwealth against the encroachments of the sovereign; and public opinion, though it may pronounce itself within certain limits, has no means of legal opposition, and must choose, at every critical moment, between submission to the royal will and rebellion.

Thus, during the whole modern history of Germany, the political and intellectual supremacy is divided. The former is monopolized by the sovereigns, the latter belongs to a small class of learned men. These two soon begin to attract each other. The kings seek the society, the advice, and support of literary men; whilst literary men court the patronage of kings, and acquire powerful influence by governing those who govern the people. From the time of Opitz there have been few men of eminence in literature or science who have not been drawn toward one of the larger or smaller courts of Germany; and the whole of our modern literature bears the marks of this union between princes and poets. It has been said that the existence of these numerous centres of civilization has proved beneficial to the growth of literature; and it has been pointed out that some of the smallest courts, such as Weimar, have raised the greatest men in poetry and science. Goethe himself gives expression to this opinion. "What has made Germany great," he says, "but the culture which is spread through the whole country in such a marvelous manner, and pervades equally all parts of the realm? And this culture, does it not emanate from the numerous courts which grant it support and patronage? Suppose we had had in Germany for centuries but two capitals, Vienna and Berlin, or but one; I should like to know how it would have fared with German civilization, or even with that general wellbeing which goes hand in hand with true civilization." In these words we hear Goethe, the minister of the petty court of Weimar, not the great poet of a great nation. Has France had more than one capital? Has England had more than one court? Great men have risen to eminence in great monarchies like France, and

they have risen to eminence in a great commonwealth
such as England, without the patronage of courts, by
the support, the sympathy, the love of a great nation.
Truly national poetry exists only where there is a
truly national life ; and the poet who, in creating his
works, thinks of a whole nation which will listen to
him and be proud of him, is inspired by a nobler passion than he who looks to his royal master, or the applause even of the most refined audience of the *dames
de la cour.* In a free country, the sovereign is the
highest and most honored representative of the national will, and he honors himself by honoring those
who have well deserved of his country. There a poet
laureate may hold an independent and dignified position, conscious of his own worth, and of the support
of the nation. But in despotic countries, the favor even
of the most enlightened sovereign is dangerous. Germany never had a more enlightened king than Frederick the Great; and yet, when he speaks of the
Queen receiving Leibnitz at court, he says, " She believed that it was not unworthy of a queen to show
honor to a philosopher; and as those who have received from heaven a privileged soul rise to the level
of sovereigns, she admitted Leibnitz into her familiar
society."

The seventeenth century saw the rise and fall of the
first and the second Silesian schools. The first is represented by men like Opitz and Weckherlin, and it exercised an influence in the North of Germany on Simon
Dach, Paul Flemming, and a number of less gifted
poets, who are generally known by the name of the
Königsberg School. Its character is pseudo-classical.
All these poets endeavored to write correctly, sedately,
and eloquently. Some of them aimed at a certain

simplicity and sincerity, which we admire particularly in Flemming. But it would be difficult to find in all their writings one single thought, one single expression, that had not been used before. The second Silesian school is more ambitious; but its poetic flights are more disappointing even than the honest prose of Opitz. The "Shepherds of the Pegnitz" had tried to imitate the brilliant diction of the Italian poets; but the modern Meistersänger of the old town of Nürnberg had produced nothing but wordy jingle. Hoffmannswaldau and Lohenstein, the chief heroes of the second Silesian school, followed in their track, and did not succeed better. Their compositions are bombastic and full of metaphors. It is a poetry of adjectives, without substance, truth, or taste. Yet their poetry was admired, praised not less than Goethe and Schiller were praised by their contemporaries, and it lived beyond the seventeenth century. There were but few men during that time who kept aloof from the spirit of these two Silesian schools, and were not influenced by either Opitz or Hoffmannswaldau. Among these independent poets we have to mention Friedrich von Logau, Andreas Gryphius, and Moscherosch. Beside these, there were some prose writers whose works are not exactly works of art, but works of original thought, and of great importance to us in tracing the progress of science and literature during the dreariest period of German history. We can only mention the "Simplicissimus," a novel full of clever miniature drawing, and giving a truthful picture of German life during the Thirty Years' War; the patriotic writings of Professor Schupp; the historical works of Professor Pufendorf (1631-94); the pietistic sermons of Spener, and of Professor Franke (1663-1727), the founder of the Orphan School at Halle; Professor Arnold's (1666–1714) Ecclesiastical History; the first political pamphlets by Professor Thomasius (1655–1728); and among philosophers, Jacob Böhme at the beginning, and Leibnitz at the end of the seventeenth century.

The second Silesian school was defeated by Gottsched, professor at Leipzig. He exercised, at the beginning of the eighteenth century, the same dictatorship as a poet and a critic which Opitz had exercised at the beginning of the seventeenth. Gottsched was the advocate of French models in art and poetry, and he used his wide-spread influence in recommending the correct and so-called classical style of the poets of the time. After having rendered good service in putting down the senseless extravagance of the school of Lohenstein, he became himself a pedantic and arrogant critic; and it was through the opposition which he roused by his "Gallomania" that German poetry was delivered at last from the trammels of that foreign school. Then followed a long literary warfare; Gottsched and his followers at Leipzig defended the French, Bodmer and his friends in Switzerland the English style of literature. The former insisted on classical form and traditional rules; the latter on natural sentiment and spontaneous expression. The question was, whether poets should imitate the works of the classics, or imitate the classics who had become classics by imitating nobody. A German professor wields an immense power by means of his journals. He is the editor; he writes in them himself, and allows others to write; he praises his friends, who are to laud him in turn; he patronizes his pupils, who are to call him master; he abuses his adversaries, and asks his allies to do the same. It was in this that Professor Gottsched triumphed for a long time over Bodmer and his party, till at last public opinion became too strong, and the dictator died the laughing-stock of Germany. It was in the very thick of this literary struggle that the great heroes of German poetry grew up, — Klopstock, Lessing, Wieland, Herder, Goethe, and Schiller. Goethe, who knew both Gottsched and Bodmer, has described that period of fermentation and transition in which his own mind was formed, and his extracts may be read as a commentary on the poetical productions of the first half of the eighteenth century. He does justice to Günther, and more than justice to Liscow. He shows the influence which men like Brockes, Hagedorn, and Haller exercised in making poetry respectable. He points out the new national life which, like an electric spark, flew through the whole country when Frederick the Great said, "*J'ai jeté le bonnet par-dessus les moulins;*" and defied, like a man, the political popery of Austria. The estimate which Goethe forms of the poets of the time, of Gleim and Uz, of Gessner and Rabener, and more especially of Klopstock, Lessing, and Wieland, should be read in the original, as likewise Herder's "Rhapsody on Shakspeare." The latter contains the key to many of the secrets of that new period of literature, which was inaugurated by Goethe himself and by those who like him could dare to be classical by being true to nature and to themselves.

My object in taking this rapid survey of German literature has been to show that the extracts which I have collected in my "German Classics" have not been chosen at random, and that, if properly used, they can be read as a running commentary on the po-

litical and social history of Germany. The history of
literature is but an applied history of civilization. As
in the history of civilization we watch the play of the
three constituent classes of society, — clergy, nobility,
and commoners, — we can see, in the history of literature, how that class which is supreme politically shows
for the time being its supremacy in the literary productions of the age, and impresses its mark on the
works of poets and philosophers.

Speaking very generally, we might say that, during
the first period of German history, the really moving,
civilizing, and ruling class was the clergy; and in the
whole of German literature, nearly to the time of the
Crusades, the clerical element predominates. The
second period is marked by the Crusades, and the triumph of Teutonic and Romantic chivalry, and the literature of that period is of a strictly correspondent
tone. After the Crusades, and during the political
anarchy that followed, the sole principle of order and
progress is found in the towns, and in the towns the
poetry of the fourteenth and fifteenth centuries finds
its new home. At last, at the time of the Reformation, when the political life of the country assumed for
a time a national character, German literature also is
for a short time national. The hopes, however, which
had been raised of a national policy and of a national
literature were soon blighted, and, from the Thirty
Years' War to the present day, the inheritance of the
nation has been divided between princes and professors. There have been moments when the princes had
to appeal to the nation at large, and to forget for a
while their royal pretensions; and these times of national enthusiam, as during the wars of Frederick the
Great, and during the wars against Napoleon, have not

failed to tell on the literature of Germany. They produced a national spirit, free from professorial narrowness, such as we find in the writings of Lessing and Fichte. But with the exception of these short lucid intervals, Germany has always been under the absolute despotism of a number of small sovereigns and great professors, and her literature has been throughout in the hands of court poets and academic critics. Klopstock, Lessing, and Schiller are most free from either influence, and most impressed with the duties which a poet owes, before all, to the nation to which he belongs. Klopstock's national enthusiasm borders sometimes on the fantastic; for, as his own times could not inspire him, he borrowed the themes of his national panegyrics from the distant past of Arminius and the German bards. Lessing looked more to his own age, but he looked in vain for national heroes. "Pity the extraordinary man," says Goethe, "who had to live in such miserable times, which offered him no better subjects than those which he takes for his works. Pity him, that in his 'Minna von Barnhelm,' he had to take part in the quarrel between the Saxons and the Prussians, because he found nothing better. It was owing to the rottenness of his time that he always took, and was forced to take, a polemical position. In his 'Emilia Galotti,' he shows his *pique* against the princes; in 'Nathan,' against the priests." But, although the subjects of these works of Lessing were small, his object in writing was always great and national. He never condescended to amuse a provincial court by masquerades and comedies, nor did he degrade his genius by pandering, like Wieland, to the taste of a profligate nobility. Schiller, again, was a poet truly national and truly liberal; and although a

man of aspirations rather than of actions, he has left a
deeper impress on the kernel of the nation than either
Wieland or Goethe. These considerations, however,
must not interfere with our appreciation of the greatness of Goethe. On the contrary, when we see the
small sphere in which he moved at Weimar, we admire the more the height to which he grew, and the
freedom of his genius. And it is, perhaps, owing to
this very absence of a strongly marked national feeling,
that in Germany the first idea of a world-literature
was conceived. "National literature," Goethe says,
" is of little importance: the age of a world-literature
is at hand, and every one ought to work in order to
accelerate this new era." Perhaps Goethe felt that
the true poet belonged to the whole of mankind, and
that he must be intelligible beyond the frontiers of his
own country. And, from this point of view, his idea
of a world-literature has been realized, and his own
works have gained their place side by side with the
works of Homer, Virgil, Dante, and Shakespeare.
But, so long as there are different languages and different nations, let each poet think and work and write
for his own people, without caring for the applause of
other countries. Science and philosophy are cosmopolitan; poetry and art are national: and those who
would deprive the Muses of their home-sprung character, would deprive them of much of their native
charms.

LIST OF EXTRACTS FOR ILLUSTRATING THE HISTORY OF GERMAN LITERATURE.

Fourth Century after Christ.

Gothic: —
    Ulfilas, Translation of the Bible; the Lord's Prayer.

Seventh Century.

Old High-German: —
    Vocabulary of St. Gall.

Eighth Century.

Old High-German: —
    Interlinear Translation of the Benedictine Rules.
    Translation of the Gospel of St. Matthew.
    Exhortation addressed to the Christian Laity.
    Literal Translations of the Hymns of the Old Church: —
        1. Deus qui cordi lumen es.
        2. Aurora lucis rutilat.
        3. Te Deum laudamus.
    The Song of Hildebrand and his son Hadubrand, — in alliterative metre.
    The Prayer from the Monastery of Wessobrun, — in alliterative metre.
    The Apostolic Creed.

Ninth Century.

Old High-German: —
    From Einhard's Life of Charlemagne, — the German names of the Months and the Winds fixed by the Emperor.
    Muspilli, or on the Last Judgment, — alliterative poem.
    The Oaths of Lewis the German and Charles the Bald, and their armies at Strassburg, 842, in Old Frankish and Old French; from the History of Nithard, the grandson of Charlemagne.
    The Heliand, or the Saviour, — old Saxon poem, in alliterative metre.
    The Krist, or the Gospel-book, — poem in rhyme by Otfried, the pupil of Hrabanus Maurus, dedicated to Lewis the German.

GERMAN LITERATURE. 45

Old High-German (continued) : —
    Translation of a Harmony of the Gospels.
    Lay on St. Peter.
    Song on the Victory gained by King Lewis III. at Saucourt, in 881, over the Normans.

TENTH CENTURY.

Old High-German : —
    Notker Teutonicus of St. Gall, —
      1. Translation of the Psalms.
      2. Treatise on Syllogisms.
      3. Translation of Aristotle.
      4. Translation of Boëthius de Consolatione.

ELEVENTH CENTURY.

Old High-German : —
    Williram's Explanation of the Song of Solomon.
    Merigarto, or the Earth, — fragment of a geographical poem.

TWELFTH CENTURY.

Middle High-German : —
    The Life of Jesus, — poem by the Nun Ava.
    Poetical Translation of the Books of Moses.
    Historical Poem on Anno, Bishop of Cologne.
    Poetical Chronicle of the Roman Emperors.
    Nortperti Tractatus de Virtutibus, translated.
    The poem of Roland, by Konrad the Priest.
    The poem of Alexander, by Lamprecht the Priest.
    Poem of Reinhart the Fox.
    Dietmar von Aist, — lyrics.
    The Spervogel, — lyrics.
    The Kürenberger, — lyrics.
    The Eneid, by Heinrich von Veldecke.

THIRTEENTH CENTURY.

Middle High-German : —
    Hartmann von Aue; extracts from his "Iwein," — a heroic poem.
    The Old Reinmar, — lyrics.
    Walther von der Vogelweide, — lyrics.
    Freidank's Bescheidenheit, — didactic poem.

Middle High-German (continued):
  Wolfram von Eschenbach, —
    1. Extracts from his " Parcival," — a heroic poem.
    2. Extracts from his " Titurel," — a heroic poem.
  Gottfried von Strassburg ; extracts from his " Tristan," — a heroic poem.
  The poem of the " Nibelunge," — epic poem.
  Thomasin von Zerclar ; extracts from his poem on manners, called " The Italian Guest."
  Neidhart von Reuenthal, — lyrics.
  Otto von Botenlaube, — lyrics.
  Gudrun, — epic poem.
  The Stricker, — extract from his satirical poem, " Amis the Priest."
  Rudolf von Ems, — extract from his " Wilhelm von Orleans."
  Christian von Hamle, — lyrics.
  Gottfried von Neifen, — lyrics.
  Ulrich von Lichtenstein, — lyrics.
  Sermon of Friar Berthold of Regensburg.
  Reinmar von Zweter, — lyrics.
  Master Stolle, — satire.
  The Marner, — lyrics.
  Master Konrad of Würzburg, —
    1. Poem.
    2. Extract from the Trojan War.
  Anonymous poet, — extract from the life of St. Elizabeth.
  Herman der Damen.
  Anonymous poet, — extract from the " Wartburg Krieg."
  Margrave Otto von Brandenburg, — lyrics.
  Heinrich, Duke of Breslau, — lyrics.
  Hugo von Trimberg, — extract from the " Renner."

FOURTEENTH CENTURY.

Middle High-German: —
  Heinrich Frauenlob, — lyrics.
  Master Johann Hadlaub, — lyrics.
  The Great Rosegarden, — popular epic poem.
  Master Eckhart, — homily.
  Hermann von Fritzlar, — life of St. Elizabeth.
  Dr. Johann Tauler, — sermon.
  Heinrich Suso.

Middle High-German (continued) : —
  Heinrich der Teichner, — fable.
  Peter Suchenwirt, — on the death of Leopold, Duke of Austria, 1386.
  Halbsuter's poem on the Battle of Sempach, 1386.
  Fritsche Closener's Strassburg Chronicle.
  Jacob Twinger's Chronicle, — on the Flagellants.

FIFTEENTH CENTURY.

Middle High-German: —
  Hugo von Montfort, — lyrics.
  Oswald von Wolkenstein, — lyrics.
  Muscatblüt, — lyrics.
  Hans von Bühel's Life of Diocletian, or The Seven Wise Masters.
  Popular Songs.
  Sacred Songs.
  The Soul's Comfort, — didactic prose.
  Michael Beheim, — Meistergesang.
  An Easter Mystery.
  Popular Rhymes.
  Caspar von der Roen's Heldenbuch, — Hildebrand and his Son.
  Niclas von Weyl's Translations, — Hieronymus at the Council of Constance.
  Veit Weber's poem on the Victory of Murten, 1476.
  Heinrich Steinhöwel's Fables.
  Sebastian Brant's "Ship of Fools."
  Johann Geiler von Kaisersberg, — sermon.
  Emperor Maximilian, — extract from the "Theuerdank."

SIXTEENTH CENTURY.

Modern High-German: —
  Martin Luther. —
    1. Sacred Song.
    2. Letter on the Diet of the Jackdaws and Crows.
    3. His Last Sermon.
  Ulrich Zwingle: —
    1. A Poem on his Illness.
    2. Criticism on Luther.
  Philipp Nicolai, — sacred songs.
  Justus Jonas, — sacred songs.

Modern High-German (continued): —
    Ulrich von Hutten, —
        1. Letter to Franz von Sickingen.
        2. Political poem.
    Sebastian Frank, —
        1. Preface to his Germania.
        2. Rudolf von Hapsburg.
        3. Maximilian der Erste.
        4. Fables.
    Burkard Waldis, — fables.
    Hans Sachs, —
        1. Sacred Song.
        2. Poem on the Death of Martin Luther.
        3. Poem on the War.
    Petermann Etterlin's Chronicle, — William Tell and Rudolf von Hapsburg.
    Ægidius Tschudi's Chronicle, — William Tell.
    Paulus Melissus Schede.
    Johann Fischart, —
        1. Exhortation addressed to the German people.
        2. Das glückhafte Schiff.
    Georg Rollenhagen, — fable.
    Popular Books, —
        1. Tyll Eulenspiegel.
        2. Dr. Faust.
    Popular Songs.

SEVENTEENTH CENTURY.

Modern High-German: —
    Martin Opitz, and the First Silesian School.
    Georg Rudolf Weckherlin.
    Anonymous Poem, — "O Ewigkeit."
    Michael Altenburg's Camp-song (Gustavus Adolphus).
    Johannes Heermann, — sacred song.
    Popular Songs.
    Johann Arndt, —
        1. Sacred Song.
        2. On the Power and Necessity of Prayer.
    Jacob Böhme, Mysterium Magnum.
    Johann Valentin Andreä.
    Friedrich Spee.
    Julius Wilhelm Zincgreff.

Modern High-German (continued):—
  Friedrich von Logau.
  Simon Dach and the Königsberg School.
  Paul Flemming.
  Paul Gerhard.
  Georg Philipp Harsdörffer and the Nürnberg School.
  Johannes Rist.
  Andreas Gryphius,—
    1. Sonnets.
    2. From the Tragedy "Cardenio and Celinde."
  Joachim Rachel,— satire.
  Johann Michael Moscherosch,— satires.
  Christoph von Grimmelshausen, Simplicissimus,— novel.
  Johann Balthasar Schupp,— on the German Language.
  Angelus Silesius.
  Hoffmannswaldau and Lobenstein,— Second Silesian School.
  Abraham a Santa Clara,— sermon.
  Philipp Jacob Spener,— on Luther.
  Gottfried Arnold,— sacred poem.
  Christian Weise.
  Hans Assmann von Abschatz.
  Friedrich R. L. von Canitz.
  Christian Wernicke.
  Gottfried Wilhelm von Leibnitz,— on the German Language.

Eighteenth Century.

Modern High-German:—
  Johann Christoph Gottsched,— Cato.
  Johann Jacob Bodmer,— Character of German Poetry.
  Barthold Heinrich Brockes.
  Johann Christian Günther.
  Nicolaus Ludwig Graf von Zinzendorf.
  Christian Ludwig Liscow.
  Friedrich von Hagedorn.
  Albrecht von Haller.
  Gottlieb Wilhelm Rabener.
  Ewald Christian von Kleist.
  Christian Fürchtegott Gellert.
  Johann Ludwig Gleim.
  Johann Peter Uz.

Modern High-German (continued): —
    Justus Möser.
    Klopstock. See below.
    Salomon Gessner.
    Johann Winckelmann.
    Lessing. See below.
    Johann Georg Hamann.
    Immanuel Kant.
    Johann August Musæus.
    Wieland. See below.
    Gottlieb Konrad Pfeffel.
    Christian Friedrich Daniel Schubart.
    Matthias Claudius.
    Johann Caspar Lavater.
    Herder. See below.
    Heinrich Jung, Stilling.
    Georg Christoph Lichtenberg.
    Gottfried August Bürger.
    Johann Heinrich Voss.
    Friedrich Leopold und Christian Grafen zu Stollberg.
    Das Siebengestirn der Dichter des achtzehnten Jahrhunderts, —
        1. Friedrich Gottlieb Klopstock.
        2. Gotthold Ephraim Lessing.
        3. Christoph Martin Wieland.
        4. Johann Gottfried von Herder.
        5. Johann Wolfgang von Goethe.
        6. Johann Christoph Friedrich von Schiller.
        7. Jean Paul Friedrich Richter.

1858.

II.

OLD GERMAN LOVE-SONGS.[1]

Seven hundred years ago! What a long time it seems! Philip Augustus, King of France; Henry II., King of England; Frederic I., the famous Barbarossa, Emperor of Germany! When we read of their times, the times of the Crusades, we feel as the Greeks felt when reading of the War of Troy. We listen, we admire, but we do not compare the heroes of St. Jean d'Acre with the great generals of the nineteenth century. They seem a different race of men from those who are now living, and poetry and tradition have lent to their royal frames such colossal proportions that we hardly dare to criticise the legendary history of their chivalrous achievements. It was a time of heroes, of saints, of martyrs, of miracles! Thomas à Becket was murdered at Canterbury, but for more than three hundred years his name lived on, and his bones were working miracles, and his soul seemed as it were embodied and petrified in the lofty pillars that surround the spot of his martyrdom. Abelard was persecuted and imprisoned, but his spirit revived in the Reformers of the sixteenth century,

[1] *Des Minnesangs Frühling.* Herausgegeben von Karl Lachmann und Moritz Haupt. Leipzig, 1857.

and the shrine of Abelard and Héloise in the Père
La Chaise is still decorated every year with garlands
of *immortelles*. Barbarossa was drowned in the same
river in which Alexander the Great had bathed his
royal limbs, but his fame lived on in every cottage of
Germany, and the peasant near the Kyffhäuser still
believes that some day the mighty Emperor will
awake from his long slumber, and rouse the people of
Germany from their fatal dreams. We dare not hold
communion with such stately heroes as Frederick the
Red-beard and Richard the Lion-heart; they seem
half to belong to the realm of fable. We feel from
our very school-days as if we could shake hands with a
Themistocles and sit down in the company of a Julius
Cæsar, but we are awed by the presence of those tall
and silent knights, with their hands folded and their
legs crossed, as we see them reposing in full armor on
the tombs of our cathedrals.

And yet, however different in all other respects,
these men, if they once lift their steel beaver and
unbuckle their rich armor, are wonderfully like ourselves. Let us read the poetry which they either
wrote themselves, or to which they liked to listen in
their castles on the Rhine or under their tents in Palestine, and we find it is poetry which a Tennyson or
a Moore, a Goethe or Heine, might have written.
Neither Julius Cæsar nor Themistocles would know
what was meant by such poetry. It is modern poetry,
— poetry unknown to the ancient world, — and who
invented it nobody can tell. It is sometimes called
Romantic, but this is a strange misnomer. Neither the
Romans, nor the lineal descendants of the Romans,
the Italians, the Provençals, the Spaniards, can claim
that poetry as their own. It is Teutonic poetry, —

purely Teutonic in its heart and soul, though its utterance, its rhyme and metre, its grace and imagery, show the marks of a warmer clime. It is called sentimental poetry, the poetry of the heart rather than of the head, the picture of the inward rather than of the outward world. It is subjective, as distinguished from objective poetry, as the German critics, in their scholastic language, are fond of expressing it. It is Gothic, as contrasted with classical poetry. The one, it is said, sublimizes nature, the other bodies forth spirit; the one deifies the human, the other humanizes the divine; the one is ethnic, the other Christian. But all these are but names, and their true meaning must be discovered in the works of art themselves, and in the history of the times which produced the artists, the poets, and their ideals. We shall perceive the difference between these two hemispheres of the Beautiful better if we think of Homer's "Helena" and Dante's "Beatrice," if we look at the "Venus of Milo" and a "Madonna" of Francia, than in reading the profoundest systems of æsthetics.

The work which has caused these reflections is a volume of German poetry, just published by Lachmann and Haupt. It is called "Des Minnesangs Frühling," — "the Spring of the Songs of Love;" and it contains a collection of the poems of twenty German poets, all of whom lived during the period of the Crusades, under the Hohenstaufen Emperors, from about 1170 to 1230. This period may well be called the spring of German poetry, though the summer that followed was but of short duration, and the autumn was cheated of the rich harvest which the spring had promised. Tieck, one of the first who gathered the flowers of that forgotten spring, describes it in glow-

ing language. "At that time," he says, "believers
sang of faith, lovers of love, knights described knightly
actions and battles; and loving, believing knights
were their chief audience. The spring, beauty, gayety,
were objects that could never tire: great duels and
deeds of arms carried away every hearer, the more
surely, the stronger they were painted; and as the
pillars and dome of the church encircle the flock, so
did religion, as the highest, encircle poetry and reality; and every heart, in equal love, humbled itself
before her." Carlyle, too, has listened with delight to
those merry songs of spring. "Then truly," he says,
"was the time of singing come; for princes and prelates, emperors and squires, the wise and the simple,
men, women, and children, all sang and rhymed, or
delighted in hearing it done. It was a universal noise
of song, as if the spring of manhood had arrived, and
warblings from every spray — not, indeed, without infinite twitterings also, which, except their gladness,
had no music — were bidding it welcome." And yet
it was not all gladness; and it is strange that Carlyle,
who has so keen an ear for the silent melancholy of
the human heart, should not have heard that tone of
sorrow and fateful boding which breaks, like a suppressed sigh, through the free and light music of that
Swabian era. The brightest sky of spring is not without its clouds in Germany, and the German heart
is never happy without some sadness. Whether we
listen to a short ditty, or to the epic ballads of the
"Nibelunge," or to Wolfram's grand poems of the
"Parcival" and the "Holy Grail," it is the same
everywhere. There is always a mingling of light
and shade, — in joy a fear of sorrow, in sorrow a ray
of hope, and throughout the whole, a silent wondering

at this strange world. Here is a specimen of an anonymous poem; and anonymous poetry is an invention peculiarly Teutonic. It was written before the twelfth century; its language is strangely simple, and sometimes uncouth. But there is truth in it; and it is truth after all, and not fiction, that is the secret of all poetry:—

> "It has pained me to the heart,
> Full many a time,
> That I yearned after that
> Which I may not have,
> Nor ever shall win.
> It is very grievous.
> I do not mean gold or silver;
> It is more like a human heart.
>
> "I trained me a falcon,
> More than a year.
> When I had tamed him,
> As I would have him,
> And had well tied his feathers
> With golden chains,
> He soared up very high,
> And flew into other lands.
>
> I saw the falcon since,
> Flying happily;
> He carried on his foot
> Silken straps,
> And his plumage was
> All red of gold. . . . .
> May God send them together,
> Who would fain be loved."

The key-note of the whole poem of the "Nibelunge," such as it was written down at the end of the twelfth, or the beginning of the thirteenth century, is "Sorrow after Joy." This is the fatal spell against which all the heroes are fighting, and fighting in vain. And as Hagen dashes the Chaplain into the waves, in order to belie the prophecy of the Mermaids, but the Chaplain rises, and Hagen rushes headlong into destruction, so Chriemhilt is bargaining and playing with the same inevitable fate, cautiously guarding her young heart against the happiness of love, that she may escape the sorrows of a broken heart. She, too, has been dreaming "of a wild young falcon that she trained for many a day, till two fierce eagles tore it." And she rushes to her mother Ute, that she may read the dream for her; and her mother tells her what it means. And then the coy maiden answers: —

> "No more, no more, dear mother, say,
> From many a woman's fortune this truth is clear as day,
> That falsely smiling Pleasure with Pain requites us ever.
> I from both will keep me, and thus will sorrow never."

But Siegfried comes, and Chriemhilt's heart does no longer cast up the bright and the dark days of life. To Siegfried she belongs; for him she lives, and for him, when "two fierce eagles tore him," she dies. A still wilder tragedy lies hidden in the songs of the "Edda," the most ancient fragments of truly Teutonic poetry. Wolfram's poetry is of the same sombre cast. He wrote his "Parcival" about the time when the songs of the "Nibelunge" were written down. The subject was taken by him from a French source. It belonged originally to the British cycle of Arthur and his knights. But Wolfram took the story merely as a skeleton, to which he himself gave a new body and soul. The glory and happiness which this world can give is to him but a shadow, — the crown for which his hero fights is that of the Holy Grail.

Faith, Love, and Honor are the chief subjects of the so-called Minnesänger. They are not what we should call erotic poets. *Minne* means love in the old German language, but it means, originally, not so much passion and desire, as thoughtfulness, reverence, and remembrance. In English *Minne* would be "Minding," and it is different therefore from the Greek *Eros*, the Roman *Amor*, and the French *Amour*. It is different also from the German *Liebe*, which means originally desire, not love. Most of the poems of the "Minnesänger" are sad rather than joyful, — joyful in sorrow, sorrowful in joy. The same feelings have since been so often repeated by poets in all the modern languages of Europe, that much of what we read in the "Minnesänger" of the twelfth and thirteenth centuries sounds stale to our ears. Yet there is a simplicity about these old songs, a want of effort, an entire absence of any attempt to please or to surprise; and we listen to them as we listen to a friend who tells us his sufferings in broken and homely words, and whose truthful prose appeals to our heart more strongly than the most elaborate poetry of a Lamartine or a Heine. It is extremely difficult to translate these poems from the language in which they are written, the so-called Middle High-German, into Modern German, — much more so to render them into English. But translation is at the same time the best test of the true poetical value of any poem, and we believe that many of the poems of the Minnesängers can bear that test. Here is another poem, very much in the style of the one quoted above, but written by a poet whose name is known, — Dietmar von Eist: —

> "A lady stood alone,
> And gazed across the heath,
> And gazed for her love.
> She saw a falcon flying.
> 'O happy falcon that thou art,
> Thou fliest wherever thou likest;
> Thou choosest in the forest
> A tree that pleases thee.
> Thus I too had done.
> I chose myself a man;
> Him my eyes selected.

> Beautiful ladies envy me for it.
> Alas! why will they not leave me my love?
> I did not desire the beloved of any one of them.
> Now woe to thee, joy of summer!
> The song of birds is gone;
> So are the leaves of the lime-tree:
> Henceforth, my pretty eyes too
> Will be overcast.
> My love, thou shouldst take leave
> Of other ladies;
> Yes, my hero, thou shouldst avoid them.
> When thou sawest me first,
> I seemed to thee in truth
> Right lovely made:
> I remind thee of it, dear man!'"

These poems, simple and homely as they may seem to us, were loved and admired by the people for whom they were written. They were copied and preserved with the greatest care in the albums of kings and queens, and some of them were translated into foreign languages. The poem which we quoted first was translated as an Italian sonnet in the thirteenth century, and has been published in Franc Trucchi's "Poesie Italiano Inedite:" —

> "Tapina me, che amava uno sparviero;
> amaval tanto ch' Io me ne moria;
> a lo richiamo ben m' era maniero
> ed unque troppo pascer no' l dovia.
> or è montato e salito sì altero,
> assai più altero che far non solìa;
> ed è assiso dentro a un verziero,
> e un' altra donna l' averà in balìa.
> Isparvier mio, ch' io t' avea nodrito;
> sonaglio d' oro ti faces portare,
> perchè nell' uccellar fossi più ardito.
> or mi salito siccome lo mare,
> ed hai rotti li getti, e sei fuggito
> quando eri fermo nel tuo uccellare."

One of the most original and thoughtful of the "Minnesänger" is the old Reinmar. His poems are given now for the first time in a correct and readable text by Lachmann and Haupt, and many a difficult passage has been elucidated by their notes. His poems, however, are not easy to read, and we should have been thankful for some more help than the editors have given us in their notes. The following is a specimen of Reinmar's poetry: —

> "High as the sun stands my heart;
> That is because of a lady who can be without change
> In her grace, wherever she be.
> She makes me free from all sorrow.
>
> "I have nothing to give her, but my own life,
> That belongs to her: the beautiful woman gives me always
> Joy, and a high mind,
> If I think of it, what she does for me.
>
> "Well is it for me that I found her so true!
> Wherever she dwell, she alone makes every land dear to me;
> If she went across the wild sea,
> There I should go; I long so much for her.
>
> "If I had the wisdom of a thousand men, it would be well
> That I keep her, whom I should serve:
> May she take care right well,
> That nothing sad may ever befall me through her.
>
> "I was never quite blessed, but through her:
> Whatever I wish to her, may she allow it to me!
> It was a blessed thing for me
> That she, the Beautiful, received me into her grace."

Carlyle, no doubt, is right when he says that, among all this warbling of love, there are infinite twitterings which, except their gladness, have little to charm us. Yet we like to read them as part of the bright history of those by-gone days. One poet sings: —

> "If the whole world was mine,
> From the Sea to the Rhine,
> I would gladly give it all,
> That the Queen of England
> Lay in my arms," etc.

Who was the impertinent German that dared to fall in love with a Queen of England? We do not know. But there can be no doubt that the Queen of England whom he adored was the gay and beautiful Eleanor of Poitou, the Queen of Henry II., who filled the heart of many a Crusader with unholy thoughts. Her daughter, too, Mathilde, who was married to Henry the Lion of Saxony, inspired many a poet of those days. Her beauty was celebrated by the Provençal Troubadours; and at the court of her husband, she encouraged several of her German vassals to follow the example of the French and Norman knights, and sing the love of Tristan and Isolt, and the adventures of the knights of Charlemagne. They must have been happy times, those times of the Crusades! Nor have they passed away without leaving their impress on the hearts and minds of the nations of Europe. The Holy Sepulchre, it is true, is still in the hands of the Infidels, and the bones of the Crusaders lie buried in unhallowed soil, and their deeds of valor are well-nigh forgotten, and their chivalrous Tournaments and their Courts of Love are smiled at by a wiser generation. But much that is noble and heroic in the feelings of the nineteenth century has its hidden roots in the thirteenth. Gothic architecture and Gothic poetry are the children of the same mother; and if the true but unadorned language of the heart, the aspirations of a real faith, the sorrow and joy of a true love, are still listened to by the nations of Europe; and if what is called the Romantic school is strong enough to hold its ground against the classical taste and its royal patrons, such as Louis XIV., Charles II., and Frederick the Great, — we owe it to those chivalrous poets who dared for the first time to be what they were, and to say what they felt, and to whom Faith, Love, and Honor were worthy subjects of poetry, though they lacked the sanction of the Periclean and Augustan ages.

The new edition of the Poems of the "Minnesänger" is a masterpiece of German scholarship. It was commenced by Lachmann, the greatest critic, after Wolf, that Germany has produced. Lachmann died before the work was finished, and Professor Haupt, his successor at Berlin, undertook to finish it. His share in the edition, particularly in the notes, is greater than that of Lachmann; and the accuracy with which the text has been restored from more than twenty MSS., is worthy of the great pupil of that great master.

1858.

III.

YE SCHYPPE OF FOOLES.[1]

THE critical periods in the history of the world are best studied in the lives of a few representative men. The history of the German Reformation assumes a living, intelligible, and human character in the biographies of the Reformers; and no historian would imagine that he understood the secret springs of that mighty revolution in Germany without having read the works of Hutten, the table-talk of Luther, the letters of Melancthon, and the sermons of Zwingle. But although it is easy to single out representative men in the great decisive struggles of history, they are more difficult to find during the preparatory periods. The years from 1450 to 1500 are as important as the years from 1500 to 1550, — nay, to the thoughtful historian, that silent period of incubation is perhaps of deeper interest than the violent outburst of the sixteenth century. But where, during those years, are the men of sufficient eminence to represent the age in which they lived? It was an age of transition and preparation, of dissatisfaction and hesitation. Like the whole of the fifteenth century, "It was rich in scholars, copious in

[1] Sebastian Brant's *Narrenschiff*. Herausgegeben von Friedrich Zarncke. Leipzig, 1857.

pedants, but poor in genius, and barren of strong thinkers." We must not look for heroes in so unheroic an age, but be satisfied with men if they be but a head taller than their contemporaries.

One of the most interesting men in whose life and writings the history of the preliminary age of the German Reformation may be studied, is Sebastian Brant, the famous author of the famous "Ship of Fools." He was born in the year 1457. The Council of Basle had failed to fulfill the hopes of the German laity as to a *reformatio ecclesiæ in capite et membris*. In the very year of Brant's birth, Martin Meyer, the Chancellor of Mayence, had addressed his letter to his former friend, Œneas Sylvius, — a national manifesto, in boldness and vigor only surpassed by the powerful pamphlet of Luther, "To the Nobility of the German Nation." Germany seemed to awaken at last to her position, and to see the dangers that threatened her political and religious freedom. The new movement which had taken place in Italy in classical learning, supported chiefly by Greek refugees, began to extend its quickening influence beyond the Alps. Æneas Sylvius, afterwards Pope Pius II., 1458, writes in one of his letters, that poets were held in no estimation in Germany, though he admits that their poetry is less to be blamed for this than their patrons, the princes, who care far more for any trifles than for poetry. The Germans, he says, do not care for science nor for a knowledge of classical literature, and they have hardly heard the name of Cicero or any other orator. In the eyes of the Italians, the Germans were barbarians; and when Constantine Lascaris saw the first specimen of printing, he was told by the Italian priests that this invention had lately been made *apud barbaros in urbe*.

Germaniæ. They were dangerous neighbors — these barbarians, who could make such discoveries as the art of printing; and Brant lived to see the time when Joh. Cæsarius was able to write to a friend of his: "At this moment, Germany, if she does not surpass Italy, at least need not, and will not, yield to her, not so much on account of her empire, as for her wonderful fecundity in learned men, and the almost incredible growth of learning."

This period of slow but steady progress, from the invention of printing to the Council of Worms, is bridged over by the life of Sebastian Brant, who lived from 1457 to 1521. Brant was very early the friend of Peter Schott, and through him had been brought in contact with a circle of learned men, who were busily engaged in founding one of the first schools of classical learning at Schlettstadt. Men like Jac. Wimpheling, Joh. Torrentinus, Florentius Hundius, and Johannes Hugo, belonged to that society. Brant afterwards went to Basle to study law. Basle was then a young university. It had only been founded in 1459, but it was already a successful rival of Heidelberg. The struggle between the Realists and Nominalists was then raging all over Europe, and it divided the University of Basle into two parties, each of them trying to gain influence and adherents among the young students. It has been usual to look upon the Realists as the Conservative, and upon the Nominalists as the Liberal party of the fifteenth century. But although at times this was the case, philosophical opinions, on which the differences between these two parties were founded, were not of sufficient strength to determine for any length of time the political and religious bias of either school. The Realists were chiefly supported by the Dominicans, the Nominalists by the Franciscans; and there is always a more gentle expression beaming in the eyes of the followers of the seraphic Doctor, particularly if contrasted with the stern frown of the Dominican. Ockam himself was a Franciscan, and those who thought with him were called *doctores renovatores* and *sophistæ*. Suddenly, however, the tables were turned. At Oxford, the Realists, in following out their principles in a more independent spirit, had arrived at results dangerous to the peace of the Church. As philosophers, they began to carry out the doctrines of Plato in good earnest; as reformers, they looked wistfully to the early centuries of the Christian Church. The same liberal and independent spirit reached from Oxford to Prague, and the expulsion of the German nation from that university may be traced to the same movement. The Realists were at that time no longer in the good odor of orthodoxy; and, at the Council of Constanz, the Nominalists, such as Joh. Gerson and Petrus de Alliaco, gained triumphs which seemed for a time to make them the arbiters of public opinion in Germany, and to give them the means of securing the Church against the attacks of Huss on one side, and against the more dangerous encroachments of the Pope and the monks on the other. This triumph, however, was of short duration. All the rights which the Germans seemed to have conquered at the Councils of Constanz and Basle were sacrificed by their own Emperor. No one dared to say again what Gregory von Heimburg had said to the Italian clergy, — "Quid fines alienos invaditis? quid falcem vestram in messem alienam extenditis?" Under Æneas Sylvius, the power of the Pope in Germany was as absolute as ever. The Nominalist party lost all the ground which it had gained before. It was looked upon with suspicion by Pope and Emperor. It was banished from courts and universities, and the disciples of the Realistic school began a complete crusade against the followers of Ockam.

Johannes Heynlin a Lapide, a former head of a house in Paris, migrated to Basle, in order to lend his influence and authority to the Realist party in that rising university. Trithemius says of him: "Hic doctrinam corum Parisiensium qui reales appellantur primus ad Basiliensium universitatem transtulit, ibidemque plantavit, roboravit et auxit." This Johannes Heynlin a Lapide, however, though a violent champion of the then victorious Realist party, was by no means a man without liberal sentiments. On many points the Realists were more tolerant, or at least more enlightened, than the Nominalists. They counted among themselves better scholars than the adherents of Ockam. They were the first and foremost to point out the uselessness of the dry scholastic system of teaching grammar and logic, and nothing else. And though they cherished their own ideas as to the supreme authority of the Pope, the divine right of the Emperor, or the immaculate conception of the Virgin (a dogma denied by the Dominicans, and defended by the Franciscans), they were always ready to point out abuses and to suggest reforms. The age in which they lived was not an age of decisive thought or decisive action. There was a want of character in individuals as well as in parties; and the points in which they differed were of small importance, though they masked differences of greater weight. At Basle, the men who were gathered round Johannes a Lapide were what we should call Liberal Conservatives, and it is among

them that we find Sebastian Brant. Basle could then
boast of some of the most eminent men of the time.
Besides Agricola, and Wimpheling, and Geiler von
Kaisersberg, and Trithemius, Reuchlin was there for
a time, and Wessel, and the Greek Kontablacos. Sebastian Brant, though on friendly terms with most of
these men, was their junior; and, among his contemporaries, a new generation grew up, more independent and more free-spoken than their masters, though
as yet very far from any revolutionary views in matters of Church or State. Feuds broke out very soon
between the old and the young schools. Locher, the
friend of Brant, — the poet who had turned his "Ship
of Fools" into Latin verse, — published a poem, in
which he attacked rather petulantly the scholastic
philosophy and theology. Wimpheling, at the request
of Geiler of Kaisersberg, had to punish him for this
audacity, and he did it in a pamphlet full of the most
vulgar abuse. Reuchlin also had given offense, and
was attacked and persecuted; but his party retaliated
by the "Epistolæ Obscurorum Virorum." Thus the
Conservative, or Realistic party became divided; and
when, at the beginning of a new century and a new
era in the history of the world, Luther raised his
voice in defense of national and religious freedom,
he was joined not only by the more advanced descendants of the Nominalistic school, but by all the
vigor, the talent, and the intellect of the old Conservatives.

Brant himself, though he lived at Strassburg up to
1521, did not join the standard of the Reformation.
He had learned to grumble, to find fault, to abuse, and
to condemn; but his time was gone when the moment
for action arrived. And yet he helped toward the

success of the Reformation in Germany. He had
been one of the first, after the discovery of printing,
to use the German language for political purposes.
His fly-sheets, his illustrated editions, had given useful hints how to address the large masses of the people. If he looked upon the world, as it then was, as
a ship of fools, and represented every weakness, vice,
and wickedness under the milder color of foolery, the
people who read his poems singled out some of his
fools, and called them knaves. The great work of
Sebastian Brant was his "Narrenschiff." It was first
published in 1497, at Basle, and the first edition,
though on account of its wood-cuts it could not have
been a very cheap book, was sold off at once. Edition
after edition followed, and translations were published
in Latin, in Low-German, in Dutch, in French, and
English. Sermons were preached on the "Narrenschiff;" Trithemius calls it *Divina Satira*, Locher
compares Brant with Dante, Hutten calls him the
new lawgiver of German poetry. The "Narrenschiff" is a work which we may still read with pleasure, though it is difficult to account for its immense
success at the time of its publication. Some historians
ascribe it to the wood-cuts. They are certainly very
clever, and there is reason to suppose that most of
them were, if not actually drawn, at least suggested
by Brant himself. Yet even a Turner has failed to
render mediocre poetry popular by his illustrations,
and there is nothing to show that the caricatures of
Brant were preferred to his satires. Now his satires,
it is true, are not very powerful, nor pungent, nor
original. But his style is free and easy. Brant is not
a ponderous poet. He writes in short chapters, and
mixes his fools in such a manner that we always meet

with a variety of new faces. It is true that all this
would hardly be sufficient to secure a decided success
for a work like his at the present day. But then we
must remember the time in which he wrote. What
had the poor people of Germany to read toward the
end of the fifteenth century? Printing had been invented, and books were published and sold with great
rapidity. People were not only fond, but proud, of
reading books. Reading was fashionable, and the first
fool who enters Brant's ship is the man who buys
books. But what were the books that were offered
for sale? We find among the early prints of the fifteenth century religious, theological, and classical
works in great abundance, and we know that the
respectable and wealthy burghers of Augsburg and
Strassburg were proud to fill their shelves with these
portly volumes. But then German aldermen had
wives, and daughters, and sons, and what were they
to read during the long winter evenings? The poetry of the thirteenth century was no longer intelligible, and the fourteenth and fifteenth centuries had
produced very little that would be to the taste of
young ladies and gentlemen. The poetry of the
"Meistersänger" was not very exhilarating. The
romances of "The Book of Heroes" had lost all
their native charms under the rough treatment they
had experienced at the hand of their latest editor,
Casper von der Roen. The so-called "Misteries"
(not mysteries) might be very well as Christmas pan-
tomimes once a year, but they could not be read for
their own sake, like the dramatic literature of later
times. The light literature of the day consisted entirely in novels; and in spite of their miserable character, their popularity was immense. Besides the

"Gesta Romanorum," which were turned into German verse and prose, we meet with French novels, such as "Lother and Maler," translated by a Countess of Nassau in 1437, and printed in 1514; "Pontus and Sidonia," translated from the French by Eleanor of Scotland, the wife of Sigismund of Austria, published 1498; "Melusina," equally from the French, published 1477. The old epic poems of "Tristan," and "Lancelot," and "Wigalois," were too long and tedious. People did not care any longer for the deep thoughts of Wolfram von Eschenbach, and the beautiful poetry of Gottfried von Strassburg. They wanted only the plot, the story, the dry bones; and these were dished up in the prose novels of the fifteenth century, and afterwards collected in the so-called "Book of Love." There was room, therefore, at that time for a work like the "Ship of Fools." It was the first printed book that treated of contemporaneous events and living persons, instead of old German battles and French knights. People are always fond of reading the history of their own times. If the good qualities of their age are brought out, they think of themselves or their friends; if the dark features of their contemporaries are exhibited, they think of their neighbors and enemies. Now, the "Ship of Fools" is just such a satire which ordinary people would read, and read with pleasure. They might feel a slight twinge now and then, but they would put down the book at the end, and 'thank God that they were not like other men. There is a chapter on Misers, — and who would not gladly give a penny to a beggar? There is a chapter on Gluttony, — and who was ever more than a little exhilarated after dinner? There is a chapter on Church-goers, — and who ever went to church for respectability's sake, or to show off a gaudy dress, or a fine dog, or a new hawk? There is a chapter on Dancing, — and who ever danced except for the sake of exercise? There is a chapter on Adultery, — and who ever did more than flirt with his neighbor's wife? We sometimes wish that Brant's satire had been a little more searching, and that, instead of his many allusions to classical fools (for his book is full of scholarship), he had given us a little more of the *chronique scandaleuse* of his own time. But he was too good a man to do this, and his contemporaries no doubt were grateful to him for his forbearance.

Brant's poem is not easy to read. Though he was a contemporary of Luther, his language differs much more from modern German than Luther's translation of the Bible. His "Ship of Fools" wanted a commentary, and this want has been supplied by one of the most learned and industrious scholars of Germany, Professor Zarncke, in his lately published edition of the "Narrenschiff." This must have been a work of many years of hard labor. Nothing that is worth knowing about Brant and his works has been omitted, and we hardly know of any commentary on Aristophanes or Juvenal in which every difficulty is so honestly met as in Professor Zarncke's notes on the German satirist. The editor is a most minute and painstaking critic. He tries to reëstablish the correct reading of every word, and he enters upon his work with as much zeal as if the world could not be saved till every tittle of Brant's poem had been restored. He is, however, not only a critic, but a sensible and honest man. He knows what is worth knowing and what is not, and he does not allow himself to be carried away by a desire to display his own superior acquirements, — a weakness, which makes so many of his colleagues forgetful of the real ends of knowledge, and the real duties of the scholar and the historian.

We have to say a few words on the English translation of Brant's "Ship of Fools." It was not made from the original, but from Locher's Latin translation. It reproduces the matter, but not the manner of the original satire. Some portions are added by the translator, Alexander Barclay, and in some parts his translation is an improvement on the original. It was printed in 1508, published 1509, and went through several editions.

The following may serve as a specimen of Barclay's translation, and of his original contributions to Brant's "Navis Stultifera:" —

"Here beginneth the 'Ship of Fooles,' and first of unprofitable bookes: —

"I am the first foole of all the whole navis,
To keep the Pompe, the Helme, and eke the Sayle:
For this is my minde, this one pleasure have I,
Of bookes to have great plentie and apparayle.
I take no wisdome by them, not yet avayle,
Nor them perceave not, and then I them despise:
Thus am I a foole, and all that sue that guise.

"That in this Ship the chiefe place I governe,
By this wide Sea with fooles wandring,
The cause is plaine and easy to discerne,
Still am I busy, bookes assembling,
For to have plentie it is a pleasant thing
In my conceyt, and to have them ay in hande:
But what they meane do I not understande.

"But yet I have them in great reverence
And honoure, saving them from filth and ordure,
By often brusshing and much diligence,
Full goodly bounde in pleasant coverture,
Of Damas, Sattin, or els of Velvet pure:
I keepe them sure, fearing least they should be lost,
For in them is the cunning wherein I me boast.

> "But if it fortune that any learned men
> Within my house fall to disputation,
> I drawe the curtaynes to shewe my bokes than,
> That they of my cunning should make probation:
> I kepe not to fall in altercation,
> And while they comment, my bookes I turne and winde,
> For all is in them, and nothing in my minde."

In the fourth chapter, "Of newe fassions and disguised garmentes," there is at the end what is called "The Lenvoy of Alexander Barclay," and in it an allusion to Henry VIII.:—

> "But ye proude galants that thus your selfe disguise,
> Be ye ashamed, beholde unto your prince:
> Consider his sadness, his honestie devise,
> His clothing expresseth his inwarde prudence,
> Ye see no example of such inconvenience
> In his highness, but godly wit and gravitie,
> Knowe him, and sorrowe for your enormitie."

1858.

IV.

LIFE OF SCHILLER.[1]

———◆———

The hundredth anniversary of the birthday of Schiller, which, according to the accounts published in the German newspapers, seems to have been celebrated in most parts of the civilized, nay, even the uncivilized world, is an event in some respects unprecedented in the literary annals of the human race. A nation honors herself by honoring her sons, and it is but natural that in Germany every town and village should have vied in doing honor to the memory of one of their greatest poets. The letters which have reached us from every German capital relate no more than what we expected. There were meetings and feastings, balls and theatrical representations. The veteran philologist, Jacob Grimm, addressed the Berlin Academy on the occasion in a soul-stirring oration; the directors of the Imperial Press at Vienna seized the opportunity to publish a splendid album, or "Schiller-

---

[1] *Rede auf Schiller*, von Jacob Grimm. Berlin, 1859. (Address on Schiller, by Jacob Grimm.)
Schiller-Buch, von Tannenberg; Wien. From the Imperial Printing Press, 1859.
Schiller's Life and Works. By Emil Palleske. Translated by Lady Wallace. London, Longman and Co., 1860.
Vie de Schiller. Par Ad. Regnier, Membre de l'Institut. Paris, Hachette, 1859.

Buch," in honor of the poet; unlimited eloquence was poured forth by professors and academicians; school children recited Schiller's ballads; the German students shouted the most popular of his songs; nor did the ladies of Germany fail in paying their tribute of gratitude to him who, since the days of the Minnesängers, had been the most eloquent herald of female grace and dignity. In the evening torch processions might be seen marching through the streets, bonfires were lighted on the neighboring hills, houses were illuminated, and even the solitary darkness of the windows of the Papal Nuncio at Vienna added to the lustre of the day.[1] In every place where Schiller had spent some years of his life, local recollections were revived and perpetuated by tablets and monuments. The most touching account of all came from the small village of Cleversulzbach. On the village cemetery, or, as it is called in German, the "God's-acre," there stands a tombstone, and on it the simple inscription, "Schiller's Mother." On the morning of her son's birthday the poor people of the village were gathered together round that grave, singing one of their sacred hymns, and planting a lime-tree in the soil which covers the heart that loved him best.

But the commemoration of Schiller's birthday was not confined to his native country. We have seen, in the German papers, letters from St. Petersburg and Lisbon, from Venice, Rome, and Florence, from Amsterdam, Stockholm, and Christiana, from Warsaw and Odessa, from Jassy and Bucharest, from Constantinople, Algiers, and Smyrna, and lately from America and Australia, all describing the festive gatherings which were suggested, no doubt, by Schiller's cosmo-

[1] See *The Times'* Special Correspondent from Vienna, November 14.

politan countrymen, but joined in most cheerfully by all the nations of the globe. Poets of higher rank than Schiller — Dante, Shakespeare, and Goethe — have never aroused such world-wide sympathies; and it is not without interest to inquire into the causes which have secured to Schiller this universal popularity. However superlative the praises which have lately been heaped on Schiller's poetry by those who cannot praise except in superlatives, we believe that it was not the poet, but the man, to whom the world has paid this unprecedented tribute of love and admiration. After reading Schiller's works we must read Schiller's life, — the greatest of all his works. It is a life not unknown to the English public, for it has been written by Carlyle. The last festivities, however, have given birth to several new biographies. Palleske's " Life of Schiller " has met with such success in Germany that it well deserved the honor which it has lately received at the hands of Lady Wallace, and under the special patronage of the Queen, of being translated into English. Another very careful and lucid account of the poet's life is due to the pen of a member of the French Institute, M. A. Regnier, the distinguished tutor of the Comte de Paris.

In reading these lives, together with the voluminous literature which is intended to illustrate the character of the German poet, we frequently felt inclined to ask one question, to which none of Schiller's biographers has returned a satisfactory answer: " What were the peculiar circumstances which brought out in Germany, and in the second half of the eighteenth century, a man of the moral character, and a poet of the creative genius, of Schiller?" Granted that he was endowed by nature with the highest talents, how did he grow to be a poet, such as we know him, different from all other German poets, and yet in thought, feeling, and language the most truly German of all the poets of Germany? Are we reduced to appeal to the mysterious working of an unknown power, if we wish to explain to ourselves why, in the same country and at the same time, poetical genius assumed such different forms as are seen in the writings of Schiller and Goethe? Is it to be ascribed to what is called individuality, a word which in truth explains nothing; or is it possible for the historian and psychologist to discover the hidden influences which act on the growing mind, and produce that striking variety of poetical genius which we admire in the works of contemporaneous poets, such as Schiller and Goethe in Germany, or Wordsworth and Byron in England? Men grow not only from within, but also from without. We know that a poet is born, — *poeta nascitur*, — but we also know that his character must be formed; the seed is given, but the furrow must be ploughed in which it is to grow; and the same grain which, if thrown on cultivated soil, springs into fullness and vigor, will dwindle away, stunted and broken, if cast upon shallow and untilled land. There are certain events in the life of every man which fashion and stamp his character; they may seem small and unimportant in themselves, but they are great and important to each of us; they mark that slight bend where two lines which had been running parallel begin to diverge, never to meet again. The Greeks call such events *epochs*, i. e. halts.

We halt for a moment, we look about and wonder, and then choose our further way in life. It is the duty of biographers to discover such epochs, such halting-points, in the lives of their heroes; and we shall endeavor to do the same in the life of Schiller by watching the various influences which determined the direction of his genius at different periods of his poetical career.

The period of Schiller's childhood is generally described with great detail by his biographers. We are told who his ancestors were. I believe they were bakers. We are informed that his mother possessed in her *trousseau*, among other things, four pairs of stockings, — three of cotton, one of wool. There are also long discussions on the exact date of his birth. We hear a great deal of early signs of genius, or rather, we should say, of things done and said by most children, but invested with extraordinary significance if remembered of the childhood of great men. To tell the truth, we can find nothing very important in what we thus learn of the early years of Schiller, nor does the poet himself in later years dwell much on the recollections of his dawning mind. If we must look for some determinating influences during the childhood of Schiller, they are chiefly to be found in the character of his father. The father was not what we should call a well-educated man. He had been brought up as a barber and surgeon; had joined a Bavarian regiment in 1745, during the Austrian war of succession; and had acted as a non-commissioned officer, and, when occasion required, as a chaplain. After the peace of Aix-la-Chapelle he had married the daughter of an innkeeper. He was a brave man, a God-fearing man, and, as is not unfrequently the case with half-educated people, a man very fond of reading. What he had failed to attain himself, he wished to see realized in his only son. The following prayer was found among the papers of the father: "And Thou, Being of all beings, I have asked Thee after the birth of my only son, that Thou wouldst add to his powers of intellect what I from deficient instruction was unable to attain. Thou hast heard me. Thanks be to Thee, bounteous Being, that Thou heedest the prayers of mortals." A man of this stamp of mind would be sure to exercise his own peculiar influence on his children. He would make them look on life, not as a mere profession, where the son has only to follow in the steps of his father; his children would early become familiar with such ideas as "*making* one's way in life," and would look forward to a steep path rather than to a beaten track. Their thoughts would dwell on the future at a time when other children live in the present only, and an adventurous spirit would be roused, without which no great work has ever been conceived and carried out.

When his children, young Frederick and his sisters, were growing up, their father read to them their morning and evening prayers; and so fond was the boy of the Old and New Testament stories that he would often leave his games in order to be present at his father's readings. In 1765 the family left Marbach on the Neckar. The father was ordered by the Duke of Wurtemberg to Lorch, a place on the frontier, where he had to act as recruiting officer. His son received his education in the house of a clergyman, began Latin at six, Greek at seven; and as far as we are able to see, he neither seems to have considered himself, nor to have been considered by his masters, as very superior to other boys. He was a good boy, tenderly attached to his parents, fond of games, and regular at school. There are but two marked features which we have an opportunity of watching in him as

a boy. He knew no fear, and he was full of the
warmest sympathy for others. The first quality secured him the respect, the second the love, of those
with whom he came in contact. His parents, who
were poor, had great difficulty in restraining his generosity. He would give away his school-books and the
very buckles off his shoes. Both his fearlessness and
universal sympathy are remarkable through the whole
of his after-life. Not even his enemies could point
out one trait of cowardice or selfishness in anything
he ever did, or said, or wrote. There are some perti-
nent remarks on the combination of these two qualities, sympathy with others and courage, by the author
of "Friends in Council."

"If greatness," he writes, "can be shut up in qualities, it
will be found to consist in courage and in openness of mind and
soul. These qualities may not seem at first to be so potent.
But see what *growth* there is in them. The education of a man
of open mind is never ended. Then with openness of soul a man
sees some way into all other souls that come near him, feels
with them, has their experience, is in himself a people. Sympathy is the universal solvent. Nothing is understood without
it. . . . Add courage to this openness, and you have a man who
can own himself in the wrong, can forgive, can trust, can adven-
ture, can, in short, use all the means that insight and sympathy
endow him with."

A plucky and warm-hearted boy, under the care
of an honest, brave, and intelligent father and a tender
and religious mother, — this is all we know and care
to know about Schiller during the first ten years of his
life. In the year 1768 there begins a new period in
the life of Schiller. His father was settled at Ludwigs-
burg, the ordinary residence of the reigning Duke of
Wurtemberg, the Duke Charles. This man was destined to exercise a decisive influence on Schiller's character. Like many German sovereigns in the middle of

the last century, Duke Charles of Wurtemberg had felt
the influence of those liberal ideas which had found so
powerful an utterance in the works of the French and
English philosophers of the eighteenth century. The
philosophy which in France was smiled at by kings
and statesmen, while it roused the people to insurrection and regicide, produced in Germany a deeper impression on the minds of the sovereigns and ruling
classes than of the people. In the time of Frederick
the Great and Joseph II. it became fashionable among
sovereigns to profess Liberalism, and to work for the
enlightenment of the human race. It is true that this
liberal policy was generally carried out in a rather despotic way, and people were emancipated and enlightened very much as the ancient Saxons were converted
by Charlemagne. We have an instance of this in the
case of Schiller. Duke Charles had founded an institution where orphans and the sons of poor officers
were educated free of expense. He had been informed that young Schiller was a promising boy, and
likely to reflect credit on his new institution, and he
proceeded without further inquiry to place him on the
list of his *protégés*, assigning to him a place at his military school. It was useless for the father to remonstrate, and explain to the Duke that his son had a
decided inclination for the Church. Schiller was sent
to the Academy in 1773, and ordered to study law.
The young student could not but see that an injustice
had been done him, and the irritation which it caused
was felt by him all the more deeply because it would
have been dangerous to give expression to his feelings.
The result was that he made no progress in the subjects which he had been commanded to study. In
1775 he was allowed to give up law, not, however, to

return to theology, but to begin the study of medicine. But medicine, though at first it seemed more attractive, failed, like law, to call forth his full energies. In the mean time another interference on the part of the Duke proved even more abortive, and to a certain extent determined the path which Schiller's genius was to take in life. The Duke had prohibited all German classics at his Academy; the boys, nevertheless, succeeded in forming a secret library, and Schiller read the works of Klopstock, Klinger, Lessing, Goethe, and Wieland's translations of Shakespeare with rapture, no doubt somewhat increased by the dangers he braved in gaining access to these treasures. In 1780, the same year in which he passed his examination and received the appointment of regimental surgeon, Schiller wrote his first tragedy, "The Robbers." His taste for dramatic poetry had been roused partly by Goethe's "Goetz von Berlichingen" and Shakespeare's plays, partly by his visits to the theatre, which, under the patronage of the Duke, was then in a very flourishing state. The choice of the subject of his first dramatic composition was influenced by the circumstances of his youth. His poetical sympathy for a character such as Karl Moor, a man who sets at defiance all the laws of God and man, can only be accounted for by the revulsion of feeling produced on his boyish mind by the strict military discipline to which all the pupils at the Academy were subjected. His sense of right and wrong was strong enough to make him paint his hero as a monster, and to make him inflict on him the punishment he merited. But the young poet could not resist the temptation of throwing a brighter light on the redeeming points in the character of a robber and murderer by pointedly placing him in contrast with the even darker shades of hypocritical respectability and saintliness in the picture of his brother Franz. The language in which Schiller paints his characters is powerful, but it is often wild and even coarse. The Duke did not approve of his former *protégé;* the very title-page of "The Robbers" was enough to offend his Serene Highness, — it contained a rising lion, with the motto "*In tyrannos.*" The Duke gave a warning to the young military surgeon, and when, soon after, he heard of his going secretly to Mannheim to be present at the first performance of his play, he ordered him to be put under military arrest. All these vexations Schiller endured, because he knew full well there was no escape from the favors of his royal protector. But when at last he was ordered never to publish again except on medical subjects, and to submit all his poetical compositions to the Duke's censorship, this proved too much for our young poet. His ambition had been roused. He had sat at Mannheim a young man of twenty, unknown, amid an audience of men and women who listened with rapturous applause to his own thoughts and words. That evening at the theatre of Mannheim had been a decisive evening, — it was an epoch in the history of his life; he had felt his power and the calling of his genius; he had perceived, though in a dim distance, the course he had to run and the laurels he had to gain. When he saw that the humor of the Duke was not likely to improve, he fled from a place where his wings were clipped and his voice silenced. Now, this flight from one small German town to another may seem a matter of very little consequence at present. But in Schiller's time it was a matter of life and death. German sovereigns were accustomed to look upon their subjects as their property. Without even the show of a trial the poet Schubart had been condemned to life-long confinement by this same Duke Charles. Schiller, in fleeing his benefactor's dominions, had not only thrown away all his chances in life, but he had placed his safety and the safety of his family in extreme danger. It was a bold, perhaps a reckless step. But whatever we may think of it in a moral point of view, as historians we must look upon it as the Hegira in the life of the poet.

Schiller was now a man of one or two and twenty, thrown upon the world penniless, with nothing to depend on but his brains. The next ten years were hard years for him; they were years of unsettledness, sometimes of penury and despair, sometimes of extravagance and folly. This third period in Schiller's life is not marked by any great literary achievements. It would be almost a blank were it not for the "Don Carlos," which he wrote during his stay near Dresden, between 1785–87. His "Fiesco" and "Cabale und Liebe," though they came out after his flight from Stuttgard, had been conceived before, and they were only repeated protests, in the form of tragedies, against the tyranny of rulers and the despotism of society. They show no advance in the growth of Schiller's mind. Yet that mind, though less productive than might have been expected, was growing as every mind grows between the years of twenty and thirty; and it was growing chiefly through contact with men. We must make full allowance for the powerful influence exercised at that time by the literature of the day (by the writings of Herder, Lessing, and Goethe), and by political events, such as the French Revolution. But if we watch Schiller's career carefully, we see that his character was chiefly moulded by his intercourse with men. His life was rich in friendships, and what mainly upheld him in his struggles and dangers was the sympathy of several high-born and high-minded persons, in whom the ideals of his own mind seemed to have found their fullest realization.

Next to our faith in God, there is nothing so essential to the healthy growth of our whole being as an unshaken faith in man. This faith in man is the great feature in Schiller's character, and he owes it to a kind Providence which brought him in contact with such noble natures as Frau von Wolzogen, Körner, Dalberg; in later years with his wife; with the Duke of Weimar, the Prince of Augustenburg, and lastly with Goethe. There was at that time a powerful tension in the minds of men, and particularly of the higher classes, which led them to do things which at other times men only aspire to do. The impulses of a most exalted morality — a morality which is so apt to end in mere declamation and deceit — were not only felt by them, but obeyed and carried out. Frau von Wolzogen, knowing nothing of Schiller except that he had been at the same school with her son, received the exiled poet, though fully aware that by doing so she might have displeased the Duke and blasted her fortunes and those of her children. Schiller preserved the tenderest attachment to this motherly friend through life, and his letters to her display a most charming innocence and purity of mind.

Another friend was Körner, a young lawyer living at Leipzig, and afterwards at Dresden — a man who had himself to earn his bread. He had learned to love Schiller from his writings; he received him at his house, a perfect stranger, and shared with the poor poet his moderate income with a generosity worthy of a prince. He, too, remained his friend through life; his son was Theodore Körner, the poet of "Lyre and Sword," who fell fighting as a volunteer for his country against French invaders.

A third friend and patron of Schiller was Dalberg. He was the coadjutor, and was to have been the successor, of the Elector of Hesse, then an ecclesiastical Electorate. His rank was that of a reigning prince, and he was made afterwards by Napoleon Fürst-Primas — Prince Primate — of the Confederation of the Rhine. But it was not his station, his wealth, and influence, it was his mind and heart which made him the friend of Schiller, Goethe, Herder, Wieland, Jean Paul, and all the most eminent intellects of his time. It is refreshing to read the letters of this Prince. Though they belong to a later period of Schiller's life, a few passages may here be quoted in order to characterize his friend and patron. Dalberg had promised Schiller a pension of 4,000 florins (not 4,000 thalers, as M. Regnier asserts) as soon as he should succeed to the Electorate, and Schiller in return had asked him for some hints with regard to his own future literary occupations. The Prince answers: "Your letter has delighted me. To be remembered by a man of your heart and mind is a true joy to me. I do not venture to determine what Schiller's comprehensive and vivifying genius is to undertake. But may I be allowed to humbly express a wish that spirits endowed with the powers of giants should ask themselves, 'How can I be most useful to mankind?' This inquiry, I think, leads most surely to immortality, and the rewards of a peaceful conscience. May you enjoy the purest happiness, and think sometimes of your

friend and servant, Dalberg." When Schiller was
hesitating between history and dramatic poetry, Dalberg's keen eye discovered at once that the stage was
Schiller's calling, and that there his influence would be
most beneficial. Schiller seemed to think that a professorial chair in a German university was a more
honorable position than that of a poet. Dalberg
writes: " Influence on mankind" (for this he knew to
be Schiller's highest ambition) "depends on the vigor
and strength which a man throws into his works.
Thucydides and Xenophon would not deny that poets
like Sophocles and Horace have had at least as much
influence on the world as they themselves." When
the French invasion threatened the ruin of Germany
and the downfall of the German sovereigns, Dalberg
writes again, in 1796, with perfect serenity: "True
courage must never fail! The friends of virtue and
truth ought now to act and speak all the more vigorously and straightforwardly. In the end, what you,
excellent friend, have so beautifully said in your
'Ideals' remains true: 'The diligence of the righteous
works slowly but surely, and friendship is soothing
comfort. It is only when I hope to be hereafter of assistance to my friends that I wish for a better fate.'"
The society and friendship of such men, who are rare
in all countries and in all ages, served to keep up in
Schiller's mind those ideal notions of mankind which
he had first imbibed from his own heart, and from the
works of philosophers. They find expression in all
his writings, but are most eloquently described in his
"Don Carlos." We should like to give some extracts
from the dialogue between King Philip and the Marquis Posa; but our space is precious, and hardly allows
us to do more than just to glance at those other friends

and companions whose nobility of mind and generosity of heart left so deep an impress on the poet's soul.

The name of Karl August, the Duke of Weimar, has acquired such a world-wide celebrity as the friend of Goethe and Schiller that we need not dwell long on his relation to our poet. As early as 1784 Schiller was introduced to him at Darmstadt, where he was invited to court to read some scenes of his "Don Carlos." The Duke gave him then the title of "Rath," and from the year 1787, when Schiller first settled at Weimar, to the time of his death, in 1804, he remained his firm friend. The friendship of the Prince was returned by the poet, who, in the days of his glory, declined several advantageous offers from Vienna and other places, and remained at the court of Weimar, satisfied with the small salary which that great Duke was able to give him.

There was but one other Prince whose bounty Schiller accepted, and his name deserves to be mentioned, not so much for his act of generosity as for the sentiment which prompted it. In 1792, when Schiller was ill and unable to write, he received a letter from the Hereditary Prince of Holstein-Augustenburg and from Count Schimmelmann. We quote from the letter: —

"Your shattered health, we hear, requires rest, but your circumstances do not allow it. Will you grudge us the pleasure of enabling you to enjoy that rest? We offer you for three years an annual present of 1,000 thalers. Accept this offer, noble man. Let not our titles induce you to decline it. We know what they are worth; we know no pride but that of being men, citizens of that great republic which comprises more than the life of single generations, more than the limits of this globe. You have to deal with men, — your brothers, — not with proud princes, who, by this employment of their wealth, would fain indulge but in a more refined kind of pride."

No conditions were attached to this present, though a situation in Denmark was offered if Schiller should wish to go there. Schiller accepted the gift so nobly offered, but he never saw his unknown friends.[1] We owe to them, humanly speaking, the last years of Schiller's life, and with them the master-works of his genius, from " Wallenstein " to " William Tell." As long as these works are read and admired, the names of these noble benefactors will be remembered and revered.

The name of her whom we mentioned next among Schiller's noble friends and companions, — we mean his wife, — reminds us that we have anticipated events, and that we left Schiller after his flight in 1782, at the very beginning of his most trying years. His hopes of success at Mannheim had failed. The director of the Mannheim theatre, also a Dalberg, declined to assist him. He spent the winter in great solitude at the country-house of Frau von Wolzogen, finishing " Cabale und Liebe," and writing " Fiesco." In the summer of 1783 he returned to Mannheim, where he received an appointment in connection with the theatre of about £40 a year. Here he stayed till 1785, when he went to Leipzig, and afterwards to Dresden, living chiefly at the expense of his friend Körner. This unsettled kind of life continued till 1787, and produced, as we saw, little more than his tragedy of " Don Carlos." In the mean time, however, his taste for history had been developed. He had been reading more systematically at Dresden, and after he had gone to Weimar in 1787 he was able to publish, in 1788, his " History of the Revolt of the

[1] The Prince of Holstein-Augustenburg was the grandfather of the present Duke and of Prince Christian of Schleswig-Holstein.

Netherlands." On the strength of this he was appointed professor at Jena in 1789, first without a salary, afterwards with about £30 a year. He tells us himself how hard he had to work: "Every day," he says, "I must compose a whole lecture and write it out, — nearly two sheets of printed matter, not to mention the time occupied in delivering the lecture and making extracts." However, he had now gained a position, and his literary works began to be better paid. In 1790 he was enabled to marry a lady of rank, who was proud to become the wife of the poor poet, and was worthy to be the "wife of Schiller." Schiller was now chiefly engaged in historical researches. He wrote his "History of the Thirty Years' War" in 1791-92, and it was his ambition to be recognized as a German professor rather than as a German poet. He had to work hard in order to make up for lost time, and under the weight of excessive labor his health broke down. He was unable to lecture, unable to write. It was then that the generous present of the Duke of Augustenburg freed him for a time from the most pressing cares, and enabled him to recover his health.

The years of thirty to thirty-five were a period of transition and preparation in Schiller's life, to be followed by another ten years of work and triumph. These intermediate years were chiefly spent in reading history and studying philosophy, more especially the then reigning philosophy of Kant. Numerous essays on philosophy, chiefly on the Good, the Beautiful, and the Sublime, were published during this interval. But what is more important, Schiller's mind was enlarged, enriched, and invigorated; his poetical genius, by lying fallow for a time, gave promise of

a richer harvest to come; his position in the world
became more honorable, and his confidence in himself was strengthened by the confidence placed in
him by all around him. A curious compliment was
paid him by the Legislative Assembly then sitting
at Paris. On the 26th of August, 1792, a decree
was passed, conferring the title of *Citoyen Français*
on eighteen persons belonging to various countries,
friends of liberty and universal brotherhood. In the
same list with Schiller were the names of Klopstock,
Campe, Washington, Kosciusko, and Wilberforce.
The decree was signed by Roland, Minister of the
Interior, and countersigned by Danton. It did not
reach Schiller till after the enthusiasm which he too
had shared for the early heroes of the French Revolution had given way to disappointment and horror.
In the month of December of the very year in which
he had been thus honored by the Legislative Assembly, Schiller was on the point of writing an appeal to
the French nation in defense of Louis XVI. The
King's head, however, had fallen before this defense
was begun. Schiller, a true friend of true liberty,
never ceased to express his aversion to the violent
proceedings of the French revolutionists. "It is
the work of passion," he said, "and not of that
wisdom which alone can lead to real liberty." He
admitted that many important ideas, which formerly
existed in books only or in the heads of a few enlightened people, had become more generally current
through the French Revolution. But he maintained
that the real principles which ought to form the basis
of a truly happy political constitution were still hidden
from view. Pointing to a volume of Kant's "Criticism of Pure Reason," he said, "There they are, and

nowhere else; the French republic will fall as rapidly as it has risen; the republican government will lapse into anarchy, and sooner or later a man of genius will appear (he may come from any place) who will make himself not only master of France, but perhaps also of a great part of Europe." This was a remarkable prophecy for a young professor of history.

The last decisive event in Schiller's life was his friendship with Goethe. It dates from 1794, and with this year begins the great and crowning period of Schiller's life. To this period belong his "Wallenstein," his "Song of the Bell," his Ballads (1797-98), his "Mary Staurt" (1800), the "Maid of Orleans" (1801), the "Bride of Messina" (1803), and "William Tell;" in fact, all the works which have made Schiller a national poet and gained for him a world-wide reputation and an immortal name.

Goethe's character was in many respects diametrically opposed to Schiller's, and for many years it seemed impossible that there should ever be a community of thought and feeling between the two. Attempts to bring together these great rivals were repeatedly made by their mutual friends. Schiller had long felt himself drawn by the powerful genius of Goethe, and Goethe had long felt that Schiller was the only poet who could claim to be his peer. After an early interview with Goethe, Schiller writes, "On the whole, this meeting has not at all diminished the idea, great as it was, which I had previously formed of Goethe; but I doubt if we shall ever come into close communication with each other. Much that interests me has already had its epoch with him; his world is not my world." Goethe had expressed the same feeling. He saw Schiller occupying the very

position which he himself had given up as untenable;
he saw his powerful genius carrying out triumphantly
"those very paradoxes, moral and dramatic, from
which he was struggling to get liberated." "No
union," as Goethe writes, "was to be dreamt of. Between two spiritual antipodes there was more interven-
ing than a simple diameter of the spheres. Antipodes
of that sort act as a kind of poles, which can never
coalesce." How the first approach between these two
opposite poles took place Goethe has himself described,
in a paper entitled "Happy Incidents." But no happy
incident could have led to that glorious friendship,
which stands alone in the literary history of the whole
world, if there had not been on the part of Schiller
his warm sympathy for all that is great and noble, and
on the part of Goethe a deep interest in every man-
ifestation of natural genius. Their differences on
almost every point of art, philosophy, and religion,
which at first seemed to separate them forever, only
drew them more closely together, when they discovered in each other those completing elements which
produced true harmony of souls. Nor is it right to
say that Schiller owes more to Goethe than Goethe to
Schiller. If Schiller received from Goethe the higher
rules of art and a deeper insight into human nature,
Goethe drank from the soul of his friend the youth and
vigor, the purity and simplicity, which we never find
in any of Goethe's works before his "Hermann and
Dorothea." And, as in most friendships, it was not
so much Goethe as he was, but Goethe as reflected in
his friend's soul, who henceforth became Schiller's
guide and guardian. Schiller possessed the art of admiring, an art so much more rare than the art of
criticising. His eye was so absorbed in all that was

great, and noble, and pure, and high in Goethe's mind, that he could not, or would not, see the defects in his character. And Goethe was to Schiller what he was to no one else. He was what Schiller believed him to be; afraid to fall below his friend's ideal, he rose beyond himself until that high ideal was reached, which only a Schiller could have formed. Without this regenerating friendship it is doubtful whether some of the most perfect creations of Goethe and Schiller would ever have been called into existence.

We saw Schiller gradually sinking into a German professor, the sphere of his sympathies narrowed, the aim of his ambition lowered. His energies were absorbed in collecting materials and elaborating his "History of the Thirty Years' War," which was published in 1792. The conception of his great dramatic Trilogy, the "Wallenstein," which dates from 1791, was allowed to languish until it was taken up again for Goethe, and finished for Goethe in 1799. Goethe knew how to admire and encourage, but he also knew how to criticise and advise. Schiller, by nature meditative rather than observant, had been most powerfully attracted by Kant's ideal philosophy. Next to his historical researches, most of his time at Jena was given to metaphysical studies. Not only his mind, but his language suffered from the attenuating influences of that rarefied atmosphere which pervades the higher regions of metaphysical thought. His mind was attracted by the general and the ideal, and lost all interest in the individual and the real. This was not a right frame of mind, either for an historian or a dramatic poet. In Goethe, too, the philosophical element was strong, but it was kept under by the practical tendencies of his mind. Schiller looked for his ideal beyond the real world ; and, like the pictures of a Raphael, his conceptions seemed to surpass in purity and harmony all that human eye had ever seen. Goethe had discovered that the truest ideal lies hidden in real life; and like the master-works of a Michael Angelo, his poetry reflected that highest beauty which is revealed in the endless variety of creation, and must there be discovered by the artist and the poet. In Schiller's early works every character was the personification of an idea. In his "Wallenstein" we meet for the first time with real men and real life. In his "Don Carlos," Schiller, under various disguises more or less transparent, acts every part himself. In "Wallenstein" the heroes of the "Thirty Years' War" maintain their own individuality, and are not forced to discuss the social problems of Rousseau, or the metaphysical theories of Kant. Schiller was himself aware of this change, though he was hardly conscious of its full bearing. While engaged in composing his "Wallenstein," he writes to a friend:—

"I do my business very differently from what I used to do. The subject seems to be so much outside me that I can hardly get up any feeling for it. The subject I treat leaves me cold and indifferent, and yet I am full of enthusiasm for my work. With the exception of two characters to which I feel attached, Max Piccolomini and Thekla, I treat all the rest, and particularly the principal character of the play, only with the pure love of the artist. But I can promise you that they will not suffer from this. I look to history for limitation, in order to give, through surrounding circumstances, a stricter form and reality to my ideals. I feel sure that the historical will not draw me down or cripple me. I only desire through it to impart life to my characters and their actions. The life and soul must come from another source, through that power which I have already perhaps shown elsewhere, and without which even the first conception of this work would, of course, have been impossible."

How different is this from what Schiller felt in

former years! In writing "Don Carlos," he laid
down as a principle, that the poet must not be the
painter but the lover of his heroes, and in his early
days he found it intolerable in Shakespeare's dreams
that he could nowhere lay his hand on the poet himself. He was then, as he himself expresses it, unable
to understand nature, except at second-hand.

Goethe was Schiller's friend, but he was also Schiller's rival. There is a perilous period in the lives of
great men, namely, the time when they begin to feel
that their position is made, that they have no more
rivals to fear. Goethe was feeling this at the time
when he met Schiller. He was satiated with applause,
and his bearing towards the public at large became
careless and offensive. In order to find men with
whom he might measure himself, he began to write on
the history of Art, and to devote himself to natural
philosophy. Schiller, too, had gained his laurels chiefly
as a dramatic poet; and though he still valued the
applause of the public, yet his ambition as a poet was
satisfied; he was prouder of his "Thirty Years' War"
than of his "Robbers" and "Don Carlos." When
Goethe became intimate with Schiller, and discovered
in him those powers which as yet were hidden to
others, he felt that there was a man with whom even
he might run a race. Goethe was never jealous of
Schiller. He felt conscious of his own great powers,
and he was glad to have those powers again called out
by one who would be more difficult to conquer than
all his former rivals. Schiller, on the other hand,
perceived in Goethe the true dignity of a poet. At
Jena his ambition was to have the title of Professor of
History; at Weimar he saw that it was a greater
honor to be called a poet, and the friend of Goethe.

When he saw that Goethe treated him as his friend, and that the Duke and his brilliant court looked upon him as his equal, Schiller, too modest to suppose he had earned such favors, was filled with a new zeal, and his poetical genius displayed for a time an almost inexhaustible energy. Scarcely had his "Wallenstein" been finished, in 1799, when he began his "Mary Stuart." This play was finished in the summer of 1800, and a new one was taken in hand in the same year, — the "Maid of Orleans." In the spring of 1801 the "Maid of Orleans" appeared on the stage, to be followed in 1803 by the "Bride of Messina," and in 1804 by his last great work, his "William Tell." During the same time Schiller composed his best ballads, his "Song of the Bell," his epigrams, and his beautiful Elegy, not to mention his translations and adaptations of English and French plays for the theatre at Weimar. After his "William Tell" Schiller could feel that he no longer owed his place by the side of Goethe to favor and friendship, but to his own work and worth. His race was run, his laurels gained. His health, however, was broken, and his bodily frame too weak to support the strain of his mighty spirit. Death came to his relief, giving rest to his mind, and immortality to his name.

Let us look back once more on the life of Schiller. The lives of great men are the lives of martyrs; we cannot regard them as examples to follow, but rather as types of human excellence to study and to admire. The life of Schiller was not one which many of us would envy; it was a life of toil and suffering, of aspiration rather than of fulfillment, a long battle with scarcely a moment of rest for the conqueror to enjoy his hard-won triumphs. To an ambitious man the

last ten years of the poet's life might seem an ample
reward for the thirty years' war of life which he had
to fight single-handed. But Schiller was too great a
man to be ambitious. Fame with him was a means,
never an object. There was a higher, a nobler aim in
his life, which upheld him in all his struggles. From
the very beginning of his career Schiller seems to have
felt that his life was not his. He never lived for himself; he lived and worked for mankind. He discovered within himself how much there was of the
good, the noble, and the beautiful in human nature;
he had never been deceived in his friends. And such
was his sympathy with the world at large that he
could not bear to see in any rank of life the image of
man, created in the likeness of God, distorted by cunning, pride, and selfishness. His whole poetry may
be said to be written on the simple text, "Be true, be
good, be noble!" It may seem a short text, but truth
is very short, and the work of the greatest teachers of
mankind has always consisted in the unflinching incul-
cation of these short truths. There is in Schiller's
works a kernel full of immortal growth, which will
endure long after the brilliant colors of his poetry have
faded away. That kernel is the man, and without it
Schiller's poetry, like all other poetry, is but the song
of sirens. Schiller's character has been subjected to
that painful scrutiny to which, in modern times, the
characters of great men are subjected; everything he
ever did, or said, or thought, has been published; and
yet it would be difficult, in the whole course of his life,
to point out one act, one word, one thought, that could
be called mean, untrue, or selfish. From the beginning
to the end Schiller remained true to himself; he never
acted a part, he never bargained with the world. We

may differ from him on many points of politics, ethics,
and religion; but though we differ, we must always
respect and admire. His life is the best commentary
on his poetry; there is never a discrepancy between
the two. As mere critics, we may be able to admire
a poet without admiring the man; but poetry, it should
be remembered, was not meant for critics only, and its
highest purpose is never fulfilled, except where, as
with Schiller, we can listen to the poet and look up to
the man.

1849.

V.

WILHELM MÜLLER.[1]
1794-1827.

SELDOM has a poet in a short life of thirty years engraven his name so deeply on the memorial tablets of the history of German poetry as Wilhelm Müller. Although the youthful efforts of a poet may be appreciated by those few who are able to admire what is good and beautiful, even though it has never before been admired by others, yet in order permanently to win the ear and heart of his people, a poet must live with the people, and take part in the movements and struggles of his age. Thus only can he hope to stir and mould the thoughts of his contemporaries, and to remain a permanent living power in the recollections of his countrymen. Wilhelm Müller died at the very moment when the rich blossoms of his poetic genius were forming fruit; and after he had warmed and quickened the hearts of the youth of Germany with the lyric songs of his own youth, only a short span of time was granted him to show the world, as he did more especially in his "Greek Songs" and "Epi-

---

[1] Preface to a new edition of Wilhelm Müller's poems, published in 1868, in the *Bibliothek der Deutschen National-literatur des achtzehnten und neunzehnten Jahrhunderts*. Leipzig, Brockhaus. Translated from the German by G. A. M.

grams," the higher goal toward which he aspired. In
these his last works one readily perceives that his poetry would not have reflected the happy dreams of
youth only, but that he could perceive the poetry of
life in its sorrows as clearly as in its joys, and depict it
in true and vivid colors.

One may, I think, divide the friends and admirers
of Wilhelm Müller into two classes: those who rejoice
and delight in his fresh and joyous songs, and those
who admire the nobleness and force of his character as
shown in the poems celebrating the war of Greek independence, and in his epigrams. All poetry is not
for every one, nor for every one at all times. There
are critics and historians of literature who cannot tolerate songs of youth, of love, and of wine; they always
ask "why?" and "wherefore?" and they demand in
all poetry, before anything else, high or deep thoughts.
No doubt there can be no poetry without thought, but
there are thoughts which are poetical without being
drawn from the deepest depths of the heart and brain,
nay, which are poetical just because they are as simple
and true and natural as the flowers of the field or the
stars of heaven. There is a poetry for the old, but
there is also a poetry for the young. The young demand in poetry an interpretation of their own youthful
feelings, and first learn truly to understand themselves through those poets who speak for them as they
would speak for themselves, had nature endowed them
with melody of thought and harmony of diction.
Youth is and will remain the majority of the world,
and will let no gloomy brow rob it of its poetic enthusiasm for young love and old wine. True, youth is
not over-critical; true, it does not know how to speak
or write in learned phrases of the merits of its favorite

poets. But for all that, where is the poet who would not rather live in the warm recollection of the never-dying youth of his nation than in voluminous encyclopædias, or even in the marble Walhallas of Germany? The story and the songs of a miller's man who loves his master's daughter, and of a miller's daughter who loves a huntsman better, may seem very trivial, commonplace, and unpoetical to many a man of forty or fifty. But there are men of forty and fifty who have never lost sight of the bright but now far-off days of their own youth, who can still rejoice with those that rejoice, and weep with those that weep, and love with those that love, — aye, who can still fill their glasses with old and young, and in whose eyes every-day life has not destroyed the poetic bloom that rests everywhere on life so long as it is lived with warm and natural feelings. Songs which, like the "Beautiful Miller's Daughter" and the "Winter Journey," could so penetrate and again spring forth from the soul of Franz Schubert, may well stir the very depths of our own hearts, without the need of fearing the wise looks of those who possess the art of saying nothing in many words. Why should poetry be less free than painting to seek for what is beautiful wherever a human eye can discover, wherever human art can imitate it? No one blames the painter if, instead of giddy peaks or towering waves, he delineates on his canvas a quiet narrow valley, filled with a green mist, and enlivened only by a gray mill and a dark brown mill-wheel, from which the spray rises like silver dust, and then floats away, and vanishes in the rays of the sun. Is what is not too common for the painter, too common for the poet? Is an idyl in the truest, warmest, softest colors of the soul, like the

"Beautiful Miller's Daughter," less a work of art than
a landscape by Ruysdael? And observe in these songs
how the execution suits the subject; their tone is
thoroughly popular, and reminds many of us, perhaps
too much, of the popular songs collected by Arnim and
Brentano in "Des Knaben Wunderhorn." But this
could not be helped. Theocritus could not write his
idyls in grand Attic Greek; he needed the homeliness of the Bœotian dialect. It was the same with
Wilhelm Müller, who must not be blamed for expressions which now perhaps, more than formerly, may
sound, to fastidious ears, too homely or commonplace.

His simple and natural conception of nature is
shown most beautifully in the "Wanderer's Songs,"
and in the "Spring Wreath from the Plauen Valley."
Nowhere do we find a labored thought or a labored
word. The lovely spring world is depicted exactly as
it is, but over all is thrown the life and inspiration of
a poet's eye and a poet's mind, which perceives and
gives utterance to what others fail to see, and silent
nature cannot utter. It is this recognition of the beautiful in what is insignificant, of greatness in what is
small, of the marvelous in ordinary life, — yes, this perception of the divine in every earthly enjoyment, —
which gives its own charm to each of Wilhelm Müller's smallest poems, and endears them so truly to
those who, amidst the hurry of life, have not forgotten
the delight of absorption in nature, who have never
lost their faith in the mystery of the divine presence
in all that is beautiful, good, and true on earth. We
need only read the "Frühlingsmahl," or "Pfingsten"
to see how a whole world, aye, a whole heaven, may
be mirrored in the tiniest drop of dew.

And as enjoyment of nature finds so clear an echo

in the poetry of Wilhelm Müller, so also does the delight which man should have in man. Drinking songs and table songs do not belong to the highest flights of poetry; but if the delights of friendly meetings and greetings belong to some of the brightest moments of human happiness, why should a poet hold them to be beneath his muse? There is something especially German in all drinking songs, and no other nation has held its wine in such honor. Can one imagine English poems on port and sherry? or has a Frenchman much to tell us of his Bordeaux, or even of his Burgundy? The reason that the poetry of wine is unknown in England and France is, that in these countries people know nothing of what lends its poetry to wine, namely, the joyous consciousness of mutual pleasure, the outpouring of hearts, the feeling of common brotherhood, which makes learned professors and divines, generals and ministers, men once more at the sound of the ringing glasses. This purely human delight in the enjoyment of life, in the flavor of the German wine, and in the yet higher flavor of the German Symposium, finds it happiest expression in the drinking songs of Wilhelm Müller. They have often been set to music by the best masters, and have long been sung by the happy and joyous. The name of the poet is often forgotten, whilst many of his songs have become popular songs, just because they were sung from the heart and soul of the German people, as the people were fifty years ago, and as the best of them still are, in spite of many changes in the Fatherland.

It is easy to see that a serious tone is not wanting even in the drinking songs. The wine was good, but the times were bad. Those who, like Wilhelm Müller, had shared in the great sufferings and the great

hopes of the German people, and who then saw that
after all the sacrifices that had been made, all was in
vain, all was again as bad or even worse than before,
could with difficulty conceal their disaffection, however
helpless they felt themselves against the brutalities of
those in power, Many, who like Wilhelm Müller
had labored to reanimate German popular feeling;
who like him had left the university to sacrifice as
common soldiers their life and life's happiness to the
freedom of the Fatherland, and who then saw how the
terror felt by the scarcely rescued princes of their de-
liverers, and the fear of foreign nations of a united
and strong Germany, joined hand in hand to destroy
the precious seed sown in blood and tears, — could not
always suppress their gloomy anger at such faint-
hearted, weak-minded policy. On the first of January, 1820, Wilhelm Müller wrote thus, in the dedication of the second part of his "Letters from Rome" to
his friend Atterbom, the Swedish poet, with whom he
had but a short time before passed the Carnival time
in Italy joyously and carelessly: "And thus I greet
you in your old sacred Fatherland, not jokingly and
merrily, like the book, whose writer seems to have become a stranger to me, but earnestly and briefly; for
the great fast of the European world, expecting the
passion, and waiting for deliverance, can endure no
indifferent shrug of the shoulders and no hollow com-
promises and excuses. He who cannot act at this
time, can yet rest and mourn." For such words,
veiled as they were, resigned as they were, the fortress
of Mayence was at that time the usual answer.

"Deutsch und frei und stark und lauter
In dem deutschen Land
Ist der Wein allein geblieben
An der Rheines Strand.

> Ist der nicht ein Demagoge,
> Wer soll einer sein?
> Mainz, du stolze Bundesfeste,
> Sperr ihn nur nicht ein." [1]

That Wilhelm Müller escaped the petty and annoying persecutions of the then police system, he owed partly to the retired life he led in his little native country, partly to his own good spirits, which prevented him from entirely sinking the man in the politician. He had some enemies in the little court, whose Duke and Duchess were personally so attached to him. A prosperous life such as his could not fail to attract envy, and his frank, guileless character gave plenty of occasion for suspicion. But the only answer which he vouchsafed to his detractors was: —

> " Und lasst mir doch mein volles Glass,
> Und lasst mir meinen guten Spass,
> Mit unsrer schlechten Zeit!
> Wer bei dem Weine singt und lacht,
> Den thut, ihr Herrn, nicht in die Acht!
> Ein Kind ist Fröhligkeit." [2]

Wilhelm Müller evidently felt that when words are not deeds, or do not lead to deeds, silence is more worthy of a man than speech. He never became a political poet, at least never in his own country. But when the rising of the Greeks appealed to those human sympathies of Christian nations which can never be

---

[1] " Free, and strong, and pure, and German,
On the German Rhine,
Nothing can be now discovered
Save alone our wine;
If the wine is not a rebel,
Then no more are we;
Mainz, thou proud and frowning fortress,
Let him wander free!"

[2] " And let me have my full glass, and let me have my hearty laugh at these wretched times! He who can sing and laugh with his wine, you need not put under the ban, my lords: mirth is a harmless child."

quite extinguished, and when here, too, the faint-
hearted policy of the great powers played and bargained over the great events in the east of Europe
instead of trusting to those principles which alone can
secure the true and lasting well-being of states, as well
as of individuals, then the long accumulated wrath of
the poet and of the man burst forth and found utterance in the songs on the Greek war of independence.
Human, Christian, political, and classical sympathies
stirred his heart, and breathed that life into his poems,
which most of them still possess. It is astonishing how
a young man in a small isolated town like Dessau,
almost shut out from intercourse with the great world,
could have followed step by step the events of the
Greek revolution, seizing on all the right, the beauty,
the grandeur of the struggle, making himself intimately
acquainted with the dominant characters, whilst he at
the same time mastered the peculiar local coloring of
the passing events. Wilhelm Müller was not only a
poet, but he was intimately acquainted with classic antiquity. He *knew* the Greeks and the Romans. And
just as during his stay in Rome he recognized at all
points the old in what was new, and everywhere
sought to find what was eternal in the eternal city, so
now with him the modern Greeks were inseparably
joined with the ancient. A knowledge of the modern
Greek language appeared to him the natural completion of the study of old Greek; and it was his acquaintance with the popular songs of modern as well as of
ancient Hellas that gave the color which imparted such
a vivid expression of truth and naturalness to his own
Greek songs. It was thus that the " Griechen Lieder " arose, which appeared in separate but rapid
numbers, and found great favor with the people. But

even these "Griechen Lieder" caused anxiety to the
paternal governments of those days: —

"Ruh und Friede will Europa — warum hast du sie gestört?
Warum mit dem Wahn der Freiheit eigenmächtig dich bethört?
Hoff' auf keines Herren Hülfe gegen eines Herren Frohn:
Auch des Türkenkaisers Polster nennt Europa einen Thron."[1]

His last poems were suppressed by the Censor, as
well as his "Hymn on the Death of Raphael Riego."
Some of these were first published long after his
death; others must have been lost whilst in the Censor's hands.

Two of the Greek songs, "Mark Bozzaris," and
"Song before Battle," may help the English reader to
form his own opinion both of the poetical genius and
of the character of Wilhelm Müller: —

MARK BOZZARI.[2]

Oeffne deine hohen Thore, Missolunghi, Stadt der Ehren,
Wo der Helden Leichen ruhen, die uns fröhlich sterben lehren,
Oeffne deine hohen Thore, öffne deine tiefen Grüfte,
Auf, und streue Lorberreiser auf den Pfad und in die Lüfte;
Mark Bozzari's edlen Leib bringen wir an dir getragen.
Mark Bozzari's! Wer darf's wagen, solchen Helden zu beklagen?
Willst zuerst du seine Wunden oder seine Siege zählen?
Keinem Sieg wird eine Wunde, keiner Wund' ein Sieg hier fehlen.
Sieh auf unsern Lanzenspitzen sich die Turbanhäupter drehen,
Sieh, wie über seiner Bahre die Osmanenfahnen wehen,
Sieh, o sieh die letzten Werke, die vollbracht des Helden Rechte
In dem Feld von Karpinisi, wo sein Stahl im Blute zechte!
In der schwarzen Geisterstunde rief er unsre Schar zusammen.
Funken sprühten unsre Augen durch die Nacht wie Wetterflammen,
Uebers Knie zerbrachen wir jauchzend unsrer Schwerter Scheiden,
Um mit Sensen einzumähen in die feisten Türkenweiden;
Und wir drückten uns die Hände, und wir strichen uns die Bärte,

[1] "Europe wants but peace and quiet: why hast thou disturbed her rest?
How with silly dreams of freedom dost thou dare to fill thy breast?
If thou rise against thy rulers, Hellas, thou must fight alone,
E'en the bolster of a Sultan, loyal Europe calls a throne."

[2] I am enabled through the kindness of Mr. Theodore Martin to supply
an excellent translation of these two poems, printed by him in 1863, in a
volume intended for private circulation only.

Und der stampfte mit dem Fusse, und der rieb an seinem Schwerte.
Da erscholl Bozzari's Stimme: "Auf, ins Lager der Barbaren!
Auf, mir nach! Verirrt euch nicht, Brüder, in der Feinde Scharen!
Sucht ihr mich, im Zelt des Paschas werdet ihr mich sicher finden.
Auf, mit Gott! Er hilft die Feinde, hilft den Tod auch überwinden!
Auf!" Und die Trompete riss er hastig aus des Bläsers Händen
Und stiess selbst hinein so hell, dass es von den Felsenwänden
Heller stets und heller musste sich verdoppelnd widerhallen;
Aber heller widerhallt' es doch in unsern Herzen allen.
Wie des Herren Blitz und Donner aus der Wolkenburg der Nächte,
Also traf das Schwert der Freien die Tyrannen und die Knechte;
Wie die Tuba des Gerichtes wird dereinst die Sünder wecken,
Also scholl durchs Türkenlager brausend dieser Ruf der Schrecken:
"Mark Bozzari! Mark Bozzari! Sulioten! Sulioten!"
Solch ein guter Morgengruss ward den Schläfern da entboten.
Und sie rüttelten sich auf, und gleich hirtenlosen Schafen
Rannten sie durch alle Gassen, bis sie aneinander trafen
Und, bethört von Todesengeln, die durch ihre Schwärme gingen,
Brüder sich in blinder Wuth stürzten in der Brüder Klingen.
Frag' die Nacht nach unsern Thaten; sie hat uns im Kampf gesehen —
Aber wird der Tag es glauben, was in dieser Nacht geschehen?
Hundert Griechen, tausend Türken: also war die Saat zu schauen
Auf dem Feld von Karpinissi, als das Licht begann zu grauen.
Mark Bozzari, Mark Bozzari, und dich haben wir gefunden —
Kenntlich nur an deinem Schwerte, kenntlich nur an deinen Wunden,
An den Wunden, die du schlugest, und an denen, die dich trafen —
Wie du es verheissen hattest, in dem Zelt des Paschas schlafen.

Oeffne deine hohen Thore, Missolunghi, Stadt der Ehren,
Wo der Helden Leichen ruhen, die uns fröhlich sterben lehren,
Oeffne deine tiefen Grüfte, dass wir in den heil'gen Stätten
Neben Helden unsern Helden zu dem langen Schlafe betten! —
Schlafe bei dem deutschen Grafen, Grafen Normann, Fels der Ehren,
Bis die Stimmen des Gerichtes alle Gräber werden leeren.

MARK BOZZARIS.

Open wide, proud Missolonghi, open wide thy portals high,
Where repose the bones of heroes, teach us cheerfully to die!
Open wide thy lofty portals, open wide thy vaults profound;
Up, and scatter laurel garlands to the breeze and on the ground!
Mark Bozzaris' noble body is the freight to thee we bear. —
Mark Bozzaris'! Who for hero great as he to weep will dare?
Tell his wounds, his victories over! Which in number greatest be?
Every victory has its wound, and every wound its victory!
See, a turbaned head is grimly set on all our lances here!
See, how the Osmanli's banner swathes in purple folds his bier!

See, O see the latest trophies, which our hero's glory sealed,
When his glaive with gore was drunken on great Karpinissi's field!
In the murkiest hour of midnight did we at his call arise;
Through the gloom like lightning-flashes flashed the fury from our eyes;
With a shout, across our knees we snapped the scabbards of our swords,
Better down to mow the harvest of the mellow Turkish hordes;
And we clasped our hands together, and each warrior stroked his beard,
And one stamped the sward, another rubbed his blade, and vowed its wierd.
Then Bozzaris' voice resounded: "On, to the barbarian's lair!
On, and follow me, my brothers, see you keep together there!
Should you miss me, you will find me surely in the Pasha's tent!
On, with God! Through Him our foemen, death itself through Him is sbent!
On!" And swift he snatched the bugle from the hands of him that blew,
And himself awoke a summons that o'er dale and mountain flew,
Till each rock and cliff made answer clear and clearer to the call,
But a clearer echo sounded in the bosom of us all!
As from midnight's battlemented keep the lightnings of the Lord
Sweep, so swept our swords, and smote the tyrants and their slavish horde;
As the trump of doom shall waken sinners in their graves that lie,
So through all the Turkish leaguer thundered his appalling cry:
"Mark Bozzaris! Mark Bozzaris! Suliotes, smite them in their lair!"
Such the goodly morning greeting that we gave the sleepers there.
And they staggered from their slumber, and they ran from street to street,
Ran like sheep without a shepherd, striking wild at all they meet;
Ran, and frenzied by Death's angels, who amidst their myriads strayed,
Brother, in bewildered fury, dashed and fell on brother's blade.
Ask the night of our achievements! It beheld us in the fight,
But the day will never credit what we did in yonder night.
Greeks by hundreds, Turks by thousands, there like scattered seed they lay,
On the field of Karpinissi, when the morning broke in gray.
Mark Bozarris, Mark Bozarris, and we found thee gashed and mown
By thy sword alone we knew thee, knew thee by thy wounds alone;
By the wounds thy hand had cloven, by the wounds that seamed thy breast,
Lying, as thou hadst foretold us, in the Pasha's tent at rest!

Open wide, proud Missolonghi, open wide thy portals high,
Where repose the bones of heroes, teach us cheerfully to die!
Open wide thy vaults! Within their holy bounds a couch we'd make,
Where our hero, laid with heroes, may his last long slumber take!
Rest beside that Rock of Honor, brave Count Normann, rest thy head,
Till, at the archangel's trumpet, all the graves give up their dead!

LIED VOR DER SCHLACHT.

Wer für die Freiheit kämpft und fällt, dess Ruhm wird blühend stehn,
Solange frei die Winde noch durch freie Lüfte wehn,
Solange frei der Bäume Laub noch rauscht im grünen Wald,
Solang' des Stromes Woge noch frei nach dem Meere wallt,
Solang' des Adlers Fittich frei noch durch die Wolken fleugt,
Solang' ein freier Odem noch aus freiem Herzen steigt.

Wer für die Freiheit kämpft und fällt, dess Ruhm wird blühend stehn,
Solange freie Geister noch durch Erd' und Himmel gehn.
Durch Erd' und Himmel schwebt er noch, der Helden Schattenrahn,
Und rauscht um uns in stiller Nacht, in hellem Sonnenschein,
Im Sturm, der stolze Tannen bricht, und in dem Lüftchen auch,
Das durch das Gras auf Gräbern spielt mit seinem leisen Hauch,
In ferner Enkel Hause noch um alle Wiegen kreist
Auf Hellas' heldenreicher Flur der freien Ahnen Geist;
Der haucht in Wunderträumen schon den zarten Säugling an
Und weiht in seinem ersten Schlaf das Kind zu einem Mann;
Den Jüngling lockt sein Ruf hinaus mit nie gefühlter Lust
Zur Stätte, wo ein Freier fiel; da greift er in die Brust
Dem Zitternden, und Schauer ziehn ihm durch das tiefe Herz,
Er weiss nicht, ob es Wonne sei, ob es der erste Schmerz.
Herab, du heil'ge Geisterschar, schwell' unsre Fahnen auf,
Beflügle unsrer Herzen Schlag und unsrer Füsse Lauf;
Wir ziehen nach der Freiheit aus, die Waffen in der Hand,
Wir ziehen aus auf Kampf und Tod für Gott, fürs Vaterland!
Ihr seid mit uns, ihr rauscht um uns, eu'r Geisterodem zieht
Mit zauberischen Tönen hin durch unser Jubellied;
Ihr seid mit uns, ihr schwebt daher, ihr aus Thermopylä,
Ihr aus dem grünen Marathon, ihr von der blauen See,
Am Wolkenfelsen Mykale, am Salaminerstrand,
Ihr all' aus Wald, Feld, Berg und Thal im weiten Griechenland!

Wer für die Freiheit kämpft und fällt, dess Ruhm wird blühend stehn,
Solange frei die Winde noch durch freie Lüfte wehn,
Solange frei der Bäume Laub noch rauscht im grünen Wald,
Solang' des Stromes Woge noch frei nach dem Meere wallt,
Solang' des Adlers Fittich frei noch durch die Wolken fleugt,
Solang' ein freier Odem noch aus freiem Herzen steigt.

SONG BEFORE BATTLE.

Whoe'er for freedom fights and falls, his fame no blight shall know,
As long as through heaven's free expanse the breezes freely blow,
As long as in the forest wild the green leaves flutter free,
As long as rivers, mountain-born, roll freely to the sea,

As long as free the eagle's wing exulting cleaves the skies,
As long as from a freeman's heart a freeman's breath doth rise.

Whoe'er for freedom fights and falls, his fame no blight shall know,
As long as spirits of the free through earth and air shall go;
Through earth and air a spirit-band of heroes moves always,
'Tis near us at the dead of night, and in the noontide's blaze,
In the storm that levels towering pines, and in the breeze that waves
With low and gentle breath the grass upon our fathers' graves.
There's not a cradle in the bounds of Hellas broad and fair,
But the spirit of our free-born sires is surely hovering there.
It breathes in dreams of fairy-land upon the infant's brain,
And in his first sleep dedicates the child to manhood's pain;
Its summons lures the youth to stand, with new-born joy possessed,
Where once a freeman fell, and there it fires his thrilling breast,
And a shudder runs through all his frame; he knows not if it be
A throb of rapture, or the first sharp pang of agony.
Come, swell our banners on the breeze, thou sacred spirit-band,
Give wings to every warrior's foot, and nerve to every hand.
We go to strike for freedom, to break the oppressor's rod,
We go to battle and to death for our country and our God.
Ye are with us, we hear your wings, we hear in magic tone
Your spirit-voice the pæan swell, and mingle with our own.
Ye are with us, ye throng around, — you from Thermopylæ,
You from the verdant Marathon, you from the azure sea,
By the cloud-capped rocks of Mykale, at Salamis, — all you
From field and forest, mount and glen, the land of Hellas through!

Whoe'er for freedom fights and falls, his fame no blight shall know,
As long as through heaven's free expanse the breezes freely blow,
As long as in the forest wild the green leaves flutter free,
As long as rivers, mountain-born, roll freely to the sea,
As long as free the eagle's wing exulting cleaves the skies,
As long as from a freeman's heart a freeman's breath doth rise.

When we remember all that was compressed into this short life, we might well believe that this ceaseless acquiring and creating must have tired and weakened and injured both body and mind. Such, however, was not the case. All who knew the poet agree in stating that he never overworked himself, and that he accomplished all he did with the most perfect ease and enjoyment. Let us only remember how his life as a student was broken into by his service during the war, how his journey to Italy occupied several years of his life, how later in Dessau he had to follow his profession as teacher and librarian, and then let us turn our thoughts to all the work of his hands and the creations of his mind, and we are astonished, not only at the amount of work done, but still more at the finished form which distinguishes all his works. He was one of the first who with Zeune, Von der Hagen, and the brothers Grimm, labored to reawaken an interest in ancient and mediæval German literature. He was a favorite pupil of Wolf, and his "Homerische Vorschule" did more than any other work at that time to propagate the ideas of Wolf. He had explored the modern languages of Europe, — French, Italian, English, and Spanish; and his critiques in all these fields of literature show how intimately acquainted he was with the best authors of these nations. Besides all this, he worked regularly for journals and enclycopædias, and was engaged co-editor of the great "Enclycopædia of Arts and Sciences," by Ersch and Gruber. He also undertook the publication of a "Library of the German Poets of the Seventeenth Century," and all this, without mentioning his poems and novels, in the short space of a life of thirty-three years.

I almost forget that I am speaking of my father; for indeed I hardly knew him, and when his scientific and poetic activity reached its end, he was far younger than I am now. I do not believe, however, that a natural affection and veneration for the poet deprives us of the right of judging. It is well said that love is blind, but love also strengthens and sharpens the dull eye, so that it sees beauty where thousands pass by unmoved. If one reads most of our critical writings, it would almost appear as if the chief duty of the reviewer were to find out the weak points and faults of every work of art. Nothing has so injured the art of criticism as this prejudice. A critic is a judge; but a judge, though he is no advocate, should also be no prosecutor. The weak points of any work of art betray themselves only too soon; but in order to discover its beauties, not only a sharp, but an experienced eye is needed; and love and sympathy are necessary above anything else. It is the heart that makes the critic, not the nose. It is well known how many of the most beautiful spots in Scotland, and Wales, and Cornwall, were not many years ago described as wastes and wildernesses. Richmond and Hampton Court were admired, people travelled also to Versailles, and admired the often admired blue sky of Italy. But poets such as Walter Scott and Wordsworth discovered the beauties of their native land. Where others had only lamented over bare and wearisome hills, they saw the battle-fields and burial-places of the primeval Titan struggles of nature. Where others saw nothing but barren moors full of heather and broom, the land in their eyes was covered as with a carpet softer and more variegated than the most precious loom of Turkey. Where others lost their temper at the gray cold fog, they marveled at the silver veil of the bride of the morning, and the gold illumination of the departing sun. Now every cockney can admire the smallest lake in Westmoreland or the barest moor in the Highlands. Why is this? Because few eyes are so dull that they cannot see what is beautiful after it has been pointed out to them, and when they know that they need not feel ashamed of admiring it. It is the same with the beauties of poetry, as with the beauties of nature. We must first discover what is beautiful in poetry, and, when it is discovered, communicate it;

otherwise the authors of Scotch ballads are but strolling singers, and the Niebelungen songs are, as Frederick the Great said, not worth powder and shot. The trade of fault-finding is quickly learnt; the art of admiration is a difficult art, at least for little minds, narrow hearts, and timid souls, who prefer treading broad and safe paths. Thus many critics and literary historians have rushed by the poems of Wilhelm Müller, just like travellers, who go on in the beaten track, passing by on the right hand and on the left the most beautiful scenes of nature, and who only stand still and open both eyes and mouth when their " Murray " tells them there is something they ought to admire. Should an old man who is at home here meet them on their way, and counsel the travellers to turn for a moment from the high road in order to accompany him through a shady path to a mill, many may feel at first full of uneasiness and distrust. But when they have refreshed themselves in the dark green valley with its lively mill stream and delicious wood fragrance, they no longer blame their guide for having called somewhat loudly to them to pause in their journey. It is such a pause that I have tried in these few introductory lines to enforce on the reader, and I believe that I too may reckon on pardon, if not on thanks, from those who have followed my sudden call.

1858.

VI.

ON THE LANGUAGE AND POETRY OF SCHLESWIG-HOLSTEIN.

AFTER all that has been written about the Schleswig-Holstein question, how little is known about those whom that question chiefly concerns, — the Schleswig-Holsteiners! There may be a vague recollection that, during the general turmoil of 1848, the German inhabitants of the Duchies rose against the Danes; that they fought bravely, and at last succumbed, not to the valor, but to the diplomacy of Denmark. But, after the treaty of London in 1852 had disposed of them as the treaty of Vienna had disposed of other brave people, they sank below the horizon of European interests, never to rise again, it was fondly hoped, till the present generation had passed away.

Yet these Schleswig-Holsteiners have an interest of their own, quite apart from the political clouds that have lately gathered round their country. Ever since we know anything of the history of Northern Europe, we find Saxon races established as the inhabitants of that northern peninsula which was then called the *Cimbric Chersonese*. The first writer who ever mentions the name of Saxons is Ptolemy,[1] and he speaks of them as settled in what is now called Schles-

[1] Ptol. II. 11, ἐπὶ τὸν αὐχένα τῆς Κιμβρικῆς Χερσονήσου Σάξονες.

wig-Holstein.[1] At the time of Charlemagne the Saxon race is described to us as consisting of three tribes: the *Ostfalai*, *Westfalai*, and *Angrarii*. The *Westphalians* were settled near the Rhine, the *Eastphalians* near the Elbe, and the intermediate country, washed by the Weser, was held by the *Angrarii*.[2] The name of Westphalia is still in existence; that of Eastphalia has disappeared, but its memory survives in the English *sterling*. Eastphalian traders, the ancestors of the merchant princes of Hamburg, were known in England by the name of *Easterlings;* and their money being of the purest quality, *easterling*, in Latin *esterlingus*, shortened to *sterling*, became the general name of pure or sterling money. The name of the third tribe, the *Angrarii*, continued through the Middle Ages as the name of a people; and to the present day, my own sovereign, the Duke of Anhalt, calls himself Duke of "*Sachsen, Engern, und Westphalen.*" But the name of the *Angrarii* was meant to fulfill another and more glorious destiny. The name *Angrarii* or *Angarii*[3] is a corruption of the older name, *Angrivarii*, the famous German race mentioned by Tacitus as the neighbors of the *Cherusci*. These *Angrivarii* are in later documents called *Anglevarii*. The termination *varii*[4] represents the same word which exists in A.-S. as *ware;* for instance, in *Cant-ware*, inhabitants of Kent, or *Cant-ware-burh*, Canterbury; *burh-ware*, inhabitants of a town, burghers. It is derived from *werian*, to defend, to hold, and may be connected with *wer*, a man.

[1] Grimm, *Geschichte der Deutschen Sprache*, p. 609. Strabo, Pliny, and Tacitus do not mention the name of Saxons.

[2] Grimm, l. c. p. 629.

[3] See *Poeta Saxo*, anno 772, in Pertz, Monum. I. 225, line 26; Grimm, l. c. p. 629.

[4] See Grimm, *Deutsche Sprache*, p. 781.

The same termination is found in *Ansivarii* or *Ampsivarii;* probably also in *Teutonoarii* instead of *Teutoni, Chattuari* instead of *Chatti.*

The principal seats of these *Angrarii* were, as we saw, between the Rhine and Elbe, but Tacitus[1] knows of *Anglii*, i. e. *Angrii*, east of the Elbe; and an offshoot of the same Saxon tribe is found very early in possession of that famous peninsula between the Schlei and the Bay of Flensburg on the eastern coast of Schleswig,[2] which by Latin writers was called *Anglia*, i. e. *Angria*. To derive the name of *Anglia* from the Latin *angulus*,[3] corner, is about as good an etymology as the kind-hearted remark of St. Gregory, who interpreted the name of *Angli* by *angeli*. From that Anglia, the *Angli*, together with the *Saxons* and *Juts*, migrated to the British Isles in the fifth century, and the name of the *Angli*, as that of the most numerous tribe, became in time the name of *Englaland*.[4] In the Latin laws ascribed to King Edward the Confessor, a curious supplement is found, which states "that the *Juts* (*Guti*) came formerly from the noble blood of the *Angli*, namely, from the state of *Engra*, and that the English came from the same blood. The Juts, therefore, like the Angli of Germany, should always be received in England as brothers, and as citizens of the realm, because the Angli of England and Germany had always intermarried, and had fought together against the Danes."[5]

[1] *Germania*, c. 40. Grimm, l. c. p. 604.
[2] Grimm, p. 641.
[3] Beda, *Hist. Eccl.* I. 15. " Porro de Anglis, hoc est, de illa patria quæ Angulus dicitur," etc. Ethelwerd, Chron. I., " Porro Anglia vetus sita est inter Saxones et Giotos, habens oppidum capitale, quod sermone Saxonico *Slesvic* nuncupatur, secundum vero Danos, *Haithaby*."
[4] Grimm, l. c. p. 630.
[5] " Guti vero similiter cum veniunt (in regnum Britanniæ) suscipi

Like the Angli of Anglia, the principal tribes clustering round the base of the Cimbric peninsula, and known by the general name of *Northalbingi* or *Transalbiani*, also *Nordleudi*, were all offshoots of the Saxon stem. Adam of Bremen (2, 15) divides them into *Tedmaregoi*, *Holcetae*, and *Sturmarii*. In these it is easy to recognize the modern names of *Dithmarschen*, *Holtseten* or *Holsten*, and *Stormarn*. It would require more space than we can afford, were we to enter into the arguments by which Grimm has endeavored to identify the *Dithmarschen* with the *Teutoni*, the *Stormarn* with the *Cimbri*, and the *Holsten* with the *Harudes*. His arguments, if not convincing, are at least highly ingenious, and may be examined by those interested in these matters, in his "History of the German Language," pp. 633–640.

For many centuries the Saxon inhabitants of those regions have had to bear the brunt of the battle between the Scandinavian and the German races. From the days when the German Emperor Otho I. (died 973) hurled his swift spear from the northernmost promontory of Jutland into the German Ocean to mark the true frontier of his empire, to the day when

---

debent, et protegi in regno suo sicut conjurati fratres, sicut propinqui et proprii cives regni hujus. Exierunt enim quondam de nobili sanguine Anglorum, scilicet de Engra civitate, et Anglici de sanguine illorum, et semper efficiuntur populus unus et gens una. Ita constituit optimus suus Rex Anglorum.... Multi vero Angli ceperunt uxores suas de sanguine et genere Anglorum Germaniæ, et quidam Angli ceperunt uxores suas de sanguine et genere Scotorum; proceres vero Scotorum, et Scoti fere omnes ceperunt uxores suas de optimo genere et sanguine Anglorum Germaniæ, et ita fuerunt tunc temporis per universum regnum Britanniæ duo in carne una.... Universi prædicti semper postea pro communi utilitate coronæ regni in simul et in unum viriliter contra Danos et Norwegienses semper steterunt; et strenuissime unanimi voluntate contra inimicos pugnaverunt, et bella atrocissima in regno gesserunt." (*Die Gesetze der Angelsachsen*, ed. Schmid, p. 296.)

Christian IX. put his unwilling pen to that Danish constitution which was to incorporate all the country north of the Eider with Denmark, they have had to share in all the triumphs and all the humiliations of the German race, to which they are linked by the strong ties of a common blood and a common language.

Such constant trials and vicissitudes have told on the character of these German borderers, and have made them what they are, a hardy and determined, yet careful and cautious race. Their constant watchings and struggles against the slow encroachments or sudden inroads of an enemy more inveterate even than the Danes, — namely, the sea, — had imparted to them from the earliest times somewhat of that wariness and perseverance which we perceive in the national character of the Dutch and the Venetians. But the fresh breezes of the German Ocean and the Baltic kept their nerves well braced and their hearts buoyant; and for muscular development the arms of these sturdy ploughers of the sea and the land can vie with those of any of their neighbors on the isles or on the Continent. *Holsten-treue*, i. e. Holstein-truth, is proverbial throughout Germany, and it has stood the test of long and fearful trials.

There is but one way of gaining an insight into the real character of a people, unless we can actually live among them for years; and that is to examine their language and literature. Now it is true that the language spoken in Schleswig-Holstein is not German, — at least not in the ordinary sense of the word, — and one may well understand how travellers and correspondents of newspapers, who have picked up their German phrases from Ollendorf, and who, on the

strength of this, try to enter into a conversation with
Holstein peasants, should arrive at the conclusion that
these peasants speak Danish, or, at all events, that
they do not speak German.

The Germans of Schleswig-Holstein are Saxons,
and all true Saxons speak Low-German, and Low-
German is more different from High-German than
English is from Lowland Scotch. Low-German, however, is not to be mistaken for vulgar German. It is
the German which from time immemorial was spoken
in the low countries and along the northern sea-coast
of Germany, as opposed to the German of the high
country, of Swabia, Thuringia, Bavaria, and Austria.
These two dialects differ from each other like Doric
and Ionic; neither can be considered as a corruption
of the other; and however far back we trace these
two branches of living speech, we never arrive at a
point when they diverge from one common source.
The Gothic of the fourth century, preserved in the
translation of the Bible by Ulfilas, is not, as has been
so often said, the mother both of High and Low German. It is to all intents and purposes Low-German,
only Low-German in its most primitive form, and more
primitive therefore in its grammatical framework than
the earliest specimens of High-German also, which
date only from the seventh or eighth century. This
Gothic, which was spoken in the east of Germany, has
become extinct. The Saxon, spoken in the north of
Germany, continues its manifold existence to the present day in the Low-German dialects, in Frisian, in
Dutch, and in English. The rest of Germany was
and is occupied by High-German. In the West the
ancient High-German dialect of the Franks has been
absorbed in French, while the German spoken from

the earliest times in the centre and south of Germany has supplied the basis of what is now called the literary and classical language of Germany.

Although the literature of Germany is chiefly High-German, there are a few literary compositions, both ancient and modern, in the different spoken dialects of the country, sufficient to enable scholars to distinguish at least nine distinct grammatical settlements; in the Low-German branch, *Gothic, Saxon, Anglo-Saxon, Frisian,* and *Dutch;* in the High-German branch, *Thuringian, Frankish, Bavarian,* and *Alemannish.* Professor Weinhold is engaged at present in publishing separate grammars of six of these dialects, namely, of *Alemannish, Bavarian, Frankish, Thuringian, Saxon,* and *Frisian:* and in his great German Grammar Jacob Grimm has been able to treat these, together with the Scandinavian tongues, as so many varieties of one common, primitive type of Teutonic speech.

But although, in the early days of German life, the Low and High German dialects were on terms of perfect equality, Low-German has fallen back in the race, while High-German has pressed forward with double speed. High-German has become the language of literature and good society. It is taught in schools, preached in church, pleaded at the bar; and, even in places where ordinary conversation is still carried on in Low-German, High-German is clearly intended to be the language of the future. At the time of Charlemagne this was not so; and one of the earliest literary monuments of the German language, the "Heliand," *i. e.* the Saviour, is written in Saxon or Low-German. The Saxon Emperors, however, did little for German literature, while the Swabian Emperors were proud of being the patrons of art and poetry.

The language spoken at their court being High-German, the ascendency of that dialect may be said to date from their days, though it was not secured till the time of the Reformation, when the translation of the Bible by Luther put a firm and lasting stamp on what has since become the literary speech of Germany.

But language, even though deprived of literary cultivation, does not easily die. Though at present people write the same language all over Germany, the towns and villages teem everywhere with dialects, both High and Low. In Hanover, Brunswick, Mecklenburg, Oldenburg, the Free Towns, and in Schleswig-Holstein, the lower orders speak their own German, generally called *Platt-Deutsch*, and in many parts of Mecklenburg, Oldenburg, Ostfriesland, and Holstein, the higher ranks too cling in their every-day conversation to this more homely dialect.[1] Children frequently

---

[1] Klaus Groth writes: "The island of Friesian speech on the continent of Schleswig between Husum and Tondern is a very riddle and miracle in the history of language, which has not been sufficiently noticed and considered. Why should the two extreme ends only of the whole Friesian coast between Belgium and Jutland have retained their mother-speech? For the Ost Friesians in Oldenburg speak simply Platt-Deutsch like the Westphalians and ourselves. Cirk Hinrich Stüremburg's so-called Ost-Friesian Dictionary has no more right to call itself Friesian than the Bremen Dictionary. Unless the whole coast has sunk into the sea, who can explain that close behind Husum, in a flat country as monotonous as a Hungarian Pusta, without any natural frontier or division, the traveller, on entering the next inn, may indeed be understood if he speaks High or Low German, nay, may receive to either an answer in pure German, but hears the host and his servants speak in words that sound quite strange to him? Equally strange is the frontier north of the Wiede-au, where Danish takes the place of Friesian. Who can explain by what process the language has maintained itself so far and no farther, a language with which one cannot travel beyond eight or ten square miles? Why should these few thousand people not have surrendered long ago this 'useless remnant of an unschooled dialect,' considering they learn at the same time Low and High German, or Low-German and Danish? In the far-stretching, straggling villages a Low-German house stands sometimes alone among Friesian houses, and vice versâ, and that has been going on for generations.

speak two languages: High-German at school, Low-German at their games. The clergyman speaks High-German when he stands in the pulpit; but when he visits the poor, he must address them in their own peculiar *Platt*. The lawyer pleads in the language of Schiller and Goethe; but when he examines his witnesses he has frequently to condescend to the vulgar tongue. That vulgar tongue is constantly receding from the towns; it is frightened away by railways, it is ashamed to show itself in parliament. But it is loved all the more by the people; it appeals to their hearts, and it comes back naturally to all who have ever talked it together in their youth. It is the same with the local patois of High-German. Even where at school the correct High-German is taught and spoken, as in Bavaria and Austria, each town still keeps its own patois, and the people fall back on it as soon as they are among themselves. When Maria Theresa went to the Burgtheater to announce to the people of Vienna the birth of a son and heir, she did not address them in high-flown literary German. She bent forward from her box, and called out: "*Hörts! der Leopold hot án Buebd:*" "Hear! Leopold has a boy." In German comedies, characters from Berlin, Leipzig, and Vienna are constantly introduced speaking their own local dialects. In Bavaria, Styria, and the Tyrol, much of the poetry of the people is written in their patois; and in some parts of Germany sermons even, and other religious tracts, continue to be published in the local vernaculars.

In the Saxon families they do not find it necessary to learn Friesian, for all the neighbors can speak Low-German; but in the Friesian families one does not hear German spoken except when there are German visitors. Since the seventeenth century German has hardly conquered a single house, certainly not a village." (*Illustrirte Deutsche Monatshefte*, 1869, p. 330.)

There are here and there a few enthusiastic champions of dialects, particularly of Low-German, who still cherish a hope that High-German may be thrown back, and Low-German restored to its rights and former dominion. Yet, whatever may be thought of the relative excellences of High and Low German, — and in several points, no doubt, Low-German has the advantage of High-German, — yet, practically, the battle between the two is decided, and cannot now be renewed. The national language of Germany, whether in the South or the North, will always be the German of Luther, Lessing, Schiller, and Goethe. This, however, is no reason why the dialects, whether of Low or High German, should be despised or banished. Dialects are everywhere the natural feeders of literary languages; and an attempt to destroy them, if it could succeed, would be like shutting up the tributaries of great rivers.

After these remarks it will be clear that, if people say that the inhabitants of Schleswig-Holstein do not speak German, there is some truth in such a statement, at least just enough of truth to conceal the truth. It might be said, with equal correctness, that the people of Lancashire do not speak English. But, if from this a conclusion is to be drawn that the Schleswig-Holsteiners, speaking this dialect, which is neither German nor Danish, might as well be taught in Danish as in German, this is not quite correct, and would deceive few if it were adduced as an argument for introducing French instead of English in the national schools of Lancashire.

The Schleswig-Holsteiners have their own dialect, and cling to it as they cling to many things which, in other parts of Germany, have been discarded as old-fashioned and useless. "*Oll Knuet hölt Hus*,"— "Stale bread lasts longest,"— is one of their proverbs. But they read their Bible in High-German; they write their newspapers in High-German, and it is in High-German that their children are taught, and their sermons preached in every town and in every village. It is but lately that Low-German has been taken up again by Schleswig-Holstein poets; and some of their poems, though intended originally for their own people only, have been read with delight, even by those who had to spell them out with the help of a dictionary and a grammar. This kind of homespun poetry is a sign of healthy national life. Like the songs of Burns in Scotland, the poems of Klaus Groth and others reveal to us, more than anything else, the real thoughts and feelings, the every-day cares and occupations, of the people whom they represent, and to whose approval alone they appeal. But as Scotland, proud though she well may be of her Burns, has produced some of the best writers of English, Schleswig-Holstein, too, small as it is in comparison with Scotland, counts among its sons some illustrious names in German literature. Niebuhr, the great traveller, and Niebuhr, the great historian, were both Schleswig-Holsteiners, though during their lifetime that name had not yet assumed the political meaning in which it is now used. Karsten Niebuhr, the traveller, was a Hanoverian by birth; but, having early entered the Danish service, he was attached to a scientific mission sent by King Frederick V. to Egypt, Arabia, and Palestine, in 1760. All the other members of that mission having died, it was left to Niebuhr, after his return in 1767, to publish the results of his own observations and of those of his companions. His "Description of Arabia," and his "Travels in Arabia and the Adjoining Countries," though published nearly a hundred years ago, are still quoted with respect, and their accuracy has hardly ever been challenged. Niebuhr spent the rest of his life as a kind of collector and magistrate at Meldorf, a small town of between two and three thousand inhabitants, in Dithmarschen. He is described as a square and powerful man, who lived to a good old age, and who, even when he had lost his eyesight, used to delight his family and a large circle of friends by telling them of the adventures in his Oriental travels, of the starry nights of the desert, and of the bright moonlight of Egypt, where, riding on his camel, he could, from his saddle, recognize every plant that was growing on the ground. Nor were the listeners that gathered round him unworthy of the old traveller. Like many a small German town, Meldorf, the home of Niebuhr, had a society consisting of a few government officials, clergymen, and masters at the public school; most of them men of cultivated mind, and quite capable of appreciating a man of Niebuhr's powers. Even the peasants there were not the mere clods of other parts of Germany. They were a well-to-do race, and by no means illiterate. Their sons received at the Gymnasium of Meldorf a classical education, and they were able to mix with ease and freedom in the society of their betters. The most hospitable house at Meldorf was that of Boie, the High Sheriff of Dithmarschen. He had formerly, at Göttingen, been the life and soul of a circle of friends who have become famous in the history of German literature, under the name of "Hainbund." That "Hainbund," or Grove-club, included Bürger, the author of "Lenore;" Voss, the translator of Homer; the Counts Stolberg, Hölty, and

others. With Goethe, too, Boie had been on terms of
intimacy, and when, in after life, he settled down at
Meldorf, many of his old friends, his brother-in-law
Voss, Count Stolberg, Claudius, and others, came to see
him and his illustrious townsman, Niebuhr. Many a
seed was sown there, many small germs began to ripen
in that remote town of Meldorf, which are yielding fruit
at the present day, not in Germany only, but here in
England. The sons of Boie, fired by the descriptions
of the old, blind traveller, followed his example, and
became distinguished as explorers and discoverers in
natural history. Niebuhr's son, young Barthold, soon
attracted the attention of all who came to see his father,
particularly of Voss; and he was enabled by their help
and advice, to lay, in early youth, that foundation of
solid learning which fitted him, in the intervals of his
checkered life, to become the founder of a new era in
the study of Ancient History. And how curious the
threads which bind together the destinies of men! how
marvellous the rays of light which, emanating from the
most distant centres, cross each other in their onward
course, and give their own peculiar coloring to characters apparently original and independent! We have
read, of late, in the Confessions of a modern St. Augustine, how the last stroke that severed his connection with the Church of England was the establishment
of the Jerusalem bishopric. But for that event, Dr.
Newman might now be a bishop, and his friends a
strong party in the Church of England. Well, that
Jerusalem bishopric owes something to Meldorf. The
young schoolboy of Meldorf was afterwards the private
tutor and personal friend of the Crown-Prince of Prussia, and he thus exercised an influence both on the
political and the religious views of King Frederick

William IV. He was likewise Prussian Ambassador
at Rome, when Bunsen was there as a young scholar,
full of schemes, and planning his own journey to the
East. Niebuhr became the friend and patron of Bunsen, and Bunsen became his successor in the Prussian
embassy at Rome. It is well known that the Jerusalem bishopric was a long-cherished plan of the King
of Prussia, Niebuhr's pupil, and that the bill for the
establishment of a Protestant bishopric at Jerusalem
was carried chiefly through the personal influence of
Bunsen, the friend of Niebuhr. Thus we see how all
things are working together for good or for evil,
though we little know of the grains of dust that are
carried along from all quarters of the globe, to tell like
infinitesimal weights in the scales that decide hereafter
the judgment of individuals and the fate of nations.

If Holstein, and more particularly Dithmarschen,
of which Meldorf had in former days been the capital,
may claim some share in Niebuhr the historian, — if he
himself, as the readers of his history are well aware,
is fond of explaining the social and political institutions
of Rome by references to what he had seen or heard
of the little republic of Dithmarschen, — it is certainly
a curious coincidence that the only worthy successor
of Niebuhr, in the field of Roman history, Theodore
Mommsen, is likewise a native of Schleswig. His History of Rome, though it did not produce so complete a
revolution as the work of Niebuhr, stands higher as a
work of art. It contains the results of Niebuhr's critical researches, sifted and carried on by a most careful
and thoughtful disciple. It is, in many respects, a
most remarkable work, particularly in Germany. The
fact that it is readable, and has become a popular book,
has excited the wrath of many critics, who evidently

consider it beneath the dignity of a learned professor that he should digest his knowledge, and give to the world, not all and everything he has accumulated in his note-books, but only what he considers really important and worth knowing. The fact, again, that he does not load his pages with references and learned notes has been treated like a *crimen læsæ majestatis;* and yet, with all the clamor and clatter that has been raised, few authors have had so little to alter or rectify in their later editions as Mommsen. To have produced two such scholars, historians, and statesmen as Niebuhr and Mommsen, would be an honor to any kingdom in Germany: how much more to the small duchy of Schleswig-Holstein, in which we have been told so often that nothing is spoken but Danish and some vulgar dialects of Low-German!

Well, even those vulgar dialects of Low-German, and the poems and novels that have been written in them by true Schleswig-Holsteiners, are well worth a moment's consideration. In looking at their language, an Englishman at once discovers a number of old acquaintances: words which we would look for in vain in Schiller or Goethe. We shall mention a few.

Black means black; in High-German it would be *schwarz.* *De black* is the black horse; *black up wit* is black on white; *gif mek kil un blak*, give me quill and ink. *Blid* is *blithe*, instead of the High-German *mild*. *Bottervogel*, or *botterhahn*, or *botterhex*, is *butterfly*, instead of *schmetterling.* It is a common superstition in the North of Germany, that one ought to mark the first butterfly one sees in spring. A white one betokens mourning, a yellow one a christening, a variegated one a wedding. *Bregen* or *brehm* is used instead of the High-German *gehirn;* it is the English *brain.*

People say of a very foolish person, that his brain is frozen, *de brehm is em verfrorn*. The peculiar English *but*, which has given so much trouble to grammarians and etymologists, exists in the Holstein *buten*, literally outside, the Dutch *buiten*, the Old-Saxon *bi-ûtan*. *Buten* in German is a regular contraction, just as *binnen*, which means inside, within, during. *Heben* is the English heaven, while the common German name is *Himmel*. *Hückup* is a sigh, and no doubt the English *hiccough*. *Düsig* is dizzy; *talkig* is talkative.

There are some curious words which, though they have a Low-German look, are not to be found in English or Anglo-Saxon. Thus *plitsch*, which is used in Holstein in the sense of clever, turns out to be a corruption of *politisch*, i. e. political. *Krüdsch* means particular or over nice; it is a corruption of *kritisch*, critical. *Katolsch* means angry, mad, and is a corruption of *catholic*, i. e. Roman Catholic. *Kränsch* means plucky, and stands for *courageux*. *Fränksch*, i. e. Frankish, means strange; *Flämsch*, i. e. Flemish, means sulky, and is used to form superlatives; *Polsch*, i. e. Polish, means wild. *Forsch* means strong and strength, and comes from the French *force*. *Klür* is a corruption of *couleur*, and *Kunkelfusen* stands for confusion or fibs.

Some idiomatic and proverbial expressions, too, deserve to be noted. Instead of saying, "The sun has set," the Holsteiners, fond as they are of their beer, particularly in the evening after a hard day's work, say, "*De Sünn geiht to Beer*," "The sun goes to beer." If you ask in the country how far it is to some town or village, a peasant will answer, "'*n Hunnblaff*," "A dog's bark," if it is quite close; or "'*n Pip Toback*," "A pipe of tobacco," meaning about half an hour. Of a conceited

fellow they say, "*Hé hört de Flégn hosten,*" "He hears
the flies coughing." If a man is full of great schemes,
he is told, "*In Gedanken fört de Bur ök in't Kutsch.*"
"In thought the peasant, too, drives in a coach." A
man who boasts is asked, "*Pracher! häst ök Lüs, oder
schuppst di man so?*" "Braggart! have you really
lice, or do you only scratch yourself as if you had?"

"*Holstein singt nicht,*" "Holstein does not sing," is a
curious proverb; and if it is meant to express the absence
of popular poetry in that country, it would be easy to
convict it of falsehood by a list of poets whose works,
though unknown to fame beyond the limits of their
own country, are cherished, and deservedly cherished,
by their own countrymen. The best known among
the Holstein poets is Klaus Groth, whose poems, published under the title of "Quickborn," *i. e.* quick bourn,
or living spring, show that there is a well of true poetical feeling in that country, and that its strains are all
the more delicious and refreshing if they bubble up in
the native accent of the country. Klaus Groth was
born in 1819. He was the son of a miller; and, though
he was sent to school, he had frequently to work in
the field in summer, and make himself generally useful. Like many Schleswig-Holsteiners, he showed a
decided talent for mathematics; but, before he was
sixteen, he had to earn his bread, and work as a clerk
in the office of a local magistrate. His leisure hours
were devoted to various studies: German, Danish,
music, psychology, successively engaged his attention.
In his nineteenth year he went to the seminary at
Tondern to prepare himself to become a schoolmaster.
There he studied Latin, French, Swedish; and, after
three years, was appointed teacher at a girls' school.
Though he had to give forty-three lessons a week, he

found time to continue his own reading, and he acquired a knowledge of English, Dutch, Icelandic, and Italian. At last, however, his health gave way, and in 1847 he was obliged to resign his place. During his illness his poetical talent, which he himself had never trusted, became a source of comfort to himself and to his friends, and the warm reception which greeted the first edition of his "Quickborn" made him what he was meant to be, — the poet of Schleswig-Holstein.

His political poems are few; and, though a true Schleswig-Holsteiner at heart, he has always declined to fight with his pen when he could not fight with his sword. In the beginning of this year, however, he published "Five Songs for Singing and Praying," which, though they fail to give an adequate idea of his power as a poet, may be of interest as showing the deep feelings of the people in their struggle for independence. The text will be easily intelligible with the help of a literal English translation.

DUTSCHE EHR AND DUTSCHE EER.

I.

Frühling, 1848.

Dar keemn Soldaten awer de Elf,
Horah, hurah, na't Nora!
Se keemn so dicht as Wagg an Wagg,
Un as en Koppel vull Korn.

Gundag, Soldaten! wo kamt jü her?
Vun alle Bargen de Krüs un Quer,
Ut dütschen Landen na't dütsche Meer —
So wannert un treckt dat Heer.

Wat liggt so eben as weert de See?
Wat schint so gel as Gold?
Dat is de Marschen er Saat un Staat,
Dat is de Holsten er Stoet.

Gundag jü Holsten op dütsche Eer!
Gundag jü Friesen ant dütsche Meer!
To leben un starben var dütsche Ehr
So wannert un treckt dat Heer.

GERMAN HONOR AND GERMAN EARTH.

Spring, 1848.

There came soldiers across the Elbe,
Hurrah, hurrah, to the North!
They came as thick as wave on wave,
And like a field full of corn.

Good day, soldiers! whence do you come?
From all the hills on the right and left,
From German lands to the German sea, —
Thus wanders and marches the host.

What lies so still as it were the sea?
What shines so yellow as gold?
The splendid fields of the Marshes they are,
The pride of the Holsten race.

Good day, ye Holsten, on German soil!
Good day, ye Friesians, on the German sea
To live and to die for German honor, —
Thus wanders and marches the host.

II.

Summer, 1851.

Dat treckt so trurig awer de Elf,
In Tritt un Schritt so swar —
De Swalw de wannert, de Hatbar treckt —
Se kamt wedder to tokum Jahr.

Ade, ade, du dütsches Heer!
" Ade, ade, du Holsten meer!
Ade op Hoffen un Wiederkehr!"
Wi truert alleen ant Meer.

De Storch kumt wedder, de Swalw de singt
So fröhlich as all tovær —
Wann kumt de dütsche Adler un bringt
Di wedder, du dütsche Ehr?

Wak op du Floth, wak op du Meer!
Wak op du Dunner, un weck de Eer!
Wi sitt op Hæpen un Wedderkehr—
Wi truert alleen ant Meer.

Summer, 1851.

They march so sad across the Elbe,
So heavy, step by step, —
The swallow wanders, the stork departs, —
They come back in the year to come.

Adieu, adieu, thou German host!
"Adieu, adieu, thou Holsten sea!
Adieu, in hope, and to meet again!"
We mourn alone by the sea.

The stork comes back, the swallow sings
As blithe as ever before, —
When will the German eagle return,
And bring thee back, thou German honor!

Wake up, thou flood! wake up, thou sea!
Wake up, thou thunder, and rouse the land!
We are sitting in hope to meet again, —
We mourn alone by the sea.

III.

Winter, 1863.

Dar kumt en Brusen as Væerjahswind,
Dat drœhnt as wær dat de Floth, —
Will't Fröhjahr kamen to Wihnachtstid?
Hülpt Gott uns sülb'n inne Noth?

Vun alle Bargen de Krüz un Quer
Dar is dat wedder dat dütsche Heer!
Dat gelt op Nu oder Nimmermehr!
So rett se, de dütsche Ehr!

Wi hört den Adler, he kumt, he kumt!
Noch eenmal hœpt wi un hœrrt!
Is't Friheit endlich, de he uns bringt?
Is't Wahrheit, wat der ut ward?

Snust hölp uns Himmel, un gelt't nl mehr!
Hülp du, un bring uns den Herzog her!

Denn wüllt wi starben vær dütsche Ehr!
Denn begravt uns in dütsche Eer!
30 December, 1863.

Winter, 1863.

There comes a blast like winter storm;
It roars as it were the flood.
Is the spring coming at Christmas-tide?
Does God himself help us in our need?

From all the hills on the right and left,
There again comes the German host!
It is to be now or never!
O, save the German honor!

We hear the eagle, he comes, he comes!
Once more we hope and wait!
Is it freedom at last he brings to us?
Is it truth what comes from thence?

Else Heaven help us, now it goes no more!
Help thou, and bring us our Duke!
Then will we die for German honor!
Then bury us in German earth!
December 30, 1863.

It is not, however, in war songs or political invective that the poetical genius of Klaus Groth shows to advantage. His proper sphere is the quiet idyl, a truthful and thoughtful description of nature, a reproduction of the simplest and deepest feelings of the human heart, and all this in the homely, honest, and heartfelt language of his own "Platt Deutsch." That the example of Burns has told on Groth, that the poetry of the Scotch poet has inspired and inspirited the poet of Schleswig-Holstein, is not to be denied. But to imitate Burns, and to imitate him successfully, is no mean achievement, and Groth would be the last man to disown his master. The poem "Min Jehann" might have been written by Burns. I shall give a free metrical translation of it, but should advise the reader

to try to spell out the original; for much of its charm
lies in its native form, and to turn Groth even into
High-German destroys his beauty as much as when
Burns is translated into English.

MIN JEHANN.

Ik wull, wi weern noch kleen, Jehann,
  Do weer de Welt so grot!
We seten op den Steen, Jehann,
  Weest noch? by Nawers Sot.
    An Heben sell de stille Maan,
    Wi segen, wa he leep,
    Un snacken, wa de Himmel hoch,
    Un wa de Sot wul deep.

Weest noch, wa still dat weer, Jehann?
  Dar röhr keen Blatt an Bom.
So is dat nu ni mehr, Jehann,
  As höchstens noch in Drom.
    Och ne, wenn do de Scheper sung —
    Alleen in't wide Feld:
    Ni wahr, Jehann? dat weer en Ton —
    De eenzige op de Welt.

Mitünner inne Schummerntid
  Denn ward mi so to Mod,
Denn löppt mi't langs den Rügg so hitt,
  As domals bi den Sot.
    Den dreih ik mi so hastl um,
    As weer ik nich alleen:
    Doch Allens, wat ik finn, Jehann,
    Dat is — ik stah un ween.

MY JOHN.

I wish we still were little, John,
  The world was then so wide!
When on the stone by neighbor's bourn
  We rested side by side.
    We saw the moon in silver veiled
    Sail silent through the sky;
    Our thoughts were deeper than the bourn,
    And as the heavens high.

You know how still it was then, John;
  All nature seemed at rest;

So is it now no longer, John,
  Or in our dreams at best!
    Think when the shepherd boy then sang
    Alone o'er all the plain,
    Aye, John, you know, that was a sound
    We ne'er shall hear again.

Sometimes now, John, the eventides
  The self-same feelings bring,
My pulses beat as loud and strong
  As then beside the spring.
    And then I turn affrighted round,
    Some stranger to descry;
    But nothing can I see, my John, —
    I am alone and cry.

The next poem is a little popular ballad, relating to a tradition, very common on the northern coast of Germany, both east and west of the peninsula, of islands swallowed by the sea, their spires, pinnacles, and roofs being on certain days still visible, and their bells audible, below the waves. One of these islands was called *Büsen*, or *Old Büsum*, and is supposed to have been situated opposite the village now called Büsen, on the west coast of Dithmarschen. Strange to say, the inhabitants of that island, in spite of their tragic fate, are represented rather in a comical light, as the Bœotians of Holstein.

WAT SIK DAT VOLK VERTELLT.

Ol Büsum.

Ol Büsen liggt int wille Haff,
  De Floth de keem an wühl en Graff.
De Floth de keem an spöl un spöl,
  Bet se de Insel ünner wühl.
Dar blev keen Steen, dar blev keen Pahl,
  Dat Water schæl dat all bendal.
Dar weer keen Beest, dar weer keen Hund,
  De ligt nu all in depen Grund.
Un Allens, wat der lev un lach,
  Dat deck de See mit depe Nach.

Mitünner in de holle Ebb
So süht man vunne Hüs' de Köpp.
Denn duht de Thorn herut at Sand,
As weert en Finger vun en Hand.
Denn hört man nach de Klocken klingn,
Denn hört man nach de Kanter singn;
Denn gelt dat lisen der de Luft:
"Begrabt den Leib in seine Gruft."

WHAT THE PEOPLE TELL.

Old Büsum.

Old Büsum sank into the waves;
The sea has made full many graves;
The flood came near and washed around,
Until the rock to dust was ground.
No stone remained, no belfry steep;
All sank into the waters deep.
There was no beast, there was no hound;
They all were carried to the ground.
And all that lived and laughed around
The sea now holds in gloom profound.
At times, when low the water falls,
The sailor sees the broken walls;
The church tower peeps from out the sand,
Like to the finger of a hand.
Then hears one low the church bells ringing
Then hears one low the sexton singing;
A chant is carried by the gust:
"Give earth to earth, and dust to dust."

In the Baltic, too, similar traditions are current of sunken islands and towns buried in the sea, which are believed to be visible at certain times. The most famous tradition is that of the ancient town of Vineta, — once, it is said, the greatest emporium in the north of Europe, — several times destroyed and built up again, till, in 1183, it was upheaved by an earthquake and swallowed by a flood. The ruins of Vineta are believed to be visible between the coast of Pomerania and the island of Rügen. This tradition has suggested one of Wilhelm Müller's — my father's — lyrical songs, published in his " Stones and Shells from the Island of

Rügen," 1825, of which I am able to give a translation by Mr. J. A. Froude.

VINETA.

I.

Aus des Meeres tiefem, tiefem Grunde
   Klingen Abendglocken dumpf und matt,
Uns zu geben wunderbare Kunde
   Von der schönen alten Wunderstadt.

II.

In der Fluthen Schooss hinabgesunken
   Blieben unten ihre Trümmer stehn,
Ihre Zinnen lassen goldne Funken
   Wiederscheinend auf dem Spiegel sehn.

III.

Und der Schiffer, der den Zauberschimmer
   Einmal sah im hellen Abendroth,
Nach derselben Stelle schifft er immer,
   Ob auch rings umher die Klippe droht.

IV.

Aus des Herzens tiefem, tiefem Grunde
   Klingt es mir, wie Glocken, dumpf und matt;
Ach, sie geben wunderbare Kunde
   Von der Liebe, die geliebt es hat.

V.

Eine schöne Welt ist da versunken,
   Ihre Trümmer blieben unten stehn,
Lassen sich als goldne Himmelsfunken
   Oft im Spiegel meiner Träume sehn.

VI.

Und dann möcht' ich tauchen in die Tiefen,
   Mich versenken in den Wiederschein,
Und mir ist als ob mich Engel riefen
   In die alte Wunderstadt herein.

VINETA.

I.

From the sea's deep hollow faintly pealing,
   Far off evening bells come sad and slow;

Faintly rise, the wondrous tale revealing
Of the old enchanted town below.

II.

On the bosom of the flood reclining,
Ruined arch and wall and broken spire,
Down beneath the watery mirror shining,
Gleam and flash in flakes of golden fire.

III.

And the boatman who at twilight hour
Once that magic vision shall have seen,
Heedless how the crags may round him lour,
Evermore will haunt the charmèd scene.

IV.

From the heart's deep hollow faintly pealing,
Far I hear them, bell-notes sad and slow,
Ah, a wild and wondrous tale revealing
Of the drownèd wreck of love below.

V.

There a world, in loveliness decaying,
Lingers yet in beauty ere it die;
Phantom forms, across my senses playing,
Flash like golden fire-flakes from the sky.

VI.

Lights are gleaming, fairy bells are ringing,
And I long to plunge and wander free,
Where I hear the angel-voices singing
In those ancient towers below the sea.

I give a few more specimens of Klaus Groth's poetry, which I have ventured to turn into English verse, in the hope that my translations, though very imperfect, may, perhaps on account of their very imperfection, excite among some of my readers a desire to become acquainted with the originals.

HE SÄ MI SO VEL.

I.

He sä mi so vel, un ik sä em keen Wort,
Un all wat ik sä, weert: Jehann, ik mutt fort!

II.

He sä mi van Lev un van Himmel un Eer,
He sä mi van allens — Ik weet ni mal mehr!

III.

He sä mi so vel, un ik sä em keen Wort,
Un all wat ik sä, weer: Johann, ik mutt fort!

IV.

He heeld mi de Hann, un he be mi so dull,
Ik schull em doch gut ween, un ob ik ni wull?

V.

Ik weer jo ni bös, awer sä doch keen Wort,
Un all wat ik sä, weer: Johann, ik mutt fort!

VI.

Nu sitt ik un denk, un denk jümmer deran
Mi dücht, ik muss seggt hebbn: Wa geern, min Johann!

VII.

Un doch, kumt dat wedder, so segg ik keen Wort,
Un hollt he mi, segg ik: Johann, ik mutt fort!

HE TOLD ME SO MUCH.

I.

Though he told me so much, I had nothing to say,
And all that I said was, John, I must away!

II.

He spoke of his true love, and spoke of all that,
Of honor and heaven, — I hardly know what.

III.

Though he told me so much, I had nothing to say,
And all that I said was, John, I must away!

IV.

He held me, and asked me, as hard as he could,
That I too should love him, and whether I would?

V.

I never was wrath, but had nothing to say,
And all that I said was, John, I must away!

VI.

I sit now alone, and I think on and on,
Why did I not say then, How gladly, my John!

VII.

Yet even the next time, O what shall I say,
If he holds me and asks me?—John, I must away!

TÖF MAL!

Se is doch de stillste vun alle to Kark!
Se is doch de schönste vun alle to Mark!
So weekli, so bleekli, un de Ogen so grot,
So blau as en Heben un deep as en Sot.

Wer kikt wul int Water, un denkt ni sin Deel?
Wer kikt wul nan Himmel, an wünscht sik ne vel?
Wer süht er in Ogen, so blau un so fram,
Un denkt ni an Engeln, un allerhand Kram?

I.

In church she is surely the stillest of all,
She steps through the market so fair and so tall,

II.

So softly, so lightly, with wondering eyes,
As deep as the sea, and as blue as the skies.

III.

Who thinks not a deal when he looks on the main?
Who looks to the skies, and sighs not again?

IV.

Who looks in her eyes, so blue and so true,
And thinks not of angels and other things too?

KEEN GRAFF IS SO BRUT.

I.

Keen Graff is so brut un keen Müer so hoch,
Wenn Twe sik man gut sünd, so drapt se sik doch.

II.

Keen Wedder so gruli, so düster keen Nacht,
Wenn Twe sik man mhn wüllt, so seht se sik sacht.

III.

Dat gif wul en Maanschin, dar schint wul en Steern,
Dat gift noch en Licht oder Lücht un Lantern.

IV.

Dar funt sik en Ledder, en Stegelsch un Steg:
Wenn Twe sik man leef hebbt — keen Sorg vaar den Weg.

I.

No ditch is so deep, and no wall is so high,
If two love each other, they'll meet by and by.

II.

No storm is so wild, and no night is so black,
If two wish to meet, they will soon find a track.

III.

There is surely the moon, or the stars shining bright,
Or a torch, or a lantern, or some sort of light;

IV.

There is surely a ladder, a step, or a stile,
If two love each other, they'll meet ere long while.

JEHANN, NU SPANN DE SCHIMMELS AN!

I.

Jehann, nu spann de Schimmels an!
Nu fahr wi na de Brut!
Un hebbt wi nix as brune Per,
Jehann, so is't ok gut!

II.

Un hebbt wi nix as swarte Per,
Jehann, so is't ok recht!
Un bün ik nich uns Weerth sin Sœn,
So bün'k sin jüngste Knecht!

III.

Un hebbt wi gar keen Per an Wag',
So hebbt wi junge Ikeen!
Un de so glücklli is as ik,
Jehann, dat wüll wi sehn!

MAKE HASTE, MY JOHN, PUT TO THE GRAYS.

I.

Make haste, my John, put to the grays,
We'll go and fetch the bride,
And if we have but two brown hacks,
They'll do as well to ride.

II.

And if we've but a pair of blacks,
We still can bear our doom,
And if I'm not my master's son,
I'm still his youngest groom.

III.

And have we neither horse nor cart,
Still strong young legs have we,—
And any happier man than I,
John, I should like to see.

DE JUNGE WETFRU.

Wenn Abends roth de Wulken treckt,
So denk ik och! an di!
So trock verbi dat ganze Heer,
Un du weerst mit derbi.

Wenn ut de Böm de Blaeder fallt,
So denk ik glik an di:
So full so manni brawe Jung,
Un du weerst mit derbi.

Denn sett ik mi so truri hin,
Un denk so vel an di,
Ik et alleen min Abendbrot —
Un du büst nich derbi.

THE SOLDIER'S WIDOW.

When ruddy clouds are driving past,
'Tis more than I can bear;
Thus did the soldiers all march by,
And thou, too, thou wert there.

When leaves are falling on the ground,
'Tis more than I can bear;

> Thus fell full many a valiant lad,
> And thou, too, thou wert there.
>
> And now I sit so still and sad,
> 'Tis more than I can bear;
> My evening meal I eat alone,
> For thou, thou art not there.

I wish I could add one of Klaus Groth's tales ("Vertellen," as he calls them), which give the most truthful description of all the minute details of life in Dithmarschen, and bring the peculiar character of the country and of its inhabitants vividly before the eyes of the reader. But, short as they are, even the shortest of them would fill more pages than could here be spared for Schleswig-Holstein. I shall, therefore, conclude this sketch with a tale which has no author, — a simple tale from one of the local Holstein newspapers. It came to me in a heap of other papers, fly-sheets, pamphlets, and books, but it shone like a diamond in a heap of rubbish; and, as the tale of "The Old Woman of Schleswig-Holstein," it may help to give to many who have been unjust to the inhabitants of the Duchies some truer idea of the stuff there is in that strong and staunch and sterling race to which England owes its language, its best blood, and its honored name.

"When the war against Denmark began again in the winter of 1863, offices were opened in the principal towns of Germany for collecting charitable contributions. At Hamburg, Messrs. L. and K. had set apart a large room for receiving lint, linen, and warm clothing, or small sums of money. One day, about Christmas, a poorly clad woman from the country stepped in and inquired, in the pure Holstein dialect, hether contributions were received here for Schleswig-Holstein. The clerk showed her to a table covered with linen rags and such like articles. But she turned away and pulled out an old leather purse, and, taking out pieces of money, began to count aloud on the counter: 'One mark, two marks, three marks,' till she had finished her ten marks. 'That makes ten marks,' she said, and shoved the little pile away. The clerk, who had watched the poor old woman while she was arranging her small copper and silver coins, asked her,—'From whom does the money come?'

"'From me,' she said, and began counting again, 'One mark, two marks, three marks.' Thus she went on emptying her purse, till she had counted out ten small heaps of coin, of ten marks each. Then, counting each heap once over again, she said: 'These are my hundred marks for Schleswig-Holstein; be so good as to send them to the soldiers.'

"While the old peasant woman was doing her sums, several persons had gathered round her; and, as she was leaving the shop, she was asked again in a tone of surprise from whom the money came.

"'From me,' she said; and, observing that she was closely scanned, she turned back, and looking the man full in the face, she added, smiling: 'It is all honest money; it won't hurt the good cause.'

"The clerk assured her that no one had doubted her honesty, but that she herself had, no doubt, often known want, and that it was hardly right to let her contribute so large a sum, probably the whole of her savings.

"The old woman remained silent for a time, but, after she had quietly scanned the faces of all present, she said: 'Surely it concerns no one how I got the money. Many a thought passed through my heart while I was counting that money. You would not ask me to tell you all? But you are kind gentlemen, and you take much trouble for us poor people. So I'll tell you whence the money came. Yes, I have known want; food has been scarce with me many a day, and it will be so again, as I grow older. But our gracious Lord watches over us. He has helped me to bear the troubles which He sent. He will never forsake me. My husband has been dead this many and many a year. I had one only son; and my John was a fine stout fellow, and he worked hard, and he would not leave his old mother. He made my home snug and comfortable. Then came the war with the Danes. All his friends joined the army; but the only son of a widow, you know, is free. So he remained at home, and no one said to him, "Come along with us," for they knew that he was a brave boy, and that it broke his very heart to stay behind. I knew it all. I watched him when the people talked of the war, or when the schoolmaster brought the newspaper. Ah, how he turned pale and red, and how he looked away, and thought his old mother did not see it! But he said nothing to me, and I said nothing to him, Gracious God, who could have thought that it was so hard to drive our oppressors out of the land? Then came the news from Fredericia! That was a dreadful night. We sat in silence opposite each other. We knew what was in our hearts, and we hardly dared to look at each other. Suddenly he rose and took my hand, and said, "Mother!" — God be praised, I had strength in that moment — "John," I said, "our time has come; go in God's name. I know how thou lovest me, and what thou hast suffered. God knows what will become of me if I am left quite alone, but our Lord Jesus Christ will forsake neither thee nor me." John enlisted as a volunteer. The day of parting came. Ah, I am making a long story of it all! John stood before me in his new uniform. "Mother," he said, "one request before we part — if it is to be "— "John," I said to him, "I know what thou meanest,— O, I shall weep, I shall weep very much when I am alone; but my time will come, and we shall meet again in the day of our Lord, John! and the land shall be free, John! the land shall be free!"'

"Heavy tears stood in the poor old woman's eyes as she repeated her sad tale; but she soon collected herself, and continued: 'I did not think then it would be so hard. The heart always hopes even against hope. But for all that' — and here the old woman drew herself up, and looked at us like a queen — 'I have never regretted that I bade him go. Then came dreadful days; but the most dreadful of all was when we read that the Germans had betrayed the land, and that they had given up our land with all our dead to the Danes! Then I called on the Lord and said, "O Lord, my God, how is that possible? Why lettest Thou the wicked triumph and allowest the just to perish?" And I was told that the Germans were sorry for what they had done, but that they could not help it. But that, gentlemen, I could never understand. We should never do wrong, nor allow wrong to be done. And, therefore, I thought, it cannot always remain so; our good Lord knows his own good time, and in his own good time He will come and deliver us. And I prayed every evening that our gracious Lord would permit me to see that day when the land should be free, and our dear dead should sleep no more in Danish soil. And, as I had no other son against that day, I saved every year what I could save, and on every Christmas Eve I placed it before me on a table, where, in former years, I had always placed a small present for my John, and I said in my heart, The war will come again, and the land will be free, and thou shalt sleep in a free grave, my only son, my John! And now, gentlemen, the poor old woman has been told that the day has come, and that her prayer has been heard, and that the war will begin again; and that is why she has brought her money, the money she saved for her son. Good morning, gentlemen,' she said, and was going quickly away.

"But, before she had left the room, an old gentleman said, loud enough for her to hear, 'Poor body! I hope she may not be deceived.'

"'Ah,' said the old woman, turning back, 'I know what you mean; I have been told all is not right yet. But have faith, men! the wicked cannot prevail against the just; man cannot prevail against the Lord. Hold to that, gentlemen; hold fast together, gentlemen! This very day I — begin to save up again.'

"Bless her, good old soul! And, if Odin were still looking out of his window in the sky as of yore, when he granted victory to the women of the Lombards, might he not say even now: —

"'When women are heroes,
What must the men be like?
Theirs is the victory;
No need of me.'"

1864.

VII.

JOINVILLE.[1]

Our attention was attracted a few months ago by a review published in the "Journal des Débats," in which a new translation of Joinville's "Histoire de Saint Louis," by M. Natalis de Wailly, a distinguished member of the French Institute, was warmly recommended to the French public. After pointing out the merits of M. de Wailly's new rendering of Joinville's text, and the usefulness of such a book for enabling boys at school to gain an insight into the hearts and minds of the Crusaders, and to form to themselves a living conception of the manners and customs of the people of the thirteenth century, the reviewer, whose name is well known in this country as well as in France by his valuable contributions to the history of medicine, dwelt chiefly on the fact that through the whole of Joinville's "Mémoires" there is no mention whatever

[1] *Histoire de St. Louis*, par Joinville. Texte rapproché du Français Moderne par M. Natalis de Wailly, Membre de l'Institut. Paris, 1865.
Œuvres de Jean Sire de Joinville, avec un texte rapproché du Français Moderne, par M. Natalis de Wailly. Paris, 1867. M. Natalis de Wailly has since published a new edition of Joinville, *Histoire de Saint Louis, par Jean Sire de Joinville, suivie du Credo et de la lettre à Louis X.; texte ramené à l'orthographe des Chartes du Sire de Joinville*. Paris, 1868. He has more fully explained the principles according to which the text of Joinville has been restored by him in his *Mémoire sur la Langue de Joinville*. Paris, 1868.

of surgeons or physicians. Nearly the whole French
army is annihilated, the King and his companions lie
prostrate from wounds and disease, Joinville himself
is several times on the point of death; yet nowhere,
according to the French reviewer, does the chronicler
refer to a medical staff attached to the army or to the
person of the King. Being somewhat startled at this
remark, we resolved to peruse once more the charming
pages of Joinville's History; nor had we to read far before we found that one passage at least had been overlooked, a passage which establishes beyond the possibility of doubt the presence of surgeons and physicians
in the camp of the French Crusaders. On page 78 of
M. de Wailly's spirited translation, in the account of
the death of Gautier d'Autrèche, we read that when
that brave knight was carried back to his tent nearly
dying, "several of the surgeons and physicians of the
camp came to see him, and not perceiving that he was
dangerously injured, they bled him on both his arms."
The result was what might be expected: Gautier
d'Autrèche soon breathed his last.

Having once opened the "Mémoires" of Joinville,
we could not but go on to the end, for there are few
books that carry on the reader more pleasantly, whether
we read them in the quaint French of the fourteenth
century, or in the more modern French in which they
have just been clothed by M. Natalis de Wailly. So
vividly does the easy gossip of the old soldier bring
before our eyes the days of St. Louis and Henry III.,
that we forget that we are reading an old chronicle,
and holding converse with the heroes of the thirteenth
century. The fates both of Joinville's "Mémoires"
and of Joinville himself suggest in fact many reflections apart from mere mediæval history; and a few of

them may here be given in the hope of reviving the impressions left on the minds of many by their first acquaintance with the old Crusader, or of inviting others to the perusal of a work which no one who takes an interest in man, whether past or present, can read without real pleasure and real benefit.

It is interesting to watch the history of books, and to gain some kind of insight into the various circumstances which contribute to form the reputation of poets, philosophers, or historians. Joinville, whose name is now familiar to the student of French history, as well as to the lover of French literature, might fairly have expected that his memory would live by his acts of prowess, and by his loyal devotion and sufferings when following the King of France, St. Louis, on his unfortunate crusade. When, previous to his departure for the Holy Land, the young Sénéchal de Champagne, then about twenty-four years of age, had made his confession to the Abbot of Cheminon; when, barefoot and in a white sheet, he was performing his pilgrimages to Blehecourt (Blechicourt), St. Urbain, and other sacred shrines in his neighborhood, and when on passing his own domain he would not once turn his eyes back on the castle of Joinville, "*pour ce que li cuers ne me attendrisist dou biau chastel que je lessoie et de mes dous enfans*" ("that the heart might not make me pine after the beautiful castle which I left behind, and after my two children"), he must have felt that, happen what might to himself, the name of his family would live, and his descendants would reside from century to century in those strong towers where he left his young wife, Alix de Grandpré, and his son and heir Jean, then but a few months old. After five years he returned from his crusade, full of honors and

full of wounds. He held one of the highest positions
that a French nobleman could hold. He was Sénéchal
de Champagne, as his ancestors had been before him.
Several members of his family had distinguished themselves in former crusades, and the services of his uncle
Geoffroi had been so highly appreciated by Richard
Cœur de Lion that he was allowed by that King to
quarter the arms of England with his own. Both at
the court of the Comtes de Champagne, who were
Kings of Navarre, and at the court of Louis IX., King
of France, Joinville was a welcome guest. He witnessed the reigns of six kings, — of Louis VIII., 1223–
26; Louis IX., or St. Louis, 1226–70; Philip III., le
Hardi, 1270–85; Philip IV., le Bel, 1285–1314; Louis
X., le Hutin, 1314–16; and Philip V., le Long, 1316–
22. Though later in life Joinville declined to follow his
beloved King on his last and fatal crusade in 1270, he
tells us himself how, on the day on which he took leave
of him, he carried his royal friend, then really on the
brink of death, in his arms from the residence of the
Comte d'Auxerre to the house of the Cordeliers. In
1282 he was one of the principal witnesses when, previous to the canonization of the King, an inquest was
held to establish the purity of his life, the sincerity of
his religious professions, and the genuineness of his self-
sacrificing devotion in the cause of Christendom.
When the daughter of his own liege lord, the Comte
de Champagne, Jeanne de Navarre, married Philip le
Bel, and became Queen of France, she made Joinville Governor of Champagne, which she had brought
as her dowry to the grandson of St. Louis. Surely,
then, when the old Crusader, the friend and counselor
of many kings, closed his earthly career, at the good
age of ninety-five, he might have looked forward to an

honored grave in the Church of St. Laurent, and to an
eminent place in the annals of his country, which were
then being written in more or less elegant Latin by
the monks of St. Denis.

But what has happened? The monkish chroniclers,
no doubt, have assigned him his proper place in their
tedious volumes, and there his memory would have
lived with that kind of life which belongs to the
memory of Geoffroi, his illustrious uncle, the friend of
Philip Augustus, the companion of Richard Cœur de
Lion, whose arms were to be seen in the Church of St.
Laurent, at Joinville, quartered with the royal arms
of England. Such parchment or hatchment glory
might have been his, and many a knight, as good as he,
has received no better, no more lasting reward for his
loyalty and bravery. His family became extinct in his
grandson. Henri de Joinville, his grandson, had no
sons; and his daughter, being a wealthy heiress, was
married to one of the Dukes of Lorraine. The Dukes
of Lorraine were buried for centuries in the same
Church of St. Laurent where Joinville reposed, and
where he had founded a chapel dedicated to his companion in arms, Louis IX., the Royal Saint of France;
and when, at the time of the French Revolution, the
tombs of St. Denis were broken open by an infuriated
people, and their ashes scattered abroad, the vaults of
the church at Joinville, too, shared the same fate, and
the remains of the brave Crusader suffered the same
indignity as the remains of his sainted King. It is
true that there were some sparks of loyalty and self-
respect left in the hearts of the citizens of Joinville.
They had the bones of the old warrior and of the
Dukes of Lorraine reinterred in the public cemetery;
and there they now rest, mingled with the dust of

their faithful lieges and subjects. But the Church of
St. Laurent, with its tombs and tombstones, is gone.
The property of the Joinvilles descended from the
Dukes of Lorraine to the Dukes of Guise, and, lastly,
to the family of Orleans. The famous Duke of Orleans, Egalité, sold Joinville in 1790, and stipulated
that the old castle should be demolished. Poplars and
fir-trees now cover the ground of the ancient castle,
and the name of Joinville is borne by a royal prince,
the son of a dethroned king, the grandson of Louis
Egalité, who died on the guillotine.

Neither his noble birth, nor his noble deeds, nor the
friendship of kings and princes, would have saved
Joinville from that inevitable oblivion which has
blotted from the memory of living men the names of
his more eminent companions, — Robert, Count of Artois; Alphonse, Count of Poitiers; Charles, Count of
Anjou; Hugue, Duke of Burgundy; William, Count
of Flanders, and many more. A little book which the
old warrior wrote or dictated, — for it is very doubtful
whether he could have written it himself, — a book
which for many years attracted nobody's attention, and
which even now we do not possess in the original language of the thirteenth or the beginning of the fourteenth centuries — has secured to the name of Jean
de Joinville a living immortality, and a fame that will
last long after the bronze statue which was erected in
his native place in 1853 shall have shared the fate of
his castle, of his church, and of his tomb. Nothing
could have been further from the mind of the old nobleman when, at the age of eighty-five, he began the
history of his royal comrade, St. Louis, than the hope
of literary fame. He would have scouted it. That
kind of fame might have been good enough for monks

and abbots, but it would never at that time have
roused the ambition of a man of Joinville's stamp.
How the book came to be written he tells us himself
in his dedication, dated in the year 1309, and addressed
to Louis le Hutin, then only King of Navarre and
Count of Champagne, but afterwards King of France.
His mother, Jeanne of Navarre, the daughter of Joinville's former liege lord, the last of the Counts of
Champagne, who was married to Philip le Bel, the
grandson of St. Louis, had asked him " to have a book
made for her, containing the sacred words and good
actions of our King, St. Looys." She died before the
book was finished, and Joinville, therefore, sent it to
her son. How it was received by him we do not
know; nor is there any reason to suppose that there
were more than a few copies made of a work which
was intended chiefly for members of the royal family
of France and of his own family. It is never quoted
by historical writers of that time ; and the first historian
who refers to it is said to be Pierre le Baud, who,
toward the end of the fifteenth century, wrote his
" Histoire de Bretagne." It has been proved that for
a long time no mention of the dedication copy occurs
in the inventories of the private libraries of the Kings
of France. At the death of Louis le Hutin his library
consisted of twenty-nine volumes, and among them the
History of St. Louis does not occur. There is, indeed,
one entry, " Quatre caiers de Saint Looys ; " but this
could not be meant for the work of Joinville, which
was in one volume. These four *cahiers* or quires of
paper were more likely manuscript notes of St. Louis
himself. His confessor, Geoffroy de Beaulieu, relates
that the King, before his last illness, wrote down with
his own hand some salutary counsels in French, of

which he, the confessor, procured a copy before the King's death, and which he translated from French into Latin.

Again, the widow of Louis X. left at her death a collection of forty-one volumes, and the widow of Charles le Bel a collection of twenty volumes; but in neither of them is there any mention of Joinville's History.

It is not till we come to the reign of Charles V. (1364—80) that Joinville's book occurs in the inventory of the royal library, drawn up in 1373 by the King's valet de chambre, Gilles Mallet. It is entered as "La vie de Saint Loys, et les fais de son voyage d'outre mer;" and in the margin of the catalogue there is a note, "Le Roy l'a par devers soy,"— "The King has it by him." At the time of his death the volume had not yet been returned to its proper place in the first hall of the Louvre; but in the inventory drawn up in 1411 it appears again, with the following description : [1] —

"Une grant partie de la vie et des fais de Monseigneur Saint Loys que fist faire le Seigneur de Joinville; très-bien escript et historié. Couvert de cuir rouge, à empreintes, à deux fermoirs d'argent. Escript de lettres de forme en françois à deux coulombes; commençant au deuxième folio 'et porceque,' et au derrenier 'en tele maniere.'"

This means, "A great portion of the life and actions of St. Louis which the Seigneur de Joinville had made, very well written and illuminated. Bound in red leather, tooled, with two silver clasps. Written in formal letters in French, in two columns, beginning on the second folio with the words "*et porceque*," and on the last with "*en tele maniere.*"

During the Middle Ages and before the discovery

[1] See Paulin Paris, p. 173.

of printing, the task of having a literary work published, or rather of having it copied, rested chiefly with the author; and as Joinville himself, at his time of life, and in the position which he occupied, had no interest in what we should call "pushing" his book, this alone is quite sufficient to explain its almost total neglect. But other causes, too, have been assigned by M. Paulin Paris and others for what seems at first sight so very strange, — the entire neglect of Joinville's work. From the beginning of the twelfth century the monks of St. Denis were the recognized historians of France. They at first collected the most important historical works of former centuries, such as Gregory of Tours, Eginhard, the so-called Archbishop Turpin, Nithard, and William of Jumièges. But beginning with the first year of Philip I., 1060–1108, the monks became themselves the chroniclers of passing events. The famous Abbot Suger, the contemporary of Abelard and St. Bernard, wrote the life of Louis le Gros; Rigord and Guillaume de Nangis followed with the history of his successors. Thus the official history of St. Louis had been written by Guillaume de Nangis long before Joinville thought of dictating his personal recollections of the King. Besides the work of Guillaume de Nangis, there was the "History of the Crusades," including that of St. Louis, written by Guillaume, Archbishop of Tyre, and translated into French, so that even the ground which Joinville had more especially selected as his own was preoccupied by a popular and authoritative writer. Lastly, when Joinville's History appeared, the chivalrous King, whose sayings and doings his old brother in arms undertook to describe in his homely and truthful style, had ceased to be an ordinary mortal. He had become a saint, and what people were anxious to know of him were legends rather than history. With all the sincere admiration which Joinville entertained for his King, he could not compete with such writers as Geoffroy de Beaulieu (Gaufridus de Belloloco), the confessor of St. Louis, Guillaume de Chartres (Guillelmus Carnotensis), his chaplain, or the confessor of his daughter Blanche, each of whom had written a life of the royal saint. Their works were copied over and over again, and numerous MSS. have been preserved of them in public and private libraries. Of Joinville one early MS. only was saved, and even that not altogether a faithful copy of the original.

The first edition of Joinville was printed at Poitiers in 1547, and dedicated to François I. The editor, Pierre Antoine de Rieux, tells us that when, in 1542, he examined some old documents at Beaufort en Valée, in Anjou, he found among the MSS. the Chronicle of King Louis, written by a Seigneur de Joinville, Sénéchal de Champagne, who lived at that time, and had accompanied the said St. Louis in all his wars. But because it was badly arranged or written in a very rude language, he had it polished and put in better order, a proceeding of which he is evidently very proud, as we may gather from a remark of his friend Guillaume de Perrière, that "it is no smaller praise to polish a diamond than to find it quite raw" (*toute brute*).

This text, which could hardly be called Joinville's, remained for a time the received text. It was reproduced in 1595, in 1596, and in 1609.

In 1617 a new edition was published by Claude Menard. He states that he found at Laval a heap of old papers, which had escaped the ravages committed by the Protestants in some of the monasteries at Anjou. When he compared the MS. of Joinville with the edition of Pierre Antoine de Rieux, he found that the ancient style of Joinville had been greatly changed. He therefore undertook a new edition, more faithful to the original. Unfortunately, however, his original MS. was but a modern copy, and his edition, though an improvement on that of 1547, was still very far from the style and language of the beginning of the fourteenth century.

The learned Du Cange searched in vain for more trustworthy materials for restoring the text of Joinville. Invaluable as are the dissertations which he wrote on Joinville, his own text of the History, published in 1668, could only be based on the two editions that had preceded his own.

It was not till 1761 that real progress was made in restoring the text of Joinville. An ancient MS. had been brought from Brussels by the Maréchal Maurice de Saxe. It was carefully edited by M. Capperonnier, and it has served, with few exceptions, as the foundation of all later editions. It is now in the Imperial Library. The editors of the "Recueil des Historiens de France" express their belief that the MS. might actually be the original. At the end of it are the words, "Ce fu escript en l'an de grâce mil CCC et IX, on moys d'octovre." This, however, is no real proof of the date of the MS. Transcribers of MSS., it is well known, were in the habit of mechanically copying all they saw in the original, and hence we find very commonly the date of an old MS. repeated over and over again in modern copies.

The arguments by which in 1839 M. Paulin Paris proved that this, the oldest MS. of Joinville, belongs not to the beginning, but to the end of the fourteenth century, seem unanswerable, though they failed to convince M. Daunou, who, in the twentieth volume of the "Historiens de France," published in 1840, still looks upon this MS. as written in 1309, or at least during Joinville's life-time. M. Paulin Paris establishes, first of all, that this MS. cannot be the same as that which was so carefully described in the catalogue of Charles V. What became of that MS. once belonging to the private library of the Kings of France, no one knows, but there is no reason, even now, why it should not still be recovered. The MS. of Joinville, which now belongs to the Imperial Library, is written by the same scribe who wrote another MS. of "La Vie et les Miracles de Saint Louis." Now, this MS. of "La Vie et les Miracles" is a copy of an older MS., which likewise exists at Paris. This more ancient MS., probably the original, and written, therefore, in the beginning of the fourteenth century, had been carefully revised before it served as the model for the later copy, executed by the same scribe who, as we saw, wrote the old MS. of Joinville. A number of letters were scratched out, words erased, and sometimes whole sentences altered or suppressed, a red line being drawn across the words which had to be omitted. It looks, in fact, like a manuscript prepared for the printer. Now, if the same copyist who copied this MS. copied likewise the MS. of Joinville, it follows that he was separated from the original of Joinville by the same interval which separates the corrected MSS. of "La Vie et les Miracles" from their original, or from the beginning of the fourteenth century. This line of argument seems to establish satisfactorily the approximate date of the oldest MS. of Joinville as belonging to the end of the fourteenth century.

Another MS. was discovered at Lucca. As it had
belonged to the Dukes of Guise, great expectations
were at one time entertertained of its value. It was
bought by the Royal Library at Paris in 1741 for 860
livres, but it was soon proved not to be older than
about 1500, representing the language of the time of
François I. rather than of St. Louis, but nevertheless
preserving occasionally a more ancient spelling than
the other MS. which was copied two hundred years
before. This MS. bears the arms of the Princess
Antoinette de Bourbon and of her husband, Claude de
Lorraine, who was "Duc de Guise, Comte d'Aumale,
Marquis de Mayence et d'Elbeuf, and Baron de Joinville." Their marriage took place in 1513; he died
in 1550, she in 1583.

There is a third MS. which has lately been discovered. It belonged to M. Brissart-Binet of Rheims,
became known to M. Paulin Paris, and was lent to M.
de Wailly for his new edition of Joinville. It seems
to be a copy of the so-called MS. of Lucca, the MS.
belonging to the Princess Antoinette de Bourbon, and
it is most likely the very copy which that Princess
ordered to be made for Louis Lasséré, canon of St.
Martin of Tours who published an abridgment of it
in 1541. By a most fortunate accident it supplies the
passages from page 88 to 112, and from page 126 to
139, which are wanting in the MS. of Lucca.

It must be admitted, therefore, that for an accurate
study of the historical growth of the French language,
the work of Joinville is of less importance than it
would have been if it had been preserved in its original
orthography, and with all the grammatical peculiarities which mark the French of the thirteenth and the
beginning of the fourteenth century. There may be

no more than a distance of not quite a hundred years between the original of Joinville and the earliest MS. which we possess. But in those hundred years the French language did not remain stationary. Even as late as the time of Montaigne, when French has assumed a far greater literary steadiness, that writer complains of its constant change. "I wrote my book," he says in a memorable passage ("Essais," liv. 3, c. 9) —

"For few people and for a few years. If it had been a subject that ought to last, it should have been committed to a more stable language (Latin). After the continual variation which has followed our speech to the present day, who can hope that its present form will be used fifty years hence? It glides from our hands every day, and since I have lived it has been half changed. We say that at present it is perfect, but every century says the same of its own. I do not wish to hold it back, if it will fly away and go on deteriorating as it does. It belongs to good and useful writers to nail the language to themselves" (*de le clouer à eux*).

On the other hand, we must guard against forming an exaggerated notion of the changes that could have taken place in the French language within the space of less than a century. They refer chiefly to the spelling of words, to the use of some antiquated words and expressions, and to the less careful observation of the rules by which in ancient French the nominative is distinguished from the oblique cases, both in the singular and the plural. That the changes do not amount to more than this can be proved by a comparison of other documents which clearly preserve the actual language of Joinville. There is a letter of his which is preserved at the Imperial Library at Paris, addressed to Louis X. in 1315. It was first published by Du Cange, afterwards by M. Daunou, in the twentieth volume of the "Historiens de France," and again by M. de Wailly. There are, likewise, some charters of Joinville, written in his *chancellerie*, and in some cases with additions from his own hand. Lastly, there is Joinville's "Credo," containing his notes on the Apostolic Creed, preserved in a manuscript of the thirteenth century. This was published in the "Collection des Bibliophiles Français," unfortunately printed in twenty-five copies only. The MS. of the "Credo," which formerly belonged to the public library of Paris, disappeared from it about twenty years ago; and it now forms No. 75 of a collection of MSS. bought in 1849 by Lord Ashburnham from M. Barrois. By comparing the language of these thirteenth century documents with that of the earliest MS. of Joinville's History, it is easy to see that although we have lost something, we have not lost very much, and that, at all events, we need not suspect in the earliest MS. any changes that could in any way affect the historical authenticity of Joinville's work.[1]

[1] In his last edition of the text of Joinville, which was published in 1868, M. de Wailly has restored the spelling of Joinville on all these points according to the rules which are observed in Joinville's charters, and in the best MSS. of the beginning of the fourteenth century. The fac-similes of nine of these charters are published at the end of M. de Wailly's *Mémoire sur la Langue de Joinville*; of others an accurate transcript is given. The authentic texts thus collected, in which we can study the French language as it was written at the time of Joinville, amount to nearly one fifth of the text of Joinville's History. To correct, according to these charters, the text of Joinville so systematically as had been done by M. de Wailly in his last edition may seem a bold undertaking; but few who have read attentively his *Mémoire* would deny that the new editor has fully justified his critical principles. Thus with regard to the terminations of the nominative and the oblique cases, where other MSS. of Joinville's History follow no principle whatever, M. de Wailly remarks: " Pour plus de simplicité j'appellerai règle du sujet singulier et règle du sujet pluriel l'usage qui consistait à distinguer, dans beaucoup de mots, le sujet du régime par une modification analogue à celle de la déclinaison latine. Or, j'ai constaté que, dans les chartes de Joinville, la règle du sujet singulier est ob-

To the historian of the French language, the language of Joinville, even though it gives us only a picture of the French spoken at the time of Charles V. or contemporaneously with Froissart, is still full of interest. That language is separated from the French of the present day by nearly five centuries, and we may be allowed to give a few instances to show the curious changes both of form and meaning which many words have undergone during that interval.

Instead of *sœur*, sister, Joinville still uses *seroeur*, which was the right form of the oblique case, but was afterwards replaced by the nominative *suer* or *sœur*. Thus, p. 424 E, we read, *quant nous menames la serour le roy*, i. e. *quand nous menâmes la sœur du roi*; but p. 466 A, *l'abbaïe que sa suer fonda*, i. e. *l'abbaïe que sa sœur fonda*. Instead of *ange*, angel, he has both *angle* and *angre*, where the *r* stands for the final *l* of *angele*, the more ancient French form of *angelus*. The same transition of final *l* into *r* may be observed in *apôtre* for *apostolus*, *chapitre* for *capitulum*, *chartre* for *cartula*, *esclandre* for *scandalum*. Instead of *vieux*, old, Joinville uses *veil* or *veel* (p. 132 C, *le veil le fil au veil*, i. e. *le vieux fils du vieux*) ; but in the nom. sing., *viex*, which is the Latin *vetulus* (p. 802 A, *li Viez de*

servée huit cent trente-cinq fois, et violée sept fois seulement; encore dois-je dire que cinq de ces violations se rencontrent dans une même charte, celle du mois de mai 1278, qui n'est connue que par une copie faite au siècle dernier. Si l'on fait abstraction de ce texte, il reste deux violations contre huit cent trente-cinq observations de la règle. La règle du sujet pluriel est observée cinq cent quatre-vingt-huit fois, et violée six fois : ce qui donne en total quatorze cent vingt-trois contre treize, en tenant compte même de six fautes commises dans le texte copié au siècle dernier. De ce résultat numérique, il faut évidemment conclure, d'abord, que l'une et l'autre règle étaient parfaitement connues et pratiquées à la chancellerie de Joinville, ensuite qu'on est autorisé à modifier le texte de l'Histoire, partout où ces règles y sont violées. (D'après un calcul approximatif, on peut croire que le copiste du quatorzième siècle a violé ces règles plus de quatre mille fois et qu'il les respectait peut-être une fois sur dix.) "

la Montaingne, i. e. *le Vieux de la Montagne;* but p. 304 A, *li messaige le Vieil,* i. e. *les messagers du Vieux.*) Instead of *coude,* m., elbow, we find *coute,* which is nearer to the Latin *cubitus,* cubit. The Latin *t* in words like *cubitus* was generally softened in old French, and was afterwards dropped altogether. As in *coude,* the *d* is preserved in *aider* for *adjutare,* in *fade* for *fatuus.* In other words, such as *chaîne* for *catena, roue* for *rota, épée* for *spatha, aimée* for *amata,* it has disappeared altogether. *True* is *voir,* the regular modification of *verum,* like *soir* of *serum,* instead of the modern French *vrai;* e. g., p. 524 B, *et sachiez que voirs estait,* i. e. *et sachez que c'était vrai.* We still find *ester,* to stand ("*Et ne pooit ester sur ses pieds,*" "He could not stand on his legs"). At present the French have no single word for "standing," which has often been pointed out as a real defect of the language. "To stand" is *ester,* in Joinville; "to be" is *estre.*

In the grammatical system of the language of Joinville we find the connecting link between the case terminations of the classical Latin and the prepositions and articles of modern French. It is generally supposed that the terminations of the Latin declension were lost in French, and that the relations of the cases were expressed by prepositions, while the *s* as the sign of the plural was explained by the *s* in the nom. plur. of nouns of the third declension. But languages do not thus advance *per saltum.* They change slowly and gradually, and we can generally discover in what is, some traces of what has been.

Now the fact is that in ancient French, and likewise in Provençal, there is still a system of declension more or less independent of prepositions. There are, so to say, three declensions in old French, of which the second is the most important and the most interesting. If we take a Latin word like *annus*, we find in old French two forms in the singular, and two in the plural. We find sing. *an-s*, *an*, plur. *an*, *ans*. If *an* occurs in the nom. sing. or as the subject, it is always *ans*; if it occur as a gen., dat., or acc., it is always *an*. In the plural, on the contrary, we find in the nom. *an*, and in all the oblique cases *ans*. The origin of this system is clear enough, and it is extraordinary that attempts should have been made to derive it from German or even from Celtic, when the explanation could be found so much nearer home. The nom. sing. has the *s*, because it was there in Latin; the nom. plur. has no *s*, because there was no *s* there in Latin. The oblique cases in the singular have no *s*, because the accusative in Latin, and likewise the gen., dat., and abl., ended either in vowels, which became mute, or in *m*, which was dropped. The oblique cases in the plural had the *s*, because it was there in the acc. plur., which became the general oblique case, and likewise in the dat. and abl. By means of these fragments of the Latin declension, it was possible to express many things without prepositions which in modern French can no longer be thus expressed. *Le fils Roi* was clearly the son of the King; *il fil Roi*, the sons of the King. Again we find *li roys*, the King, but *au roy*, to the King. Pierre Sarrasin begins his letter on the crusade of St. Louis by *A seigneur Nicolas Arode, Jehan-s Sarrasin, chambrelen-s le roy de France, salut et bonne amour.*

But if we apply the same principle to nouns of the first declension, we shall see at once that they could not have lent themselves to the same contrivance. Words like *corona* have no *s* in the nom. sing., nor in any of the oblique cases; it would therefore be in French *corone* throughout. In the plural indeed there might have been a distinction between the nom. and the acc. The nom. ought to have been without an *s*, and the acc. with an *s*. But with the exception of some doubtful passages, where a nom. plur. is supposed to occur in old French documents without an *s*, we find throughout, both in the nom. and the other cases, the *s* of the accusative as the sign of the plural.

Nearly the same applies to certain words of the third declension. Here we find indeed a distinction between the nom. and the oblique cases of the singular, such as *flor-s*, the flower, with *flor*, of the flower; but the plural is *flor-s* throughout. This form is chiefly confined to feminine nouns of the third declension.

There is another very curious contrivance by which the ancient French distinguished the nom. from the acc. sing., and which shows us again how the consciousness of the Latin grammar was by no means entirely lost in the formation of modern French. There are many words in Latin which change their accent in the oblique cases from what it was in the nominative. For instance, *cantátor*, a singer, becomes *cantatórem*, in the accusative. Now in ancient French the nom., corresponding to *cantator*, is *chántere*, but the gen. *chanteór*, and thus again a distinction is established of great importance for grammatical purposes. Most of these words followed the analogy of the second declension, and added an *s* in the nom. sing., dropped it in the nom. plur., and added it again in the oblique cases of the plural. Thus we get —

	Singular.		Plural.
Nom.	Oblique Cases.	Nom.	Oblique Cases.
chántere	chanteór	chanteór	chanteórs
From baro, barónis	barón	barón	baróns
(O. Fr. ber)			
latro, latrónis	larrón	larrón	larróns
(O. Fr. lierre)			
senior, senióris	seignór	seignór	seignórs
(O. Fr. sendre)	(sire)		

Thus we read in the beginning of Joinville's History: —

A son bon signour Looys, Jehans sires de Joinville salut et amour;

and immediately afterwards, *Chiers sire*, not *Chiers seigneur*.

If we compare this old French declension with the grammar of modern French, we find that the accusative or the oblique form has become the only recognized form, both in the singular and plural. Hence —

[Corone]	[Ans]	[Flors]	[Chántere] le chantre.
Corone	An	Flor	Chanteór le chanteur.
[Corones]	[Ans]	[Flors]	[Chanteór].
Corones	Ans	Flors	Chanteórs.

A few traces only of the old system remain in such words as *fils, bras, Charles, Jacques,* etc.

Not less curious than the changes of form are the changes of meaning which have taken place in the French language since the days of Joinville. Thus, *la viande*, which now only means meat, is used by Joinville in its original and more general sense of *victuals*, the Latin *vivenda*. For instance (p. 248 D), "*Et nous requeismes que en nous donnast la viande,*" "And we asked that one might give us something to eat." And soon after, "*Les viandes que il nous donnèrent, ce furent begniet de fourmaiges qui estoient roti au soliel, pour ce que li ver n'i venissent, et oef dur cuit de quatre jours ou de cinc*," " And the viands which they gave us were cheese-cakes roasted in the sun, that the worms might not get at them, and hard eggs boiled four or five days ago."

Payer, to pay, is still used in its original sense of pacifying or satisfying, the Latin *pacare*. Thus a priest who has received from his bishop an explanation of some difficulty and other ghostly comfort " *se tint bin pour paié* " (p. 84 C), he " considered himself well satisfied." When the King objected to certain words in the oath which he had to take, Joinville says that he does not know how the oath was finally arranged, but he adds, " *Li amiral se tindrent bien apaié*," " The admirals considered themselves satisfied " (p. 242 C). The same word, however, is likewise used in the usual sense of paying.

Noise, a word which has almost disappeared from modern French, occurs several times in Joinville; and we can watch in different passages the growth of its various meanings. In one passage Joinville relates (p. 198) that one of his knights had been killed, and was lying on a bier in his chapel. While the priest was performing his office, six other knights were talking very loud, and " *Faisoient noise au prestre*," " They annoyed or disturbed the priest ; they caused him annoyance." Here *noise* has still the same sense as the Latin *nausea*, from which it is derived. In another passage, however, Joinville uses *noise* as synonymous with *bruit* (p. 152 A), *Vint li roys d' toute sa bataille, à grant noyse et d grant bruit de trompes et nacaires*, i. e. *vint le roi avec tout son corps de bataille, à grand cris et à grand bruit de trompettes et de timbales*. Here *noise* may still mean an annoying noise, but we can see the easy transition from that to noise in general.

Another English word, "to purchase," finds its explanation in Joinville. Originally *pourchasser*, meant to hunt after a thing, to pursue it. Joinville frequently uses the expression "*par son pourchas*" (p. 458 E) in the sense of "by his endeavors." When the King had reconciled two adversaries, peace is said to have been made *par son pourchas*. "*Pourchasser*" afterwards took the sense of "procuring," "catering," and lastly, in English, of "buying."

To return to Joinville's History, the scarcity of MSS. is very instructive from an historical point of view. As far as we know at present, his great work existed for centuries in two copies only, one preserved in his own castle, the other in the library of the Kings of France. We can hardly say that it was published, even in the restricted sense which that word had during the fourteenth century, and there certainly is no evidence that it was read by any one except by members of the royal family of France, and possibly by descendants of Joinville. It exercised no influence; and if two or three copies had not luckily escaped (one of them, it must be confessed, clearly showing the traces of mice's teeth), we should have known very little indeed either of the military or of the literary achievements of one who is now ranked among the chief historians of France, or even of Europe. After Joinville's History had once emerged from its obscurity, it soon became the fashion to praise it, and to praise it somewhat indiscriminately. Joinville became a general favorite both in and out of France; and after all had been said in his praise that might be truly and properly said, each successive admirer tried to add a little more, till at last, as a matter of course, he was compared to Thucydides, and lauded for the graces of his style, the vigor of his language, the subtlety of his mind, and his worship of the harmonious and the beautiful, in such a manner that the old bluff soldier would have been highly perplexed and disgusted, could he have listened to the praises of his admirers. Well might M. Paulin Paris say, "I shall not stop to praise what everybody has praised before me; to recall the graceful *naïveté* of the good Sénéchal, would it not be, as the English poet said, 'to gild the gold and paint the lily white?'"

It is surprising to find in the large crowd of indiscriminate admirers a man so accurate in his thoughts and in his words as the late Sir James Stephen. Considering how little Joinville's History was noticed by his contemporaries, how little it was read by the people before it was printed during the reign of François I., it must seem more than doubtful whether Joinville really deserved a place in a series of lectures, "On the Power of the Pen in France." But, waiving that point, is it quite exact to say, as Sir James Stephen does, "that three writers only retain, and probably they alone deserve, at this day the admiration which greeted them in their own, — I refer to Joinville, Froissart, and to Philippe de Comines?" And is the following a sober and correct description of Joinville's style? —

"Over the whole picture the genial spirit of France glows with all the natural warmth which we seek in vain among the dry bones of earlier chroniclers. Without the use of any didactic forms of speech, Joinville teaches the highest of all wisdom — the wisdom of love. Without the pedantry of the schools, he occasionally exhibits an eager thirst of knowledge, and a graceful facility of imparting it, which attest that he is of the lineage of the great father of history, and of those modern historians who have taken Herodotus for their model." (Vol. ii. pp. 209, 219.)

Now, all this sounds to our ears just an octave too
high. There is some truth in it, but the truth is spoilt
by being exaggerated. Joinville's book is very pleasant
to read, because he gives himself no airs, and tells
us as well as he can what he recollects of his excellent
King, and of the fearful time which they spent together
during the crusade. He writes very much as
an old soldier would speak. He seems to know that
people will listen to him with respect, and that they
will believe what he tells them. He does not weary
them with arguments. He rather likes now and then
to evoke a smile, and he maintains the glow of attention
by thinking more of his hearers than of himself.
He had evidently told his stories many times before he
finally dictated them in the form in which we read
them, and this is what gives to some of them a certain
finish and the appearance of art. Yet, if we speak of
style at all,—not of the style of thought, but of the
style of language,—the blemishes in Joinville's History
are so apparent that one feels reluctant to point
them out. He repeats his words, he repeats his remarks,
he drops the thread of his story, begins a new
subject, leaves it because, as he says himself, it would
carry him too far, and then, after a time, returns to it
again. His descriptions of the scenery where the
camp was pitched, and the battles fought, are neither
sufficiently broad nor sufficiently distinct to give the
reader that view of the whole which he receives from
such writers as Cæsar, Thiers, Carlyle, or Russell.
Nor is there any attempt at describing or analyzing
the character of the principal actors in the crusade of
St. Louis, beyond relating some of their remarks or
occasional conversations. It is an ungrateful task to
draw up these indictments against a man whom one

probably admires much more sincerely than those who bespatter him with undeserved praise. Joinville's book is readable, and it is readable even in spite of the antiquated and sometimes difficult language in which it is written. There are few books of which we could say the same. What makes his book readable is partly the interest attaching to the subject of which it treats, but far more the simple, natural, straightforward way in which Joinville tells what he has to tell. From one point of view it may be truly said that no higher praise could be bestowed on any style than to say that it is simple, natural, straightforward, and charming. But if his indiscriminate admirers had appreciated this artless art, they would not have applied to the pleasant gossip of an old general epithets that are appropriate only to the masterpieces of classical literature.

It is important to bear in mind what suggested to Joinville the first idea of writing his book. He was asked to do so by the Queen of Philip le Bel. After the death of the Queen, however, Joinville did not dedicate his work to the King, but to his son, who was then the heir apparent. This may be explained by the fact that he himself was Sénéchal de Champagne, and Louis, the son of Philip le Bel, Comte de Champagne. But it admits of another and more probable explanation. Joinville was dissatisfied with the proceedings of Philip le Bel, and from the very beginning of his reign he opposed his encroachments on the privileges of the nobility and the liberties of the people. He was punished for his opposition, and excluded from the assemblies in Champagne in 1287; and though his name appeared again on the roll in 1291, Joinville then occupied only the sixth instead of the first place. In

1314 matters came to a crisis in Champagne, and Joinville called together the nobility in order to declare openly against the King. The opportune death of Philip alone prevented the breaking out of a rebellion. It is true that there are no direct allusions to these matters in the body of Joinville's book, yet an impression is left on the reader that he wrote some portion of the Life of St. Louis as a lesson to the young prince to whom it is dedicated. Once or twice, indeed, he uses language which sounds ominous, and which would hardly be tolerated in France, even after the lapse of five centuries. When speaking of the great honor which St. Louis conferred on his family, he says " that it was, indeed, a great honor to those of his descendants who would follow his example by good works, but a great dishonor to those who would do evil. For people would point at them with their fingers, and would say that the sainted King from whom they descended would have despised such wickedness." There is another passage even stronger than this. After relating how St. Louis escaped from many dangers by the grace of God, he suddenly exclaims, " Let the King who now reigns (Philip le Bel) take care, for he has escaped from as great dangers — nay, from greater ones — than we ; let him see whether he cannot amend his evil ways, so that God may not strike him and his affairs cruelly."

This surely is strong language, considering that it was used in a book dedicated to the son of the then reigning King. To the father of Philip le Bel, Joinville seems to have spoken with the same frankness as to his son ; and he tells us himself how he reproved the King, Philip le Hardi, for his extravagant dress, and admonished him to follow the example of his father. Similar remarks occur again and again; and though the Life of St. Louis was certainly not written merely for didactic purposes, yet one cannot help seeing that it was written with a practical object. In the introduction Joinville says, " I send the book to you, that you and your brother and others who hear it may take an example, and that they may carry it out in their life, for which God will bless them." And again (p. 268), " These things shall I cause to be written, that those who hear them may have faith in God in their persecutions and tribulations, and God will help them, as He did me." Again (p. 380), " These things I have told you, that you may guard against taking an oath without reason, for, as the wise say, 'He who swears readily, forswears himself readily.' "

It seems, therefore, that when Joinville took to dictating his recollections of St. Louis, he did so partly to redeem a promise given to the Queen, who, he says, loved him much, and whom he could not refuse, partly to place in the hands of the young princes a book full of historical lessons which they might read, mark, and inwardly digest.

And well might he do so, and well might his book be read by all young princes, and by all who are able to learn a lesson from the pages of history; for few kings, if any, did ever wear their crowns so worthily as Louis IX. of France; and few saints, if any, did deserve their halo better than St. Louis. Here lies the deep and lasting interest of Joinville's work. It allows us an insight into a life which we could hardly realize, nay, which we should hardly believe in, unless we had the testimony of that trusty witness, Joinville, the King's friend and comrade. The legendary lives of St. Louis would have destroyed in the eyes of posterity the real greatness and the real sanctity of the King's character. We should never have known the man, but only his saintly caricature. After reading Joinville, we must make up our mind that such a life as he there describes was really lived, and was lived in those very palaces which we are accustomed to consider as the sinks of wickedness and vice. From other descriptions we might have imagined Louis IX. as a bigoted, priest-ridden, credulous King. From Joinville we learn that, though unwavering in his faith, and most strict in the observance of his religious duties, the King was by no means narrow in his sympathies, or partial to the encroachments of priestcraft. We find Joinville speaking to the King on subjects of religion with the greatest freedom, and as no courtier would have dared to speak during the later years of Louis XIV.'s reign. When the King asked him whether in the holy week he ever washed the feet of the poor, Joinville replied that he would never wash the feet of such villains. For this remark he was, no doubt, reproved by the King, who, as we are told by Beaulieu, with the most unpleasant details, washed the feet of the poor every Saturday. But the reply, though somewhat irreverent, is, nevertheless, highly creditable to the courtier's frankness. Another time he shocked his royal friend still more by telling him, in the presence of several priests, that he would rather have committed thirty mortal sins than be a leper. The King said nothing at the time, but he sent for him the next day, and reproved him in the most gentle manner for his thoughtless speech.

Joinville, too, with all the respect which he entertained for his King, would never hesitate to speak his mind when he thought that the King was in the wrong. On one occasion the Abbot of Cluny presented the King with two horses, worth five hundred *livres*. The next day the Abbot came again to the King to discuss some matters of business. Joinville observed that the King listened to him with marked attention. After the Abbot was gone, he went to the King, and said, "'Sire, may I ask you whether you listened to the Abbot more cheerfully because he presented you yesterday with two horses?' The King meditated for a time, and then said to me, 'Truly, yes.' 'Sire,' said I, 'do you know why I asked you this question?' 'Why?' said he. 'Because, Sire,' I said, 'I advise you, when you return to France, to prohibit all sworn counselors from accepting anything from those who have to bring their affairs before them. For you may be certain, if they accept anything, they will listen more cheerfully and attentively to those who give, as you did yourself with the Abbot of Cluny.'"

Surely a king who could listen to such language is not likely to have had his court filled with hypocrites, whether lay or clerical. The bishops, though they might count on the King for any help he could give them in the great work of teaching, raising, and comforting the people, tried in vain to make him commit an injustice in defense of what they considered religion. One day a numerous deputation of prelates asked for an interview. It was readily granted. When they appeared before the King, their spokesman said, "Sire, these lords who are here, archbishops and bishops, have asked me to tell you that Christianity is perishing at your hands." The King signed himself with the cross, and said, "Tell me how can that be?" "Sire," he said, "it is because people care so little nowadays for excommunication that they would rather die excommunicated than have themselves absolved and give satisfaction to the Church. Now, we pray you, Sire, for the sake of God, and because it is your duty, that you command your provosts and bailiffs that by seizing the goods of those who allow themselves to be excommunicated for the space of one year, they may force them to come and be absolved." Then the King replied that he would do this willingly with all those of whom it could be *proved* that they were in the wrong (which would, in fact, have given the King jurisdiction in ecclesiastical matters). The bishops said that they could not do this at any price; they would never bring their causes before his court. Then the King said he could not do it otherwise, for it would be against God and against reason. He reminded them of the case of the Comte de Bretagne, who had been excommunicated by the prelates of Brittany for the space of seven years, and who, when he appealed to the Pope, gained his cause, while the prelates were condemned. "Now then," the King said, "if I had forced the Comte de Bretagne to get absolution from the prelates after the first year, should I not have sinned against God and against him?"

This is not the language of a bigoted man; and if we find in the life of St. Louis traces of what in our age we might feel inclined to call bigotry or credulity, we must consider that the religious and intellectual atmosphere of the reign of St. Louis was very different from our own. There are, no doubt, some of the sayings and doings recorded by Joinville of his beloved King which at present would be unanimously condemned even by the most orthodox and narrow-minded. Think of an assembly of theologians in the monastery of Cluny who had invited a distinguished rabbi to discuss certain points of Christian doctrine with them. A knight, who happened to be staying with the abbot, asked for leave to open the discussion, and he addressed the Jew in the following words: "Do you believe that the Virgin Mary was a virgin and Mother of God?" When the Jew replied, "No!" the knight took his crutch and felled the poor Jew to the ground. The King, who relates this to Joinville, draws one very wise lesson from it — namely, that no one who is not a very good theologian should enter upon a controversy with Jews on such subjects. But when he goes on to say that a layman who hears the Christian religion evil spoken of should take to the sword as the right weapon of defense, and run it into the miscreant's body as far as it would go, we perceive at once that we are in the thirteenth and not in the nineteenth century. The punishments which the King inflicted for swearing were most cruel. At Cesarea, Joinville tells us that he saw a goldsmith fastened to a ladder, with the entrails of a pig twisted round his neck right up to his nose, because he had used irreverent language. Nay, after his return from the Holy Land, he heard that the King ordered a man's nose and lower lip to be burnt for the same offense. The Pope himself had to interfere to prevent St. Louis from inflicting on blasphemers mutilation and death. "I would myself be branded with a hot iron," the King said, "if thus I could drive away all swearing from my kingdom." He himself, as Joinville assures us, never used an oath, nor did he pronounce the name of the Devil except when reading the lives of the saints. His soul, we cannot doubt, was grieved when he heard the names which to him were the most sa-

cred, employed for profane purposes; and this feeling
of indignation was shared by his honest chronicler.
"In my castle," says Joinville, "whosoever uses bad
language receives a good pommeling, and this has
nearly put down that bad habit." Here again we see
the upright character of Joinville. He does not, like
most courtiers, try to outbid his sovereign in pious indignation; on the contrary, while sharing his feelings,
he gently reproves the King for his excessive zeal and
cruelty, and this after the King had been raised to the
exalted position of a saint.

To doubt of any points of the Christian doctrine
was considered at Joinville's time, as it is even now,
as a temptation of the Devil. But here again we see
at the court of St. Louis a wonderful mixture of toler-
ance and intolerance. Joinville, who evidently spoke
his mind freely on all things, received frequent re-
proofs and lessons from the King; and we hardly know
which to wonder at most, the weakness of the arguments, or the gentle and truly Christian spirit in which
the King used them. The King once asked Joinville
how he knew that his father's name was Symon.
Joinville replied he knew it because his mother had
told him so. "Then," the King said, "you ought
likewise firmly to believe all the articles of faith which
the Apostles attest, as you hear them sung every Sunday in the Creed." The use of such an argument by
such a man leaves an impression on the mind that the
King himself was not free from religious doubts and
difficulties, and that his faith was built upon ground
which was apt to shake. And this impression is confirmed by a conversation which immediately follows
after this argument. It is long, but it is far too important to be here omitted. The Bishop of Paris had

told the King, probably in order to comfort him after receiving from him the confession of some of his own religious difficulties, that one day he received a visit from a great master in divinity. The master threw himself at the Bishop's feet and cried bitterly. The Bishop said to him, —

" ' Master, do not despair; no one can sin so much that God could not forgive him.'

" The master said, ' I cannot help crying, for I believe I am a miscreant; for I cannot bring my heart to believe the sacrament of the altar, as the holy Church teaches it, and I know full well that it is the temptation of the enemy.'

" ' Master,' replied the Bishop, ' tell me, when the enemy sends you this temptation, does it please you ? '

" And the master said, ' Sir, it pains me as much as anything can pain.'

" ' Then I ask you,' the Bishop continued, ' would you take gold or silver in order to avow with your mouth anything that is against the sacrament of the altar, or against the other sacred sacraments of the Church?'

" And the master said, ' Know, sir, that there is nothing in the world that I should take; I would rather that all my limbs were torn from my body than openly avow this.'

" ' Then,' said the Bishop, ' I shall tell you something else. You know that the King of France made war against the King of England, and you know that the castle which is nearest to the frontier is La Rochelle, in Poitou. Now, I shall ask you, if the King had trusted you to defend La Rochelle, and he had trusted me to defend the Castle of Laon, which is in the heart of France, where the country is at peace, to whom ought the King to be more beholden at the end of the war, — to you who had defended La Rochelle without losing it, or to me who kept the Castle of Laon?'

"'In the name of God,' said the master, 'to me who had kept La Rochelle with losing it.'

"'Master,' said the Bishop, 'I tell you that my heart is like the Castle of Laon (Montlehcri), for I feel no temptation and no doubt as to the sacrament of the altar; therefore, I tell you, if God gives me one reward because I believe firmly and in peace, He will give you four, because you keep your heart for Him in this fight of tribulation, and have such good-will toward Him that for no earthly good, nor for any pain inflicted on your body, you would forsake Him. Therefore, I say to you, be at ease; your state is more pleasing to our Lord than my own.'"

When the master had heard this, he fell on his knees before the Bishop, and felt again at peace.

Surely, if the cruel punishment inflicted by St. Louis on blasphemers is behind our age, is not the love, the humility, the truthfulness of this Bishop, — is not the spirit in which he acted toward the priest, and the spirit in which he related this conversation to the King, somewhat in advance of the century in which we live?

If we only dwell on certain passages of Joinville's memoirs, it is easy to say that he and his King, and the whole age in which they moved, were credulous, engrossed by the mere formalities of religion, and fanatical in their enterprise to recover Jerusalem and the Holy Land. But let us candidly enter into their view of life, and many things which at first seem strange and startling will become intelligible. Joinville does not relate many miracles; and such is his good faith

that we may implicitly believe the facts, such as he
states them, however we may differ as to the interpretation by which, to Joinville's mind, these facts assumed a miraculous character. On their way to the
Holy Land it seems that their ship was windbound for
several days, and that they were in danger of being
taken prisoners by the pirates of Barbary. Joinville
recollected the saying of a priest who had told him
that, whatever had happened in his parish, whether too
much rain or too little rain, or anything else, if he
made three processions for three successive Saturdays,
his prayer was always heard. Joinville, therefore,
recommended the same remedy. Seasick as he was,
he was carried on deck, and the procession was formed
round the two masts of the ship. As soon as this was
done, the wind rose, and the ship arrived at Cyprus the
third Saturday. The same remedy was resorted to a
second time, and with equal effect. The King was
waiting at Damietta for his brother, the Comte de
Poitiers, and his army, and was very uneasy about the
delay in his arrival. Joinville told the legate of the
miracle that had happened on their voyage to Cyprus.
The legate consented to have three processions on
three successive Saturdays, and on the third Saturday
the Comte de Poitiers and his fleet arrived before Damietta. One more instance may suffice. On their
return to France a sailor fell overboard, and was left
in the water. Joinville, whose ship was close by, saw
something in the water; but, as he observed no struggle, he imagined it was a cask. The man, however,
was picked up; and when asked why he did not exert
himself, he replied that he saw no necessity for it. As
soon as he fell into the water he commended himself
to *Nostre Dame*, and she supported him by his shoul-

ders till he was picked up by the King's galley. Joinville had a window painted in his chapel to commemorate this miracle; and there, no doubt, the Virgin would be represented as supporting the sailor exactly as he described it.

Now, it must be admitted that before the tribunal of the ordinary philosophy of the nineteenth century, these miracles would be put down either as inventions or as exaggerations. But let us examine the thoughts and the language of that age, and we shall take a more charitable, and, we believe, a more correct view. Men like Joinville did not distinguish between a general and a special providence, and few who have carefully examined the true import of words would blame him for that. Whatever happened to him and his friends, the smallest as well as the greatest events were taken alike as so many communications from God to man. Nothing could happen to any one of them unless God willed it. "God wills it," they exclaimed, and put the cross on their breasts, and left house and home, and wife and children, to fight the infidels in the Holy Land. The King was ill and on the point of death, when he made a vow that if he recovered, he would undertake a crusade. In spite of the dangers which threatened him and his country, where every vassal was a rival, in spite of the despair of his excellent mother, the King fulfilled his vow, and risked not only his crown, but his life, without a complaint and without a regret. It may be that the prospect of Eastern booty, or even of an Eastern throne, had some part in exciting the pious zeal of the French chivalry. Yet if we read of Joinville, who was then a young and gay nobleman of twenty-four, with a young wife and a beautiful castle in Champagne, giving up everything, confessing his sins, making reparation, performing pilgrimages, and then starting for the East, there to endure for five years the most horrible hardships; when we read of his sailors singing a *Veni, Creator Spiritus*, before they hoisted their sails; when we see how every day, in the midst of pestilence and battle, the King and his Sénéchal and his knights say their prayers and perform their religious duties; how in every danger they commend themselves to God or to their saints; how for every blessing, for every escape from danger, they return thanks to Heaven, — we easily learn to understand how natural it was that such men should see miracles in every blessing vouchsafed to them, whether great or small, just as the Jews of old, in that sense the true people of God, saw miracles, saw the finger of God in every plague that visited their camp, and in every spring of water that saved them from destruction. When the Egyptians were throwing the Greek fire into the camp of the Crusaders, St. Louis raised himself in his bed at the report of every discharge of those murderous missiles, and, stretching forth his hands towards heaven, he said, crying, "Good Lord God, protect my people." Joinville, after relating this, remarks, "And I believe truly that his prayers served us well in our need." And was he not right in this belief, as right as the Israelites were when they saw Moses lifting up his heavy arms, and they prevailed against Amalek? Surely this belief was put to a hard test when a fearful plague broke out in the camp, when nearly the whole French army was massacred, when the King was taken prisoner, when the Queen, in childbed, had to make her old chamberlain swear that he would kill her at the first approach of the enemy, when the small remnant of that mighty French army had to purchase its return to France by a heavy ransom. Yet nothing could shake Joinville's faith in the ever-ready help of our Lord, of the Virgin, and of the saints. "Be certain," he writes, "that the Virgin helped us, and she would have helped us more if we had not offended her, her and her Son, as I said before." Surely, with such faith, credulity ceases to be credulity. Where there is credulity without that living faith which sees the hand of God in everything, man's indignation is rightly roused. That credulity leads to self-conceit, hypocrisy, and unbelief. But such was not the credulity of Joinville or of his King, or of the Bishop who comforted the great master in theology. A modern historian would not call the rescue of the drowning sailor, nor the favorable wind which brought the Crusaders to Cyprus, nor the opportune arrival of the Comte de Poitiers miracles, because the word "miracle" has a different sense with us from what it had during the Middle Ages, from what it had at the time of the Apostles, and from what it had at the time of Moses. Yet to the drowning sailor his rescue was miraculous; to the despairing King the arrival of his brother was a godsend; and to Joinville and his crew, who were in imminent danger of being carried off as slaves by Moorish pirates, the wind that brought them safe to Cyprus was more than a fortunate accident. Our language differs from the language of Joinville, yet in our heart of hearts we mean the same thing.

And nothing shows better the reality and healthiness of the religion of those brave knights than their cheerful and open countenance, their thorough enjoyment of all the good things of this life, their freedom in thought and speech. You never catch Joinville

canting, or with an expression of blank solemnity.
When his ship was surrounded by the galleys of the
Sultan, and when they held a council as to whether
they should surrender themselves to the Sultan's fleet
or to his army on shore, one of his servants objected to
all surrender. "Let us all be killed," he said to Joinville, "and then we shall all go straight to Paradise."
His advice, however, was not followed, because, as
Joinville says, "we did not believe it."

If we bear in mind that Joinville's History was written after Louis has been raised to the rank of a saint,
his way of speaking of the King, though always respectful, strikes us, nevertheless, as it must have struck
his contemporaries, as sometimes very plain and familiar. It is well known that an attempt was actually
made by the notorious Jesuit, le Père Hardouin, to
prove Joinville's work as spurious, or, at all events, as
full of interpolations, inserted by the enemies of the
Church. It was an attempt which thoroughly failed,
and which was too dangerous to be repeated; but, on
reading Joinville after reading the life and miracles of
St. Louis, one can easily understand that the soldier's
account of the brave King was not quite palatable or
welcome to the authors of the legends of the royal
saint. At the time when the King's bones had begun
to work wretched miracles, the following story could
hardly have sounded respectful: "When the King was
at Acre," Joinville writes, "some pilgrims on their
way to Jerusalem wished to see him. Joinville went
to the King, and said, 'Sire, there is a crowd of people who have asked me to show them the royal saint,
though *I* have no wish as yet to kiss your bones.'
The King laughed loud, and asked me to bring the
people."

In the thick of the battle, in which Joinville received five wounds and his horse fifteen, and when death seemed almost certain, Joinville tells us that the good Count of Soissons rode up to him and chaffed him, saying, "Let these dogs loose, for, *par la quoife Dieu*," — as he always used to swear, — "we shall still talk of this day in the rooms of our ladies."

The Crusades and the Crusaders, though they are only five or six centuries removed from us, have assumed a kind of romantic character, which makes it very difficult even for the historian to feel towards them the same human interest which we feel for Cæsar or Pericles. Works like that of Joinville are most useful in dispelling that mist which the chroniclers of old and the romances of Walter Scott and others have raised round the heroes of these holy wars. St. Louis and his companions, as described by Joinville, not only in their glistening armor, but in their everyday attire, are brought nearer to us, become intelligible to us, and teach us lessons of humanity which we can learn from men only, and not from saints and heroes. Here lies the real value of real history. It makes us familiar with the thoughts of men who differ from us in manners and language, in thought and religion, and yet with whom we are able to sympathize, and from whom we are able to learn. It widens our minds and our hearts, and gives us that true knowledge of the world and of human nature in all its phases which but few can gain in the short span of their own life, and in the narrow sphere of their friends and enemies. We can hardly imagine a better book for boys to read or for men to ponder over; and we hope that M. de Wailly's laudable efforts may be crowned with complete success, and that, whether in France or in England, no student of history will in future imagine that he knows the true spirit of the Crusades and the Crusaders who has not read once, and more than once, the original Memoirs of Joinville, as edited, translated, and explained by the eminent Keeper of the Imperial Library at Paris, M. Natalis de Wailly. 1868.

VIII.

THE JOURNAL DES SAVANTS AND THE JOURNAL DE TRÉVOUX.[1]

For a hundred persons who, in this country, read the " Revue des Deux Mondes," how many are there who read the " Journal des Savants ? " In France the authority of that journal is indeed supreme; but its very title frightens the general public, and its blue cover is but seldom seen on the tables of the *salles de lecture*. And yet there is no French periodical so well suited to the tastes of the better class of readers in England. Its contributors are all members of the Institut de France; and, if we may measure the value of a periodical by the honor which it reflects on those who form its staff, no journal in France can vie with the " Journal des Savants." At the present moment we find on its roll such names as Cousin, Flourens, Villemain, Mignet, Barthélemy Saint-Hilaire, Naudet, Prosper Mérimé, Littré, Vitet — names which, if now and then seen on the covers of the " Revue des Deux Mondes," the " Revue Contemporaine," or the " Revue Moderne," confer an exceptional lustre on these fortnightly or monthly issues. The articles which are

[1] *Table Méthodique des Mémoires de Trévoux* (1701-1775), précédée d'une Notice Historique. Par le Père P. C. Sommervogel, de la Compagnie de Jésus. 3 vols. Paris, 1864-65.

admitted into this select periodical may be deficient
now and then in those outward charms of diction by
which French readers like to be dazzled; but what in
France is called *trop savant, trop lourd*, is frequently
far more palatable than the highly spiced articles which
are no doubt delightful to read, but which, like an excellent French dinner, make you almost doubt whether
you have dined or not. If English journalists are bent
on taking for their models the fortnightly or monthly
contemporaries of France, the " Journal des Savants "
might offer a much better chance of success than the
more popular *revues*. We should be sorry indeed to
see any periodical published under the superintendence
of the " Ministre de l'Instruction Publique," or of any
other member of the Cabinet; but, apart from that, a
literary tribunal like that formed by the members of
the " Bureau du Journal des Savants " would certainly
be a great benefit to literary criticism. The general
tone that runs through their articles is impartial and
dignified. Each writer seems to feel the responsibility
which attaches to the bench from which he addresses
the public, and we can of late years recall hardly any
case where the dictum of " noblesse oblige " has been
disregarded in this the most ancient among the purely
literary journals of Europe.

The first number of the " Journal des Savants "
was published more than two hundred years ago, on
the 5th of January, 1655. It was the first small
beginning in a branch of literature which has since
assumed immense proportions. Voltaire speaks of it
as " le père de tous les ouvrages de ce genre, dont
l'Europe est aujourd'hui remplie." It was published
at first once a week, every Monday; and the responsible editor was M. de Sallo, who, in order to avoid the

retaliations of sensitive authors, adopted the name of Le Sieur de Hedouville, the name, it is said, of his *valet de chambre*. The articles were short, and in many cases they only gave a description of the books, without any critical remarks. The Journal likewise gave an account of important discoveries in science and art, and of other events that might seem of interest to men of letters. Its success must have been considerable, if we may judge by the number of rival publications which soon sprang up in France and in other countries of Europe. In England, a philosophical journal on the same plan was started before the year was over. In Germany, the "Journal des Savants" was translated into Latin by F. Nitzschius in 1668, and before the end of the seventeenth century the "Giornale de' Letterati" (1668), the "Bibliotheca Volante" (1677), the "Acta Eruditorum" (1682), the "Nouvelles de la République des Lettres" (1684), the "Bibliothèque Universelle et Historique" (1686), the "Histoire des Ouvrages des Savants" (1687), and the "Monatliche Unterredungen" (1689), had been launched in the principal countries of Europe. In the next century it was remarked of the journals published in Germany, " Plura dixeris pullulasse brevi tempore quam fungi nascuntur unâ nocte."

Most of these journals were published by laymen, and represented the purely intellectual interests of society. It was but natural, therefore, that the clergy also should soon have endeavored to possess a journal of their own. The Jesuits, who at that time were the most active and influential order, were not slow to appreciate this new opportunity for directing public opinion, and they founded in 1701 their famous journal, the "Mémoires de Trévoux." Famous indeed it

might once be called, and yet at present how little is
known of that collection! how seldom are its volumes
called for in our public libraries! It was for a long
time the rival of the "Journal des Savants." Under
the editorship of Le Père Berthier it fought bravely
against Diderot, Voltaire, and other heralds of the
French Revolution. It weathered even the fatal year
of 1762, but, after changing its name, and moderating
its pretensions, it ceased to appear in 1782. The long
rows of its volumes are now piled up in our libraries
likes rows of tombstones, which we pass by without
even stopping to examine the names and titles of those
who are buried in these vast catacombs of thought.

It was a happy idea that led the Père P. C. Sommervogel, himself a member of the order of the Jesuits, to examine the dusty volumes of the "Journal de Trévoux," and to do for it the only thing that could be done to make it useful once more, at least to a certain degree, namely, to prepare a general index of the numerous subjects treated in its volumes, on the model of the great index, published in 1753, of the "Journal des Savants." His work, published at Paris in 1865, consists of three volumes. The first gives an index of the original dissertations; the second and third, of the works criticised in the "Journal de Trévoux." It is a work of much smaller pretensions than the index to the "Journal des Savants;" yet, such as it is, it is useful, and will amply suffice for the purposes of those few readers who have from time to time to consult the literary annals of the Jesuits in France.

The title of the "Mémoires de Trévoux" was taken from the town of Trévoux, the capital of the principality of Dombes, which Louis XIV. had conferred on the Duc de Maine, with all the privileges of a sovereign. Like Louis XIV., the young prince gloried in the title of a patron of art and science, but, as the pupil of Madame de Maintenon, he devoted himself even more zealously to the defense of religion. A printing-office was founded at Trévoux, and the Jesuits were invited to publish a new journal, "où l'on eût principalement en vûë la défense de la religion." This was the " Journal de Trévoux," published for the first time in February, 1701, under the title of " Mémoires pour l'Histoire des Sciences et des Beaux Arts, recueillis par l'ordre de Son Altesse Sérénissime, Monseigneur Prince Souvernin de Dombes." It was entirely and professedly in the hands of the Jesuits, and we find among its earliest contributors such names as Catrou, Tournemine, and Hardouin. The opportunities for collecting literary and other intelligence enjoyed by the members of that order were extraordinary. We doubt whether any paper, even in our days, has so many intelligent correspondents in every part of the world. If any astronomical observation was to be made in China or America, a Jesuit missionary was generally on the spot to make it. If geographical information was wanted, eye-witnesses could write from India or Africa to state what was the exact height of mountains or the real direction of rivers. The architectural monuments of the great nations of antiquity could easily be explored and described, and the literary treasures of India or China or Persia could be ransacked by men ready for any work that required devotion and perseverance, and that promised to throw additional splendor on the order of Loyola. No missionary society has ever understood how to utilize its resources in the interest of science like the Jesuits; and if our own missionaries may on many points take warning from the history of the Jesuits, on that one point at least they might do well to imitate their example.

Scientific interests, however, were by no means the chief motive of the Jesuits in founding their journal, and the controversial character began soon to preponderate in their articles. Protestant writers received but little mercy in the pages of the "Journal de Trévoux," and the battle was soon raging in every country of Europe between the flying batteries of the Jesuits and the strongholds of Jansenism, of Protestantism, or of liberal thought in general. Le Clerc was attacked for his "Harmonia Evangelica;" Boileau even was censured for his "Epître sur l'Amour de Dieu." But the old lion was too much for his reverend satirists. The following is a specimen of his reply:—

> "Mes Révérends Pères en Dieu,
>   Et mes confrères en Satire,
>   Dans vos Ecrits dans plus d'un lieu
> Je voy qu'à mes dépens vous affectés de rire;
> Mais ne craignés-vous point, que pour rire de Vous,
> Ralisant Juvénal, refeuilletant Horace,
> Je ne ranime encor ma satirique audace?
> Grands Aristarques de Trévoux,
> N'allés point de nouveau faire courir aux armes,
> Un athlète tout prest à prendre son congé,
> Qui par vos traits malins au combat rengagé
> Peut encore aux Rieurs faire verser des larmes.
> Apprenés un mot de Régnier,
> Notre célèbre Devancier,
>   *Corsaires attaquans Corsaires*
> *Ne font pas*, dit-il, *leurs affaires.*"

Even stronger language than this became soon the fashion in journalistic warfare. In reply to an attack on the Marquis Orsi, the "Giornale de' Letterati d'Italia" accused the "Journal de Trévoux" of *mensogna* and *impostura*, and in Germany the "Acta Eruditorum Lipsiensium" poured out even more violent invectives against the Jesuitical critics. It is wonderful how well Latin seems to lend itself to the expression of angry abuse. Few modern writers have excelled the following tirade, either in Latin or in German: —

"Quæ mentis stupiditas! At si qua est, Jesuitarum est. . . . Res est intoleranda, Trevoltianos Jesuitas, toties contusos, iniquissimum in suis diariis tribunal erexisse, in eoque non ratione duce, sed animi impotentia, non æquitatis legibus, sed præjudiciis, non veritatis lance, sed affectus aut odi pondere, optimis exquisitissimisque operibus detrahere, pessima ad cœlum usque laudibus efferre: ignaris auctoribus, modo secum sentiant, aut sibi faveant, ubique blandiri, doctissimos sibi non plane plenequo deditos plus quam canino dente mordere."

What has been said of other journals was said of the "Journal de Trévoux:" —

"Les auteurs de ce journal, qui a son mérite, sont constants à louer tous les ouvrages de ceux qu'ils affectionnent, et pour éviter une froide monotonie, ils exercent quelquefois la critique sur les écrivans à qui rien ne les oblige de faire grâce."

It took some time before authors became at all reconciled to these new tribunals of literary justice. Even a writer like Voltaire, who braved public opinion more than anybody, looked upon journals, and the influence which they soon gained in France and abroad, as a great evil. "Rien n'a plus nui à la littérature," he writes, " plus répandu le mauvais goût, et plus confondu le vrai avec le faux." Before the establishment of literary journals, a learned writer had indeed little to fear. For a few years, at all events, he was allowed to enjoy the reputation of having published a book; and this by itself was considered a great distinction by the world at large. Perhaps his book was never noticed at all, or, if it was, it was only criticised in one of those elaborate letters which the learned men of the

sixteenth and seventeenth centuries used to write to
each other, which might be forwarded indeed to one or
two other professors, but which never influenced public
opinion. Only in extreme cases a book would be
answered by another book, but this would necessarily
require a long time; nor would it at all follow that
those who had read and admired the original work
would have an opportunity of consulting the volume
that contained its refutation. This happy state of things
came to an end after the year 1665. Since the invention of printing, no more important event had
happened in the republic of letters than the introduction of a periodical literature. It was a complete revolution, differing from other revolutions only by the
quickness with which the new power was recognized
even by its fiercest opponents.

The power of journalism, however, soon found its
proper level, and the history of its rise and progress,
which has still to be written, teaches the same lesson
as the history of political powers. Journals which
defended private interests, or the interests of parties,
whether religious, political, or literary, never gained
that influence which was freely conceded to those who
were willing to serve the public at large in pointing out
real merit wherever it could be found, and in unmask-
ing pretenders, to whatever rank they might belong.
The once all-powerful organ of the Jesuits, the "Journal de Trévoux," has long ceased to exist, and even to
be remembered; the "Journal des Savants" still
holds, after more than two hundred years, that eminent
position which was claimed for it by its founder, as the
independent advocate of justice and truth.

IX.

CHASOT.[1]

HISTORY is generally written *en face.* It reminds us occasionally of certain royal family pictures, where the centre is occupied by the king and queen, while their children are ranged on each side like organ-pipes, and the courtiers and ministers are grouped behind, according to their respective ranks. All the figures seem to stare at some imaginary spectator, who would require at least a hundred eyes to take in the whole of the assemblage. This place of the imaginary spectator falls generally to the lot of the historian, and of those who read great historical works; and perhaps this is inevitable. But it is refreshing for once to change this unsatisfactory position, and, instead of always looking straight in the faces of kings, and queens, and generals, and ministers, to catch, by a side-glance, a view of the times, as they appeared to men occupying a less central and less abstract position than that of the general historian. If we look at the Palace of Versailles from the terrace in front of the edifice, we are impressed with its broad magnificence, but we are soon tired, and all that is left in our memory is a vast expanse of windows, columns, statues, and wall. But let us retire to some of the *bosquets* on each side of the main

[1] *Chasot: a Contribution to the History of Frederic the Great and his Time.* By Kurd von Schlözer. Berlin. 1856.

avenue, and take a diagonal view of the great mansion of Louis XIV., and though we lose part of the palace, the whole picture gains in color and life, and it brings before our mind the figure of the great monarch himself, so fond of concealing part of his majestic stateliness under the shadow of those very groves where we are sitting.

It was a happy thought of M. Kurd von Schlözer to try a similar experiment with Frederic the Great, and to show him to us, not as the great king, looking history in the face, but as seen near and behind another person, for whom the author has felt so much sympathy as to make him the central figure of a very pretty historical picture. This person is Chasot. Frederic used to say of him, *C'est le matador de ma jeunesse*, — a saying which is not found in Frederic's works, but which is nevertheless authentic. One of the chief magistrates of the old Hanseatic town of Lübeck, Syndicus Curtius, — the father, we believe, of the two distinguished scholars, Ernst and Georg Curtius, — was at school with the two sons of Chasot, and he remembers these royal words, when they were repeated in all the drawing-rooms of the city where Chasot spent many years of his life. Frederic's friendship for Chasot is well known, for there are two poems of the king addressed to this young favorite. They do not give a very high idea either of the poetical power of the monarch, or of the moral character of his friend; but they contain some manly and straightforward remarks, which make up for a great deal of shallow declamation. This young Chasot was a French nobleman, a fresh, chivalrous, buoyant nature, — adventurous, careless, extravagant, brave, full of romance, happy with the happy, and galloping through life like a true cavalry officer. He met Frederic in 1734. Louis XV. had taken up the cause of Stanislas Lesczynski, King of Poland, his father-in-law, and Chasot served in the French army which, under the Duke of Berwick, attacked Germany on the Rhine, in order to relieve Poland from the simultaneous pressure of Austria and Russia. He had the misfortune to kill a French officer in a duel, and was obliged to take refuge in the camp of the old Prince Eugène. Here the young Prince of Prussia soon discovered the brilliant parts of the French nobleman, and when his father, Frederic William I., no longer allowed him to serve under Eugène, he asked Chasot to follow him to Prussia. The years from 1735 to 1740 were happy years for the prince, though he, no doubt, would have preferred taking an active part in the campaign. He writes to his sister : —

"J'aurais répondu plus tôt, si je n'avais été très-affligé de ce que le roi ne veut pas me permettre d'aller en campagne. Je le lui ai demandé quatre fois, et lui ai rappelé la promesse qu'il m'en avait faite ; mais point de nouvelle ; il m'a dit qu'il avait des raisons très-cachées qui l'en empêchaient. Je le crois, car je suis persuadé qu'il ne les sait pas lui-même."

But, as he wished to be on good terms with his father, he stayed at home, and travelled about to inspect his future kingdom. "C'est un peu plus honnête qu'en Sibérie," he writes, "mais pas de beaucoup." Frederic, after his marriage, took up his abode in the Castle of Rheinsberg, near Neu-Ruppin, and it was here that he spent the happiest part of his existence. M. de Schlözer has described this period in the life of the king with great art ; and he has pointed out how Frederic, while he seemed to live for nothing but pleasure,—shooting, dancing, music, and poetry,—was given at the same time to much more serious occupations,—reading and composing works on history, strategy, and philosophy, and maturing plans which, when the time of their execution came, seemed to spring from his head full-grown and full-armed. He writes to his sister, the Markgravine of Baireuth, in 1737:—

"Nous nous divertissons de rien, et n'avons aucun soin des choses de la vie, qui la rendent désagréable et qui jettent du dégoût sur les plaisirs. Nous faisons la tragédie et la comédie, nous avons bal, mascarade, et musique à toute sauce. Voilà un abrégé de nos amusements."

And again, he writes to his friend Suhm, at Petersburg:—

"Nous allons représenter l'*Œdipe* de Voltaire, dans lequel je ferai le héros de théâtre; j'ai choisi le rôle de Philoctète."

A similar account of the royal household at Rheinsberg is given by Bielfeld:—

"C'est ainsi que les jours s'écoulent ici dans une tranquillité assaisonnée de tous les plaisirs qui peuvent flatter une âme raisonnable. Chère de roi, vin des dieux, musique des anges, promenades délicieuses dans les jardins et dans les bois, parties sur l'eau, culture des lettres et des beaux-arts, conversation spirituelle, tout concourt à répandre dans ce palais enchanté des charmes sur la vie."

Frederic, however, was not a man to waste his time in mere pleasure. He shared in the revelries of his friends, but he was perhaps the only person at Rheinsberg who spent his evenings in reading Wolff's "Metaphysics." And here let us remark, that this German prince, in order to read that work, was obliged to have the German translated into French by his friend Suhm, the Saxon minister at Petersburg. Chasot, who had no very definite duties to perform at

Rheinsberg, was commissioned to copy Suhm's manuscript, — nay, he was nearly driven to despair when he had to copy it a second time, because Frederic's monkey, Mimi, had set fire to the first copy. We have Frederic's opinion on Wolff's "Metaphysics," in his "Works," vol. i. p. 263 : —

"Les universités prospéraient en même temps. Halle et Francfort étaient fournies de savants professeurs : Thomasius, Gundling, Ludewig, Wolff, et Stryke tenaient le premier rang pour la célébrité et faisaient nombre de disciples. Wolff commenta l'ingénieux système de Leibnitz sur les monades, et noya dans un déluge de paroles, d'arguments, de corollaires, et de citations, quelques problèmes que Leibnitz avait jetées peut-être comme une amorce aux métaphysiciens. Le professeur de Halle écrivait laborieusement nombre de volumes, qui, au lieu de pouvoir instruire des hommes faits, servirent tout au plus de catéchisme de didactique pour des enfants. Les monades ont mis aux prises les métaphysiciens et les géomètres d'Allemagne, et ils disputent encore sur la divisibilité de la matière."

In another place, however, he speaks of Wolff with greater respect, and acknowledges his influence in the German universities. Speaking of the reign of his father, he writes : —

"Mais la faveur et les brigues remplissaient les chaires de professeurs dans les universités ; les dévots, qui se mêlent de tout, acquirent une part à la direction des universités ; ils y persécutaient le bon sens, et surtout la classe des philosophes : Wolff fut exilé pour avoir déduit avec un ordre admirable les preuves sur l'existence de Dieu. La jeune noblesse qui se vouait aux armes, crût déroger en étudiant, et comme l'esprit humain donne toujours dans les excès, ils regardèrent l'ignorance comme un titre de mérite, et le savoir comme une pédanterie absurde."

During the same time, Frederic composed his "Refutation of Macchiavelli," which was published in 1740, and read all over Europe ; and besides the gay parties of the court, he organized the somewhat mysterious society of the *Ordre de Bayard*, of which his brothers, the Duke Ferdinand of Brunswick, the Duke Wilhelm of Brunswick-Bevern, Keyserling, Fouqué, and Chasot, were members. Their meetings had reference to serious political matters, though Frederic himself was never initiated by his father into the secrets of Prussian policy till almost on his death-bed. The king died in 1740, and Frederic was suddenly called away from his studies and pleasures at Rheinsberg, to govern a rising kingdom which was watched with jealousy by all its neighbors. He describes his state of mind, shortly before the death of his father, in the following words : —

"Vous pouvez bien juger que je suis assez tracassé dans la situation où je me trouve. On me laisse peu de repos, mais l'intérieur est tranquille, et je puis vous assurer que je n'ai jamais été plus philosophe qu'en cette occasion-ci. Je regarde avec des yeux d'indifférence tout ce qui m'attend, sans désirer la fortune ni la craindre, plein de compassion pour ceux qui souffrent, d'estime pour les honnêtes gens, et de tendresse pour mes amis."

As soon, however as he had mastered his new position, the young king was again the patron of art, of science, of literature, and of social improvements of every kind. Voltaire had been invited to Berlin, to organize a French theatre, when suddenly the news of the death of Charles VI., the Emperor of Germany, arrived at Berlin. How well Frederic understood what was to follow, we learn from a letter to Voltaire : —

"Mon cher Voltaire, — L'événement le moins prévu du monde m'empêche, pour cette fois, d'ouvrir mon âme à la vôtre comme d'ordinaire, et de bavarder comme je le voudrais. L'empereur est mort. Cette mort dérange toutes mes idées pacifiques, et je crois qu'il s'agira, au mois de juin, plutôt de poudre à canon, de soldats, de tranchées, que d'actrices, de ballets et de théâtre."

He was suffering from fever, and he adds: —

"Je vais faire passer ma fièvre, car j'ai besoin de ma machine, et il en faut tirer à présent tout le parti possible."

Again he writes to Algarotti: —

"Une bagatelle comme est la mort de l'empereur ne demande pas de grands mouvements. Tout était prévu, tout était arrangé. Ainsi il ne s'agit que d'exécuter des desseins que j'ai roulés depuis long temps dans ma tête."

We need not enter into the history of the first Silesian war; but we see clearly from these expressions, that the occupation of Silesia, which the house of Brandenburg claimed by right, had formed part of the policy of Prussia long before the death of the emperor; and the peace of Breslau, in 1742, realized a plan which had probably been the subject of many debates at Rheinsberg. During this first war, Chasot obtained the most brilliant success. At Mollwitz, he saved the life of the king; and the following account of this exploit was given to M. de Schlözer by members of Chasot's family: An Austrian cavalry officer, with some of his men, rode up close to the king. Chasot was near. "Where is the king?" the officer shouted; and Chasot, perceiving the imminent danger, sprang forward, declared himself to be the king, and sustained for some time single-handed the most violent combat with the Austrian soldiers. At last he was rescued by his men, but not without having received a severe wound across his forehead. The king thanked him, and Voltaire afterwards celebrated his bravery in the following lines: —

"Il me souvient encore de ce jour mémorable
Où l'illustre Chasot, ce guerrier formidable,
Sauva par sa valeur le plus grand de nos rois.
O Prusse! élève un temple à ses fameux exploits."

Chasot soon rose to the rank of major, and received

large pecuniary rewards from the king. The brightest event, however, of his life was still to come; and this was the battle of Hohenfriedberg, in 1745. In spite of Frederic's successes, his position before that engagement was extremely critical. Austria had concluded a treaty with England, Holland and Saxony against Prussia. France declined to assist Frederic, Russia threatened to take part against him. On the 19th of April, the king wrote to his minister: —

"La situation présente est aussi violente que désagréable. Mon parti est tout pris. S'il s'agit de se battre, nous le ferons en désespérés. Enfin, jamais crise n'a été plus grande que la mienne. Il faut laisser au temps de débrouiller cette fusée, et au destin, s'il y en a un, à décider de l'événement."

And again: —

"J'ai jeté le bonnet pardessus les moulins; je me prépare à tous les événements qui peuvent m'arriver. Que la fortune me soit contraire ou favorable, cela ne m'abaissera ni m'enorgueillira; et s'il faut périr, ce sera avec gloire et l'épée à la main."

The decisive day arrived — "le jour le plus décisif de ma fortune." The night before the battle, the king said to the French ambassador — "Les ennemis sont où je les voulais, et je les attaque demain;" and on the following day the battle of Hohenfriedberg was won. How Chasot distinguished himself, we may learn from Frederic's own description: —

"Muse dis-moi, comment en ces moments
Chasot brilla, faisant voler des têtes,
De maints uhlans faisant de vrais squelettes,
Et des hossards, devant lui s'echappant,
Fendant les uns, les autres transperçant,
Et, maniant sa flamberge tranchante,
Mettait en fuite, et donnait l'épouvante
Aux ennemis effarés et tremblants.
Tel Jupiter est peint armé du foudre,
Et tel Chasot réduit l'uhlan en poudre."

In his account of the battle, the king wrote: —

"Action inouïe dans l'histoire, et dont le succès est dû aux Généraux Gessler et Submettau, au Colonel Schwerin et au brave Major Chasot, dont la valeur et la conduite se sont fait connaître dans trois batailles également."

And in his "Histoire de mon Temps," he wrote: —

"Un fait aussi rare, aussi glorieux, mérite d'être écrit en lettres d'or dans les fastes prussiens. Le Général Schwerin, le Major Chasot et beaucoup d'officiers s'y firent un nom immortel."

How, then, is it that, in the later edition of Frederic's "Histoire de mon Temps," the name of Chasot is erased? How is it that, during the whole of the Seven Years' War, Chasot is never mentioned? M. de Schlözer gives us a complete answer to this question, and we must say that Frederic did not behave well to the *matador de sa jeunesse*. Chasot had a duel with a Major Bronickowsky, in which his opponent was killed. So far as we can judge from the documents which M. de Schlözer has obtained from Chasot's family, Chasot had been forced to fight; but the king believed that he had sought a quarrel with the Polish officer, and, though a court-martial found him not guilty, Frederic sent him to the fortress of Spandau. This was the first estrangement between Chasot and the king; and though after a time he was received again at court, the friendship between the king and the young nobleman who had saved his life had received a rude shock.

Chasot spent the next few years in garrison at Treptow; and, though he was regularly invited by Frederic to be present at the great festivities at Berlin, he seems to have been a more constant visitor at the small court of the Duchess of Strelitz, not far from his garrison, than at Potsdam. The king employed him on a diplomatic mission, and in this also Chasot was

successful. But notwithstanding the continuance of
this friendly intercourse, both parties felt chilled, and
the least misunderstanding was sure to lead to a rupture. The king, jealous perhaps of Chasot's frequent
visits at Strelitz, and not satisfied with the drill of his
regiment, expressed himself in strong terms about
Chasot at a review in 1751. The latter asked for
leave of absence in order to return to his country and
recruit his health. He had received fourteen wounds
in the Prussian service, and his application could not be
refused. There was another cause of complaint, on
which Chasot seems to have expressed himself freely.
He imagined that Frederic had not rewarded his services with sufficient liberality. He expressed himself
in the following words: —

"Je ne sais quel malheureux guignon poursuit le roi : mais ce guignon se reproduit dans tout ce que sa majesté entreprend ou ordonne. Toujours ses vues sont bonnes, ses plans sont sages, réfléchis et justes ; et toujours le succès est nul ou très-imparfait, et pourquoi ? Toujours pour la même cause ! parce qu'il manque un louis à l'exécution ! un louis de plus, et tout irait à merveille. Son guignon veut que partout il retienne ce maudit louis ; et tout se fait mal."

How far this is just, we are unable to say. Chasot
was reckless about money, and whatever the king
might have allowed him, he would always have wanted
one louis more. But on the other hand, Chasot was
not the only person who complained of Frederic's parsimony ; and the French proverb, "On ne peut pas
travailler pour le roi de Prusse," probably owes its
origin to the complaints of Frenchmen who flocked to
Berlin at that time in great numbers, and returned
home disappointed. Chasot went to France, where he
was well received, and he soon sent an intimation to
the king that he did not mean to return to Berlin. In

1752 his name was struck off the Prussian army-list. Frederic was offended, and the simultaneous loss of many friends, who either died or left his court, made him *de mauvaise humeur.* It is about this time that he writes to his sister: —

"J'étudie beaucoup, et cela me soulage réellement; mais lorsque mon esprit fait des retours sur les temps passés, alors les plaies du cœur se rouvrent et je regrette inutilement les pertes que j'ai faites."

Chasot, however, soon returned to Germany, and probably in order to be near the court of Strelitz, took up his abode in the old free town of Lübeck. He became a citizen of Lübeck in 1754, and in 1759 was made commander of its militia. Here his life seems to have been very agreeable, and he was treated with great consideration and liberality. Chasot was still young, as he was born in 1716, and he now thought of marriage. This he accomplished in the following manner. There was at that time an artist of some celebrity at Lübeck, — Stefano Torelli. He had a daughter whom he had left at Dresden to be educated, and whose portrait he carried about on his snuff-box. Chasot met him at dinner, saw the snuff-box, fell in love with the picture, and proposed to the father to marry his daughter Camilla. Camilla was sent for. She left Dresden, travelled through the country, which was then occupied by Prussian troops, met the king in his camp, received his protection, arrived safely at Lübeck, and in the same year was married to Chasot. Frederic was then in the thick of the Seven Years' War, but Chasot, though he was again on friendly terms with the king, did not offer him his sword. He was too happy at Lübeck with his Camilla, and he made himself useful to the king by sending him recruits.

One of the recruits he offered was his son, and in a letter, April 8, 1760, we see the king accepting this young recruit in the most gracious terms: —

"J'accepte volontiers, cher de Chasot, la recrue qui vous doit son être, et je serai parrain de l'enfant qui vous naîtra, au cas que ce soit un fils. Nous tuons les hommes, tandis que vous en faites."

It was a son, and Chasot writes: —

"Si ce garçon me ressemble, Sire, il n'aura pas une goutte de sang dans ses veines qui ne soit à vous."

M. de Schlözer, who is himself a native of Lübeck, has described the later years of Chasot's life in that city with great warmth and truthfulness. The diplomatic relations of the town with Russia and Denmark were not without interest at that time, because Peter III., formerly Duke of Holstein, had declared war against Denmark in order to substantiate his claims to the Danish crown. Chasot had actually the pleasure of fortifying Lübeck, and carrying on preparations for war on a small scale, till Peter was dethroned by his wife, Catherine. All this is told in a very comprehensive and humorous style; and it is not without regret that we find ourselves in the last chapter, where M. de Schlözer describes the last meetings of Chasot and Frederic in 1779, 1784, and 1785. Frederic had lost nearly all his friends, and he was delighted to see the *matador de sa jeunesse* once more. He writes: —

"Une chose qui n'est presque arrivée qu'à moi est que j'ai perdu tous mes amis de cœur et mes anciennes connaissances ; ce sont des plaies dont le cœur saigne long-temps, que la philosophie apaise, mais que sa main ne saurait guérir."

How pleasant for the king to find at least one man with whom he could talk of the old days of Rheinsberg, — of Fräulein von Schack and Fräulein von Walmoden, of Cæsarion and Jordan, of Mimi and le Tourbillon! Chasot's two sons entered the Prussian service, though, in the manner in which they are received, we find Frederic again acting more as king than as friend. Chasot in 1784 was still as lively as ever, whereas the king was in bad health. The latter writes to his old friend, " Si nous ne nous revoyons bientôt, nous ne nous reverrons jamais; " and when Chasot had arrived, Frederic writes to Prince Heinrich, " Chasot est venu ici de Lübeck; il ne parle que de mangeaille, de vins de Champagne, du Rhin, de Madère, de Hongrie, et du faste de messieurs les marchands de la bourse de Lübeck."

Such was the last meeting of these two knights of the *Ordre de Bayard*. The king died in 1786, without seeing the approach of the revolutionary storm which was soon to upset the throne of the Bourbons. Chasot died in 1797. He began to write his memoirs in 1789, and it is to some of their fragments, which had been preserved by his family, and were handed over to M. Kurd de Schlözer, that we owe this delightful little book. Frederic the Great used to complain that Germans could not write history:—

" Ce siècle ne produisit aucun bon historien. On chargea Teissier d'écrire l'histoire de Brandebourg : il en fit le panégyrique. Pufendorf écrivit la vie de Frédéric-Guillaume, et, pour ne rien omettre, il n'oublia ni ses clercs de chancellerie, ni ses valets de chambre dont il put recueillir les noms. Nos auteurs ont, ce me semble, toujours péché, faute de discerner les choses essentielles des accessoires, d'éclaircir les faits, de reserrer leur prose traînante et excessivement sujette aux inversions, aux nombreuses épithètes, et d'écrire en pédants plutôt qu'en hommes de génie."

We believe that Frederic would not have said this

of a work like that of M. de Schlözer; and as to Chasot,
it is not too much to say that, after the days of Mollwitz
and Hohenfriedberg, the day on which M. de Schlözer
undertook to write his biography was perhaps the most
fortunate for his fame.

1854.

X.

SHAKESPEARE.[1]

The city of Frankfort, the birthplace of Goethe, sends her greeting to the city of Stratford-on-Avon, the birthplace of Shakespeare. The old free town of Frankfort, which, since the days of Frederick Barbarossa, has seen the Emperors of Germany crowned within her walls, might well at all times speak in the name of Germany. But to-day she sends her greeting, not as the proud mother of German Emperors, but as the prouder mother of the greatest among the poets of Germany; and it is from the very house in which Goethe lived, and which has since become the seat of "the Free German Institute for Science and Art," that this message of the German admirers and lovers of Shakespeare has been sent, which I am asked to present to you, the Mayor and Council of Stratford-on-Avon.

When honor was to be done to the memory of Shakespeare, Germany could not be absent, for next to Goethe and Schiller there is no poet so truly loved by us, so thoroughly our own, as your Shakespeare. He is no stranger with us, no mere classic, like Homer, or Virgil, or Dante, or Corneille, whom we admire as we

[1] Speech delivered at Stratford-on-Avon on the 23d of April, 1864, the Tercentenary of Shakespeare's birth.

admire a marble statue. He has become one of ourselves, holding his own place in the history of our literature, applauded in our theatres, read in our cottages, studied, known, loved, "as far as sounds the German tongue." There is many a student in Germany who has learned English solely in order to read Shakespeare in the original, and yet we possess a translation of Shakespeare with which few translations of any work can vie in any language. What we in Germany owe to Shakespeare must be read in the history of our literature. Goethe was proud to call himself a pupil of Shakespeare. I shall at this moment allude to one debt of gratitude only which Germany owes to the poet of Stratford-on-Avon. I do not speak of the poet only, and of his art, so perfect because so artless; I think of the man with his large, warm heart, with his sympathy for all that is genuine, unselfish, beautiful, and good; with his contempt for all that is petty, mean, vulgar, and false. It is from his plays that our young men in Germany form their first ideas of England and the English nation, and in admiring and loving him we have learned to admire and to love you who may proudly call him your own. And it is right that this should be so. As the height of the Alps is measured by Mont Blanc, let the greatness of England be measured by the greatness of Shakespeare. Great nations make great poets, great poets make great nations. Happy the nation that possesses a poet like Shakespeare. Happy the youth of England whose first ideas of this world in which they are to live are taken from his pages. The silent influence of Shakespeare's poetry on millions of young hearts in England, in Germany, in all the world, shows the almost superhuman power of human genius. If we

look at that small house, in a small street of a small
town of a small island, and then think of the world-
embracing, world-quickening, world-ennobling spirit
that burst forth from that small garret, we have learned
a lesson and carried off a blessing for which no pilgrim-
age would have been too long. Though the great
festivals which in former days brought together people
from all parts of Europe to worship at the shrine of
Canterbury exist no more, let us hope, for the sake of
England, more even than for the sake of Shakespeare,
that this will not be the last Shakespeare festival in the
annals of Stratford-on-Avon. In this cold and critical
age of ours the power of worshipping, the art of admiring, the passion of loving what is great and good
are fast dying out. May England never be ashamed
to show to the world that she can love, that she can
admire, that she can worship the greatest of her
poets! May Shakespeare live on in the love of each
generation that grows up in England! May the youth
of England long continue to be nursed, to be fed, to
be reproved and judged by his spirit! With that
nation — that truly English, because truly Shake-
spearian nation — the German nation will always be
united by the strongest sympathies; for, superadded
to their common blood, their common religion, their
common battles and victories, they will always have in
Shakespeare a common teacher, a common benefactor,
and a common friend.

April, 1864.

XI.

BACON IN GERMANY.[1]

"IF our German philosophy is considered in England and in France as German dreaming, we ought not to render evil for evil, but rather to prove the groundlessness of such accusations by endeavoring ourselves to appreciate, without any prejudice, the philosophers of France and England, such as they are, and doing them that justice which they deserve; especially as, in scientific subjects, injustice means ignorance." With these words M. Kuno Fischer introduces his work on Bacon to the German public; and what he says is evidently intended, not as an attack upon the conceit of French, and the exclusiveness of English philosophers, but rather as an apology which the author feels that he owes to his own countrymen. It would seem, indeed, as if a German was bound to apologize for treating Bacon as an equal of Leibnitz, Kant, Hegel, and Schelling. Bacon's name is never mentioned by German writers without some proviso that it is only by a great stretch of the meaning of the word, or by courtesy, that he can be called a philosopher. His philosophy, it is maintained, ends where all true philosophy begins; and his style or method has frequently been described

[1] Franz Baco von Verulam: *Die Realphilosophie und ihr Zeitalter.* Von Kuno Fischer. Leipzig. Brockhaus. 1856.

as unworthy of a systematic thinker. Spinoza, who has exercised so great an influence on the history of thought in Germany, was among the first who spoke slightingly of the inductive philosopher. When treating of the causes of error, he writes, "What he (Bacon) adduces besides, in order to explain error, can easily be traced back to the Cartesian theory; it is this, that the human will is free and more comprehensive than the understanding, or, as Bacon expresses himself in a more confused manner, in the forty-ninth aphorism, 'The human understanding is not a pure light, but obscured by the will.'" In works on the general history of philosophy, German authors find it difficult to assign any place to Bacon. Sometimes he is classed with the Italian school of natural philosophy, sometimes he is contrasted with Jacob Boehme. He is named as one of the many who helped to deliver mankind from the thralldom of scholasticism. But any account of what he really was, what he did to immortalize his name, and to gain that prominent position among his own countrymen which he has occupied to the present day, we should look for in vain even in the most complete and systematic treatises on the history of philosophy published in Germany. Nor does this arise from any wish to depreciate the results of English speculation in general. On the contrary, we find that Hobbes, Locke, Berkeley, and Hume are treated with great respect. They occupy well-marked positions in the progress of philosophic thought. Their names are written in large letters on the chief stations through which the train of human reasoning passed before it arrived at Kant and Hegel. Locke's philosophy took for a time complete possession of the German mind, and called forth some of the most important

and decisive writings of Leibnitz; and Kant himself
owed his commanding position to the battle which he
fought and won against Hume. Bacon alone has
never been either attacked or praised, nor have his
works, as it seems, ever been studied very closely by
Germans. As far as we can gather, their view of
Bacon and of English philosophy is something as
follows. Philosophy, they say, should account for experience; but Bacon took experience for granted. He
constructed a cyclopædia of knowledge, but he never
explained what knowledge itself was. Hence philosophy, far from being brought to a close by his "Novum
Organon," had to learn again to make her first steps
immediately after his time. Bacon had built a magnificent palace, but it was soon found that there was
no staircase in it. The very first question of all philosophy, "How do we know?" or, "How can we
know?" had never been asked by him. Locke, who
came after him, was the first to ask it, and he endeavored to answer it in his "Essay concerning Human
Understanding." The result of his speculations was,
that the mind is a *tabula rasa*, that this *tabula rasa* becomes gradually filled with sensuous perceptions, and
that these sensuous perceptions arrange themselves
into classes, and thus give rise to more general ideas
or conceptions. This was a step in advance; but there
was again one thing taken for granted by Locke, —
the perceptions. This led to the next step in English
philosophy, which was made by Berkeley. He asked the
question, "What are perceptions?" and he answered
it boldly: "Perceptions are the things themselves, and
the only cause of these perceptions is God." But this
bold step was in reality but a bold retreat. Hume accepted the results both of Locke and Berkeley. He

admitted with Locke that the impressions of the senses are the source of all knowledge; he admitted with Berkeley that we know nothing beyond the impressions of our senses. But when Berkeley speaks of the cause of these impressions, Hume points out that we have no right to speak of anything like cause and effect, and that the idea of causality, of necessary sequence, on which the whole fabric of our reasoning rests, is an assumption; inevitable, it may be, yet an assumption. Thus English philosophy, which seemed to be so settled and positive in Bacon, ended in the most unsettled and negative skepticism in Hume; and it was only through Kant that, according to the Germans, the great problem was solved at last, and men again knew *how* they knew.

From this point of view, which we believe to be that generally taken by German writers of the historical progress of modern philosophy, we may well understand why the star of Bacon should disappear almost below their horizon. And if those only are to be called philosophers who inquire into the causes of our knowledge, or into the possibility of knowing and being, a new name must be invented for men like him, who are concerned alone with the realities of knowledge. The two are antipodes, — they inhabit two distinct hemispheres of thought. But German Idealism, as M. Kuno Fischer says, would have done well if it had become more thoroughly acquainted with its opponent: —

"And if it be objected," he says, "that the points of contact between German and English philosophy, between Idealism and Realism, are less to be found in Bacon than in other philosophers of his kind; that it was not Bacon, but Hume, who influenced Kant; that it was not Bacon, but Locke, who induced Leibnitz; that Spinoza, if he received any impulse at all from those quarters, received it from Hobbes, and not from Bacon, of whom he speaks in several places very contemptuously,—I answer, that it was Bacon whom Des Cartes, the acknowledged founder of dogmatic Idealism, chose for his antagonist. And as to those realistic philosophers who have influenced the opposite side of philosophy in Spinoza, Leibnitz, and Kant, I shall be able to prove that Hobbes, Locke, Hume, are all descendants of Bacon, that they have their roots in Bacon, that without Bacon they cannot be truly explained and understood, but only be taken up in a fragmentary form, and, as it were, plucked off. Bacon is the creator of realistic philosophy. Their age is but a development of the Baconian germs; every one of their systems is a metamorphosis of Baconian philosophy. To the present day, realistic philosophy has never had a greater genius than Bacon, its founder; none who has manifested the truly realistic spirit that feels itself at home in the midst of life, in so comprehensive, so original and characteristic, so sober, and yet at the same time so ideal and aspiring a manner; none, again, in whom the limits of this spirit stand out in such distinct and natural relief. Bacon's philosophy is the most healthy and quite inartificial expression of Realism. After the systems of Spinoza and Leibnitz had moved me for a long time, had filled, and, as it were, absorbed me, the study of Bacon was to me like a new life, the fruits of which are gathered in this book."

After a careful perusal of M. Fischer's work, we believe that it will not only serve in Germany as a useful introduction to the study of Bacon, but that it will be read with interest and advantage by many persons in England who are already acquainted with the chief works of the philosopher. The analysis which he gives of Bacon's philosophy is accurate and complete; and, without indulging in any lengthy criticisms, he has thrown much light on several important points. He first discusses the aim of his philosophy, and characterizes it as Discovery in general, as the conquest of nature by man (*Regnum hominis, interpretatio naturæ*). He then enters into the means which it supplies for accomplishing this conquest, and which consist chiefly in experience:—

"The chief object of Bacon's philosophy is the establishment and extension of the dominion of man. The means of accomplishing this we may call culture, or the application of physical powers toward human purposes. But there is no such culture without discovery, which produces the means of culture; no discovery without science, which understands the laws of nature; no science without natural science; no natural science without an interpretation of nature; and this can only be accomplished according to the measure of our experience."

M. Fischer then proceeds to discuss what he calls the negative or destructive part of Bacon's philosophy (*pars destruens*),— that is to say, the means by which the human mind should be purified and freed from all preconceived notions before it approaches the interpretation of nature. He carries us through the long war which Bacon commenced against the idols of traditional or scholastic science. We see how the *idola tribus*, the *idola specus*, the *idola fori*, and the *idola theatri*, are destroyed by his iconoclastic philosophy. After all these are destroyed, there remains nothing but uncertainty and doubt; and it is in this state of nudity, approaching very nearly to the *tabula rasa* of Locke, that the human mind should approach the new temple of nature. Here lies the radical difference between Bacon and Des Cartes, between Realism and Idealism. Des Cartes also, like Bacon, destroys all former knowledge. He proves that we know nothing for certain. But after he has deprived the human mind of all its imaginary riches, he does not lead it on, like Bacon, to a study of nature, but to a study of itself as the only subject which can be known for certain, *Cogito, ergo sum*. His philosophy leads to a study of the fundamental laws of knowing and being; that of Bacon enters at once into the gates of nature, with the innocence of a child (to use his own expression) who enters the kingdom of God. Bacon speaks, indeed, of a *Philosophia prima* as a kind of introduction to Divine, Natural, and Human Philosophy; but he does not discuss in this preliminary chapter the problem of the possibility of knowledge, nor was it with him the right place to do so. It was destined by him as a "receptacle for all such profitable observations and axioms as fall not within the compass of the special parts of philosophy or sciences, but are more common, and of a higher stage." He mentions himself some of these axioms, such as — "*Si inæqualibus æqualia addas, omnia erunt inæqualia;*" "*Quæ in eodem tertio conveniunt, et inter se conveniunt;*" "*Omnia mutantur, nil interit.*" The problem of the possibility of knowledge would generally be classed under metaphysics; but what Bacon calls *Metaphysique* is, with him, a branch of philosophy treating only on Formal and Final Causes, in opposition to *Physique*, which treats on Material and Efficient Causes. If we adopt Bacon's division of philosophy, we might still expect to find the fundamental problem discussed in his chapter on Human Philosophy; but here, again, he treats man only as a part of the continent of Nature, and when he comes to consider the substance and nature of the soul or mind, he declines to enter into this subject, because "the true knowledge of the nature and state of soul must come by the same inspiration that gave the substance." There remains, therefore, but one place in Bacon's cyclopædia where we might hope to find some information on this subject, — namely, where he treats on the faculties and functions of the mind, and in particular, of understanding and reason. And here he dwells indeed on the doubtful evidence of the senses as one of the causes of error so frequently pointed out by other philosophers. But he remarks that, though they charged the deceit upon the senses, their chief errors arose from a different cause, from the weakness of their intellectual powers, and from the manner of collecting and concluding upon the reports of the senses. And he then points to what is to be the work of his life, — an improved system of invention, consisting of the *Experientia Literata*, and the *Interpretatio Naturæ*.

It must be admitted, therefore, that one of the problems which has occupied most philosophers, — nay, which, in a certain sense, may be called the first impulse to all philosophy, — the question whether we can know anything, is entirely passed over by Bacon; and we may well understand why the name and title of philosopher has been withheld from one who looked upon human knowledge as an art, but never inquired into its causes and credentials. This is a point which M. Fischer has not overlooked; but he has not always kept it in view, and in wishing to secure to Bacon his place in the history of philosophy, he has deprived him of that more exalted place which Bacon himself wished to occupy in the history of the world. Among men like Locke, Hume, Kant, and Hegel, Bacon is, and always will be, a stranger. Bacon himself would have drawn a very strong line between their province and his own. He knows where their province lies; and if he sometimes speaks contemptuously of formal philosophy, it is only when formal philosophy has encroached on his own ground, or when it breaks into the enclosure of revealed religion, which he wished to be kept sacred. There, he holds, the human mind should not enter, except in the attitude of the Semnones, with chained hands.

Bacon's philosophy could never supplant the works of Plato and Aristotle, and though his method might prove useful in every branch of knowledge, — even in the most abstruse points of logic and metaphysics, — yet there has never been a Baconian school of philosophy, in the sense in which we speak of the school of Locke or Kant. Bacon was above or below philosophy. Philosophy, in the usual sense of the word, formed but a part of his great scheme of knowledge. It had its place therein, side by side with history, poetry, and religion. After he had surveyed the whole universe of knowledge, he was struck by the small results that had been obtained by so much labor, and he discovered the cause of this failure in the want of a proper method of investigation and combination. The substitution of a new method of invention was the great object of his philosophical activity; and though it has been frequently said that the Baconian method had been known long before Bacon, and had been practiced by his predecessors with much greater success than by himself or his immediate followers, it was his chief merit to have proclaimed it, and to have established its legitimacy against all gainsayers. M. Fischer has some very good remarks on Bacon's method of induction, particularly on the *instantiæ prærogativæ* which, as he points out, though they show the weakness of his system, exhibit at the same time the strength of his mind, which rises above all the smaller considerations of systematic consistency, where higher objects are at stake.

M. Fischer devotes one chapter to Bacon's relation to the ancient philosophers, and another to his views on poetry. In the latter, he naturally compares Bacon with his contemporary, Shakespeare. We recommend this chapter, as well as a similar one in a work on

Shakespeare by Gervinus, to the author of the ingenious discovery that Bacon was the real author of Shakespeare's plays. Besides an analysis of the constructive part of Bacon's philosophy, or the *Instauratio Magna*, M. Fischer gives us several interesting chapters, in which he treats of Bacon as an historical character, of his views on religion and theology, and of his reviewers. His defense of Bacon's political character is the weakest part of his work. He draws an elaborate parallel between the spirit of Bacon's philosophy and the spirit of his public acts. Discovery, he says, was the object of the philosopher; success that of the politician. But what can be gained by such parallels? We admire Bacon's ardent exertions for the successful advancement of learning, but, if his acts for his own advancement were blamable, no moralist, whatever notions he may hold on the relation between the understanding and the will, would be swayed in his judgment of Lord Bacon's character by such considerations. We make no allowance for the imitative talents of a tragedian, if he stands convicted of forgery, nor for the courage of a soldier, if he is accused of murder. Bacon's character can only be judged by the historian, and by a careful study of the standard of public morality in Bacon's times. And the same may be said of the position which he took with regard to religion and theology. We may explain his inclination to keep religion distinct from philosophy by taking into account the practical tendencies of all his labors. But there is such a want of straightforwardness, and we might almost say, of real faith, in his theological statements, that no one can be surprised to find that, while he is taken as the representative of orthodoxy by some, he has been attacked by others as the most dangerous and insidious enemy of Christianity. Writers of the school of De Maistre see in him a decided atheist and hypocrite.

In a work on Bacon, it seems to have become a necessity to discuss Bacon's last reviewer, and M. Fischer therefore breaks a lance with Mr. Macaulay. We give some extracts from this chapter (page 858 *seq.*), which will serve, at the same time, as a specimen of our author's style : —

"Mr. Macaulay pleads unconditionally in favor of practical philosophy, which he designates by the name of Bacon, against all theoretical philosophy. We have two questions to ask: 1. What does Mr. Macaulay mean by the contrast of practical and theoretical philosophy, on which he dwells so constantly? and 2. What has his own practical philosophy in common with that of Bacon?

"Mr. Macaulay decides on the fate of philosophy with a ready formula, which, like many of the same kind, dazzles by means of words which have nothing behind them, — words which become more obscure and empty the nearer we approach them. He says, Philosophy was made for Man, not Man for Philosophy. In the former case it is practical; in the latter, theoretical. Mr. Macaulay embraces the first, and rejects the second. He cannot speak with sufficient praise of the one, nor with sufficient contempt of the other. According to him, the Baconian philosophy is practical; the pre-Baconian, and particularly the ancient philosophy, theoretical. He carries the contrast between the two to the last extreme, and he places it before our eyes, not in its naked form, but veiled in metaphors, and in well-chosen figures of speech, where the imposing and charming image always represents the practical, the repulsive the theoretical, form of philosophy. By this play he carries away the great mass of people, who, like children, always run after images. Practical philosophy is not so much a conviction with him, but it serves him to make a point; whereas theoretical philosophy serves as an easy butt. Thus the contrast between the two acquires a certain dramatic charm. The reader feels moved and excited by the subject before him, and forgets the scientific question. His fancy is caught by a kind of metaphor-

ical imagery, and his understanding surrenders what is due to
it. . . . What is Mr. Macaulay's meaning in rejecting theoretical philosophy, because philosophy is here the object, and man
the means; whereas he adopts practical philosophy, because
man is here the object, and philosophy the means? What do
we gain by such comparisons, as when he says that practical
and theoretical philosophy are like works and words, fruits and
thorns, a high-road and a treadmill? Such phrases always remind us of the remark of Socrates: They are said indeed, but
are they well and truly said? According to the strict meaning
of Mr. Macaulay's words, there never was a practical philosophy;
for there never was a philosophy which owed its origin to practical considerations only. And there never was a theoretical
philosophy, for there never was a philosophy which did not receive its impulse from a human want, that is to say, from a
practical motive. This shows where playing with words must
always lead. He defines theoretical and practical philosophy
in such a manner that his definition is inapplicable to any kind
of philosophy. His antithesis is entirely empty. But if we
drop the antithesis, and only keep to what it means in sober and
intelligible language, it would come to this, — that the value of
a theory depends on its usefulness, on its practical influence on
human life, on the advantage which we derive from it. Utility
alone is to decide on the value of a theory. Be it so. But who
is to decide on utility? If all things are useful which serve to
satisfy human wants, who is to decide on our wants? We take
Mr. Macaulay's own point of view. Philosophy should be
practical; it should serve man, satisfy his wants, or help to satisfy them; and if it fails in this, let it be called useless and hollow. But if there are wants in human nature which demand to
be satisfied, which make life a burden unless they are satisfied,
is that not to be called practical which answers to these wants?
And if some of them are of that peculiar nature that they can
only be satisfied by knowledge, or by theoretical contemplation,
is this knowledge, is this theoretical contemplation, not useful, —
useful even in the eyes of the most decided Utilitarian? Might
it not happen that what he calls theoretical philosophy seems
useless and barren to the Utilitarian, because his ideas of men
are too narrow? It is dangerous, and not quite becoming, to
lay down the law, and say from the very first, 'You must not
have more than certain wants, and therefore you do not want
more than a certain philosophy!' If we may judge from Mr.

Macaulay's illustrations, his ideas of human nature are not very
liberal. 'If we were forced,' he says, ' to make our choice between the first shoemaker and Seneca, the author of the books
on Anger, we should pronounce for the shoemaker. It may be
worse to be angry than to be wet. But shoes have kept millions from being wet; and we doubt whether Seneca ever kept
anybody from being angry.' I should not select Seneca as the
representative of theoretical philosophy, still less take those for
my allies whom Mr. Macaulay prefers to Seneca, in order to
defeat theoretical philosophers. Brennus threw his sword into
the scale in order to make it more weighty. Mr. Macaulay
prefers the awl. But whatever he may think about Seneca,
there is another philosopher more profound than Seneca, but in
Mr. Macaulay's eyes likewise an unpractical thinker. And yet
in him the power of theory was greater than the powers of nature and the most common wants of man. His meditations
alone gave Socrates his serenity when he drank the fatal poison.
Is there, among all evils, one greater than the dread of death?
And the remedy against this, the worst of all physical evils, is
it not practical in the best sense of the word? True, some
people might here say, that it would have been more practical
if Socrates had fled from his prison, as Criton suggested, and
had died an old and decrepit man in Bœotia. But to Socrates
it seemed more practical to remain in prison, and to die as the
first witness and martyr of the liberty of conscience, and to rise
from the sublime height of his theory to the seats of the immor-
tals. Thus it is the want of the individual which decides on
the practical value of an act or of a thought, and this want depends on the nature of the human soul. There is a difference
between individuals in different ages, and there is a difference
in their wants. . . . As long as the desire after knowledge lives
in our hearts, we must, with the purely practical view of satisfying this want, strive after knowledge in all things, even in
those which do not contribute towards external comfort, and
have no use except that they purify and invigorate the mind.
. . . . What is theory in the eyes of Bacon? ' A temple in
the human mind, according to the model of the world.' What
is it in the eyes of Mr. Macaulay? A snug dwelling, according
to the wants of practical life. The latter is satisfied if knowledge is carried far enough to enable us to keep ourselves dry.
The magnificence of the structure, and its completeness according to the model of the world, is to him useless by-work, super-

fluous and even dangerous luxury. This is the view of a
respectable rate-payer, not of a Bacon. Mr. Macaulay reduces
Bacon to his own dimensions, while he endeavors at the same
time to exalt him above all other people. . . . Bacon's own
philosophy was, like all philosophy, a theory; It was the theory
of the inventive mind. Bacon has not made any great discoveries himself. He was less inventive than Leibnitz, the German
metaphysician. If to make discoveries be practical philosophy,
Bacon was a mere theorist, and his philosophy nothing but the
theory of practical philosophy. . . . How far the spirit of
theory reached in Bacon may be seen in his own works. He
did not want to fetter theory, but to renew and to extend it to
the very ends of the universe. His practical standard was not
the comfort of the individual, but human happiness, which in-
volves theoretical knowledge. . . . That Bacon is not the
Bacon of Mr. Macaulay. What Bacon wanted was new, and it
will be eternal. What Mr. Macaulay and many people at the
present day want, in the name of Bacon, is not new, but novel.
New is what opposes the old, and serves as a model for the future.
Novel is what flatters our times, gains sympathies, and dies
away. . . . And history has pronounced her final verdict. It is
the last negative instance which we oppose to Mr. Macaulay's
assertion. Bacon's philosophy has not been the end of all theories, but the beginning of new theories, — theories which flowed
necessarily from Bacon's philosophy, and not one of which was
practical in Mr. Macaulay's sense. Hobbes was the pupil of
Bacon. His ideal of a State is opposed to that of Plato on all
points. But one point it shares in common, — It is as unpractical a theory as that of Plato. Mr. Macaulay, however, calls
Hobbes the most acute and vigorous spirit. If, then, Hobbes
was a practical philosopher, what becomes of Macaulay's politics? And if Hobbes was not a practical philosopher, what becomes of Mr. Macaulay's philosophy, which does homage to the
theories of Hobbes?"

We have somewhat abridged M. Fischer's argument,
for, though he writes well and intelligibly, he wants
condensation; and we do not think that his argument
has been weakened by being shortened. What he
has extended into a volume of nearly five hundred
pages, might have been reduced to a pithy essay of

one or two hundred, without sacrificing one essential fact, or injuring the strength of any one of his arguments. The art of writing in our times is the art of condensing; and those who cannot condense write only for readers who have more time at their disposal than they know what to do with.

Let us ask one question in conclusion. Why do all German writers change the thoroughly Teutonic name of Bacon into Baco? It is bad enough that we should speak of Plato; but this cannot be helped. But unless we protest against Baco, *gen.* Baconis, we shall soon be treated to Newto, Newtonis, or even to Kans, Kantis.

1857.

XII.

A GERMAN TRAVELLER IN ENGLAND.[1]

A. D. 1598.

LESSING, when he was Librarian at Wolfenbüttel, proposed to start a review which should only notice forgotten books, — books written before reviewing was invented, published in the small towns of Germany, never read, perhaps, except by the author and his friends, then buried on the shelves of a library, properly labeled and catalogued, and never opened again, except by an inquisitive inmate of these literary mausoleums. The number of those forgotten books is great, and as in former times few authors wrote more than one or two works during the whole of their lives, the information which they contain is generally of a much more substantial and solid kind than our literary palates are now accustomed to. If a man now travels to the unexplored regions of Central Africa, his book is written and out in a year. It remains on the draw-

---

[1] *Pauli Hentzneri J. C. Itinerarium Germaniæ, Galliæ, Angliæ, Italiæ:* cum Indice Locorum, Rerum, atque Verborum commemorabilium. Huic libro accessère norâ hâc editione — 1. Monita Peregrinatoria duorum doctissimorum virorum; itemque Lucerti auctoris Epi'oms Præcognitorum Historicorum, antehac non edita. Noribergæ, Typis Abrahami Wagenmanni, sumptibus sui ipsius et Johan. Güntzelii, anno MDCXXIX.

ing-room table for a season; it is pleasant to read, easy
to digest, and still easier to review and to forget. Two
or three hundred years ago this was very different.
Travelling was a far more serious business, and a man
who had spent some years in seeing foreign countries,
could do nothing better than employ the rest of his
life in writing a book of travels, either in his own language, or, still better, in Latin. After his death his
book continued to be quoted for a time in works on
history and geography, till a new traveller went over
the same ground, published an equally learned book,
and thus consigned his predecessor to oblivion. Here
is a case in point: Paul Hentzner, a German, who, of
course, calls himself Paulus Hentznerus, travelled in
Germany, France, England, and Italy; and after his
return to his native place in Silesia, he duly published
his travels in a portly volume, written in Latin.
There is a long title-page, with dedications, introductions, a preface for the *Lector benevolus*, Latin verses,
and a table showing what people ought to observe in
travelling. Travelling, according to our friend, is the
source of all wisdom; and he quotes Moses and the
Prophets in support of his theory. We ought all to
travel, he says, — " vita nostra peregrinatio est; " and
those who stay at home like snails (*cochlearum instar*)
will remain " inhumani, insolentes, superbi," etc.

It would take a long time to follow Paulus Hentznerus through all his peregrinations; but let us see
what he saw in England. He arrived here in the year
1598. He took ship with his friends at *Depa*, vulgo
Dieppe, and after a boisterous voyage, they landed at
Rye. On their arrival they were conducted to a *No-
tarius*, who asked their names, and inquired for what
object they came to England. After they had satisfied

his official inquiries, they were conducted to a *Diversorium*, and treated to a good dinner, *pro regionis more*, according to the custom of the country. From *Rye* they rode to *London*, passing *Flimwoll*, *Tumbridge*, and *Chepsted* on their way. Then follows a long description of London, its origin and history, its bridges, churches, monuments, and palaces, with extracts from earlier writers, such as Paulus Jovius, Polydorus Vergilius, etc. All inscriptions are copied faithfully, not only from tombs and pictures, but also from books which the travellers saw in the public libraries. Whitehall seems to have contained a royal library at that time, and in it Hentzner saw, besides Greek and Latin MSS., a book written in French by Queen Elizabeth, with the following dedication to Henry VIII.: —

"A Tres haut et Tres puissant et Redouble Prince Henry VIII. de ce nom, Roy d'Angleterre, de France, et d'Irlande, defenseur de la foy, Elizabeth, sa Tres humble fille, rend salut et obedience."

After the travellers had seen St. Paul's, Westminster, the House of Parliament, Whitehall, Guildhall, the Tower, and the Royal Exchange, commonly called *Bursa*, — all of which are minutely described, — they went to the theatres and to places *Ursorum et Taurorum venationibus destinata*, where bears and bulls, tied fast behind, were baited by bull-dogs. In these places, and everywhere, in fact, as our traveller says, where you meet with Englishmen, they use *herba nicotiana*, which they call by an American name *Tobaca* or *Paetum*. The description deserves to be quoted in the original: —

"Fistulæ in hunc finem ex argillâ factæ orificio posteriori dictam herbam probe exiccatam, ita ut in pulverem facile redigi possit, immittunt, et igne admoto accendunt, unde fumus ab anteriori parte ore attrahitur, qui per nares rursum, tamquam per infurnibulum exit, et phlegma ac capitis defluxiones magnâ copiâ secum educit."

After they had seen everything in London — not omitting the ship in which Francis Drake, *nobilissimus pyrata*, was said to have circumnavigated the world, — they went to Greenwich. Here they were introduced into the presence-chamber, and saw the Queen. The walls of the room were covered with precious tapestry, the floor strewed with hay. The Queen had to pass through on going to chapel. It was a Sunday, when all the nobility came to pay their respects. The Archbishop of Canterbury and the Bishop of London were present. When divine service began, the Queen appeared, preceded and followed by the court. Before her walked two barons, carrying the sceptre and the sword, and between them the Great Chancellor of England with the seal. The Queen is thus minutely described: —

"She was said (*rumor erat*) to be fifty-five years old. Her face was rather long, white, and a little wrinkled. Her eyes small, black, and gracious; her nose somewhat bent; her lips compressed, her teeth black (from eating too much sugar). She had ear-rings of pearls; red hair, but artificial, and wore a small crown. Her breast was uncovered (as is the case with all unmarried ladies in England), and round her neck was a chain with precious gems. Her hands were graceful, her fingers long. She was of middle stature, but stepped on majestically. She was gracious and kind in her address. The dress she wore was of white silk, with pearls as large as beans. Her cloak was of black silk with silver lace, and a long train was carried by a marchioness. As she walked along she spoke most kindly with many people, some of them ambassadors. She spoke English, French, and Italian; but she knows also Greek and Latin, and understands Spanish, Scotch, and Dutch. Those whom she addressed bent their knees, and some she lifted up with her hand. To a Bohemian nobleman of the name of Slawata, who had brought some letters to the Queen, she gave her right hand after taking off her glove, and he kissed it. Wherever she turned her eyes, people fell on their knees."

There was probably nobody present who ventured to scrutinize the poor Queen so impertinently as Paulus Hentznerus. He goes on to describe the ladies who followed the Queen, and how they were escorted by fifty knights. When she came to the door of the chapel, books were handed to her, and the people called out, "God save the Queen Elizabeth!" whereupon the Queen answered, "I thanke you myn good peuple." Prayers did not last more than half an hour, and the music was excellent. During the time that the Queen was in chapel, dinner was laid, and this again is described in full detail.

But we cannot afford to tarry with our German observer, nor can we follow him to Grantbridge (Cambridge) or Oxenford, where he describes the colleges and halls (each of them having a library), and the life of the students. From Oxford he went to Woodstock, then back to Oxford, and from thence to Henley and Madenhood to Windsor. Eton also was visited, and here, he says, sixty boys were educated gratuitously, and afterwards sent to Cambridge. After visiting Hampton Court and the royal palace of Nonesuch, our travellers returned to London.

We shall finish our extracts with some remarks of Hentzner on the manners and customs of the English: —

"The English are grave, like the Germans, magnificent at home and abroad. They carry with them a large train of followers and servants. These have silver shields on their left arm, and a pig-tail. The English excel in dancing and music. They are swift and lively, though stouter than the French. They shave the middle portion of the face, but leave the hair untouched on each side. They are good sailors and famous pirates; clever, perfidious, and thievish. About three hundred are hanged in London every year. At table they are more civil than the French. They eat less bread, but more meat, and they dress it well. They throw much sugar into their wine. They suffer frequently from leprosy, commonly called the white leprosy, which is said to have come to England in the time of the Normans. They are brave in battle, and always conquer their enemies. At home they brook no manner of servitude. They are very fond of noises that fill the ears, such as explosions of guns, trumpets, and bells. In London, persons who have got drunk are wont to mount a church tower, for the sake of exercise, and to ring the bells for several hours. If they see a foreigner who is handsome and strong, they are sorry that he is not an Anglicus, — *vulgo* Englishman."

On his return to France, Hentzner paid a visit to Canterbury, and, after seeing some ghosts on his journey, arrived safely at Dover. Before he was allowed to go on board, he had again to undergo an examination, to give his name, to explain what he had done in England, and where he was going; and, lastly, his luggage was searched most carefully, in order to see whether he carried with him any English money, for nobody was allowed to carry away more than ten pounds of English money: all the rest was taken away and handed to the royal treasury. And thus farewell, Carissime Hentzneri! and slumber on your shelf until the eye of some other benevolent reader, glancing at the rows of forgotten books, is caught by the quaint lettering on your back, "*Hentzneri Itin.*"

1857.

XIII.

CORNISH ANTIQUITIES.[1]

It is impossible to spend even a few weeks in Cornwall without being impressed with the air of antiquity which pervades that county, and seems, like a morning mist, half to conceal and half to light up every one of its hills and valleys. It is impossible to look at any pile of stones, at any wall, or pillar, or gate-post, without asking one's self the question, Is this old, or is this new? Is it the work of Saxon, or of Roman, or of Celt? Nay, one feels sometimes tempted to ask, Is this the work of Nature or of man?

> "Among these rocks and stones, methinks I see
> More than the heedless impress that belongs
> To lonely Nature's casual work : they bear
> A semblance strange of power intelligent,
> And of design not wholly worn away." — *Excursion.*

The late King of Prussia's remark about Oxford, that in it everything old seemed new, and everything new seemed old, applies with even greater truth to Cornwall. There is a continuity between the present and the past of that curious peninsula, such as we seldom find in any other place. A spring bubbling up in a natural granite basin, now a meeting-place for Bap-

---

[1] *Antiquities, Historical and Monumental, of the County of Cornwall.* By William Borlase, LL. D. London, 1769.
A Week at the Land's End. By J. T. Blight. London, 1861.

tists or Methodists, was but a few centuries ago a holy well, attended by busy friars, and visited by pilgrims, who came there "nearly lame," and left the shrine "almost able to walk." Still further back the same spring was a centre of attraction for the Celtic inhabitants, and the rocks piled up around it stand there as witnesses of a civilization and architecture certainly more primitive than the civilization and architecture of Roman, Saxon, or Norman settlers. We need not look beyond. How long that granite buttress of England has stood there, defying the fury of the Atlantic, the geologist alone, who is not awed by ages, would dare to tell us. But the historian is satisfied with antiquities of a more humble and homely character; and in bespeaking the interest, and, it may be, the active support of our readers, in favor of the few relics of the most ancient civilization of Britain, we promise to keep within strictly historical limits, if by historical we understand, with the late Sir G. C. Lewis, that only which can be authenticated by contemporaneous monuments.

But even thus, how wide a gulf seems to separate us from the first civilizers of the West of England, from the people who gave names to every headland, bay, and hill of Cornwall, and who first planned those lanes that now, like throbbing veins, run in every direction across that heath-covered peninsula! No doubt it is well known that the original inhabitants of Cornwall were Celts, and that Cornish is a Celtic language; and that, if we divide the Celtic languages into two classes, Welsh with Cornish and Breton forms one class, the *Cymric;* while the Irish with its varieties, as developed in Scotland and the Isle of Man, forms another class, which is called the *Gaelic* or *Gadhelic.*

It may also be more or less generally known that Celtic, with all its dialects, is an Aryan or Indo-European language, closely allied to Latin, Greek, German, Slavonic, and Sanskrit, and that the Celts, therefore, were not mere barbarians, or people to be classed together with Finns and Lapps, but heralds of true civilization wherever they settled in their world-wide migrations, the equals of Saxons and Romans and Greeks, whether in physical beauty or in intellectual vigor. And yet there is a strange want of historical reality in the current conceptions about the Celtic inhabitants of the British Isles; and while the heroes and statesmen and poets of Greece and Rome, though belonging to a much earlier age, stand out in bold and sharp relief on the table of a boy's memory, his notions of the ancient Britons may generally be summed up "in houses made of wicker-work, Druids with long white beards, white linen robes, and golden sickles, and warriors painted blue." Nay, strange to say, we can hardly blame a boy for banishing the ancient bards and Druids from the scene of real history, and assigning to them that dark and shadowy corner where the gods and heroes of Greece live peacefully together with the ghosts and fairies from the dreamland of our own Saxon forefathers. For even the little that is told in "Little Arthur's History of England" about the ancient Britons and the Druids is extremely doubtful. Druids are never mentioned before Cæsar. Few writers, if any, before him were able to distinguish between Celts and Germans, but spoke of the barbarians of Gaul and Germany as the Greeks spoke of Scythians, or as we ourselves speak of the negroes of Africa, without distinguishing between races so different from each other as Hottentots and Kaffirs. Cæsar was one of the first writers who knew of an ethnological distinction between Celtic and Teutonic barbarians, and we may therefore trust him when he says that the Celts had Druids, and the Germans had none. But his further statements about these Celtic priests and sages are hardly more trustworthy than the account which an ordinary Indian officer at the present day might give us of the Buddhist priests and the Buddhist religion of Ceylon. Cæsar's statement that the Druids worshipped Mercury, Apollo, Mars, Jupiter, and Minerva, is of the same base metal as the statements of more modern writers that the Buddhists worship the Trinity, and that they take Buddha for the Son of God. Cæsar most likely never conversed with a Druid, nor was he able to control, if he was able to understand, the statements made to him about the ancient priesthood, the religion and literature of Gaul. Besides, Cæsar himself tells us very little about the priests of Gaul and Britain; and the thrilling accounts of the white robes and the golden sickles belong to Pliny's "Natural History," by no means a safe authority in such matters.[1]

We must be satisfied, indeed, to know very little

[1] Plin. *H. N.* xvi. c. 44. "Non est omittenda in ea re et Galliarum admiratio. Nihil habent Druidæ (ita suos appellant magos) visco et arbore in qua gignatur (si modo sit robur) sacratius. Jam per se roborum eligunt lucos, nec ulla sacra sine ea fronde conficiunt, ut inde appellati quoque interpretatione Græca possint Druidæ videri. Enimvero quidquid adnascatur illis, e cœlo missum potant signumque esse electæ ab ipso deo arboris. Est autem id rarum admodum inventu et repertum magna religione petitur, et ante omnia sexta luna, quæ principia mensium annorumque his facit, et sæculi post tricesimum annum, quia jam virium abunde habeat, nec sit sui dimidia. Omnia sanantem appellantes suo vocabulo, sacrificiis epulisque rite sub arbore præparatis, duos admovent candidi coloris tauros, quorum cornua tunc primum vinciantur. Sacerdos candida veste cultus arborem scandit, falce aurea demetit; candido id excipitur sago. Tum deinde victimas immolant, precantes ut suum donum deus prosperum faciat his quibus dederit."

about the mode of life, the forms of worship, the religious doctrines, or the mysterious wisdom of the Druids and their flocks. But for this very reason it is most essential that our minds should be impressed strongly with the historical reality that belongs to the Celtic inhabitants, and to the work which they performed in rendering these islands for the first time fit for the habitation of man. That historical lesson, and a very important lesson it is, is certainly learned more quickly, and yet more effectually, by a visit to Cornwall or Wales, than by any amount of reading. We may doubt many things that Celtic enthusiasts tells us; but where every village and field, every cottage and hill, bear names that are neither English, nor Norman, nor Latin, it is difficult not to feel that the Celtic element has been something real and permanent in the history of the British Isles. The Cornish language is no doubt extinct, if by extinct we mean that it is no longer spoken by the people. But in the names of towns, castles, rivers, mountains, fields, manors, and families, and in a few of the technical terms of mining, husbandry, and fishing, Cornish lives on, and probably will live on, for many ages to come. There is a well-known verse: —

"By Tre, Ros, Pol, Lan, Caer, and Pen,
You may know most Cornish men." [1]

But it will hardly be believed that a Cornish antiquarian, Dr. Bannister, who is collecting materials for a glossary of Cornish proper names, has amassed no less than 2,400 names with Tre, 500 with Pen, 400 with Ros, 300 with Lan, 200 with Pol, and 200 with Caer.

[1] *Tre*, homestead; *ros*, moor, pastland, a common; *pol*, a pool; *lan*, an enclosure, church; *caer*, town; *pen*, head.

A language does not die all at once, nor is it always possible to fix the exact date when it breathed its last. Thus, in the case of Cornish, it is by no means easy to reconcile the conflicting statements of various writers as to the exact time when it ceased to be the language of the people, unless we bear in mind that what was true with regard to the higher classes was not so with regard to the lower, and likewise that in some parts of Cornwall the vitality of the language might continue, while in others its heart had ceased to beat. As late as the time of Henry VIII., the famous physician Andrew Borde tells us that English was not understood by many men and women in Cornwall. "In Cornwal is two speeches," he writes; "the one is naughty Englyshe, and the other the Cornyshe speche. And there be many men and women the which cannot speake one worde of Englyshe, but all Cornyshe." During the same King's reign, when an attempt was made to introduce a new church service composed in English, a protest was signed by the Devonshire and Cornish men utterly refusing this new English:—

"We will not receive the new Service, because it is but like a Christmas game; but we will have our old Service of Matins, Mass, Evensong, and Procession, in Latin as it was before. And so we the Cornish men (whereof certain of us understand no English) utterly refuse this new English."[1]

Yet in the reign of Elizabeth, when the liturgy was appointed by authority to take the place of the mass, the Cornish, it is said,[2] desired that it should be in the English language. About the same time we are told

[1] Cranmer's Works, ed. Jenkyns, vol. II. p. 230.
[2] Observations on an ancient Manuscript, entitled *Passio Christi*, by —— Scawen, Esq., 1777, p. 26.

that Dr. John Moreman[1] taught his parishioners the Lord's Prayer, the Creed, and the Ten Commandments, in the English tongue. From the time of the Reformation onward, Cornish seems constantly to have lost ground against English, particularly in places near Devonshire. Thus Norden, whose description of Cornwall was probably written about 1584, though not published till 1728, gives a very full and interesting account of the struggle between the two languages:—

"Of late," he says (p. 26), "the Cornishe men have muche conformed themselves to the use of the Englishe tounge, and their Englishe is equall to the beste, espetially in the easterne partes; even from Truro eastwarde it is in manner wholly Englishe. In the weste parte of the countrye, as in the hundreds of Penwith and Kerrier, the Cornishe tounge is moste in use amongste the inhabitantes, and yet (whiche is to be marveyled), though the husband and wife, parentes and children, master and servantes, doe mutually communicate in their native language, yet ther is none of them in manner but is able to convers with a straonger in the Englishe tounge, unless it be some obscure people, that seldome conferr with the better sorte: But it seemeth that in few yeares the Cornishe language willbe by litle and litle abandoned."

Carew, who wrote about the same time, goes so far as to say that most of the inhabitants "can no word of Cornish, but very few are ignorant of the English, though they sometimes affect to be." This may have been true with regard to the upper classes, particularly in the west of Cornwall, but it is nevertheless a fact that, as late as 1640, Mr. William Jackman, the vicar of Feock,[2] was forced to administer the sacrament in Cornish, because the aged people did not understand English; nay, the rector of Landewednak

---

[1] Borlase's *Natural History of Cornwall*, p. 315.
[2] Ibid.

preached his sermons in Cornish as late as 1678. Mr. Scawen, too, who wrote about that time, speaks of some old folks who spoke Cornish only, and would not understand a word of English; but he tells us at the same time that Sir Francis North, the Lord Chief Justice, afterwards Lord Keeper, when holding the assizes at Lanceston in 1678, expressed his concern at the loss and decay of the Cornish language. The poor people, in fact, could speak, or at least understand, Cornish, but he says, " They were laughed at by the rich, who understood it not, which is their own fault in not endeavoring after it." About the beginning of the last century, Mr. Ed. Lhuyd (died 1709), the keeper of the Ashmolean Museum, was still able to collect from the mouths of the people a grammar of the Cornish language, which was published in 1707. He says that at this time Cornish was only retained in five or six villages towards the Land's End; and in his " Archæologia Britannica " he adds, that although it was spoken in most of the western districts from the Land's End to the Lizard, " a great many of the inhabitants, especially the gentry, do not understand it, there being no necessity thereof in regard there's no Cornish man but speaks good English." It is generally supposed that the last person who spoke Cornish was Dolly Pentreath, who died in 1778, and to whose memory Prince Louis Lucien Bonaparte has lately erected a monument in the churchyard at Paul. The inscription is : —

" Here lieth interred Dorothy Pentreath, who died in 1778, said to have been the last person who conversed in the ancient Cornish, the peculiar language of this country from the earliest records till it expired in this parish of St. Paul. This stone is erected by the Prince Louis Lucien Bonaparte, in union with the Rev. John Garret, vicar of St. Paul, June, 1860."

It seems hardly right to deprive the old lady of her fair name; but there are many people in Cornwall who maintain that when travellers and grandees came to see her, she would talk anything that came into her head, while those who listened to her were pleased to think that they had heard the dying echoes of a primeval tongue.[1] There is a letter extant, written in Cornish by a poor fisherman of the name of William Bodener. It is dated July 3, 1776, that is, two years before the death of Dolly Pentreath; and the writer says of himself in Cornish:—

"My age is threescore and five. I am a poor fisherman. I learnt Cornish when I was a boy. I have been to sea with my father and five other men in the boat, and have not heard one word of English spoke in the boat for a week together. I never saw a Cornish book. I learned Cornish going to sea with old men. There is not more than four or five in our town can talk Cornish now,—old people fourscore years old. Cornish is all forgot with young people."[2]

It would seem, therefore, that Cornish died with the

[1] Her age was certainly mythical, and her case forms a strong confirmation of the late Sir G. C. Lewis's skepticism on that point. Dolly Pentreath is generally believed to have died at the age of one hundred and two. Dr. Borlase, who knew her, and has left a good description of her, stated that, about 1774, she was in her eighty-seventh year. This, if she died in 1778, would only bring her age to ninety one. But Mr. Haliwell, who examined the register at Paul, found that Dolly Pentreath was baptized in 1714; so that, unless she was baptized late in life, this supposed centenarian had only reached her sixty-fourth year at the time of her death, and was no more than sixty when Dr. Borlase supposed her to be eighty-seven. Another instance of extraordinary old age is mentioned by Mr. Scawen (p. 25), about a hundred years earlier. "Let not the old woman be forgotten," he says, "who died about two years since, who was one hundred and sixty-four years old, of good memory, and healthful at that age, living in the parish of Gulthian, by the charity mostly of such as came purposely to see her, speaking to them (in default of English) by an interpreter, yet partly understanding it. She married a second husband after she was eighty, and buried him after he was eighty years of age."

[2] *Specimens of Cornish Provincial Dialects*, by Uncle Jan Tremoodle. London, 1846: p. 52.

last century, and no one now living can boast to have
heard its sound when actually spoken for the sake of
conversation. It seems to have been a melodious and
yet by no means an effeminate language, and Scawen
places it in this respect above most of the other Celtic
dialects : —

"Cornish," he says, "Is not to be gutturally pronounced, as
the Welsh for the most part is, nor mutteringly, as the Armor-
ick, nor whiningly as the Irish (which two latter qualities seem
to have been contracted from their servitude), but must be
lively and manly spoken, like other primitive tongues."

Although Cornish must now be classed with the
extinct languages, it has certainly shown a marvelous
vitality. More than four hundred years of Roman occupation, more than six hundred years of Saxon and
Danish sway, a Norman conquest, a Saxon Reformation, and civil wars, have all passed over the land;
but, like a tree that may bend before a storm but is not
to be rooted up, the language of the Celts of Cornwall
has lived on in an unbroken continuity for at least two
thousand years. What does this mean? It means
that through the whole of English history to the acces-
sion of the House of Hanover, the inhabitants of Cornwall and the western portion of Devonshire, in spite
of intermarriages with Romans, Saxons, and Normans,
were Celts, and remained Celts. People speak indeed of blood, and intermingling of blood, as determin-
ing the nationality of a people ; but what is meant by
blood? It is one of those scientific idols, that crumble
to dust as soon as we try to define or grasp them ; it is
a vague, hollow, treacherous term, which, for the present at least, ought to be banished from the dictionary
of every true man of science. We can give a scientific definition of a Celtic language; but no one has

yet given a definition of Celtic blood, or a Celtic skull.
It is quite possible that hereafter chemical differences
may be discovered in the blood of those who speak a
Celtic, and of those who speak a Teutonic language.
It is possible, also, that patient measurements, like
those lately published by Professor Huxley, in the
"Journal of Anatomy and Physiology," may lead in
time to a really scientific classification of skulls, and
that physiologists may succeed in the end in carrying
out a classification of the human race, according to
tangible and unvarying physiological criteria. But
their definitions and their classifications will hardly
ever square with the definitions or classifications of the
student of language, and the use of common terms can
only be a source of constant misunderstandings. We
know what we mean by a Celtic language, and in the
grammar of each language we are able to produce a
most perfect scientific definition of its real character.
If, therefore, we transfer the term Celtic to people, we
can, if we use our words accurately, mean nothing but
people who speak a Celtic language, the true exponent,
aye, the very life of Celtic nationality. Whatever people, whether Romans, or Saxons, or Normans, or, as
some think, even Phœnicians and Jews, settled in
Cornwall, if they ceased to speak their own language
and exchanged it for Cornish, they are, before the tribunal of the science of language, Celts, and nothing
but Celts; while, whenever Cornishmen, like Sir
Humphrey Davy or Bishop Colenso, have ceased to
speak Cornish, and speak nothing but English, they are
no longer Celts, but true Teutons or Saxons, in the
only scientifically legitimate sense of that word.
Strange stories, indeed, would be revealed, if blood
ould cry out and tell of its repeated mixtures since

the beginning of the world. If we think of the early
migrations of mankind; of the battles fought before
there were hieroglyphics to record them; of conquests,
leadings into captivity, piracy, slavery, and coloniza-
tion, all without a sacred poet to hand them down to
posterity, — we shall hesitate, indeed, to speak of
pure races, or unmixed blood, even at the very dawn
of real history. Little as we know of the early history of Greece, we know enough to warn us against
looking upon the Greeks of Asia or Europe as an
unmixed race. Ægyptus, with his Arabian, Ethio-
pian, and Tyrian wives; Cadmus, the son of Libya;
Phœnix, the father of Europa, — all point to an intercourse of Greece with foreign countries, whatever
else their mythological meaning may be. As soon
as we know anything of the history of the world,
we know of wars and alliances between Greeks and
Lydians and Persians, of Phœnician settlements all
over the world, of Carthaginians trading in Spain and
encamped in Italy, of Romans conquering and coloniz-
ing Gaul, Spain, Britain, the Danubian Principalities
and Greece, Western Asia and Northern Africa.
Then again, at a later time, follow the great ethnic
convulsions of Eastern Europe, and the devastation
and re-population of the ancient seats of civilization by
Goths, and Lombards, and Vandals, and Saxons;
while at the same time, and for many centuries to
come, the few strongholds of civilization in the East
were again and again overwhelmed by the irresistible
waves of Hunnish, Mongolic, and Tartaric invaders.
And, with all this, people at the latter end of the
nineteenth century venture to speak, for instance,
of pure Norman blood as something definite or defina-
ble, forgetting how the ancient Norsemen carried their

wives away from the coasts of Germany or Russia, from Sicily or from the very Piræus; while others married whatever wives they could find in the North of France, whether of Gallic, Roman, or German extraction, and then settled in England, where they again contracted marriages with Teutonic, Celtic, or Roman damsels. In our own days, if we see the daughter of an English officer and an Indian Ranee married to the son of a Russian nobleman, how are we to class the offspring of that marriage? The Indian Ranee may have had Mongol blood, so may the Russian nobleman; but there are other possible ingredients of pure Hindu and pure Slavonic, of Norman, German, and Roman blood, — and who is the chemist bold enough to disengage them all? There is, perhaps, no nation which has been exposed to more frequent admixture of foreign blood, during the Middle Ages, than the Greeks. Professor Fallmerayer maintained that the Hellenic population was entirely exterminated, and that the people who at the present day call themselves Greeks are really Slavonians. It would be difficult to refute him by arguments drawn either from the physical or the moral characteristics of the modern Greeks as compared with the many varieties of the Slavonic stock. But the following extract from "Felton's Lectures on Greece, Ancient and Modern," contains the only answer that can be given to such charges, without point or purpose: "In one of the courses of lectures," he says, "which I attended in the University of Athens, the Professor of History, a very eloquent man as well as a somewhat fiery Greek, took this subject up. His audience consisted of about two hundred young men from every part of Greece. His indignant comments on the learned

German, that notorious Μισέλλην or Greek-hater, as
he stigmatized him, were received by his hearers with
a profound sensation. They sat with expanded
nostrils and flashing eyes — a splendid illustration of
the old Hellenic spirit, roused to fury by the charge of
barbarian descent. 'It is true,' said the eloquent
professor, 'that the tide of barbaric invaders poured
down like a deluge upon Hellas, filling with its surg-
ing floods our beautiful plains, our fertile valleys.
The Greeks fled to their walled towns and mountain
fastnesses. By and by the water subsided and the soil
of Hellas reappeared. The former inhabitants descended from the mountains as the tide receded,
resumed their ancient lands and rebuilt their ruined
habitations, and, the reign of the barbarians over,
Hellas was herself again.' Three or four rounds of
applause followed the close of the lectures of Professor
Manouses, in which I heartily joined. I could not
help thinking afterwards what a singular comment on
the German anti-Hellenic theory was presented by this
scene, — a Greek professor in a Greek university,
lecturing to two hundred Greeks in the Greek language, to prove that the Greeks were Greeks, and not
Slavonians."[1]

And yet we hear the same arguments used over
and over again, not only with regard to the Greeks,
but with regard to many other modern nations; and
even men whose minds have been trained in the
school of exact science, use the term "bloods," in this
vague and thoughtless manner. The adjective Greek
may connote many things, but what it denotes is
language. People who speak Greek as their mother

[1] *Greece, Ancient and Modern*, by C. C. Felton. Boston, 1867, vol. II. p. 314.

tongue are Greeks, and if a Turkish-speaking inhabitant of Constantinople could trace his pedigree straight to Pericles, he would still be a Turk, whatever his name, his faith, his hair, features, and stature — whatever his blood might be. We can classify languages, and as languages presuppose people that speak them, we can so far classify mankind, according to their grammars and dictionaries; while all who possess scientific honesty must confess and will confess that, as yet, it has been impossible to devise any truly scientific classification of skulls, to say nothing of blood, or bones, or hair. The label on one of the skulls in the Munich Collection, "Etruscan-Tyrol, or Inca-Peruvian," characterizes not too unfairly the present state of ethnological craniology. Let those who imagine that the great outlines, at least, of a classification of skulls have been firmly established, consult Mr. Brace's useful manual of "The Races of the World," where he has collected the opinions of some of the best judges on the subject. We quote a few passages:[1] —

"Dr. Bachmann concludes, from the measurements of Dr. Tiedemann and Dr. Morton, that the negro skull, though less than the European, is within one inch as large as the Persian and the Armenian, and three square inches larger than the Hindu and Egyptian. The scale is thus given by Dr. Morton: European skull, 87 cubic inches; Malay, 85; Negro 83; Mongol, 82; Ancient Egyptian, 80; American, 79. The ancient Peruvians and Mexicans, who constructed so elaborate a civilization, show a capacity only of from 75 to 79 inches. .... Other observations by Huschke make the average capacity of the skull of Europeans 40.88 oz.; of Americans, 39.13; of Mongols, 38.39; of Negroes, 37.57; of Malays, 36.41."

"Of the shape of the skull, as distinctive of different origin,

[1] *The Races of the Old World: A manual of Ethnology.* By Charles L. Brace. London, 1863, p. 362 seq.

"M. J. Weber has said there is no proper mark of a
race from the cranium so firmly attached that it may
found in some other race. Tiedemann has met with
... whose skulls bore all the characters of the negro race;
... inhabitant of Nukahiwa, according to Silesius and Blu-
...h, agreed exactly in his proportions with the Apollo
Belvedere."

Professor Huxley, in his "Observations on the
Human Skulls of Engis and Neanderthal," printed in
Sir Charles Lyell's "Antiquity of Man," p. 81, remarks that " the most capacious European skull yet
measured had a capacity of 114 cubic inches, the
smallest (as estimated by weight of brain) about 55
cubic inches; while, according to Professor Schaaff-
hausen, some Hindu skulls have as small a capacity
as 46 cubic inches (27 oz. of water);" and he sums
up by stating that "cranial measurements alone afford
no safe indication of race."

And even if a scientific classification of skulls were
to be carried out, if, instead of merely being able to
guess that this may be an Australian and this a Malay
skull, we were able positively to place each individual
skull under its own definite category, what should we
gain in the classification of mankind? Where is the
bridge from skull to man in the full sense of that
word? Where is the connecting link between the
cranial proportions and only one other of man's characteristic properties, such as language? And what
applies to skulls applies to color and all the rest.
Even a black skin and curly hair are mere outward
accidents as compared with language. We do not
classify parrots and magpies by the color of their
plumage, still less by the cages in which they live;
and what is the black skin or the white skin but the
mere outward covering, not to say the mere cage, in

which that being which we call man lives, moves, and has his being? A man like Bishop Crowther, though a negro in blood, is, in thought and speech, an Aryan. He speaks English, he thinks English, he acts English; and, unless we take English in a purely historical, and not in its truly scientific, i. e. linguistic sense, he is English. No doubt there are many influences at work — old proverbs, old songs and traditions, religious convictions, social institutions, political prejudices, besides the soil, the food, and the air of a country — that may keep up, even among people who have lost their national language, that kind of vague similarity which is spoken of as national character.[1] This is a subject on which many volumes have been written, and yet the result has only been to supply newspapers with materials for international insults or international courtesies, as the case may be. Nothing sound or definite has been gained by such speculations, and in an age that prides itself on the careful observance of the rules of inductive reasoning, nothing is more surprising than the sweeping assertions with regard to national character, and the reckless way in which casual observations that may be true of one, two, three, or it may be ten or even a hundred individuals, are extended to millions. However, if there is one safe exponent of national character, it is language. Take away the language of a people, and you destroy at once that powerful chain

[1] Cornish proverbs have lived on after the extinction of Cornish, and even as translated into English they naturally continue to exercise their own peculiar spell on the minds of men and children. Such proverbs are: —
"It is better to keep than to beg."
"Do good; for thyself thou dost it."
"Speak little, speak well, and well will be spoken again."
"There is no down without eye, no hedge without ears."

of tradition in thought and sentiment which holds all the generations of the same race together, if we may use an unpleasant simile, like the chain of a gang of galley-slaves. These slaves, we are told, very soon fall into the same pace, without being aware that their movements depend altogether on the movements of those who walk before them. It is nearly the same with us. We imagine we are altogether free in our thoughts, original and independent, and we are not aware that our thoughts are manacled and fettered by language, and that, without knowing and without perceiving it, we have to keep pace with those who walked before us thousands and thousands of years ago. Language alone binds people together, and keeps them distinct from others who speak different tongues. In ancient times particularly, "languages and nations" meant the same thing; and even with us our real ancestors are those whose language we speak, the fathers of our thoughts, the mothers of our hopes and fears. Blood, bones, hair, and color, are mere accidents, utterly unfit to serve as principles of scientific classification for that great family of living beings, the essential characteristics of which are thought and speech, not fibrine, serum, coloring matter, or whatever else enters into the composition of blood.

If this be true, the inhabitants of Cornwall, whatever the number of Roman, Saxon, Danish, or Norman settlers within the boundaries of that county may have been, continued to be Celts as long as they spoke Cornish. They ceased to be Celts when they ceased to speak the language of their forefathers. Those who can appreciate the charms of genuine antiquity will not, therefore, find fault with the enthusiasm of Daines

Barrington or Sir Joseph Banks in listening to the strange utterances of Dolly Pentreath; for her language, if genuine, carried them back and brought them, as it were, into immediate contact with people who, long before the Christian era, acted an important part on the stage of history, supplying the world with two of the most precious metals, more precious then than gold or silver, with copper and tin, the very materials, it may be, of the finest works of art in Greece, aye, of the armor wrought for the heroes of the Trojan War, as described so minutely by the poets of the "Iliad." There is a continuity in language which nothing equals, and there is an historical genuineness in ancient words, if but rightly interpreted, which cannot be rivaled by manuscripts, or coins, or monumental inscriptions.

But though it is right to be enthusiastic about what is really ancient in Cornwall, — and there is nothing so ancient as language, — it is equally right to be discriminating. The fresh breezes of antiquity have intoxicated many an antiquarian. Words, purely Latin or English, though somewhat changed after being admitted into the Cornish dictionary, have been quoted as the originals from which the Roman or English were in turn derived. The Latin *liber*, book, was supposed to be derived from the Welsh *llyvyr*; *litera*, letter, from Welsh *llythyr*; *persona*, person, from Welsh *person*, and many more of the same kind. Walls built within the memory of men have been admitted as relics of British architecture; nay, Latin inscriptions of the simplest character have but lately been interpreted by means of Cornish, as containing strains of a mysterious wisdom. Here, too, a study of the language gives some useful hints as to the proper method of disentangling the truly ancient from the more modern elements. Whatever in the Cornish dictionary cannot be traced back to any other source, whether Latin, Saxon, Norman, or German, may safely be considered as Cornish, and therefore as ancient Celtic. Whatever in the antiquities of Cornwall cannot be claimed by Romans, Saxons, Danes, or Normans, may fairly be considered as genuine remains of the earliest civilization of this island, as the work of the Celtic discoverers of Britain.

The Cornish language is by no means a pure or unmixed language, — at least we do not know it in its pure state. It is, in fact, a mere accident that any literary remains have been preserved, and three or four small volumes would contain all that is left to us of Cornish literature. "There is a poem," to quote Mr. Norris, "which we may by courtesy call epic, entitled 'Mount Calvary.'" It contains 259 stanzas of eight lines each, in heptasyllabic metre, with alternate rhyme. It is ascribed to the fifteenth century, and was published for the first time by Mr. Davies Gilbert in 1826.[1] There is, besides, a series of dramas, or mystery-plays, first published by Mr. Norris for the University Press of Oxford, in 1858. The first is called "The Beginning of the World," the second "The Passion of our Lord," the third "The Resurrection." The last is interrupted by another play, "The Death of Pilate." The oldest MS. in the Bodleian Library belongs to the fifteenth century, and Mr. Norris is not inclined to refer the composition of these plays to a much earlier date. Another MS., likewise in the Bodleian Library, contains both the text and a

[1] A critical edition, with some excellent notes, was published by Mr. Whitley Stokes under the title of *The Passion*. MSS. of it exist at the British Museum and at the Bodleian. One of the Bodleian MSS. (Gough, Cornwall, 3) contains an English translation by Keigwyn, made in 1682.

translation by Keigwyn (1695). Lastly, there is another sacred drama, called "The Creation of the World, with Noah's Flood." It is in many places copied from the dramas, and, according to the MS., it was written by William Jordan in 1611. The oldest MS. belongs again to the Bodleian Library, which likewise possesses a MS. of the translation by Keigwyn in 1691.[1]

These mystery-plays, as we may learn from a passage in Carew's "Survey of Cornwall" (p. 71), were still performed in Cornish in his time, i. e. at the beginning of the seventeenth century. He says: —

"Pastimes to delight the minde, the Cornish men have Guary miracles and three mens songs; and, for the exercise of the body, hunting, hawking, shooting, wrastling, hurling, and such other games.

"The Guary miracle — in English, a miracle-play — is a kind of enterlude, compiled in Cornish out of some Scripture history, with that grossenes which accompanied the Romanes vetus Comedia. For representing it, they raise an earthen amphitheatre in some open field, having the diameter of his enclosed playne some forty or fifty foot. The country people flock from all sides, many miles off, to heare and see it, for they have therein devils and devices, to delight as well the eye as the eare; the players conne not their parts without booke, but are prompted by one called the Ordinary, who followeth at their back with the booke in his hand, and telleth them softly what they must pronounce aloud. Which manner once gave occasion to a pleasant conceyted gentleman, of practising a mery pranke; for he undertaking (perhaps of set purpose) an actor's roome, was accordingly lessoned (beforehand) by the Ordinary, that he

[1] In the MS. in the British Museum, the translation is said by Mr. Norris to be dated 1693 (vol. II. p. 440). It was published in 1827 by Davies Gilbert; and a critical edition was prepared by Mr. Whitley Stokes, and published with an English translation in 1863. Mr. Stokes leaves it doubtful whether William Jordan was the author, or merely the copyist, and thinks the text may belong to an earlier date, though it is decidedly more modern than the other specimens of Cornish which we possess in the dramas, and in the poem of *The Passion*.

must say after him. His turn came. Quoth the Ordinary, Goe forth man and shew thy selfe. The gentleman steps out upon the stage, and like a bad Clarke in Scripture matters, cleaving more to the letter than the sense, pronounced those words aloud. Oh! (sayes the fellowe softly in his eare) you marre all the play. And with this his passion the actor makes the audience in like sort acquainted. Hereon the prompter falls to flat rayling and cursing in the bitterest termes he could devise; which the gentleman, with a set gesture and countenance, still soberly related, untill the Ordinary, driven at last into a madde rage, was faine to give all over. Which trousse, though it brake off the enterlude, yet defrauded not the beholders, but dismissed them with a great deale more sport and laughter than such Guaries could have afforded."[1]

Scawen, at the end of the seventeenth century, speaks of these miracle-plays, and considers the suppression of the *Guirrimears*,[2] or Great Plays or Speeches,[3] as one of the chief causes of the decay of the Cornish language.

"These *Guirrimears*," he says, "which were used at the great conventions of the people, at which they had famous interludes celebrated with great preparations, and not without shows of devotion in them, solemnized in great and spacious downs of great capacity, encompassed about with earthen banks, and some in part stone-work, of largeness to contain thousands, the shapes of which remain in many places at this day, though the use of them long since gone. . . . This was a great means to keep in use the tongue with delight and admiration. They had recita-

[1] *Guare*, in Cornish, means a play, a game; the Welsh *gware*.
[2] According to Lhuyd, *gwirimir* would be a corruption of *gwarimirkle*, i. e. a miracle-play. Norris, vol ii. p. 455.
[3] In some lines written in 1693, on the origin of the Oxford *Terræ filius*, we read:—

"These undergraduates' oracles
Deduced from Cornwall's *guary* miracles,—
From immemorial custom there
They raise a turfy theatre!
When from a passage underground,
By frequent crowds encompassed round,
Out leaps some little Mephistopheles,
Who e'en of all the mob the offal is," etc.

tions in them, poetical and divine, one of which I may suppose this small relique of antiquity to be, in which the passion of our Saviour, and his resurrection, is described."

If to these mystery-plays and poems we add some versions of the Lord's Prayer, the Commandments, and the Creed, a protestation of the bishops in Britain to Augustine the monk, the Pope's legate, in the year 600 after Christ (MS. Gough, 4), the first chapter of Genesis, and some songs, proverbs, riddles, a tale and a glossary, we have an almost complete catalogue of what a Cornish library would be at the present day.

Now if we examine the language as preserved to us in these fragments, we find that it is full of Norman, Saxon, and Latin words. No one can doubt, for instance, that the following Cornish words are all taken from Latin, that is, from the Latin of the Church:—

Abat, an abbot; Lat. *abbas*.
Alter, altar; Lat. *altare*.
Apostol, apostle; Lat. *apostolus*.
Clauster, cloister; Lat. *claustrum*.
Colom, dove; Lat. *columba*.
Gwespar, vespers; Lat. *vesper*.
Cantuil, candle; Lat. *candela*.
Cantuilbren, candlestick; Lat. *candelabrum*.
Ail, angel; Lat. *angelus*.
Archail, archangel; Lat. *archangelus*.

Other words, though not immediately connected with the service and the doctrine of the Church, may nevertheless have passed from Latin into Cornish, either directly from the daily conversation of monks, priests, and schoolmasters, or indirectly from English or Norman, in both of which the same Latin words had naturally been adopted, though slightly modified according to the phonetic peculiarities of each. Thus:—

Ancar, anchor; the Latin, *ancora*. This might have come indirectly through English or Norman-French.

Aradar, plough; the Latin, *aratrum*. This must have come direct from Latin, as it does not exist in Norman or English.

Arghans, silver; *argentum*.

Keghin, kitchen; *coquina*. This is taken from the same Latin word from which the Romance languages formed *cuisine*, *cucina*; not from the classical Latin, *culina*.

Liver, book; *liber*, originally the bark of trees on which books were written.

Dinair, coin; *denarius*. *Seth*, arrow; *sagitta*. *Caus*, cheese; *caseus*. *Caul*, cabbage; *caulis*.

These words are certainly foreign words in Cornish and the other Celtic languages in which they occur, and to attempt to supply for some of them a purely Celtic etymology shows a complete want of appreciation both of the history of words and of the phonetic laws that govern each family of the Indo-European languages. Sometimes, no doubt, the Latin words have been considerably changed and modified, according to the phonetic peculiarities of the dialects into which they were received. Thus, *gwespar* for *vesper*, *seth* for *sagitta*, *caus* for *caseus*, hardly look like Latin words. Yet no real Celtic scholar would claim them as Celtic; and the Rev. Robert Williams, the author of the "Lexicon Cornu-Britannicum," in speaking of a list of words borrowed from Latin by the Welsh during the stay of the Romans in Britain, is no doubt right in stating "that it will be found much more extensive than is generally imagined."

Latin words which have reached the Cornish after they had assumed a French or Norman disguise, are, for instance,—

Emperur, instead of Latin *imperator* (Welsh, *ymherawdwr*).

Laian, the French *loyal*, but not the Latin *legalis*. Likewise, *dislaian*, disloyal.

Fruit, fruit; Lat. *fructus*; French, *fruit*.
Funten, fountain, commonly pronounced *fenton*; Lat. *fontana*; French, *fontaine*.
Gromersy, i. e. grand mercy, thanks.
Hoyz, hoyz, hoyz! hear, hear! The Norman-French, *Oyez*.

The town-crier of Aberconwy may still be heard prefacing his notices with the shout of " Hoyz, hoyz, hoyz!" which in other places has been corrupted to " O yes."

The following words, adopted into Cornish and other Celtic dialects, clearly show their Saxon origin: —

Cafor, a chafer; Germ. *käfer*. *Craft*, art, craft. *Redior*, a reader. *Store*, a stork. *Let*, hindrance, let; preserved in the German, *verletzen*.[1]

[1] The following extract from a Cornish paper gives some curious words still current among the people: —

"A few weeks since a correspondent in the *Cornish Telegraph* remarked a few familiar expressions which we West country folks are accustomed to use in so vague a sense that strangers are often rather puzzled to know precisely what we mean. He might also have added to the list many old Cornish words, still in common use, as *skaw* for the elder-tree; *skaw-dower*, water elder; *skaw-cow*, nightshade; *banael*, broom; *skedgewith*, privet; *griglans*, heath; *padrypaw* (from *padzar*, four?), the small gray lizard; *meryon*, the ant; *guilkon*, the frog (which retains its English name when in the water); *pol-crouick* (literally pool-toad) is the name given to a small fish with a head much like that of a toad, which is often found in the pools (*pulons*) left by the receding tide among the rocks along shore; *siman*, the sand-lance; *bul-horn*, the shell-snail; *dumble-dory*, the black-beetle (but this may be a corruption of the dor-beetle). A small, solid wheel has still the old name of *druckhar*. Finely pulverized soil is called *grues*. The roots and other light matter harrowed up on the surface of the ground for burning we call *tabs*. The harvest-home and harvest-feast, *guildize*. *Plum* means soft; *quril*, withered; *crum*, crooked; *brayans*, crumbs; with a few other terms more rarely used.

"Many of our ordinary expressions (often mistaken for vulgar provincialisms) are French words slightly modified, which were probably introduced into the West by the old Norman families who long resided there. For instance: a large apron to come quite round, worn for the sake of keeping the under-clothing clean, is called a *touser* (*tout-serre*); a game of running romps, is a *courant* (from *courir*). Very rough play is a regular *cow's courant*. Going into a neighbor's for a spell of friendly chat is going to *cursey* (*causer*) a bit. The loins are called the *cheens* (old French,

Considering that Cornish and other Celtic dialects are members of the same family to which Latin and German belong, it is sometimes difficult to tell at once whether a Celtic word was really borrowed, or whether it belongs to that ancient stock of words which all the Aryan languages share in common. This is a point which can be determined by scholars only, and by means of phonetic tests. Thus the Cornish *huir*, or *hoer*, is clearly the same word as the Latin *soror*, sister. But the change of *s* into *h* would not have taken place if the word had been simply borrowed from Latin, while many words beginning with *s* in Sanskrit, Latin, and German, change the *s* into *h* in Cornish as well as in Greek and Persian. The Cornish *hoer*, sister, is indeed curiously like the Persian *khâher*, the regular representative of the Sanskrit *svasar*, the Latin *soror*. The same applies to *braud*, brother, *dedh*, day, *dri*, three, and many more words which form the primitive stock of Cornish, and were common to all the Aryan languages before their earliest dispersion.

What applies to the language of Cornwall, applies with equal force to the other relics of antiquity of that curious county. It has been truly said that Cornwall is poor in antiquities, but it is equally true that it is rich in antiquity. The difficulty is to discriminate, and to distinguish what is really Cornish or Celtic from what may be later additions, of Roman, Saxon, Danish, and Norman origin. Now here, as

echine). The plant sweet-leaf, a kind of St. John's wort, here called *tad-sen*, is the French *tout-srius* (heal all). There are some others which, however, are not peculiar to the West; as *kickshaws* (*quelque chose*), etc. We have also many inverted words, as *sawp* for wasp, *cruds* for curds, etc. Then again we call a fly a *flea*; and a flea a *fly*; and the smallest stream of water a river." — W. B.

we said before, the safest rule is clearly the same as that which we followed in our analysis of language. Let everything be claimed for English, Norman, Danish, and Roman sources that can clearly be proved to come from thence; but let what remains unclaimed be considered as Cornish or Celtic. Thus, if we do not find in countries exclusively inhabited by Romans or Saxons anything like a cromlech, surely we have a right to look upon these strange structures as remnants of Celtic times. It makes no difference if it can be shown that below these cromlechs coins have occasionally been found of the Roman Emperors. This only proves that even during the days of Roman supremacy the Cornish style of public monuments, whether sepulchral or otherwise, remained. Nay, why should not even a Roman settled in Cornwall have adopted the monumental style of his adopted country? Roman and Saxon hands may have helped to erect some of the cromlechs which are still to be seen in Cornwall, but the original idea of such monuments, and hence their name, is purely Celtic.

Cromlêh in Cornish, or *cromlech* in Welsh, means a bent slab, from the Cornish *crom*, bent, curved, rounded, and *lêh*, a slab. Though many of these cromlechs have been destroyed, Cornwall still possesses some fine specimens of these ancient stone tripods. Most of them are large granite slabs, supported by three stones fixed in the ground. These supporters are likewise huge flat stones, but the capstone is always the largest, and its weight inclining towards one point, imparts strength to the whole structure. At Lanyon, however, where the top-stone of a cromlech was thrown down in 1816 by a violent storm, the supporters remained standing, and the capstone was replaced in 1824, though not, it would seem, at its original height. Dr. Borlase relates that in his time the monument was high enough for a man to sit on horseback under it. At present such a feat would be impossible, the coverstone being only about five feet from the ground. These cromlechs, though very surprising when seen for the first time, represent in reality one of the simplest achievements of primitive architecture. It is far easier to balance a heavy weight on three uneven props than to rest it level on two or four even supporters. There are, however, cromlechs resting on four or more stones, these stones forming a kind of chamber, or a *kist-vaen*, which is supposed to have served originally as a sepulchre. These structures presuppose a larger amount of architectural skill; still more so the gigantic portals of Stonehenge, which are formed by two pillars of equal height, joined by a superincumbent stone. Here weight alone was no longer considered sufficient for imparting strength and safety, but holes were worked in the upper stones, and the pointed tops of the pillars were fitted into them. In the slabs that form the cromlechs we find no such traces of careful workmanship; and this, as well as other considerations, would support the opinion, that in Stonehenge we have one of the latest specimens of Celtic architecture. Marvelous as are the remains of that primitive style of architectural art, the only real problem they offer is, how such large stones could have been brought together from a distance, and how such enormous weights could have been lifted up. The first question is answered by ropes

---

[1] *Quarterly Review*, vol. cviii. p. 200.

and rollers; and the mural sculptures of Nineveh show us what can be done by such simple machinery. We there see the whole picture of how these colossal blocks of stone were moved from the quarry on to the place where they were wanted. Given plenty of time, and plenty of men and oxen, and there is no block that could not be brought to its right place by means of ropes and rollers. And that our forefathers did not stint themselves either in time, or in men, or other cattle, when engaged in erecting such monuments, we know even from comparatively modern times. Under Harold Harfagr, two kings spent three whole years in erecting one single tumulus; and Harold Blatand is said to have employed the whole of his army and a vast number of oxen in transporting a large stone which he wished to place on his mother's tomb. As to the second question, we can readily understand how, after the supporters had once been fixed in the ground, an artificial mound might be raised, which, when the heavy slab had been rolled up on an inclined plane, might be removed again, and thus leave the heavy stone poised in its startling elevation.

As skeletons have been found under some of the cromlechs, there can be little doubt that the chambers inclosed by them, the so-called *kist-vaens*, were intended to receive the remains of the dead, and to perpetuate their memory. And as these sepulchral monuments are most frequent in those parts of the British Isles which from the earliest to the latest times were inhabited by Celtic people, they may be considered as representative of the Celtic style of public

---

[1] Saxo Grammaticus, *Historia Danica*, lib. x. p. 167; ed. Francofurt. 1576.

sepulture. *Kist-vaen*, or *cist-vaen*, means a stone-chamber, from *cista*, a chest, and *vaen*, the modified form of *maen* or *mên*, stone. Their size is, with few exceptions, not less than the size of a human body. But although these monuments were originally sepulchral, we may well understand that the burying-places of great men, of kings, or priests, or generals, were likewise used for the celebration of other religious rites. Thus we read in the Book of Lecan, " that Amhalgaith built a cairn, for the purpose of holding a meeting of the Hy-Amhalgaith every year, and to view his ships and fleet going and coming, and as a place of interment for himself."[1] Nor does it follow, as some antiquarians maintain, that every structure in the style of a cromlech, even in England, is exclusively Celtic. We imitate pyramids and obelisks: why should not the Saxons have built the Kitts Cotty House, which is found in a thoroughly Saxon neighborhood, after Celtic models and with the aid of Celtic captives? This cromlech stands in Kent, on the brow of a hill about a mile and a half from Aylesford, to the right of the great road from Rochester to Maidstone. Near it, across the Medway, are the stone circles of Addington. The stone on the south side is 8 ft. high by 7½ broad, and 2 ft. thick; weight, about 8 tons. That on the north is 8 ft. by 8, and 2 thick; weight, 8 tons 10 cwt. The end stone, 5 ft. 6 in. high by 5 ft. broad; thickness, 14 in.; weight, 2 tons 8¼ cwt. The impost is 11 ft. long by 8 ft. broad, and 2 ft. thick; weight, 10 tons 7 cwt. It is higher, therefore, than the Cornish cromlechs, but in other respects it is a true specimen of that class of Celtic monuments. The cover-stone of the cromlech at Molfra is 9 ft. 8. in. by 14 ft. 3 in.; its supporters

[1] Quoted in Petrie, *Eccles. Architecture of Ireland*, p. 107.

are 5 ft. high. The cover-stone of the Chûn cromlech measures 12½ ft. in length and 11 ft. in width. The largest slab is that at Lanyon, which measures 18½ ft. in length and 9 ft. at the broadest part.

The cromlechs are no doubt the most characteristic and most striking among the monuments of Cornwall. Though historians have differed as to their exact purpose, not even the most careless traveller could pass them by without seeing that they do not stand there without a purpose. They speak for themselves, and they certainly speak in a language that is neither Roman, Saxon, Danish, nor Norman. Hence in England they may, by a kind of exhaustive process of reasoning, be claimed as relics of Celtic civilization. The same argument applies to the cromlechs and stone avenues of Carnac, in Brittany. Here, too, language and history attest the former presence of Celtic people; nor could any other race, that influenced the historical destinies of the North of Gaul, claim such structures as their own. Even in still more distant places, in the South of France, in Scandinavia, or Germany, where similar monuments have been discovered, they may, though more hesitatingly, be classed as Celtic, particularly if they are found near the natural high roads on which we know that the Celts in their westward migrations preceded the Teutonic and Slavonic Aryans. But the case is totally different when we hear of cromlechs, cairns, and kist-vaens in the North of Africa, in Upper Egypt, on the Lebanon, near the Jordan, in Circassia, or in the South of India. Here, and more particularly in the South of India, we have no indications whatever of Celtic Aryans; on the contrary, if that name is taken in its strict scientific meaning, it would be impossible to account for the presence of Celtic Aryans in those southern latitudes at any time after the original dispersion of the Aryan family. It is very natural that English officers living in India should be surprised at monuments which cannot but remind them of what they had seen at home, whether in Cornwall, Ireland, or Scotland. A description of some of these monuments, the so-called Pandoo Coolies in Malabar, was given by Mr. J. Babington, in 1820, and published in the third volume of the "Transactions of the Literary Society of Bombay," in 1823. Captain Congreve called attention to what he considered Scythic Druidical remains in the Nilghiri hills, in a paper published in 1847, in the "Madras Journal of Literature and Science," and the same subject was treated in the same journal by the Rev. W. Taylor. A most careful and interesting description of similar monuments has lately been published in the "Transactions of the Royal Irish Academy," by Captain Meadows Taylor, under the title of "Description of Cairns, Cromlechs, Kist-vaens, and other Celtic, Druidical, or Scythian Monuments in the Dekhan." Captain Taylor found these monuments near the village of Rajunkolloor, in the principality of Shorapoor, an independent native state, situated between the Bheema and Krishna rivers, immediately above their junction. Others were discovered near Huggeritgi, others on the hill of Yemmee Gooda, others again near Shapoor, Hyderabad, and other places. All these monuments in the South of India are no doubt extremely interesting; but to call them Celtic, Druidical, or Scythic, is unscientific, or, at all events, exceedingly premature. There is in all architectural monuments a natural or rational, and a conventional, or, it may be, irrational element. A striking agreement in purely conventional features may justify the assumption that monuments so far distant from each others as the cromlechs of Anglesea and the "Mori-Munni" of Shorapoor owe their origin to the same architects, or to the same races. But an agreement in purely natural contrivances goes for nothing, or, at least, for very little. Now there is very little that can be called conventional in a mere stone pillar, or in a cairn, that is, an artificial heap of stones. Even the erection of a cromlech can hardly be claimed as a separate style of architecture. Children, all over the world, if building houses with cards, will build cromlechs; and people, all over the world, if the neighborhood supplies large slabs of stone, will put three stones together to keep out the sun or the wind, and put a fourth stone on the top to keep out the rain. Before monuments like those described by Captain Meadows Taylor can be classed as Celtic or Druidical, a possibility, at all events, must be shown that Celts, in the true sense of the word, could ever have inhabited the Dekhan. Till that is done, it is better to leave them anonymous, or to call them by their native names, than to give to them a name which is apt to mislead the public at large, and to encourage theories which exceed the limits of legitimate speculation.

Returning to Cornwall, we find there, besides the cromlechs, pillars, holed stones, and stone circles, all of which may be classed as public monuments. They all bear witness to a kind of public spirit, and to a certain advance in social and political life, at the time of their erection. They were meant for people living at the time, who understood their meaning, if not as messages to posterity, and, if so, as truly historical monuments; for history begins when the living begin to care about a good opinion of those who come after them. Some of the single Cornish pillars tell us little indeed; nothing, in reality, beyond the fact that they were erected by human skill, and with some human purpose. Some of these monoliths seem to have been of a considerable size. In a village called Mên Perhen, in Constantine parish, there stood, "about five years ago," — so Dr. Borlase relates in the year 1769, — a large pyramidal stone, twenty feet above the ground, and four feet in the ground; it made above twenty stone posts for gates when it was clove up by the farmer who gave the account to the Doctor.[1] Other stones, like the Mên Scrifa, have inscriptions, but these inscriptions are Roman, and of comparatively late date. There are some pillars, like the Pipers at Bolleit, which are clearly connected with the stone circles close by, remnants, it may be, of old stone avenues, or beacons, from which signals might be sent to other distant settlements. The holed stones, too, are generally found in close proximity to other large stone monuments. They are called *mên-an-tol*, hole-stones, in Cornwall; and the name of *tol-men*, or *dol-men*, which is somewhat promiscuously used by Celtic antiquarians, should be restricted to monuments of this class, *toll* being the Cornish word for *hole*, *mên* for *stone*, and *an* the article. French antiquarians, taking *dol* or *tól* as a corruption of *tabula*, use *dolman* in the sense of tablestones, and as synonymous with *cromlech*, while they frequently use *cromlech* in the sense of stone circles. This can hardly be justified, and leads at all events to much confusion.

The stone circles, whether used for religious or judicial purposes, — and there was in ancient times very lit-

[1] Borlase, *Antiquities of Cornwall*, p. 162.

tle difference between the two, — were clearly intended for solemn meetings. There is a very perfect circle at Boscawen-ûn, which consisted originally of nineteen stones. Dr. Borlase, whose work on the Antiquities of the County of Cornwall contains the most trustworthy information as to the state of Cornish antiquities about a hundred years ago, mentions three other circles which had the same number of stones, while others vary from twelve to seventy-two.

"The figure of these monuments," he says, "is either simple, or compounded. Of the first kind are exact circles; elliptical or semicircular. The construction of these is not always the same, some having their circumference marked with large separate stones only; others having ridges of small stones intermixed, and sometimes walls and seats, serving to render the inclosure more complete. Other circular monuments have their figure more complex and varied, consisting, not only of a circle, but of some other distinguishing properties. In or near the centre of some stands a stone taller than the rest, as at Boscawen-Ûn; in the middle of others, a kist-vaen. A cromlêh distinguishes the centre of some circles, and one remarkable rock that of others; some have only one line of stones in their circumference, and some have two; some circles are adjacent, some contiguous, and some include, and some intersect each other. Sometimes urns are found in or near them. Some are curiously erected on geometrical plans, the chief entrance facing the cardinal points of the heavens; some have avenues leading to them, placed exactly north and south, with detached stones, sometimes in straight lines to the east and west, sometimes triangular. These monuments are found in many foreign countries, in Iceland, Sweden, Denmark, and Germany, as well as in all the Isles dependent upon Britain (the Orkneys, Western Isles, Jersey, Ireland, and the Isle of Man), and in most parts of Britain itself."

Modern traditions have everywhere clustered round these curious stone circles. Being placed in a circular order, so as to make an area for dancing, they were naturally called *Dawns-mên*, i. e. dancing stones.

This name was soon corrupted into dancemen, and a legend sprang up at once to account for the name, namely, that these men had danced on a Sunday and been changed into stones. Another corruption of the same name into *Danis-mên* led to the tradition that these circles were built by the Danes. A still more curious name for these circles is that of " *Nine Maidens*," which occurs at Boscawen-ûn, and in several other places in Cornwall. Now the Boscawen-ûn circle consists of nineteen stones, and there are very few " Nine Maidens" that consist of nine stones only. Yet the name prevails, and is likewise supported by local legends of nine maidens having been changed into stones for dancing on a Sunday, or some other misdeed. One part of the legend may perhaps be explained by the fact that *mêdn* would be a common corruption in modern Cornish for *mên*, stone, as *pen* becomes *pedn*, and *gwyn*, *gwydn*, etc., and that the Saxons mistook Cornish *mêdn* for their own *maiden*. But even without this, legends of a similar character would spring up wherever the popular mind is startled by strange monuments, the history and purpose of which has been forgotten. Thus Captain Meadows Taylor tells us that at Vibat-Hullie the people told him " that the stones were men who, as they stood marking out the places for the elephants of the king of the dwarfs, were turned into stone by him, because they would not keep quiet." And M. de Cambry, as quoted by him, says in regard to Carnac, " that the rocks were believed to be an army turned into stone, or the work of the Croins, — men or demons, two or three feet high, who carried these rocks in their hands, and placed them there."

A second class of Cornish antiquities comprises private buildings, whether castles or huts or caves.

What are called castles in Cornwall are simple intrenchments, consisting of large and small stones piled up about ten or twelve feet high, and held together by their own weight, without any cement. There are everywhere traces of a ditch, then of a wall; sometimes, as at Chûn Castle, of another ditch and another wall; and there is generally some contrivance for protecting the principal entrance by walls overlapping the ditches. Near these castles barrows are found, and in several cases there are clear traces of a communication between them and some ancient Celtic villages and caves, which seem to have been placed under the protection of these primitive strongholds. Many of the cliffs in Cornwall are fortified towards the land by walls and ditches, thus cutting off these extreme promontories from communication with the land, as they are by nature inaccessible from the sea. Some antiquarians ascribed these castles to the Danes, the very last people, one would think, to shut themselves up in such hopeless retreats. Here, too, as in other cases, a popular etymology may have taken the place of an historical authority, and the Cornish word for castle being *Dinas* as in *Castle-an-Dinas*, *Pendennis*, etc., the later Saxon-speaking population may have been reminded by *Dinas* of the Danes, and on the strength of this vague similarity have ascribed to these pirates the erection of the Cornish castles.

It is indeed difficult, with regard to these castles, to be positive as to the people by whom they were constructed. Tradition and history point to Romans and Saxons, as well as to Celts; nor is it at all unlikely that many of these half-natural, half-artificial strongholds, though originally planned by the Celtic inhabitants, were afterwards taken possession of and strengthened by Romans or Saxons.

But no such doubts are allowed with regard to Cornish huts, of which some striking remains have been preserved in Cornwall and other parts of England, particularly in those which, to the very last, remained the true home of the Celtic inhabitants of Britain. The houses and huts of the Romans were rectangular, nor is there any evidence to show that the Saxon ever approved of the circular style in domestic architecture.

If, then, we find these so-called bee-hive huts in places peculiarly Celtic, and if we remember that so early a writer as Strabo[1] was struck with the same strange style of Celtic architecture, we can hardly be suspected of Celtomania, if we claim them as Celtic workmanship, and dwell with a more than ordinary interest on these ancient chambers, now long deserted and nearly smothered with ferns and weeds, but in their general planning, as well as in their masonry, clearly exhibiting before us something of the arts and the life of the earliest inhabitants of these isles. Let anybody who has a sense of antiquity, and who can feel the spark which is sent on to us through an unbroken chain of history, when we stand on the Acropolis or on the Capitol, or when we read a ballad of Homer or a hymn of the Veda, — nay, if we but read in a proper spirit a chapter of the Old Testament too, — let such a man look at the Celtic huts at Bosprennis or Chysauster, and discover for himself, through the ferns and brambles, the old gray walls, slightly sloping inward, and arranged according to a design that cannot be mistaken; and miserable as these shapeless clumps may appear to the thoughtless traveller, they will convey to the true historian a lesson which he could hardly learn anywhere else. The

[1] Strabo, iv. 197: τοῖς δ' οἴκοις ἐκ σανίδων καὶ γέρρων ἔχουσι μεγάλοις θολοειδέσι, ὄροφον πολὺν ἐπιβάλλοντες.

ancient Britons will no longer be a mere name to him, no mere Pelasgians or Tyrrhenians. He has seen their homes and their handiwork; he has stood behind the walls which protected their lives and property; he has touched the stones which their hands piled up rudely, yet thoughtfully. And if that small spark of sympathy for those who gave the honored name of Britain to these islands has once been kindled among a few who have the power of influencing public opinion in England, we feel certain that something will be done to preserve what can still be preserved of Celtic remains from further destruction. It does honor to the British Parliament that large sums are granted, when it is necessary, to bring to these safe shores whatever can still be rescued from the ruins of Greece and Italy, of Lycia, Pergamos, Palestine, Egypt, Babylon, or Nineveh. But while explorers and excavators are sent to those distant countries, and the statues of Greece, the coffins of Egypt, and the winged monsters of Nineveh, are brought home in triumph to the portals of the British Museum, it is painful to see the splendid granite slabs of British cromlechs thrown down and carted away, stone circles destroyed to make way for farming improvements, and ancient huts and caves broken up to build new houses and stables, with the stones thus ready to hand. It is high time, indeed, that something should be done; and nothing will avail but to place every truly historical monument under national protection. Individual efforts may answer here and there, and a right spirit may be awakened from time to time by local societies; but during intervals of apathy mischief is done that can never be mended; and unless the damaging of national monuments, even though they should stand on private ground, is made a misdemeanor, we doubt whether, two hundred years hence, any enterprising explorer would be as fortunate as Mr. Layard and Sir H. Rawlinson have been in Babylon and Nineveh, and whether one single cromlech would be left for him to carry away to the National Museum of the Maoris. It is curious that the willful damage done to Logan Stones, once in the time of Cromwell by Shrubsall, and more recently by Lieutenant Goldsmith, should have raised such indignation, while acts of Vandalism, committed against real antiquities, are allowed to pass unnoticed. Mr. Scawen, in speaking of the mischief done by strangers in Cornwall, says: —

"Here, too, we may add, what wrong another sort of strangers has done to us, especially in the civil wars, and in particular by destroying of Mincamber, a famous monument, being a rock of infinite weight, which, as a burden, was laid upon other great stones, and yet so equally thereon poised up by Nature only, as a little child could instantly move it, but no one man or many remove it. This natural monument all travellers that came that way desired to behold; but in the time of Oliver's usurpation, when all monumental things became despicable, one Shrubsall, one of Oliver's heroes, then Governor of Pendennis, by labor and much ado, caused to be undermined and thrown down, to the great grief of the country; but to his own great glory, as he thought, doing it, as he said, with a small cane in his hand. I myself have heard him to boast of this act, being a prisoner then under him."

Mr. Scawen, however, does not tell us that this Shrubsall, in throwing down the Mincamber, i. e. the Mênamber, acted very like the old missionaries in felling the sacred oaks in Germany. Merlin, it was believed, had proclaimed that this stone should stand until England had no king; and as Cornwall was a stronghold of the Stuarts, the destruction of this loyal stone may have seemed a matter of wise policy.

Even the foolish exploit of Lieutenant Goldsmith, in 1824, would seem to have had some kind of excuse. Dr. Borlase had asserted " that it was *morally* impossible that any lever, or indeed force, however applied in a mechanical way, could remove the famous Logan rock at Trereen Dinas from its present position." Ptolemy, the son of Hephæstion, had made a similar remark about the Gigonian rock,[1] stating that it might be stirred with the stalk of an asphodel, but could not be removed by any force. Lieutenant Goldsmith, living in an age of experimental philosophy, undertook the experiment, in order to show that it was *physically* possible to overthrow the Logan; and he did it. He was, however, very properly punished for this unscientific experiment, and he had to replace the stone at his own expense.

As this matter is really serious, we have drawn up a short list of acts of Vandalism committed in Cornwall within the memory of living man. That list could easily be increased, but even as it is, we hope it may rouse the attention of the public:—

Between St. Ives and Zennor, on the lower road over Tregarthen Downs, stood a Logan rock. An old man, perhaps ninety years of age, told Mr. Hunt, who mentions this and other cases in the preface to his charming collection of Cornish tales and legends, that he had often logged it, and that it would make a noise which could *be heard for miles*.

At Balnoon, between Nancledrea and Knill's Steeple, some miners came upon "two slabs of granite cemented together," which covered a walled grave three feet square, an ancient kist-vaen. In it they found an

---

[1] Cf. Photius, *Bibliotheca*, ed. Bekker, p. 148, l. 32: περὶ τῆς παρὰ τὸν ὠκεανὸν Γιγωνίαν πέτρας, καὶ ὅτι μόνῳ ἀσφοδελῷ κινεῖται, πρὸς πᾶσαν βίαν ἀκατανόητος οὖσα.

earthenware vessel, containing some black earth and a leaden spoon. The spoon was given to Mr. Praed, of Trevethow; the kist-vaen was utterly destroyed.

In Bosprennis Cross there was a very large coit or cromlech. It is said to have been fifteen feet square, and not more than one foot thick in any part. This was broken in two parts some years since, and taken to Penzance to form the beds of two ovens.

The curious caves and passages at Chysauster have been destroyed for building purposes within living memory.

Another Cornishman, Mr. Bellows, reports as follows : —

" In a field between the recently discovered Beehive hut and the Boscawen-ûn circle, out of the public road, we discovered part of a 'Nine Maidens,' perhaps the third of the circle, the rest of the stones being dragged out and placed against the hedge, to make room for the plough."

The same intelligent antiquarian remarks : —

" The Boscawen-ûn circle seems to have consisted originally of twenty stones. Seventeen of them are upright, two are down, and a gap exists of exactly the double space for the twentieth. We found the missing stone not twenty yards off. A farmer had removed it, and made it into a gate-post. He had cut a road through the circle, and in such a manner that he was obliged to remove the offending stone to keep it straight. Fortunately the present proprietress is a lady of taste, and has surrounded the circle with a good hedge to prevent further Vandalism."

Of the Mên-an-tol, at Boleit, we have received the following description from Mr. Botterell, who supplied Mr. Hunt with so many of his Cornish tales : —

" These stones are from twenty to twenty-five feet above the surface, and we were told by some folks of Boleit that more than ten feet had been sunk near, without finding the base. The Mên-an-tol have both been displaced, and removed a considerable distance from their original site. They are now placed in a hedge, to form the side of a gateway. The upper portion of one is so much broken that one cannot determine the angle, yet that it worked to an angle is quite apparent. The other is turned downward, and serves as the hanging-post of a gate. From the head being buried so deep in the ground, only part of the hole (which is in both stones about six inches diameter) could be seen; though the hole is too small to pop the smallest, or all but the smallest, baby through, the people call them *crick-stones*, and maintain they were so called before they were born. Crick-stones were used for dragging people through, to cure them of various diseases."

The same gentleman, writing to one of the Cornish papers, informs the public that a few years ago a rock known by the name of Garrack-zans might be seen in the town-place of Sawah, in the parish of St. Levan; another in Roskestal, in the same parish. One is also said to have been removed from near the centre of Trereen, by the family of Jans, to make a grander approach to their mansion. The ruins, which still remain, are known by the name of the Jans House, although the family became extinct soon after perpetrating what was regarded by the old inhabitants as a sacrilegious act. The Garrack-zans may still be remaining in Roskestal and Sawah, but, as much alteration has recently taken place in these villages, in consequence of building new farm-houses, making new roads, etc., it is a great chance if they have not been either removed or destroyed.

Mr. J. T. Blight, the author of one of the most useful little guide-books of Cornwall, " A Week at the Land's End," states that some eight or ten years ago the ruins of the ancient Chapel of St. Eloy, in St. Burian, were thrown over the cliff by the tenant of the estate, without the knowledge or permission of the owner of the property. Chûn Castle, he says, one of the finest examples of early military architecture in this kingdom, has for many years been resorted to as a sort of quarry. The same applies to Castle-an-Dinas.

From an interesting paper on Castallack Round by the same antiquarian, we quote the following passages, showing the constant mischief that is going on, whether due to downright Vandalism or to ignorance and indifference:—

"From a description of Castallack Round, in the parish of St. Paul, written by Mr. Crozier, perhaps fourteen or fifteen years ago, it appears that there was a massive outer wall, with an entrance on the south; from which a colonnade of stones led to an inner inclosure, also formed with stones, and nine feet in diameter. Mr. Halliwell, so recently as 1861, refers to the avenue of upright stones leading from the outer to the inner inclosure.

"On visiting the spot a few days ago (in 1863), I was surprised to find that not only were there no remains of an avenue of stones, but that the existence of an inner inclosure could scarcely be traced. It was, in fact, evident that some modern Vandal had been at work. A laborer, employed in the field close by, with a complaisant smile, informed me that the old Round had been dug into last year, for the sake of the stones. I found, however, enough of the work left to be worthy of a few notes, sufficient to show that it was a kindred structure to that at Kerris, known as the Roundago, and described and figured in Borlase's 'Antiquities of Cornwall.' . . . Mr. Crozier also refers to a stone, five feet high, which stood within a hundred yards of the Castallack Round, and from which the Pipers at Boleit could be seen.

"The attention of the Royal Institution of Cornwall has been repeatedly called to the destruction of Cornish antiquities, and the interference of landed proprietors has been frequently invoked in aid of their preservation; but it unfortunately happens, in most cases, that important remains are demolished by the tenants without the knowledge or consent of the landlords. On comparing the present condition of the Castallack Round with a description of its appearance so recently as in 1861, I find that the greater and more interesting part has been barbarously and irreparably destroyed; and I regret to say, I could draw up a long list of ancient remains in Cornwall, partially or totally demolished within the last few years."

We can hardly hope that the wholesome superstition which prevented people in former days from desecrating their ancient monuments will be any protection to them much longer, though the following story shows that some grains of the old leaven are still left in the Cornish mind. Near Carleen, in Breage, an old cross has been removed from its place, and now does duty as a gate-post. The farmer occupying the farm where the cross stood, set his laborer to sink a pit in the required spot for the gate-post, but when it was intimated that the cross standing at a little distance off was to be erected therein, the man absolutely refused to have any hand in the matter, not on account of the beautiful or the antique, but for fear of the old people. Another farmer related that he had a neighbor who "haeled down a lot of stoans called the Roundago, and sold 'em for building the docks at Penzance. But not a penny of the money he got for 'em ever prospered, and there wasn't wan of the hosses that haeld 'em that lived out the twelvemonth; and they do say that some of the stoans do weep blood, but I don't believe that."

There are many antiquarians who affect to despise the rude architecture of the Celts, nay, who would think the name of architecture disgraced if applied to cromlechs and bee-hive huts. But even these will perhaps be more willing to lend a helping hand in protecting the antiquities of Cornwall when they hear that even ancient Norman masonry is no longer safe in that country. An antiquarian writes to us from Cornwall: " I heard of some farmers in Meneage (the Lizard district) who dragged down an ancient well and rebuilt it. When called to task for it, they said, ' The ould thing was so shaky that a wasn't fit to be seen, so we thought we'd putten to rights and build'un up *fitty.*'"

Such things, we feel sure, should not be, and would not be, allowed any longer, if public opinion, or the public conscience, was once roused. Let people laugh at Celtic monuments as much as they like, if they will only help to preserve their laughing-stocks from destruction. Let antiquarians be as skeptical as they like, if they will only prevent the dishonest withdrawal of the evidence against which their skepticism is directed. Are lake-dwellings in Switzerland, are flint-deposits in France, is kitchen-rubbish in Denmark, so very precious, and are the magnificent cromlechs, the curious holed stones, and even the rock-basins of Cornwall, so contemptible? There is a fashion even in scientific tastes. For thirty years M. Boucher de Perthes could hardly get a hearing for his flint-heads, and now he has become the centre of interest for geologists, anthropologists, and physiologists. There is every reason to expect that the interest, once awakened in the early history of our own race, will go on increasing; and two hundred years hence the antiquarians and anthropologists of the future will call us hard names if they find out how we allowed these relics of the earliest civilization of England to be destroyed. It is easy to say, What is there in a holed stone? It is a stone with a hole in it, and that is all. We do not wish to propound new theories; but in order to show how full of interest even a stone with a hole in it may become, we will just mention that the *Mên-an-tol*, or the holed stone which stands in one of the fields near Lanyon, is flanked by two other stones standing erect on each side. Let any one go there to watch a sunset about the time of the

autumnal equinox, and he will see that the shadow
thrown by the erect stone would fall straight through
the hole of the *Mên-an-tol*. We know that the great
festivals of the ancient world were regulated by the
sun, and that some of these festive seasons — the winter solstice about Yule-tide or Christmas, the vernal
equinox about Easter, the summer solstice on Mid-
summer-eve, about St. John Baptist's day, and the
autumnal equinox about Michaelmas — are still kept,
under changed names and with new objects, in our own
time. This *Mên-an-tol* may be an old dial erected
originally to fix the proper time for the celebration of
the autumnal equinox; and though it may have been
applied to other purposes likewise, such as the curing
of children by dragging them several times through the
hole, still its original intention may have been astronomical. It is easy to test this observation, and to find
out whether the same remark does not hold good of
other stones in Cornwall, as, for instance, the Two
Pipers. We do not wish to attribute to this guess as
to the original intention of the *Mên-an-tol* more importance than it deserves, nor would we in any way countenance the opinion of those who, beginning with Cæsar,
ascribe to the Celts and their Druids every kind of
mysterious wisdom. A mere shepherd, though he had
never heard the name of the equinox, might have
erected such a stone for his own convenience, in order
to know the time when he might safely bring his flocks
out, or take them back to their safer stables. But this
would in no way diminish the interest of the *Mên-an-tol*.
It would still remain one of the few relics of the childhood of our race; one of the witnesses of the earliest
workings of the human mind in its struggle against,
and in its alliance with, the powers of nature; one of

the vestiges of the first civilization of the British Isles.
Even the Romans, who carried their Roman roads in a
straight line through the countries they had conquered,
undeterred by any obstacles, unawed by any sanctu-
aries, respected, as can hardly be doubted, Silbury
Hill, and made the road from Bath to London diverge
from the usual straight line, instead of cutting through
that time-honored mound. Would the engineers of
our railways show a similar regard for any national
monument, whether Celtic, Roman, or Saxon? When
Charles II., in 1663, went to see the Celtic remains of
Abury, sixty-three stones were still standing within the
intrenched inclosure. Not quite a hundred years later
they had dwindled down to forty-four, the rest having
been used for building purposes. Dr. Stukeley, who
published a description of Abury in 1743, tells us that
he himself saw the upper stone of the great cromlech
there broken and carried away, the fragments of it
making no less than twenty cart-loads. After another
century had passed, seventeen stones only remained
within the great inclosure, and these, too, are being
gradually broken up and carted away. Surely such
things ought not to be. Let those whom it concerns
look to it before it is too late. These Celtic monuments
are public property as much as London Stone, Corona-
tion Stone, or Westminster Abbey, and posterity will
hold the present generation responsible for the safe
keeping of the national heirlooms of England.[1]

[1] The following extract from a Cornish newspaper, July 15, 1869, shows
the necessity of imperial legislation on this subject to prevent irreparable
mischief: —

"The ruthless destruction of the Tolmen, in the parish of Constantine,
which has been so much deplored, has had the effect, we are glad to say,
of drawing attention to the necessity of taking measures for the preservation of the remaining antiquities and objects of curiosity and interest in the
county. In a recent number of the *West Briton* we called attention to the

threatened overthrow of another of our far-famed objects of great interest, — the Cheesewring, near Liskeard; and we are now glad to hear that the committee of the Royal Institution of Cornwall have requested three gentlemen who take great interest in the preservation of antiquities — Mr. William Jory Henwood, F. G. S., etc., Mr. N. Hare, Jr., of Liskeard, and Mr. Whitley, one of the secretaries of the Royal Institution — to visit Liskeard for the purpose of conferring with the agents of the lessors of the Cheesewring granite quarries — the Duchy of Cornwall — and with the lessees of the works, Messrs. Freeman, of Penryn, who are themselves greatly anxious that measures should be taken for the preservation of that most remarkable pile of rocks known as the Cheesewring. We have no doubt that the measures to be adopted will prove successful; and with regard to any other antiquities or natural curiosities in the county, we shall be glad to hear from correspondents, at any time, if they are placed in peril of destruction, in order that a public announcement of the fact may become the means of preserving them."

July, 1857.

XIV.

ARE THERE JEWS IN CORNWALL?

THERE is hardly a book on Cornish history or antiquities in which we are not seriously informed that at some time or other the Jews migrated to Cornwall, or worked as slaves in Cornish mines. Some writers state this simply as a fact requiring no further confirmation; others support it by that kind of evidence which Herodotus, no doubt, would have considered sufficient for establishing the former presence of Pelasgians in different parts of Greece, but which would hardly have satisfied Niebuhr, still less Sir G. C. Lewis. Old smelting-houses, they tell us, are still called *Jews' houses* in Cornwall; and if, even after that, anybody could be so skeptical as to doubt that the Jews, after the destruction of Jerusalem, were sent in large numbers to work as slaves in the Cornish mines, he is silenced at once by an appeal to the name of *Marazion*, the well-known town opposite St. Michael's Mount, which means the "bitterness of Zion," and is also called *Market Jew*. Many a traveller has no doubt shaken his unbelieving head, and asked himself how it is that no real historian should ever have mentioned the migration of the Jews to the Far West, whether it took place under Nero or under one of the later Flavian

Emperors. Yet all the Cornish guides are positive on the subject, and the *primâ facie* evidence is certainly so startling that we can hardly wonder if certain anthropologists discovered even the sharply marked features of the Jewish race among the sturdy fishermen of Mount's Bay.

Before we examine the facts on which this Jewish theory is founded,—facts, as will be seen, chiefly derived from names of places, and other relics of language,—it will be well to inquire a little into the character of the Cornish language, so that we may know what kind of evidence we have any right to expect from such a witness.

The ancient language of Cornwall, as is well known, was a Celtic dialect, closely allied to the languages of Brittany and Wales, and less nearly, though by no means distantly, related to the languages of Ireland, Scotland, and the Isle of Man. Cornish began to die out in Cornwall about the time of the Reformation, being slowly but surely supplanted by English, till it was buried with Dolly Pentreath and similar worthies about the end of the last century.[1] Now there is in most languages, but more particularly in those which are losing their consciousness or their vitality, what, by a name borrowed from geology, may be called a *metamorphic process*. It consists chiefly in this, that words, as they cease to be properly understood, are slightly changed, generally with the object of imparting to them once more an intelligible meaning. This new meaning is mostly a mistaken one, yet it is not only readily accepted, but the word in its new dress and with its new character is frequently made to support facts or fictions which could be supported by no

[1] See p. 245.

other evidence. Who does not believe that *sweetheart* has something to do with *heart?* Yet it was originally formed like *drunk-ard, dull-ard,* and *nigg-ard;* and poets, not grammarians, are responsible for the mischief it may have done under its plausible disguise. By the same process, *shamefast,* formed like *steadfast* and still properly spelt by Chaucer and in the early editions of the Authorized Version of the Bible, has long become *shamefaced,* bringing before us the blushing roses of a lovely face. The *Vikings,* mere pirates from the *viks* or creeks of Scandinavia, have, by the same process, been raised to the dignity of kings; just as *coat cards* — the king, and queen, and knave in their gorgeous gowns — were exalted into *court cards.*

Although this kind of metamorphosis takes place in every language, yet it is most frequent in countries where two languages come in contact with each other, and where, in the end, one is superseded by the other. *Robertus Curtus,* the eldest son of the Conqueror, was by the Saxons called *Curt-hose.* The name of *Oxford* contains in its first syllable an old Celtic word, the well-known term for water or river, which occurs as *ux* in *Uxbridge,* as *ex* in *Exmouth,* as *ax* in *Axmouth,* and in many more disguises down to the *whisk* of *whiskey,* the Scotch *Usquebaugh.*[1] In the name of the *Isis,* and of the suburb of *Osney,* the same Celtic word has been preserved. The Saxons kept the Celtic name of the river, and they called the place where one of the Roman roads crossed the river Ox, *Oxford.* The name, however, was soon mistaken, and interpreted as purely Saxon; and if any one should doubt that Oxford was a kind of *Bosphorus,* and meant a ford for

[1] See Isaac Taylor's *Words and Places,* p. 212. The Ock joins the Thames near Abingdon.

oxen, the ancient arms of the city were readily appealed to in order to cut short all doubts on the subject. The Welsh name *Ryt-ychen* for Oxford was a retranslation into Welsh of an original Celtic name, to which a new form and a new meaning had been given by the Saxon conquerors.

Similar accidents happened to Greek words after they were adopted by the people of Italy, particularly by the Romans. The Latin *orichalcum*, for instance, is simply the Greek word ὀρείχαλκος, from ὄρος, mountain, and χαλκός, copper. Why it was called mountain-copper, no one seems to know. It was originally a kind of fabulous metal, brought to light from the brains of the poet rather than from the bowels of the earth. Though the poets, and even Plato, speak of it as, after gold, the most precious of metals, Aristotle sternly denies that there ever was any real metal corresponding to the extravagant descriptions of the ὀρείχαλκος. Afterwards the same word was used in a more sober and technical sense, though it is not always easy to say when it means copper, or bronze (*i. e.* copper and tin), or brass (*i. e.* copper and zinc). The Latin poets not only adopted the Greek word in the fabulous sense in which they found it used in Homer, but forgetting that the first portion of the name was derived from the Greek ὄρος, hill, they pronounced and even spelt it as if derived from the Latin *aurum*, gold, and thus found a new confirmation of its equality with gold, which would have greatly surprised the original framers of that curious compound.[1]

In a county like Cornwall, where the ancient Celtic dialect continued to be spoken, though disturbed and

[1] See the learned essay of M. Rossignol, "De l'Orichalque : Histoire du Cuivre et de ses Alliages," in his work, *Les Métaux dans l'Antiquité*. Paris, 1863.

overlaid from time to time by Latin, Saxon, and Norman, where Celts had to adopt certain Saxon and Norman, and Saxons and Normans certain Celtic words, we have a right to expect an ample field for observing this metamorphic process, and for tracing its influence in the transformation of names, and in the formation of legends, traditions, nay even, as we shall see, in the production of generally accepted historical facts. To call this process *metamorphic*, using that name in the sense given to it by geologists, may at first sight seem pedantic and far-fetched. But if we see how a new language forms what may be called a new stratum covering the old language; how the life or heat of the old language, though apparently extinct, breaks forth again through the superincumbent crust, destroys its regular features and assimilates its stratified layers with its own igneous or volcanic nature, our comparison, though somewhat elaborate, will be justified to a great extent, and we shall only have to ask our geological readers to make allowance for this, that, in languages, the foreign element has always to be considered as the superincumbent stratum, Cornish forming the crust to English or English to Cornish, according as the speaker uses the one or the other as his native or as his acquired speech.

Our first witness in support of this metamorphic process is Mr. Scawen, who lived about two hundred years ago, a true Cornishman, though he wrote in English, or in what he is pleased so to call. In blaming the Cornish gentry and nobility for having attempted to give to their ancient and honorable names a kind of Norman varnish, and for having adopted new-fangled coats of arms, Mr. Scawen remarks on the several mistakes, intentional or unintentional, that occurred in this foolish process. "The grounds of two several mistakes," he writes, "are very obvious: 1st, upon the *Tre* or *Ter*; 2d, upon the *Ross* or *Rose*. *Tre* or *Ter* in Cornish commonly signifies a town, or rather place, and it has always an adjunct with it. *Tri* is the number 3. Those men willingly mistake one for another. And so, in French heraldry terms, they used to fancy and contrive those with any such three things as may be like, or cohere with, or may be adapted to anything or things in their surnames, whether very handsome or not is not much stood upon. Another usual mistake is upon *Ross*, which, as they seem to fancy, should be a Rose, but *Ross* in Cornish is a vale or valley. Now for this their French-Latin tutors, when they go into the field of Mars, put them in their coat armor prettily to smell out a Rose or flower (a fading honor instead of a durable one); so any three such things, agreeable perhaps a little to their names, are taken up and retained from abroad, when their own at home have a much better scent and more lasting."

Some amusing instances of what may be called Saxon puns on Cornish words have been communicated to me by a Cornish friend of mine, Mr. Bellows. "The old Cornish name for Falmouth," he writes, "was *Penny come quick*,[1] and they tell a most improbable story to account for it. I believe the whole compound is the Cornish *Pen y cwm gwic*, 'Head of the creek valley.' In like manner they have turned *Bryn uhella* (highest hill) into *Brown Willy*, and *Cwm ty goed* (woodhouse valley) into *Come to good*." To this might be added the common etymologies of *Helstone* and *Camelford*. The former name has nothing to do with the Saxon *helstone*, a covering stone, or with the infernal regions,

[1] There is another Penny come quick near Falmouth.

but meant "place on the river;" the latter, in spite of the camel in the arms of the town, meant the ford of the river Camel. A frequent mistake arises from the misapprehension of the Celtic *dun*, hill, which enters in the composition of many local names, and was changed by the Saxons into *town* or *tun*. Thus *Melidunum* is now *Moulton*, *Seccan-dun* is *Seckington*, and *Beamdun* is *Bampton*.[1]

This transformation of Celtic into Saxon or Norman terms is not confined, however, to the names of families, towns, and villages; and we shall see how the fables to which it has given rise have not only disfigured the records of some of the most ancient families in Cornwall, but have thrown a haze over the annals of the whole county.

Returning to the Jews in their Cornish exile, we find, no doubt, as mentioned before, that even in the Ordnance maps the little town opposite St. Michael's Mount is called *Marazion* and *Market Jew*. *Marazion* sounds decidedly like Hebrew, and might signify *Márah*, "bitterness, grief," *Zion*, "of Zion." M. Esquiros, a believer in Cornish Jews, thinks that *Mara* might be a corruption of the Latin *Amara*, bitter; but he forgets that this etymology would really defeat its very object, and destroy the Hebrew origin of the name. The next question therefore is, What is the real origin of the name *Marazion*, and of its *alias*, *Market Jew?* It cannot be too often repeated that inquiries into the origin of local names are, in the first place, historical, and only in the second place, philological. To attempt an explanation of any name, without having first traced it back to the earliest form in which we can find it, is to set at defiance the plainest rules of the

[1] Isaac Taylor, *Words and Places*, p. 402.

science of language as well as of the science of history. Even if the interpretation of a local name should be right, it would be of no scientific value without the preliminary inquiry into its history, which frequently consists in a succession of the most startling changes and corruptions. Those who are at all familiar with the history of Cornish names of places will not be surprised to find the same name written in four or five, nay, in ten different ways. The fact is that those who pronounced the names were frequently ignorant of their real import, and those who had to write them down could hardly catch their correct pronunciation. Thus we find that Camden calls Marazion *Merkiu*; Carew, *Marcaiew*. Leland in his "Itinerary" (about 1538) uses the names *Markesin, Markine* (vol. iii. fol. 4); and in another place (vol. vii. fol. 119) he applies, it would seem, to the same town the name of *Marasdeythyon*. William of Worcester (about 1478) writes promiscuously *Markysyoo* (p. 103), *Marchew* and *Margew* (p. 133), *Marchasyowe* and *Markysyow* (p. 98). In a charter of Queen Elizabeth, dated 1595, the name is written *Marghasiewe;* in another of the year 1313, *Markesion;* in another of 1309, *Markasyon;* in another of Richard, Earl of Cornwall (*Rex Romanorum*, 1257), *Marchadyon*, which seems the oldest, and at the same time the most primitive form.[1] Besides these, Dr. Oliver has found in different title-

[1] It has been objected that *Marchadyon* could not be called the original form, because by a *carta Alani comitis Britanniae*, sealed, according to Dugdale's *Monasticon Anglicanum*, by Alan, anno incarnationis domini MCXL, ten shillings per annum were granted to the monks of St. Michael, due from a fair held at *Merdresem* or *Merdresein*. Until, however, it has been proved that *Merdresem* is the same place and the same name as *Marchadyon*, or that the latter sprang from the former, *Marchadyon* in the charter of Richard, Earl of Cornwall, 1257, may for our immediate purpose be treated as the root from which all the other names branched off. See Oliver, *Monasticon Exon*. p. 52.

deeds the following varieties of the same name:—
Marghasion, Markesiow, Marghasiew, Maryazion, and
Marazion. The only explanation of the name which
we meet with in early writers, such as Leland, Camden, and Carew, is that it meant "Thursday Market."
Leland explains *Marasdeythyon* by *forum Jovis.*
Camden explains *Merkiu* in the same manner, and
Carew takes *Marcaiew* as originally *Markas diew,* i. e.
"Thursdaies market, for then it useth this traffike."

This interpretation of *Marhasdiew* as Thursday Market, appears at first very plausible, and it has at all
events far better claims on our acceptance than the
modern Hebrew etymology of "Bitterness of Zion."
But, strange to say, although from a charter of Robert,
Earl of Cornwall, it appears that the monks of the
Mount had the privilege of holding a market on Thursday (*die quintæ feriæ*), there is no evidence, and no
probability, that a town so close to the Mount as Marazion ever held a market on the same day.[1] Thursday
in Cornish was called *deyow,* not *diew.* The only additional evidence we get is this, that in the taxation of
Bishop Walter Bronescombe, made August 12, 1261,
and quoted in Bishop Stapledon's register of 1319, the
place is called *Markesion de parvo mercato,*[2] and that
in a charter of Richard, King of the Romans and Earl
of Cornwall, permission was granted to the prior of St.
Michael's Mount that three markets, which formerly
had been held in *Marghasbigan,* on ground not belonging to him, should in future be held on his own ground

---

[1] If a market was held on the "dimidia terra hida" granted by Robert to the monks, this difficulty would disappear.

[2] In the Additional Supplement (p. 4), Dr. Oliver gives the more correct reading, "*de Markesion, de parvo Mercato, Brerannek, Penmedel, Trevesborne.*" It depends on the comma after *Markesion* whether *parvus Mercatus* is a separate place or not.

in *Marchadyon*. *Parvus mercatus* is evidently the same place as *Marghasbigan*, for *Marghas-bigan* means in Cornish the same as *Mercatus parvus*, namely, "Little Market." The charter of Richard, Earl of Cornwall, is more perplexing, and it would seem to yield no sense, unless we again take *Marchadyon* as a mere variety of *Marghasbigan*, and suppose that the privilege granted to the prior of St. Michael's Mount consisted really in transferring the fair from land in Marazion not belonging to him, to land in Marazion belonging to him. Anyhow, it is clear that in *Marazion* we have some kind of name for market.

The old Cornish word for market is *marchas*, a corruption of the Latin *mercatus*. Originally the Cornish word must have been *marchad*, and this form is preserved in Armorican, while in Cornish the *ch* gradually sunk to *h*, and the final *d* to *s*. This change of *d* into *s* is of frequent occurrence in modern as compared with ancient Cornish, and the history of our word will enable us, to a certain extent, to fix the time when that change took place. In the charter of Richard, Earl of Cornwall (about 1257), we find *Marchadyon;* in a charter of 1309, *Markasyon*. The change of *d* into *s* had taken place during these fifty years.[1] But what is the termination *yon?* Considering that Marazion is called the Little Market, I should like to see in *yon* the diminutive Cornish suffix, corresponding to the Welsh *yn*. But if this should be objected to, on the ground that no such diminutives occur in the literary

---

[1] Dr. Bannister remarks that *Markasion* occurs as early as 1261, in the taxation of Bishop Walter Bronescombe, as quoted in Bishop Stapledon's register of 1313. If that be so, the original form and its dialectic varieties would have existed almost contemporaneously, but the evidence that *Markasion* was used by Bishop Bronescombe is indirect. See Oliver, *Monast. Exon.* p. 28.

monuments of the Cornish language, another explanation is open, which was first suggested to me by Mr. Bellows: *Marchadion* may be taken as a perfectly regular plural in Cornish, and we should then have to suppose that, instead of being called the Market or the Little Market, the place was called, from its three statute markets, "The Markets." And this would help us to explain, not only the gradual growth of the name Marazion, but likewise, I think, the gradual formation of "Market Jew;" for another termination of the plural in Cornish is *ieu*, which, added to *Marchad*, would give us *Marchadieu*.[1]

Now it is perfectly true that no real Cornishman, I mean no man who spoke Cornish, would ever have taken *Marchadieu* for Market Jew, or Jews' Market. The name for Jew in Cornish is quite different. It is *Edhow, Yedhow, Yudhow*, corrupted likewise into *Ezow*; plural, *Yedhewon*, etc. But to a Saxon ear the Cornish name *Marchadieu* might well convey the idea of *Market Jew*, and thus, by a metamorphic process, a name meaning in Cornish the Markets would give rise in a perfectly natural manner, not only to the two names, Marazion and Market Jew, but likewise to the historical legends of Jews settled in the county of Cornwall.[2]

[1] On the termination of the plural in Cornish, see Mr. Whitley Stokes's excellent remarks in his edition of *The Passion*, p. 79; also in Kuhn's *Beiträge*, III. 151; and Norris, *Cornish Drama*, vol. II. p. 229. My attention has since been called to the fact that *markas* occurs in the plural as *markasow*, in the *Cornish Drama*, vol. I. p. 248; and as *s* under such circumstances may become *j* (cf. *arahasnee*, Creat. line 29, but *ennhajowe*, Creat. line 67), *Markajow* would come still nearer to *Market Jew*. Dr. Bannister remarks that in Armorican, market is *marched*, plural *marchadow*, corrupted into *marchajou*.

[2] The following note from a Cornish paper gives some important facts as to the date of the name of *Market Jew*:—

"Among the State Papers at the Record Office, there is a letter from Ralph

298 ARE THERE JEWS IN CORNWALL?

But there still remain the *Jews' houses*, the name given, it is said, to the old, deserted smelting-houses

Conway to Secretary Cope, dated 3d October, 1634, which mentions the name of *Market-jew*.

"In another, dated 7th February, 1634-5, Sir James Bagg informs the Lords of the Admiralty that the endeavors of Mr. Basset, and other gentlemen in the west of Cornwall, to save the cargo of a wrecked Spanish galleon which broke from her moorings in Gwavas Lake, near Penzance, were opposed by a riotous multitude, consisting of the inhabitants of Mousehole and *Marka-jew*, who maintained their unlawful proceedings with the cry of 'One and All!' threatening with death the servants of the Crown, and compelling them to avoid their fury by leaping down a high cliff.

"In another of the same date, from Ralph Bird, of Saltram, to Francis Basset, the rebels of Mousehole, with their fellow-rebels of *Market Jew*, are spoken of, as having menaced the life of any officer who should come to their houses to search for certain hides that mysteriously disappeared from the deck of the galleon one boisterous night, and were probably transferred to Mousehole in the cork-boat of Mr. Keigwin, of that place; and various methods are suggested for administering punishment to the outrageous barbarians.

"In consequence of these complaints, the Lords of the Admiralty wrote to Sir Henry Marten, on the 12th of February of the same year, concerning 'the insolency' committed by the inhabitants of Mousehole and *Markusew* requesting that the offenders may be punished, and, if necessary, the most notorious of them sent to London for trial.

"In *Magna Britannia et Hibernia*, 1720, p. 308, *Merkju* is mentioned as being 'a little market-town which takes its name from the market on Thursdays, it being a contraction of *Market-Jupiter*, i. e. as 'tis now called *Market Jew*, or rather *Ju*.'

"Norden, who was born about 1548, says in his *Speculi Britannia*, which was published in 1723, that *Marca-iew* (*Marca-iew* in margin) signifies in English, 'market on the Thursday.' In an old map, apparently drawn by hand, which appears to have been inserted in this book after it was published, *Market Jew* is given, and in the map issued with the book *Market Jew*.

"The map of Cornwall, contained in *Camden's Britannia*, by Gibson, 1772, gives *Market-Jew*. The edition 1789, by Gough, states at page 8, that '*Merkiu* signifies the *Market of Jupiter*, from the market being held on a Thursday, the day sacred to Jupiter.'

"Carew's *Survey of Cornwall*, ed. 1769, p. 156, has the following:— 'Over against the Mount frontith a towne of petty fortune, pertinently named *Marcaiew*, or *Markas diew*, in English "the Thursdaies market."' In the edition published in 1811, p. 378, it is stated in . . . . that *Marasion* means 'market on the Strand,' the name r to its situation, 'for *Zion* answers to the Latin *litus*.'"

in Cornwall, and in Cornwall only. Though, in the absence of any historical evidence as to the employment of this term *Jews' house* in former ages, it will be more difficult to arrive at its original form and meaning, yet an explanation offers itself which, by a procedure very similar to that which was applied to *Marazion* and *Market Jew*, may account for the origin of this name likewise.

The Cornish name for house was originally *ty*. In modern Cornish, however, to quote from Lhuyd's Grammar, *t* has been changed to *tsh*, as *ti*, thou, *tshei*; *ty*, a house, *tshey*; which *tsh* is also sometimes changed to *dzh*, as *ol mein y dzhyi*, "all in the house." Out of this *dzhyi* we may easily understand how a Saxon mouth and a Saxon ear might have elicited a sound somewhat like the English *Jew*.

But we do not get at *Jews' house* by so easy a road, if indeed we get at it at all. We are told that a smelting-house was called a White-house, in Cornish *Chiwidden*, *widden* standing for *gwydn*, which is a corruption of the old Cornish *gwyn*, white. This name of Chiwidden is a famous name in Cornish hagiography. He was the companion of St. Perran, or St. Piran, the most popular saint among the mining population of Cornwall.

Mr. Hunt, who in his interesting work, "The Popular Romances of the West of England," has assigned a separate chapter to Cornish saints, tells us how St. Piran, while living in Ireland, fed ten Irish kings and their armies, for ten days together, with three cows. Notwithstanding this and other miracles, some of these kings condemned him to be cast off a precipice into the sea, with a millstone round his neck. St. Piran, however, floated on safely to Cornwall, and he landed, on the 5th of March, on the sands which still bear his name, *Perranzabuloe*, or *Perran on the Sands*.

The lives of saints form one of the most curious subjects for the historian, and still more for the student of language; and the day, no doubt, will come when it will be possible to take those wonderful conglomerates of fact and fiction to pieces, and, as in one of those huge masses of graywacke or rubblestone, to assign each grain and fragment to the stratum from which it was taken, before they were all rolled together and cemented by the ebb and flow of popular tradition. With regard to the lives of Irish and Scotch and British saints, it ought to be stated, for the credit of the pious authors of the "Acta Sanctorum," that even they admit their tertiary origin. "During the twelfth century," they say, "when many of the ancient monasteries in Ireland were handed over to monks from England, and many new houses were built for them, these monks began to compile the acts of the saints with greater industry than judgment. They collected all they could find among the uncertain traditions of the natives and in obscure Irish writings, following the example of Jocelin, whose work on the acts of St. Patrick had been received everywhere with wonderful applause. But many of them have miserably failed, so that the foolish have laughed at them, and the wise been filled with indignation." ("Bollandi Acta," 5th of March, p. 390, B). In the same work (p. 392, A), it is pointed out that the Irish monks, whenever they heard of any saints in other parts of England whose names and lives reminded them of Irish saints, at once concluded that they were of Irish origin; and that the people in some parts of England, as they possessed no written acts of their popular saints, were glad to identify their own with the famous saints of the Irish Church. This has evidently happened in the case of St. Piran. St. Piran, in one of his characters, is certainly a truly Cornish saint; but when the monks in Cornwall heard the wonderful legends of the Irish saint, St. Kiran, they seem to have grafted their own St. Piran on the Irish St. Kiran. The difference in the names must have seemed less to them than to us; for words which in Cornish are pronounced with *p*, are pronounced, as a rule, in Irish with *k*. Thus, head in Cornish is *pen*, in Irish *ceann*; son is *map*, in Irish *mac*. The town built at the eastern extremity of the wall of Severus, was called *Penguaul*, i. e. *pen*, caput, *guaul*, walls; the English call it *Penel-tun*; while in Scotch it was pronounced *Cenail*.[1] That St. Kiran had originally nothing to do with St. Piran can still be proved, for the earlier Lives of St. Kiran, though full of fabulous stories, represent him as dying in Ireland. His saint's day was the 5th of March; that of St. Piran, the 2d of May. The later Lives, however, though they say nothing as yet of the millstone, represent St. Kiran, when a very old man, as suddenly leaving his country in order that he might die in Cornwall. We are told that suddenly, when already near his death, he called together his little flock, and said to them: " My dear brothers and sons, according to a divine disposition I must leave Ireland and go to Cornwall, and wait for the end of my life there. I cannot resist the will of God." He then sailed to Cornwall, and built himself a house, where he performed many miracles. He was buried in Cornwall on the sandy sea, fifteen miles from Petrokstowe, and twenty-five miles from Mousehole.[2]

[1] H. R. C. Brandes, *Kelten und Germanen*, p. 52.
[2] Capgrave, *Legenda Anglia*, fol. 269.

In this manner the Irish and the Cornish saints, who originally had nothing in common but their names, became amalgamated,[1] and the saint's day of St. Piran was moved from the 2d of May to the 5th of March. Yet although thus welded into one, nothing could well be imagined more different than the characters of the Irish and of the Cornish saint. The Irish saint lived a truly ascetic life; he preached, wrought miracles, and died. The Cornish saint was a jolly miner, not always very steady on his legs.[2] Let us hear what the Cornish have to tell of him. His name occurs in several names of places, such as Perran Zabuloe, Perran Uthno, in Perran the Little, and in Perran Arworthall. His name, pronounced Perran, or Piran, has been further corrupted into Picras, and Picrous, though some authorities suppose that this is again a different saint from St. Piran. Anyhow, both St. Perran and St. Picras live in the memory of the Cornish miner as the discoverers of tin; and the tinners' great holiday, the Thursday before Christmas, is still called Picrou's day.[3] The legend relates that St. Piran, when still in Cornwall, employed a heavy black stone as a part of his fire-place. The fire was more intense than usual, and a stream of beautiful white metal flowed out of the fire. Great was the joy of

---

[1] "Within the land of Meneke or Menegland, is a paroch chirche of S. Keveryn, otherwise Piranus."—Leland. "Piran and Keveryn were different persons." See Gough's edition of *Camden*, vol. i. p. 14.

[2] Carew, *Survey* (ed. 1602), p. 58. "From which civility, in the fruitful age of Canonization, they stepped a degree farder to holines, and helped to stuffe the Church Kalender with divers saints, either made or borne Cornish. Such was Keby, son to Solomon, prince of Cor.; such *Perrn*, who (if my author the Legend lye not) after that (like another Johannes de temporibus) he had lived two hundred yeres with perfect health, took his last rest in a Cornish parish, which there-through he endowed with his name."

[3] Hunt's *Popular Romances*, vol ii. p. 19.

the saint, and he communicated his discovery to St.
Chiwidden. They examined the stone together, and
Chiwidden, who was learned in the learning of the
East, soon devised a process for producing this metal
in large quantities. The two saints called the Cornishmen together. They told them of their treasures, and
they taught them how to dig the ore from the earth,
and how, by the agency of fire, to obtain the metal.
Great was the joy in Cornwall, and many days of feast-
ing followed the announcement. Mead and metheg-
lin, with other drinks, flowed in abundance ; and vile
rumor says the saints and their people were rendered
equally unstable thereby. "Drunk as a Perraner"
has certainly passed into a proverb from that day.

It is quite clear from these accounts that the legendary discoverer of tin in Cornwall was originally a totally different character from the Irish saint, St. Kiran.
If one might indulge in a conjecture, I should say that
there probably was in the Celtic language a root *kar*,
which in the Cymbric branch would assume the form
par. Now *cair* in Gaelic means to dig, to raise ; and
from it a substantive might be derived, meaning dig-
ger or miner. In Ireland, *Kiran* seems to have been
simply a proper name, like Smith or Baker, for there
is nothing in the legends of St. Kiran that points to
mining or smelting. In Cornwall, on the contrary,
St. Piran, before he was engrafted on St. Kiran, was
probably nothing but a personification or apotheosis of
the Miner, as much as Dorus was the personification
of the Dorians, and Brutus the first King of Britain.

The rule, "noscitur a sociis," may be applied to St.
Piran. His friend and associate, St. Chiwidden, or
St. Whitehouse, is a personification of the white-house,
i. e. the smelting-house, without which St. Piran, the

miner, would have been a very useless saint. If Chywidden, *i. e.* the smelting-house, became the St. Chywidden, why should we look in the Cornish St. Piran for anything beyond Piran, *i. e.* the miner?

However, what is of importance to us for our present object is not St. Piran, but St. Chywidden, the white-house or smelting-house. We are looking all this time for the original meaning of the Jews' houses, and the question is, how can we, starting from Chywidden, arrive at Jews'-house? I am afraid we can not do so without a jump or two; all we can do is to show that they are jumps which language herself is fond of taking, and which therefore we must not shirk, if we wish to ride straight after her.

Well, then, the first jump which language frequently takes is this, that instead of using a noun with a qualifying adjective, such as white-house, the noun by itself is used without any such qualification. This can, of course, be done with very prominent words only, words which are used so often, and which express ideas so constantly present to the mind of the speaker, that no mistake is likely to arise. In English, "the House" is used for the House of Commons; in later Latin "domus" was used for the House of God. Among fisherman in Scotland "fish" means salmon. In Greek $\lambda i\theta os$, stone, in the feminine, is used for the magnet, originally $M\alpha\gamma\nu\tilde{\eta}\tau\iota s$ $\lambda i\theta os$ while the masculine $\lambda i\theta os$ means a stone in general. In Cornwall, *ore* by itself means copper ore only, while tin ore is called black tin. In times, therefore, when the whole attention of Cornwall was absorbed by mining and smelting, and when smelting-houses were most likely the only large buildings that seemed to deserve the name of houses, there is nothing extraordinary in *tshey* or *dzhyi*, even without *widden*, white, having become the recognized name for smelting-houses.

But now comes a second jump, and again one that can be proved to have been a very favorite one with many languages. When people speaking different languages live together in the same country, they frequently, in adopting a foreign term, add to it, by way of interpretation, the word that corresponds to it in their own language. Thus *Portsmouth* is a name half Latin and half English. *Portus* was the Roman name given to the harbor. This was adopted by the Saxons, but interpreted at the same time by a Saxon word, namely, *mouth*, which really means harbor. This interpretation was hardly intentional, but arose naturally. *Port* first became a kind of proper name, and then *mouth* was added, so that "the mouth of Port," *i. e.* of the place called *Portus* by the Romans, became at last Portsmouth. But this does not satisfy the early historians, and, as happens so frequently when there is anything corrupt in language, a legend springs up almost spontaneously to remove all doubts and difficulties. Thus we read in the venerable Saxon Chronicle under the year 501, "that Port came to Britain with his two sons, Bieda and Maegla, with two ships, and their place was called Portsmouth; and they slew a British man, a very noble man."[1] Such is the growth of legends, aye, and in many cases the growth of history.

Formed on the same principle as Portsmouth we find such words as *Hayle-river*, the Cornish *hal* by itself meaning salt marsh, moor, or estuary; *Treville* or *Trou-ville*, where the Celtic *tre*, town, is explained by the French *ville*; the *Cotswold* Hills, where the Celtic word *cot*, wood, is explained by the Saxon *wold* or

[1] Saxon Chronicle, ed. Earle, p. 14, and his note, Preface, p. ix.

weald, a wood. In *Dun-bar-ton*, the Celtic word *dun*, hill, is explained by the Saxon *bar* for *byrig*, burg, *ton* being added to form the name of the town that rose up under the protection of the hill-castle. In *Penhow* the same process has been suspected; *how*, the German Höhe,[1] expressing nearly the same idea as *pen*, head. In Constantine, in Cornwall, one of the large stones with rock-basins is called the *Mên-rock*,[2] rock being simply the interpretation of the Cornish *mên*.

If, then, we suppose that in exactly the same manner the people of Cornwall spoke of *Tshey-houses*, or *Dshyi-houses*, is it so very extraordinary that this hybrid word should at last have been interpreted as *Jew-houses* or *Jews' houses?* I do not say that the history of the word can be traced through all its phases with the same certainty as that of Marazion; all I maintain is that, in explaining its history, no step has been admitted that cannot be proved by sufficient evidence to be in strict keeping with the well-known movements, or, if it is respectful to say so, the well-known antics of language.

Thus vanish the Jews from Cornwall; but there still remain the *Saracens*. One is surprised to meet with Saracens in the West of England; still more, to hear of their having worked in the tin-mines, like the Jews. According to some writers, however, Saracen is only another name for Jews, though no explanation is given why this detested name should have been applied to the Jews in Cornwall, and nowhere else. This view is held, for instance, by Carew, who writes:

---

[1] This *how*, according to Professor Earle, appears again in the *Hoe*, a high down at Plymouth, near the citadel; in *Hoxton* (Cheshire), in *Howgate*, *Howe of Fife*, and other local names. See also Halliwell, s. v. Hoes, and Hogh; Kemble's *Codex Diplomaticus*, Nos. 563, 663, 754.

[2] Hunt, vol. I. p. 187.

"The Cornish maintain these works to have been very ancient, and the first wrought by the Jews with pickaxes of holm, box, hartshorn; they prove this by the names of those places yet enduring, to wit, *Attall-Sarazin* (or, as in some editions, *Sazarin*); in English, the Jews' Offcast."

Camden (p. 69) says: "We are taught from Diodorus and Æthicus that the ancient Britons had worked hard at the mines, but the Saxons and Normans seem to have neglected them for a long time, or to have employed the labor of Arabs or Saracens, for the inhabitants call deserted shafts, *Attall-Sarazin*, i. e. the leavings of the Saracens."

Thus, then, we have not only the Saracens in Cornwall admitted as simply a matter of history, but their presence actually used in order to prove that the Saxons and Normans neglected to work the mines in the West of England.

A still more circumstantial account is given by Hals, as quoted by Gilbert in his "Parochial History of Cornwall." Here we are told that King Henry III., by proclamation, let out all Jews in his dominions at a certain rent to such as would poll and rifle them, and amongst others to his brother Richard, King of the Romans, who, after he had plundered their estates, committed their bodies, as his slaves, to labor in the tin-mines of Cornwall; the memory of whose workings is still preserved in the names of several tin works, called *Towle Sarasin*, and corruptly *Attall Saracen*; i. e. the refuse or outcast of Saracens; that is to say, of those Jews descended from Sarah and Abraham. Other works were called *Whele Etherson* (alias *Ethewon*), the Jews' Works, or Unbelievers' Works, in Cornish.

Here we see how history is made; and if our inquiries led to no other result, they would still be useful as a warning against putting implicit faith in the statements of writers who are separated by several centuries from the events they are relating. Here we have men like Carew and Camden, both highly cultivated, learned, and conscientious, and yet neither of them hesitating, in a work of historical character, to assert as a fact, what, after making every allowance, can only be called a very bold guess. Have we any reason to suppose that Herodotus and Thucydides, when speaking of the original abodes of the various races of Greece, of their migrations, their wars and final settlements, had better evidence before them, or were more cautious in using their evidence, than Camden and Carew? And is it likely that modern scholars, however learned and however careful, can ever arrive at really satisfactory results by sifting and arranging and rearranging the ethnological statements of the ancients, as to the original abodes or the later migrations of Pelasgians, Tyrrhenians, Thracians, Macedonians, and Illyrians, or even of Dorians, Æolians, and Ionians? What is Carew's evidence in support of his statement that the Jews first worked the tin-mines of Cornwall? Simply the sayings of the people in Cornwall, who support their sayings by the name given to deserted mines, *Attall Sarazin*. Now admitting that *Attall Sarazin*, or *Attall Sazarin*, meant the refuse of the Saracens, how is it possible, in cold blood, to identify the Saracens with Jews, and where is there a tittle of evidence to prove that the Jews were the first to work these mines, — mines, be it remembered, which, according to the same Carew, were certainly worked before the beginning of our era?

But leaving the Jews of the time of Nero, let us examine the more definite and more moderate statements of Hals and Gilbert. According to them, the deserted shafts are called by a Cornish name meaning the refuse of the Saracens, because, as late as the thirteenth century, the Jews were sent to work in these mines. It is difficult, no doubt, to prove a negative, and to show that no Jews ever worked in the mines of Cornwall. All that can be done, in a case like this, is to show that no one has produced an atom of evidence in support of Mr. Gilbert's opinion. The Jews were certainly ill treated, plundered, tortured, and exiled during the reign of the Plantagenet kings; but that they were sent to the Cornish mines, no contemporary writer has ever ventured to assert. The passage in Matthew Paris, to which Mr. Gilbert most likely alludes, says the very contrary of what he draws from it. Matthew Paris says that Henry III. extorted money from the Jews, and that when they petitioned for a safe conduct, in order to leave England altogether, he sold them to his brother Richard, " ut quos Rex excoriaverat, Comes evisceraret." [1] But this selling of the Jews meant no more than that, in return for money advanced him by his brother, the Earl of Cornwall, the King pawned to him, for a number of years, the taxes, legitimate or illegitimate, which could be extorted from the Jews. That this was the real meaning of the bargain between the King and his brother, the Earl of Cornwall, can be proved by the document printed in Rymer's " Fœdera," vol. i. p. 543, " De Judæis Comiti Cornubiæ assignatis, pro solutione pecuniæ sibi a Rege debitæ." [2] Anyhow, there is not a single word about

[1] Matthew Paris, *Opera*, ed. Wats, p. 902.
[2] See *Rymeri Fœdera*, A. D. 1255, tom. i. p. 543.

the Jews having been sent to Cornwall, or having had to work in the mines. On the contrary, Matthew Paris says, "*Comes pepercit iis,*" "the Earl spared them."

After thus looking in vain for any truly historical evidence in support of Jewish settlements in Cornwall, I suppose they may in future be safely treated as a "verbal myth," of which there are more indeed in different chapters of history, both ancient and modern, than is commonly supposed. As in Cornwall the name of a market has given rise to the fable of Jewish settlements, the name of another market in Finland led to the belief that there were Turks settled in that northern country. *Abo*, the ancient capital of Finland, was called *Turku*, which is the Swedish word *torg*, market. Adam of Bremen, enumerating the various tribes adjoining the Baltic, mentions *Turci* among the rest, and these *Turci* were by others mistaken for Turks.[1]

Even after such myths have been laid open to the very roots, there is a strong tendency not to drop them altogether. Thus Mr. H. Merivale is far too good an historian to admit the presence of Jews in Cornwall as far back as the destruction of Jerusalem.[2] He knows there is no evidence for it, and he would not repeat a mere fable, however plausible. Yet Marazion and the Jews' houses evidently linger in his memory, and he throws out a hint that they may find an historical explanation in the fact that under the Plantagenet kings the Jews commonly farmed or wrought the mines. Is there any contemporary evi-

[1] See Adam Bremensis' *De Situ Daniæ*, ed. Lindenbruch, p. 126; Buckle's *History of Civilization*, vol. i. p. 273.

[2] Carew, *Survey* (ed? 1602), p. 8: "and perhaps under one of those Flavians, the Jewish workmen made here their first arrival."

dence even for this? I do not think so. Dr. Borlase, indeed, in his "Natural History of Cornwall" (p. 190), says, "In the time of King John, I find the product of tin in this county very inconsiderable, the right of working for tin being as yet wholly in the King, the property of tinners precarious and unsettled, and what tin was raised was engrossed and managed by the Jews, to the great regret of the barons and their vassals." It is a pity that Dr. Borlase should not have given his authority, but there is little doubt that he simply quoted from Carew. Carew tells us how the Cornish gentlemen borrowed money from the merchants of London, giving them tin as security (p. 14); and though he does not call the merchants Jews, yet he speaks of them as usurers, and reproves their "cut throats and abominable dealing." He continues afterwards, speaking of the same usurers (p. 16), "After such time as the Jewes by their extreme dealing had worne themselves, first out of the love of the English inhabitants, and afterwards out of the land itselfe, and so left the mines unwrought, it hapned, that certaine gentlemen, being lords of seven tithings in Blackmoore, whose grounds were best stored with this minerall, grewe desirous to renew this benefit," etc. To judge from several indications, this is really the passage which Dr. Borlase had before him when writing of the Jews as engrossing and managing the tin that was raised, and in that case neither is Carew a contemporary witness, nor would it follow from what he says that one single Jew ever set foot on Cornish soil, or that any Jews ever tasted the actual bitterness of working in the mines.

Having thus disposed of the Jews, we now turn to

the Saracens in Cornwall. We shall not enter upon
the curious and complicated history of that name. It
is enough to refer to a short note in Gibbon,[1] in order
to show that Saracen was a name known to Greeks
and Romans, long before the rise of Islam, but never
applied to the Jews by any writer of authority, not
even by those who saw in the Saracens "the children
of Sarah."

What, then, it may be asked, is the origin of the
expression *Attal Sarazin* in Cornwall? *Attal*, or *Atal*,
is said to be a Cornish word, the Welsh *Adhail*, and
means refuse, waste.[2] As to *Sarazin*, it is most likely
another Cornish word, which by a metamorphic process, has been slightly changed in order to yield some
sense intelligible to Saxon speakers. We find in Cornish *tarad*, meaning a piercer, a borer; and, in another
form, *tardar* is distinctly used, together with axe and
hammer, as the name of a mining implement. The
Latin *taratrum*, Gr. τέρετρον, Fr. *tarière*, all come from
the same source. If from *tarad* we form a plural, we
get *taradion*. In modern Cornish we find that *d* sinks
down to *s*, which would give us *taras*,[3] and plural *tarasion*. Next, the final *l* of *atal* may, like several
final *l*'s in the closely allied language of Brittany, have

---

[1] Gibbon, chap. l. "The name which, used by Ptolemy and Pliny in a more confined, by Ammianus and Procopius in a larger sense, has been derived, ridiculously, from Sarah, the wife of Abraham, obscurely from the village of Saraka, more plausibly from the Arabic words, which signify a *thievish* character, or *Oriental* situation. Yet the last and most popular of these etymologies is refuted by Ptolemy, who expressly remarks the western and southern position of the Saracens, then an obscure tribe on the borders of Egypt. The appellation cannot therefore allude to any *national* character; and, since it was imported by strangers, it must be found, not in the Arabic, but in a foreign language."

[2] See R. Williams, *Lexicon Cornu-Britannicum*, s. v.

[3] "It may be given as a rule, without exception, that words ending with *t* or *d* in Welsh or Briton, do, if they exist in Cornish, turn *t* or *d* to *s*." —Norris, vol. ii. p. 207.

infected the initial *t* of *tarasion*, and changed it to *th*, which *th*, again, would, in modern Cornish, sink down to *s*.[1] Thus *atal tharasion* might have been intended for the refuse of the borings, possibly the refuse of the mines; but pronounced in Saxon fashion, it might readily have been mistaken for the Atal or refuse of the Sarasion or Saracens.

POSTSCRIPT.

The essay on the presence of Jews in Cornwall has given rise to much controversy; and as I republish it here without any important alterations, I feel it incumbent to say a few words in answer to the objections that have been brought forward against it. No one, I think, can read my essay without perceiving that what I question is not the presence of single Jews in Cornwall, but the migration of large numbers of Jews into the extreme West of Britain, whether at the time of the Phœnicians, or at the period of the destruction of Jerusalem, or under the Flavian princes, or even at a later time. The Rev. Dr. Bannister in a paper on "the Jews in Cornwall," published in the Journal of the Royal Institution of Cornwall, 1867, does indeed represent me as having maintained "that one single Jew never set foot on Cornish soil!" But if my readers will refer to the passage thus quoted from my essay by Dr. Bannister, they will see that it was not meant in that sense. In the passage thus quoted with inverted commas,[2] I simply argued that from certain words used by Carew, on which great stress had been laid, it would not even follow "that one single Jew ever set foot on Cornish soil," which surely is very different from saying that I maintained that no single Jew ever set foot on Cornish soil. It would in-

[1] "The frequent use of *th* instead of *s* shows that (in Cornish) the sound was not so definite as in English." — Norris, vol. ii. p. 224.

Another explanation of *Atal Sarasin* has been suggested by an eminent Cornish scholar: "I should explain *sarasin*," he writes, "as from *sarasin*, a Med. Lat. *stritium*, cf. *ex-sarritum*, *ex saritore* in Diez, E. W. ii. 283, s. v. *Essart*. *Atal* cannot be W. *adhail*. I would identify it with the Fr. *attelle*, splint. It occurs in O. 427, meaning 'fallow.' *Atal sarasin* I should explain as 'dug-up splinters or shingle,' and *towls (toll) sarasin* as a 'dug-up hole or excavation.'"

[2] See p. 311, l. 30.

deed be the most extraordinary fact if Cornwall had never been visited by Jews. If it were so, Cornwall would stand alone, as far as such an immunity is concerned, among all the countries of Europe. But it is one thing for Jews to be scattered about in towns,[1] or even for one or two Jews to have actually worked in tin mines, and quite another to speak of towns receiving Hebrew names in Cornwall, and of deserted tin-mines being called the workings of the Jews. To explain such startling facts, if facts they be, a kind of Jewish exodus to Cornwall had to be admitted, and was admitted as long as such names as *Marazion* and *Attal Sarazin* were accepted in their traditional meaning. My own opinion was that these names had given rise to the assumed presence of Jews in Cornwall, and not that the presence of Jews in Cornwall had given rise to these names.

If, therefore, it could be proved that some Jewish families had been settled in Cornwall in very early times, or that a few Jewish slaves had been employed as miners, my theory would not at all be affected. But I must say that the attempts at proving even so much have been far from successful. Surely the occurrence of Old Testament names among the people of Cornwall, such as Abraham, Joseph, or Solomon (there is a Solomon, Duke of Cornwall), does not prove that their bearers were Jews. Again, if we read in the time of Edward II. that "John Peverel held Hametethy of Roger le Jeu," we may be quite certain that *le Jeu* does not mean "the Jew," and that in the time of Edward II. no John Peverel held land of a Jew. Again, if in the time of Edward III. we read of one "Abraham, the tinner, who employed 300 men in the stream-works of Brodhok," it would require stronger proof than the mere name to make us believe that this Abraham was a Jew.

I had endeavored to show that there was no evidence as to the Earl of Cornwall, the brother of Henry III., having employed Jews in the Cornish mines, and had pointed out a passage from Rymer's "Fœdera" where it is stated that the Earl spared them (*pepercit*). Dr. Bannister remarks: "Though we are told that he spared them, might not this be similar to Joseph's brethren sparing him, — by committing their bodies as his slaves to work in the tin-mines?" It might be so, no doubt, but we do not know it. Again, Dr. Bannister remarks: "Jerome tells us

[1] "History of the Exchequer," London, 1711, p. 168: "Et quod nullus Judæus recepietur in aliqua Villa sine speciali licentia Regis, nisi in Villis illis in quibus Judæi manere consueverunt" (37 Henry III).

that when Titus took Jerusalem, an incredible number of Jews were sold like horses, and dispersed over the face of the whole earth. The account given by Josephus is, that of those spared after indiscriminate slaughter, some were dispersed through the provinces for the use of the theatres, as gladiators; others were sent to the Egyptian mines, and others sold as slaves. If the Romans at this time worked the Cornish mines, why may not some have been sent here?" I can only answer, as before; they may have been, no doubt, but we do not know it.

I had myself searched very carefully for any documents that might prove the presence even of single Jews in Cornwall, previous to the time when they were banished the realm by Edward I. But my inquiries had not proved more successful than those of my predecessors. Pearce, in his "Laws and Customs of the Stanaries," published in London, 1725, shares the common belief that the Jews worked in the Cornish mines. "The tinners," he says (p. ii), "call the antient works by the name of the Working of the Jews, and it is most manifest, that there were Jews inhabiting here until 1291; and this they prove by the names yet enduring, viz. Attall Sarazin, in English, The Jews Feast." But in spite of his strong belief in the presence of Jews in Cornwall, Pearce adds: "But whether they had liberty to work and search for tin, does not appear, because they had their dwellings chiefly in great Towns and Cities; and being great Usurers, were in that year banished out of England, to the number of 15,060, by the most noble Prince, Edward I."

At last, however, with the kind assistance of Mr. Macray, I discovered a few real Jews in Cornwall in the third year of King John, 1202, namely, one *Simon de Dena*, one *Deulone, the son of Samuel*, and one *Aaron*. Some of their monetary transactions are recorded in the "Rotulus Cancellarii vel Antigraphum Magni Rotuli Pipæ de tertio anno Regni Regis Johannis" (printed under the direction of the Commissioners of the Public Records in 1863, p. 96), and we have here not only their names as evidence of their Jewish origin, but they are actually spoken of as "*praedictus Judæus*." Their transactions, however, are purely financial, and do not lead us to suppose that the Jews, in order to make tin, condescended, in the time of King John or at any other time, to the drudgery of working in tin-mines.

July, 1867.

XV.

THE INSULATION OF ST. MICHAEL'S MOUNT.[1]

St. Michael's Mount in Cornwall is so well known to most people, either from sight or from report, that a description of its peculiar features may be deemed almost superfluous; but in order to start fair, I shall quote a short account from the pen of an eminent geologist, Mr. Pengelly, to whom I shall have to refer frequently in the course of this paper.

"St. Michael's Mount in Cornwall," he says, "is an island at very high water, and, with rare exceptions, a peninsula at very low water. The distance from Marazion Cliff, the nearest point of the mainland, to spring-tide high-water mark on its own strand, is about 1680 feet. The total isthmus consists of the outcrop of highly inclined Devonian slate and associated rocks, and in most cases is covered with a thin layer of gravel or sand. At spring-tides, in still weather, it is at high-water about twelve feet below, and at low-water six feet above, the sea level. In fine weather it is dry from four to five hours every tide; but occasionally, during very stormy weather and neap tides, it is impossible to cross from the mainland for two or three days together.

[1] Read before the Ashmolean Society, Oxford, November 25, 1867.

"The Mount is an outlier of granite, measuring at its base about five furlongs in circumference, and rising to the height of one hundred and ninety-five feet above mean tide. At high-water it plunges abruptly into the sea, except on the north or landward side, where the granite comes into contact with slate. Here there is a small plain occupied by a village. . . . The country immediately behind or north of the town of Marazion consists of Devonian strata, traversed by traps and elvans, and attains a considerable elevation."

At the meeting of the British Association in 1865, Mr. Pengelly, in a paper on "The Insulation of St. Michael's Mount in Cornwall," maintained that the change which converted that Mount from a promontory into an island must have taken place, not only within the human period, but since Cornwall was occupied by a people speaking the Cornish language. As a proof of this somewhat startling assertion, he adduced the ancient British name of St. Michael's Mount, signifying *the Hoar rock in the wood*. Nobody would think of applying such a name to the Mount in its present state; and as we know that during the last two thousand years the Mount has been, as it is now, an island at high, and a promontory at low tide, it would indeed seem to follow that its name must have been framed before the destruction of the ancient forest by which it was once surrounded, and before the separation of the Mount from the mainland.

Sir Henry James, in a "Note on the Block of Tin dredged in Falmouth Harbor," asserts, it is true, that there are trees growing on the Mount in sufficient numbers to have justified the ancient descriptive name of "the Hoar rock in the wood;" but though there are traces of trees visible on the engravings published a hundred years ago, in Dr. Borlase's "Antiquities of Cornwall," these are most likely due to artistic embellishment only. At present no writer will discover in St. Michael's Mount what could fairly be called either trees or a wood, even in Cornwall.

That the geographical change from a promontory into a real island did not take place during the last two thousand years, is proved by the description which Diodorus Siculus, a little before the Christian era, gives of St. Michael's Mount. "The inhabitants of the promontory of Belerium," he says (lib. v. c. 22), " were hospitable, and, on account of their intercourse with strangers, eminently civilized in their habits. These are the people who work the tin, which they melt into the form of astragali, and then carry it to an island in front of Britain, called *Ictis*. This island is left dry at low tide, and they then transport the tin in carts from the shore. Here the traders buy it from the natives, and carry it to Gaul, over which it travels on horseback in about thirty days to the mouths of the Rhone." That the Island of Ictis, described by Diodorus, is St. Michael's Mount, seems, to say the least, very probable, and was at last admitted even by the late Sir G. C. Lewis. In fact, the description which Diodorus gives answers so completely to what St. Michael's Mount is at the present day, that few would deny that if the Mount ever was a " Hoar rock in the wood," it must have been so before the time of which Diodorus speaks, that is, at least before the last two thousand years. The nine apparent reasons why St. Michael's Mount cannot be the Ictis of Diodorus, and their refutation, may be seen in Mr. Pengelly's paper " On the Insulation of St. Michael's Mount," p. 6, seq.

Mr. Pengelly proceeded to show that the geological

change which converted the promontory into an island may be due to two causes. First, it may have taken place in consequence of the encroachment of the sea. This would demand a belief that at least 20,000 years ago Cornwall was inhabited by men who spoke Cornish. Secondly, this change may have taken place by a general subsidence of the land, and this is the opinion adopted by Mr. Pengelly. No exact date was assigned to this subsidence, but Mr. Pengelly finished by expressing his decided opinion that, subsequent to a period when Cornwall was inhabited by a race speaking a Celtic language, St. Michael's Mount was "a hoar rock in the wood," and has since become insulated by powerful geological changes.

In a more recent paper read at the Royal Institution (April 5, 1867), Mr. Pengelly has somewhat modified his opinion. Taking for granted that at some time or other St. Michael's Mount was a peninsula and not yet an island, he calculates that it must have taken 16,800 years before the coast line could have receded from the Mount to the present cliffs. He arrived at this result by taking the retrocession of the cliffs at ten feet in a century, the distance between the Mount and the mainland being at present 1,680 feet.

If, however, the severance of the Mount from the mainland was the result, not of retrocession, but of the subsidence of the country, — a rival theory which Mr. Pengelly still admits as possible, — the former calculation would fail, and the only means of fixing the date of this severance would be supplied by the remains found in the forests that were carried down by that subsidence, and which are supposed to belong to the mammoth era. This mammoth era, we are told, is anterior to the lake-dwellings of Switzerland, and the kitchenmiddens of Denmark, for in neither of these have any remains of the mammoth been discovered. The mammoth, in fact, did not outlive the age of bronze, and before the end of that age, therefore, St. Michael's Mount must be supposed to have become an island.

In all these discussions it is taken for granted that St. Michael's Mount was at one time unquestionably a "hoar rock in the wood," and that the land between the Mount and the mainland was once covered by a forest which extended along the whole of the seaboard. That there are submerged forests along that seaboard is attested by sufficient geological evidence; but I have not been able to discover any proof of the unbroken continuity of that shore-forest, still less of the presence of vegetable remains in the exact locality which is of interest to us, namely between the Mount and the mainland. It is true that Dr. Borlase discovered the remains of trunks of trees on the 10th of January, 1757; but he tells us that these forest trees were not found round the Mount, but midway betwixt the piers of St. Michael's Mount and Penzance, that is to say, about one mile distant from the Mount; also, that one of them was a willow-tree with the bark on it, another a hazel-branch with the bark still fat and glossy. The place where these trees were found was three hundred yards below full-sea mark, where the water is twelve feet deep when the tide is in.

Carew, also, at an earlier date, speaks of roots of mighty trees found in the sand about the Mount, but without giving the exact place. Lelant (1533–40) knows of "Spere Heddes, Axis for Warre, and Swerdes of Copper wrapped up in lynist, scant perishid," that had been found of late years near the

THE INSULATION OF ST. MICHAEL'S MOUNT.

Mount, in St. Hilary's parish, in tin works; but he places the land that had been devoured of the sea between Penzance and Mousehole, i. e. more than two miles distant from the Mount.

The value of this kind of geological evidence must of course be determined by geologists. It is quite possible that the remains of trunks of trees may still be found on the very isthmus between the Mount and the mainland; but it is, to say the least, curious that, even in the absence of such stringent evidence, geologists should feel so confident that the Mount once stood on the mainland, and that exactly the same persuasion should have been shared by people long before the name of geology was known. There is a powerful spell in popular traditions, against which even men of science are not always proof, and is just possible that if the tradition of the "hoar rock in the wood" had not existed, no attempts would have been made to explain the causes that severed St. Michael's Mount from the mainland. But even then the question remains, How was it that people quite guiltless of geology should have framed the popular name of the Mount, and the popular tradition of its former connection with the mainland? Leaving, therefore, for the present all geological evidence out of view, it will be an interesting inquiry to find out, if possible, how people that could not have been swayed by any geological theories, should have been led to believe in the gradual insulation of St. Michael's Mount.

The principal argument brought forward by non-geological writers in support of the former existence of a forest surrounding the Mount, is the Cornish name of St. Michael's Mount, *Cara clowse in cowse*, which in Cornish is said to mean "the hoar rock in the wood."

In his paper read before the British Association at Manchester, Mr. Pengelly adduced that very name as irrefragable evidence that Cornish, *i. e.* a Celtic language, an Aryan language, was spoken in the extreme west of Europe about 20,000 years ago. In his more recent paper Mr. Pengelly has given up this position, and he considers it improbable that any philologer could now give a trustworthy translation of a language spoken 20,000 years ago. This may be or not; but before we build any hypothesis on that Cornish name, the first question which an historian has to answer is clearly this : —

What authority is there for that name? Where does it occur for the first time? and does it really mean what it is supposed to mean?

Now the first mention of the Cornish name, as far as I am aware, occurs in Richard Carew's "Survey of Cornwall," which was published in 1602. It is true that Camden's "Britannia" appeared earlier, in 1586, and that Camden (p. 72), too, mentions "the Mons Michaelis, *Dinsol* olim, ut in libro Laudavensi habetur, incolis *Careg Cowse*,[1] i. e. rupis cana." But it will be seen that he leaves out the most important part of the old name, nor can there be much doubt that Camden received his information about Cornwall direct from Carew, before Carew's "Survey of Cornwall" was published.

After speaking of "the countrie of Lionesse which the sea hath ravined from Cornwall betweene the lands end and the Isles of Scilley," Carew continues (p. 3), "Moreover, the ancient name of Saint Michael's Mount was *Cara-clowse in Cowse*, in Eng-

[1] In Gough's edition of Camden the name is given "Careg cowse in clowse, i. e. the heavy rock in the wood."

lish, The hoare Rocke in the Wood; which now is at everie floud incompassed by the Sea, and yet at some low ebbes, rootes of mightie trees are discryed in the sands about it. The like overflowing hath happened in Plymmouth Haven, and divers other places." Now while in this place Carew gives the name *Cara-clowse in Cowse*, it is very important to remark that on page 154, he speaks of it again as " *Cara Cowz in Clowze*, that is, the hoare rock in the wood."

The original Cornish name, whether it was *Cara clowse in Cowse*, or *Cara Cowz in Clowze*, cannot be traced back beyond the end of the sixteenth century, for the Cornish Pilchard song in which the name likewise occurs is much more recent, at least in that form in which we possess it. The tradition, however, that St. Michael's Mount stood in a forest, and even the Saxon designation, " the Hoar rock in the wood," can be followed up to an earlier date.

At least one hundred and twenty-five years before Carew's time, William of Worcester, though not mentioning the Cornish name, not only gives the Mount the name of " hoar rock of the wood," but states distinctly that St. Michael's Mount was formerly six miles distant from the sea, and surrounded by a dense forest: " PREDICTUS LOCUS OPACISSIMA PRIMO CLAUDEBATUR SYLVA, AB OCEANO MILIARIBUS DISTANS SEX." As William of Worcester never mentions the Cornish name, it is not likely that his statement should merely be derived from the supposed meaning of *Cara Cowz in Clowze*, and it is but fair to admit that he may have drawn from a safer source of information. We must therefore inquire more closely into the credibility of this important witness. He is an important witness, for, if it were not for him, I believe we should never

have heard of the insulation of St. Michael's Mount
at all. The passage in question occurs in William of
Worcester's Itinerary, the original MS. of which is
preserved in Corpus Christi College at Cambridge. It
was printed at Cambridge by James Nasmith, in the
year 1778, from the original MS., but, as it would
seem, without much care. William Botoner, or, as he
is commonly called, William of Worcester, was born
at Bristol in 1415, and educated at Oxford about 1434.
He was a member of the *Aula Cervina*, which at that
time belonged to Balliol College. His "Itinerarium"
is dated 1478. It hardly deserves the grand title
which it bears, "Itinerarium, sive liber memorabilium
Will. W. in viagio de Bristol usque ad montem St.
Michaelis." It is not a book of travels in our sense of
the word, and it was hardly destined for the public in
the form in which we possess it. It is simply a note-
book in which William entered anything that interested him during his journey; and it contains not only
his own observations, but all sorts of extracts, copies,
notices, thrown together without any connecting
thread. He hardly tells us that he has arrived at St.
Michael's Mount before he begins to copy a notice
which he found posted up in the church. This notice
informed all comers that Pope Gregory had remitted a
third of their penances to all who should visit this church
and give to it benefactions and alms. It can be fully
proved that this notice, which was intended to attract
pilgrims and visitors, repeats *ipsissimis verbis* the charter of Leofric, Bishop of Exeter, who exempted the
church and convent from all episcopal jurisdiction.
This was in the year 1088, when St. Michael's Mount
was handed over by Robert, Earl of Mortain, half-
brother of William the Conqueror, to the Abbey of St.

Michel in Normandy. This charter may be seen in Dr. Oliver's " Monasticon Diocesis Exoniensis," 1846. The passage copied by William of Worcester from a notice in the church of St. Michael's Mount occurs at the end of the original charter: "*Et omnibus illis qui illam ecclesiam suis cum beneficiis elemosinis expetierint et visitaverint, tertiam partem penitentiarum condonamus.*"

Though it is not quite correct to say that this condonation was granted by Pope Gregory, yet it is perfectly true that it was granted by the Bishop of Exeter at the command and exhortation of the Pope, "*Jussione et exhortatione domini reverentissimi Gregorii.*" The date also given by William, 1070, cannot be correct, for Gregory occupied the papal throne from 1073–86. It was Gregory VII., not Gregory VI., as printed by Dr. Oliver.

Immediately after this memorandum in William's diary we meet with certain notes on the apparitions of St. Michael. He does not say from what source he takes his information on the subject, but we may suppose that he either repeated what he heard from the monks in conversation, or that he copied from some MS. in their library. In either case it is startling to read that there was an apparition of the Archangel St. Michael in Mount *Tumba*, formerly called *the Horerock in the wodd*. St. Michael seems indeed to have paid frequent visits to his worshippers, if we may trust the "Chronicon apparitionum et gestorum S. Michaelis Archangeli," published by Mich. Naveus, in 1632. Yet his visits were not made at random, and even Naveus finds it difficult to substantiate any apparition of St. Michael so far north as Cornwall, except by invectives against the *impudenta et ignorantia* of Protestant heretics who dared to doubt such occurrences.

But this short sentence of William contains one word which is of great importance for our purposes. He says that "the Hore-rock in the wodd" was formerly called *Tumba*. Is there any evidence of this?

The name *Tumba*, as far as we know, belonged originally to Mont St. Michel in Normandy. There a famous and far better authenticated apparition of St. Michael is related to have taken place in the year 708, which led to the building of a church and monastery by Autbert, Bishop of Avranches. The church was built in close imitation of the Church of St. Michael in Mount Garganus in Apulia, which had been founded as early as 493.[1] If, therefore, William of Worcester relates an apparition of St. Michael in Cornwall at about the same date, in 710, it is clear that Mont St. Michel in Normandy has here been confounded by him with St. Michael's Mount in Cornwall. In order to explain this strange confusion, and the consequences which it entailed, it will be necessary to bear in mind the peculiar relations which existed between the two ecclesiastical establishments, perched the one on the island rock of St. Michel in Normandy, the other on St. Michael's Mount in Cornwall. In physical structure there is a curious resemblance between the two mounts. Both are granite islands, and both so near the coast that at low water a dry passage is open to them from the mainland. The Mount on the Norman coast is larger and more distant from the coast than St. Michael's Mount, yet for all that their general likeness is very striking. Now Mont St. Michel was called *Tumba* at least as far back as the tenth century. Mabillon, in his "Annales Benedictini" (vol. ii. p. 18), quotes from an ancient author the following explana-

[1] *Baronii Annales*, anno 493.

tion of the name. "Now this place, to use the words of an ancient author, is called *Tumba* by the inhabitants, because, emerging as it were from the sands like a hill, it rises up by the space of two hundred cubits, everywhere surrounded by the ocean; it is six miles distant from the shore, between the mouths of the rivers Segia and Senuna, six miles distant from Avranches, looking westward, and dividing Avranches from Brittany. Here the sea by its recess allows twice a passage to the pious people who proceed to the threshold of St. Michael the Archangel." "Hic igitur locus, ut verbis antiqui autoris utar, *Tumba* vocitatur ab incolis, ideo quod in morem tumuli, quasi ab arenis emergens, ad altum SPATIO DUCENTORUM CUBITORUM porrigitur, OCEANO UNDIQUE CINCTUS, SEX MILLIBUS AB ÆSTU OCEANI, inter ostia situs, ubi immergunt se mari flumina Segia (Sée) et Senuna (Selure), ab Abrincatensi urbe (Avranches) sex distans millibus; oceanum prospectans, Abrincatensem pagum dirimit a Britannia. Illic mare suo recessu devotis populis desideratum bis præbet iter petentibus limina beati Michaelis archangeli."

This fixes *Tumba* as the name of Mont St. Michel before the tenth century, for the ancient author from whom Mabillon quotes wrote before the middle of the tenth century, and before Duke Richard had replaced the priests of St. Michel by Benedictine monks. *Tumba* remained, in fact, the recognized name of the Norman Mount, and has survived to the present day. The church and monastery there were called "*in monte Tumba*," or "*ad duas Tumbas*," there being in reality two islands, the principal one called *Tumba*, the smaller *Tumbella* or *Tumbellana*. This name of *Tumbellana* was afterwards changed into *tumba Helenæ*, giving rise to various legends about Elaine, one of the heroines of the Arthurian cycle; nay, the name was cited by learned antiquarians as a proof of the ancient worship of Belus in these northern latitudes.

The history of Mont St. Michel in Normandy is well authenticated, particularly during the period which is of importance to us. Mabillon, quoting from the chronicler who wrote before the middle of the tenth century, relates how Autbert, the Bishop of Avranches, had a vision, and after having been thrice admonished by St. Michael, proceeded to build on the summit of the Mount a church under the patronage of the Archangel. This was in 708, or possibly a few years earlier, if Pagius is right in fixing the dedication of the temple in 707.[1] Mabillon points out that this chronicler says nothing as yet of the miracles related by later writers, particularly of the famous hole in the Bishop's skull, which it was believed St. Michael had made when on exhorting him the third time to build his church, he gently touched him with his archangelic finger. In doing this the finger went through the skull, and left a hole. The perforated skull did not interfere with the Bishop's health, and it was shown after his death as a valuable relic. The new church was dedicated by Autbert himself, and the day of the dedication (xvii. Kalend. Novemb.) was celebrated, not only in France, but also in England, as is shown by a decree of the Synod held at Oxford in 1222. The further history of the church and monastery of St. Michel may be read with all its minute details in Mabillon, or in the "Neustria Pia" (p. 371), or in the "Gallia Christiana" (vol. ix. p.

[1] *Baronii Annales*, anno 709.

517 E, 870 A). What is of interest to us is that soon after the Conquest, when the ecclesiastical property of England had fallen into the hands of her Norman conquerors, Robert, Earl of Mortain and Cornwall, the half-brother of William the Conqueror, endowed the Norman with the Cornish Mount. A priory of Benedictine monks had existed on the Cornish Mount for some time, and had been richly endowed in 1044 by Edward the Confessor. Nay, if we may trust the charter of Edward the Confessor, it would seem that, even at that time, the Cornish Mount and its priory had been granted by him to the Norman Abbey, for the charter is witnessed by Norman bishops, and its original is preserved in the Abbey of Mont St. Michel. In that case William the Conqueror or his half-brother Robert would only have restored the Cornish priory to its rightful owners, the monks of Mont St. Michel, who had well deserved the gratitude of the Conqueror by supplying him after the Conquest with six ships and a number of monks, destined to assist in the restoration of ecclesiastical discipline in England. After that time the Cornish priory shared the fate of other so-called alien priories or cells. The prior was bound to visit in person or by proxy the mother-house every year, and to pay sixteen marks of silver as an acknowledgment of dependence. Whenever a war broke out between England and France, the foreign priories were seized, though some, and among them the priory of St. Michael's Mount obtained in time a distinct corporate character, and during the reigns of Henry IV. and Henry V. were exempted from seizure during war.

Under these circumstances we can well understand how in the minds of the monks, who spent their lives partly in the mother-house, partly in its dependencies, there was no very clear perception of any difference between the founders, benefactors, and patrons of these twin establishments. A monk brought up at Mont St. Michel would repeat as an old man the legends he had heard about St. Michel and Bishop Aubert, even though he was ending his days in the priory of the Cornish Mount. Relics and books would likewise travel from one place to the other, and a charter originally belonging to the one might afterwards form part of the archives of another house.

After these preliminary remarks, let us look again at the memoranda which William of Worcester made at St. Michael's Mount, and it will appear that what we anticipated has actually happened, and that a book originally belonging to Mont St. Michel in Normandy, and containing the early history of that monastery, was transferred (either in the original or in a copy) to Cornwall, and there used by William of Worcester in the belief that it contained the early history of the Cornish Mount and the Cornish priory.

The Memorandum of William of Worcester runs thus: "Apparicio Sancti Michaelis in monte Tumba, antea vocata le Hore-rok in the wodd; et fuerunt tam boscus quam prata et terra arabilis inter dictum montem et insulas Syllyo, et fuerunt 140 ecclesiæ parochiales inter istum montem et Sylly submersæ.

"Prima apparicio Sancti Michaelis in monte Gorgon in regno Apuliæ fuit anno Christi 391. Secunda apparicio fuit circa annum domini 710 in . Tumba in Cornubia juxta mare.

"Tertia apparicio Romæ fuit; tempore Gregorii papæ legitur accidisse: nam tempore magnæ pestilenciæ, etc.

"Quarta apparicio fuit in ierarchiis nostrorum angelorum.

"Spacium loci montis Sancti Michaelis est DUCENTORUM CUBITORUM UNDIQUE OCEANO CINCTUM, et religiosi monachi dicti loci. Abrincensis antistes Aubertus nomine, ut in honore Sancti Michaelis construeret . . . . predictus LOCUS OPACISSIMA PRIMO CLAUDEBATUR SYLVA, AB OCEANO MILIARIBUS DISTANS SEX, aptissimam præbens latebram ferarum, in quo loco olim comperimus MONACHOS domino servientes."

The text is somewhat corrupt and fragmentary, but may be translated as follows:—

"The apparition of St. Michael in the Mount Tumba, formerly called the Hore-rock in the wodd; and there were a forest and meadows and arable land between the said mount and the Syllye Isles, and there were 140 parochial churches swallowed by the sea between that mount and Sylly.

"The first apparition of St. Michael in Mount Gorgon in the Kingdom of Apulia was in the year 891. The second apparition was about the year 710, in Tumba in Cornwall by the sea.

"The third apparition is said to have happened at Rome in the time of Pope Gregory: for at the time of the great pestilence, etc.

"The fourth apparition was in the hierarchies of our angels.

"The space of St. Michael's Mount is 200 cubits; it is everywhere surrounded by the sea, and there are religious monks of that place. The head of Abrinca, Aubertus by name, that he might erect a church[1] in

---

[1] I have added *church*, for Mr. Munro, who kindly collated this passage for me, informs me that the C. C. C. MS. gives distinctly *alem* where the editor has left a lacuna.

honor of St. Michael. The aforesaid place was at first enclosed by a very dense forest, six miles distant from the ocean, furnishing a good retreat for wild animals. In which place we heard that formerly monks serving the Lord," etc.

The only way to explain this jumble is to suppose that William of Worcester made these entries in his diary while walking up and down in the Church of St. Michael's Mount, and listening to one of the monks, reading to him from a MS. which had been brought from Normandy, and referred in reality to the early history of the Norman, but not of the Cornish Mount. The first line, "Apparicio Sancti Michaelis in monte Tumba," was probably the title or the heading of the MS. Then William himself added, "antea vocata le Hore-rok in the wodd," a name which he evidently heard on the spot, and which no doubt conveyed to him the impression that the rock had formerly stood in the midst of a wood. For instead of continuing his account of the apparitions of St. Michael, he quotes a tradition in support of the former existence of a forest surrounding the Mount. Only, strange to say, instead of producing the evidence which he produced afterwards in confirmation of St. Michael's Mount having been surrounded by a dense forest, he here gives the tradition about Lionesse, the sunken land between the Land's End and the Scylly Isles. This is evidently a mistake, for no other writer ever supposed the sunken land of Lionesse to have reached as far as St. Michael's Mount.

Then follows the entry about the four apparitions of St. Michael. Here we must read *in monte Gargano*" instead of " *in monte Gorgon*." Opinions vary as to the exact date of the apparition in Mount Gar-

ganus in the South of Italy, but 391 is certainly far too
early, and has to be changed into 491 or 493. In the
second apparition, all is right, if we leave out " in
Cornubia juxta mare," which was added either by
William or by the monk who was showing him the
book. It refers to the well-known apparition of St.
Michael at Avranches. The third and fourth apparitions are of no consequence to us.

As we read on, we come next to William's own
measurements, fixing the extent of St. Michael's Mount
at two hundred cubits. After that we are met by a
passage which, though it hardly construes, can be
understood in one sense only, namely, as giving an
account of the Abbey of St. Michel in Normandy. I
suppose it is not too bold if I recognize in *Aubertus
Autbertus*, and in *Abrincensis antistes*, the *Abrinca-
tensis episcopus* or *antistes*, the Bishop of Avranches.

Now it is well known that the Mont St. Michel in
Normandy was believed to have been originally surrounded by forests and meadows. Du Moustier in the
" Neustria Pia" relates (p. 371), " Hæc rupes anti-
quitus Mons erat cinctus sylvis et saltibus," " This rock
was of old a mount surrounded by forests and meadows." But this is not all. In the old chronicle of Mont
St. Michel, quoted by Mabillon, which was written before the middle of the tenth century, the same account
is given; and if we compare that account with the
words used by William of Worcester, we can no longer
doubt that the old chronicle, or, it may be, a copy of
it, had been brought from France to England, and that
what was intended for a description of the Norman
abbey and its neighborhood was taken, intentionally or
unintentionally, as a description of the Cornish Mount.
These are the words of the Norman chronicler, as

quoted by Mabillon, compared with the passage in William of Worcester: —

Mont St. Michel.	*St. Michael's Mount.*
"Addit idem auctor hunc locum OPACISSIMA OLIM SILVA CLAUSUM fuisse, et MONACHOS IBIDEM INHABITASSE duasque ad suum usque tempus extitisse ecclesias quas illi scilicet monachi incolebant."	"Prædictus LOCUS OPACISSIMA OLIM CLAUDERATUR sylva ab oceano miliaribus distans sex, aptissimam præbens latebram ferarum, in quo loco olim comperimus MONACHOS DOMINO SERVIENTES."

"The same author adds that this place was formerly inclosed by a very dense forest, and that monks dwelt there, and that two churches existed there up to his own time, which those monks inhabited."

The words CLAUSUM OPACISSIMA SILVA are decisive. The phrase AB OCEANO MILIARIBUS DISTANS SEX, too, is taken from an earlier passage of the same author, quoted above, which passage may likewise have supplied the identical phrases OCEANO UNDIQUE CINCTUS, and the SPATIUM DUCENTORUM CUBITORUM, which are hardly applicable to St. Michael's Mount. The "two churches *still* existing in Mont St. Michel," had to be left out, for there was no trace of them in St. Michael's Mount. But the monks who lived in them were retained, and to give a little more life, the wild beasts were added. Even the expression of *antistes* instead of *episcopus* occurs in the original, where we read, "Hæc loci facies erat ante sancti Michaelis apparitionem hoc anno factam religiosissimo Autberto Abrincatensi episcopo, admonentis se velle ut sibi in ejus montis vertice ecclesia sub ipsius patrocinio erigeretur. Hærenti ANTISTITI tertio idem intimatum," etc.

Thus vanishes the testimony of William of Worcester, so often quoted by Cornish antiquarians, as to the dense forest by which St. Michael's Mount in Cornwall was once surrounded, and all the evidence that remains to substantiate the former presence of trees on and around the Cornish Mount is reduced to the name "the Hoar rock in the wood," given by William, and the Cornish names of *Cara clowse in Cowse* or *Cara Cowz in Clowze*, given by Carew. How much or how little dependence can be placed on old Cornish names of places and their supposed meaning has been shown before in the case of Marazion. Carew certainly did not understand Cornish, nor did the people with whom he had intercourse; and there is no doubt that he wrote down the Cornish names as best he could, and without any attempt at deciphering their meaning. He was told that " Cara clowse in Cowse " meant the " Hoar rock in the Wood," and he had no reason to doubt it. Even a very small knowledge of Cornish would have enabled Carew or anybody else at his time to find out that *cowz* might be meant for the Cornish word for wood, and that *careg* was rock. *Clowse* too might easily be taken in the sense of gray, as gray in Cornish was *glos*. Then why should we hesitate to accept *Cara clowse in cowse* as the ancient Cornish name of the Mount, and why object to Mr. Pengelly's argument that it must have been given at a time when the Mount was surrounded by a very dense forest, and that *a fortiori* at that distant period Cornish must have been the spoken language of Cornwall?

The first objection is that the old word for " wood " in Cornish was *cuit* with a final *t*, and that the change of a final *t* into *z* is a phonetic corruption which takes place only in the later stage of the Cornish language. The ancient Cornish *cuit*, " wood," occurs in Welsh as *coed*, in Armorican as *koat* and *koad*, and is supposed to exist in Cornish names of places, such as *Penquite*,

Kilquite, etc. *Cowz*, therefore, could not have occurred in a Cornish name supposed to have been formed at least 2,000 if not 20,000 years ago.

This thrust might, no doubt, be parried by saying that the name of the Mount would naturally change with the general changes of the Cornish language. Yet this is not always the case with proper names, as may be seen by the names just quoted, *Penquite* and *Kilquite*. At all events, we begin to see how uncertain is the ground on which we stand.

If we take the facts, scanty and uncertain as they are, we may admit that, at the time of William of Worcester, the Mount had most likely a Latin, a Cornish, and a Saxon appellation. It is curious that William should say nothing of a Cornish name, but only quote the Saxon one. However, this Saxon name, "the Hoar rock in the Wood" sounds decidedly like a translation, and is far too long and cumbrous for a current name. *Michelstow* is mentioned by others as the Saxon name of the Mount (Naveus, p. 233). The Latin name given to the Mount, but only after it had become a dependency of Mont St. Michel in Normandy, was, as we saw from William of Worcester's diary, *Mons Tumba* or *Mons Tumba in Cornubia*, and after his time the name of *St. Michael in Tumbâ* or in *Monte Tumbâ* is certainly used promiscuously for the Cornish and Norman mounts.[1] Now *tumba*, after

---

[1] Thomas Crammer sends a dispensation, in 1537, to the Rev. John Arscott, archpresbyter of the ecclesia St. Michaelis in Monte Tumba Exoniensis diocesis. (*Monasticon Dioc. Exon.* p. 30:) Dr. Oliver remarks, "It may be worth while to observe, that when St. Michael "in procella," or "in periculo maris," is named in the old records, the foreign house is meant. But St. Michael "in Tumbâ," or "Monte Tumbâ," is a name occasionally applied to both houses." It would have been interesting to determine the exact date when this latter name is for the first time applied to the Cornish Mount.

meaning hillock, became the recognized name for tomb, and the mediæval Latin *tumba*, too, was always understood in that sense. If, therefore, the name " Mons in tumba " had to be rendered in Cornish for the benefit of the Cornish-speaking monks of the Benedictine priory, *tumba* would actually be taken in the sense of tomb. One form of the Cornish name, as preserved by Carew, is *Cara cowz in clowze;* and this, if interpreted without any preconceived opinion, would mean in Cornish " the old rock of the tomb." *Cara* stands for *carak*, a rock. *Cowz* is meant for *coz*, the modern Cornish and Armorican form corresponding to the ancient Cornish *coth*, old.[1] *Clowze* is a modern and somewhat corrupt form in Cornish, corresponding to the Welsh *clawdh*, a tomb. *Cladh-va*, in Cornish, means a burying-place; and *cluddu*, to bury, has been preserved as a Cornish verb, corresponding to the Welsh *cladhu*. In Gaelic, too, *cladh* is a tomb or burying-place; and in Armorican, which generally follows the same phonetic changes as the Cornish, we actually find *kleuz* and *klôz* for tomb or inclosure. (See Le Gonidec, " Dict. Breton-Français," s. v.) The *en* might either be the Cornish preposition *yn*, or it may have been intended for the article in the genitive, *an*. The old rock in the tomb, i. e. *in tumbâ*, or the old rock of the tomb, Cornish *carag goz an cloz*, would be intelligible and natural renderings of the Latin *Mons in tumba*.

But though this would fully account for the origin of the Cornish name as preserved by Carew, it would still leave the Saxon appellation the " Hore rock in the wodd " unexplained. How could William of Worces-

[1] *Passion*, ed. W. S. p. 95. Coth, Bret. kôz = O. Celtic cottæ (Atecotti "perantiqui").

ter have got hold of this name? Let us remember that William does not mention any Cornish name of the Mount, and that nothing is ever said at his time of the "Hore rock in the wodd" being a translation of an old Cornish name. All we know is that the monks of the Mount used that name, and it is hardly likely that so long and cumbrous a name should ever have been used much by the people in the neighborhood. How the monks of St. Michael's Mount came to call their place the "Hore rock in the wodd" at the time of William of Worcester, and probably long before his time, is, however, not difficult to explain, after we have seen how they transferred the traditions which originally referred to Mont St. Michel to their own monastery. Having told the story of the "*sylva opacissima*" by which their mount was formerly surrounded to many visitors, as they told it to William of Worcester, the name of the "Hore rock in the wodd" might easily spring up among them, and be kept up within the walls of their priory. Nor is there any evidence that in this peculiar form the name ever spread beyond their walls. But it is possible that here, too, language may have played some tricks. The number of people who used these names and kept them alive can never have been large, and hence they were exposed much more to accidents arising from ignorance and individual caprice than names of villages or towns which are in the keeping of hundreds and thousands of people. The monks of St. Michael's Mount may in time have forgotten the exact purport of "Carn cowz in clowze," "the old rock of the tomb," really the "Mons in tumba;" and their minds being full of the old forest by which they believed *their* island, like Mont St. Michel, to have been formerly surrounded, what wonder if *cara cowz in clowze* glided away into *cara clowse in cowze*, and thus came to confirm the old tradition of the forest. For *cowz* would at once be taken as the modern Cornish word for wood, corresponding to the old Cornish *cuit*, while *clowse* might, with a little effort, be identified with the Cornish *glos*, gray, the Armorican *glâz*. Carew, it should be observed, sanctions both forms, the original one, *cara cowz in clowze*, "the old rock of the tomb," and the other *cara clowse in cowze*, meaning possibly "the gray rock in the wood." The sound of the two is so like that, particularly to the people not very familiar with the language, the substitution of one for the other would come very naturally; and as a reason could more easily be given for the latter than for the former name, we need not be surprised if in the few passages where the name occurs *after Carew's* time, the secondary name, apparently confirming the monkish legend of the dense forest that once surrounded St. Michael's Mount, should have been selected in preference to the former, which, but to a scholar and an antiquarian, sounded vague and meaningless.

If my object had been to establish any new historical fact, or to support any novel theory, I should not have indulged so freely in what to a certain extent may be called mere conjecture. But my object was only to point out the uncertainty of the evidence which Mr. Pengelly has adduced in support of a theory which would completely revolutionize our received views as to the early history of language and the migrations of the Aryan race. At first sight the argument used by Mr. Pengelly seems unanswerable. Here is St. Michael's Mount, which, according to geological evidence, may formerly have been part

of the mainland. Here is an old Cornish name for
St. Michael's Mount, which means "the gray rock in
the wood." Such a name, it might well be argued,
could not have been given to the island after it had
ceased to be a gray rock in the wood; therefore it
must have been given previous to the date which
geological chronology fixes for the insulation of St.
Michael's Mount. That date varies from 16,000 to
20,000 years ago. And as the name is Cornish, it
follows that Cornish-speaking people must have lived
in Cornwall at that early geological period.

Nothing, as I said, could sound more plausible;
but before we yield to the argument, we must surely
ask, Is there no other way of explaining the names
Cara cowz in clowze and *Cara clowse in cowze?* And
here we find—

(1.) That the legend of the dense forest by which
the Mount was believed to have been surrounded
existed, so far as we know, before the earliest occurrence of the Cornish name, and that it owes its
origin entirely to a mistake which can be accounted
for by documentary evidence. A legend told of
Mont St. Michel had been transferred *ipsissimis verbis* to St. Michael's Mount, and the monks of that
priory repeated the story which they found in their
chronicle to all who came to visit their establishment
in Cornwall. They told the name, among others, to
William of Worcester, and to prevent any incredulity
on his part, they gave him chapter and verse from
their chronicle, which he carefully jotted down in his
diary.[1]

[1] It was suggested to me that the *opacissima sylva* may even have a
more distant origin. There seems as little evidence of a dense forest having surrounded Mont St. Michel in Normandy as there was in the case of
St. Michael's Mount in Cornwall. Now as the first apparition of St.

(2.) We find that when the Cornish name first occurs, it lends itself, in one form, to a very natural interpretation, which does not give the meaning of "Hore rock in the wodd," but shows the name *Cara cowz in clowze* to have been a literal rendering of the Latin name "Mons in tumba," originally the name of Mont St. Michel, but at an early date applied in charters to St. Michael's Mount.

(3.) We find that the second form of the Cornish name, namely, *cara clowse in cowze*, may either be a merely metamorphic corruption of *cara cowz in clowze*, readily suggested and supported by the new meaning which it yielded of "gray rock in the wood;" or, even if we accept it as an original name, that it would be no more than a name framed by the Cornish-speaking monks of the Mount, in order to embody the same spurious tradition which had given rise to the name of "Hore rock in the wodd."

I need hardly add that in thus arguing against Mr. Pengelly's conclusions, I do not venture to touch his geological arguments. St. Michael's Mount may have been united with the mainland; it may, for all we know, have been surrounded by a dense forest; and it may be perfectly possible geologically to fix the date when that forest was destroyed, and the Mount severed, so far as it is severed, from the Cornish coast. All I protest against is that any one of these facts could be proved, or even supported, by the Cornish name of the Mount, whether *cara cowz in clowze*, or *cara clowse in cowze*, or by the English name, communicated by William of Worcester, "the

Michael is supposed to have taken place in Mount Garganus, i. e. Monte Gargano or Monte di S. Angelo, in Apulia, may not " the dense forest " have wandered with the archangel from the " quercets Gargani " (Hor. Od. ii. 9, 7) to Normandy, and thence to Cornwall?

Hore rock in the wodd," or finally by the legend which gave rise to these names, and which, as can be proved by irrefragable evidence, was transplanted by mistake from the Norman to the Cornish coast. The only question which, in conclusion, I should like to address to geologists, is this: As geologists are obliged to leave it doubtful whether the insulation of St. Michael's Mount was due to the washing of the sea-shore, or to a general subsidence of the country, may it not have been due to neither of these causes, and may not the Mount have always been that kind of half-island which it certainly was two thousand years ago?

1867.

XVI.

BUNSEN.[1]

Ours is, no doubt, a forgetful age. Every day brings new events rushing in upon us from all parts of the world; and the hours of real rest, when we might ponder over the past, recall pleasant days, gaze again on the faces of those who are no more, are few indeed. Men and women disappear from this busy stage, and though for a time they had been the radiating centres of social, political, or literary life, their places are soon taken by others, — "the place thereof shall know them no more." Few only appear again after a time, claiming once more our attention through the memoirs of their lives, and then either flitting away forever among the shades of the departed, or assuming afresh a power of life, a place in history, and an influence on the future often more powerful even than that which they exercised on the world while living in it. To call the great and good thus back from the grave is no easy task; it requires not only the power of a *vates sacer*, but the heart of a loving friend. Few

---

[1] *A Memoir of Baron Bunsen*, by his widow, Baroness Bunsen. 2 vols. 8vo. Longmans, 1868.

Christian Carl Josias Freiherr von Bunsen. Aus seinen Briefen und nach eigener Erinnerung geschildert, von seiner Wittwe. Deutsche Ausgabe, durch neue Mittheilungen vermehrt von Friedrich Nippold. Leipzig, 1868.

men live great and good lives; still fewer can write them; nay, often, when they have been lived and have been written, the world passes by unheeding, as crowds will pass without a glance by the portraits of a Titian or a Van Dyke. Now and then, however, a biography takes root, and then acts, as a lesson, as no other lesson can act. Such biographies have all the importance of an *Ecce Homo*, showing to the world what man can be, and permanently raising the ideal of human life. It was so in England with the life of Dr. Arnold; it was so more lately with the life of Prince Albert; it will be the same with the life of Bunsen.

It seems but yesterday that Bunsen left England; yet it was in 1854 that his house in Carlton Terrace ceased to be the refreshing oasis in London life which many still remember, and that the powerful, thoughtful, beautiful, loving face of the Prussian Ambassador was seen for the last time in London society. Bunsen then retired from public life, and after spending six more years in literary work, struggling with death, yet reveling in life, he died at Bonn on the 28th of November, 1860. His widow has devoted the years of her solitude to the noble work of collecting the materials for a biography of her husband; and we have now in two large volumes all that could be collected, or, at least, all that could be conveniently published, of the sayings and doings of Bunsen, the scholar, the statesman, and, above all, the philosopher and the Christian. Throughout the two volumes the outward events are sketched by the hand of the Baroness Bunsen; but there runs, as between wooded hills, the main stream of Bunsen's mind, the outpourings of his heart, which were given so freely and fully in his letters to his friends. When such materials exist, there can be no more satisfactory kind of biography than that of introducing the man himself, speaking unreservedly to his most intimate friends on the great events of his life. This is an autobiography, in fact, free from all drawbacks. Here and there that process, it is true, entails a greater fullness of detail than is acceptable to ordinary readers, however highly Bunsen's own friends may value every line of his familiar letters. But general readers may easily pass over letters addressed to different persons, or treating of subjects less interesting to themselves, without losing the thread of the story of the whole life; while it is sometimes of great interest to see the same subject discussed by Bunsen in letters addressed to different people. One serious difficulty in these letters is that they are nearly all translations from the German, and in the process of translation some of the original charm is inevitably lost. The translations are very faithful, and they do not sacrifice the peculiar turn of German thought to the requirements of strictly idiomatic English. Even the narrative itself betrays occasionally the German atmosphere in which it was written, but the whole book brings back all the more vividly to those who knew Bunsen the language and the very expressions of his English conversation. The two volumes are too bulky, and one's arms ache while holding them; yet one is loth to put them down, and there will be few readers who do not regret that more could not have been told us of Bunsen's life.

All really great and honest men may be said to live three lives: there is one life which is seen and accepted by the world at large, a man's outward life; there is a second life which is seen by a man's most intimate friends, his household life; and there is a third life, seen only by the man himself and by Him who searcheth the heart, which may be called the inner or heavenly life. Most biographers are and must be satisfied with giving the two former aspects of their hero's life, — the version of the world, and that of his friends. Both are important, both contain some truth, though neither of them the whole truth. But there is a third life, a life led in communion with God, a life of aspiration rather than of fulfillment, — that life which we see, for instance, in St. Paul, when he says, "The good that I would, I do not; but the evil which I would not, that I do." It is but seldom that we catch a glimpse of those deep springs of human character which cannot rise to the surface even in the most confidential intercourse, which in every-day life are hidden from a man's own sight, but which break forth when he is alone with his God in secret prayer, — aye, in prayers without words. Here lies the charm of Bunsen's life. Not only do we see the man, the father, the husband, the brother, that stands behind the ambassador, but we see behind the man his angel beholding the face of his Father which is in heaven. His prayers, poured forth in the critical moments of his life, have been preserved to us, and they show us what the world ought to know, that our greatest men can also be our best men, and that freedom of thought is not incompatible with sincere religion. Those who knew Bunsen well, know how that deep, religious undercurrent of his soul was constantly bubbling up and breaking forth in his conversations, startling even the mere worldling by an earnestness that frightened away every smile. It was said of him that he could drive out devils, and he certainly could, with his solemn, yet loving voice, soften hearts that would yield to no other appeal, and see with one look through that mask which man wears but too often in the masquerade of the world. Hence his numerous and enduring friendships, of which these volumes contain so many sacred relics. Hence that confidence reposed in him by men and women who had once been brought in contact with him. To those who can see with their eyes only, and not with their hearts, it may seem strange that Sir Robert Peel, shortly before his death, should have uttered the name of Bunsen. To those who know that England once had prime ministers who were found praying on their knees before they delivered their greatest speeches, Sir Robert Peel's recollection, or, it may be, desire of Bunsen in the last moments of his life has nothing strange. Bunsen's life was no ordinary life, and the memoirs of that life are more than an ordinary book. That book will tell in England and in Germany far more than in the Middle Ages the life of a new saint; nor are there many saints whose real life, if sifted as the life of Bunsen has been, would bear comparison with that noble character of the nineteenth century.

Bunsen was born in 1791 at Corbach, a small town in the small principality of Waldeck. His father was poor, but a man of independent spirit, of moral rectitude, and of deep religious convictions. Bunsen, the son of his old age, distinguished himself at school, and was sent to the University of Marburg at the age of seventeen. All he had then to depend on was an exhibition of about £7 a year, and a sum of £15, which his father had saved for him to start him in life. This may seem a small sum; but if we want to know how much of paternal love and self-denial it represented, we ought to read an entry in his father's diary: "Account of cash receipts by God's mercy obtained for transcribing law documents between 1793 and 1814, — sum total 3,020 thalers 23 groschen," that is to say, about £22 per annum. Did any English Duke ever give his son a more generous allowance, — more than two-thirds of his own annual income? Bunsen began by studying divinity, and actually preached a sermon at Marburg, in the Church of St. Elizabeth. Students in divinity are required in Germany to preach sermons as part of their regular theological training, and before they are actually ordained. Marburg was not then a very efficient university, and, not finding there what he wanted, Bunsen after a year went to Göttingen, chiefly attracted by the fame of Heyne. He soon devoted himself entirely to classical studies: and in order to support himself, — for £7 per annum will not support even a German student, — he accepted the appointment of assistant teacher of Greek and Hebrew at the Göttingen gymnasium, and also became private tutor to a young American, Mr. Astor, the son of the rich American merchant. He was thus learning and teaching at the same time, and he acquired by his daily intercourse with his pupil a practical knowledge of the English language. While at Göttingen he carried off, in 1812, a prize for an essay on "The Athenian Law of Inheritance," which attracted more than usual attention, and may, in fact, be looked upon as one of the first attempts at Comparative Jurisprudence. In 1713 he writes from Göttingen: —

"Poor and lonely did I arrive in this place. Heyne received me, guided me, bore with me, encouraged me, showed me in himself the example of a high and noble energy and indefatigable activity in a calling which was not that to which his merit entitled him; he might have superintended and administered and maintained an entire kingdom."

The following passage from the same letter deserves to be quoted as coming from the pen of a young man of twenty-two: —

"Learning annihilates itself, and the most perfect is the first submerged; for the next age scales with ease the height which cost the preceding the full vigor of life."

After leaving the university Bunsen travelled in Germany with young Astor, and made the acquaintance of Frederic Schlegel at Vienna, of Jacobi, Schelling, and Thiersch at Munich. He was all that time continuing his own philological studies, and we see him at Munich attending lectures on Criminal Law, and making his first beginning in the study of Persian. When on the point of starting for Paris with his American pupil, the news of the glorious battle of Leipzig (October, 1813) disturbed their plans, and he resolved to settle again at Göttingen till peace should have been concluded. Here, while superintending the studies of Mr. Astor, he plunged into reading of the most varied character. He writes (p. 51): —

"I remain firm, and strive after my earliest purpose in life, more felt, perhaps, than already discerned, — namely, to bring over into my own knowledge and into my own Fatherland the language and the spirit of the solemn and distant East. I would for the accomplishment of this object even quit Europe, in order to draw out of the ancient well that which I find not elsewhere."

This is the first indication of an important element in Bunsen's early life, his longing for the East, and his all but prophetic anticipation of the great results which a study of the ancient language of India would one day yield, and the light it would shed on the darkest pages in the ancient history of Greece, Italy, and Germany. The study of the Athenian law of inheritance seems first to have drawn his attention to the ancient codes of Indian law, and he was deeply

impressed by the discovery that the peculiar system
of inheritance which in Greece existed only in the
petrified form of a primitive custom, sanctioned by
law, disclosed in the laws of Manu its original purport and natural meaning. This one spark excited
in Bunsen's mind that constant yearning after a
knowledge of Eastern and more particularly of Indian
literature which very nearly drove him to India in
the same adventurous spirit as Anquetil Duperron
and Czoma de Körös. We are now familiar with
the great results that have been obtained by a study
of the ancient languages and religion of the East; but
in 1813 neither Bopp nor Grimm had begun to publish, and Frederic Schlegel was the only one who in
his little pamphlet, "On the Language and the
Wisdom of the Indians" (1808), had ventured to
assert a real intellectual relationship between Europe
and India. One of Bunsen's earliest friends, Wolrad
Schumacher, related that even at school Bunsen's
mind was turned towards India. "Sometimes he
would let fall a word about India which was unac-
countable to me, as at that time I connected only a
geographical conception with that name" (p. 17).

While thus engaged in his studies at Göttingen, and
working in company with such friends as Brandis, the
historian of Greek philosophy; Lachmann, the editor
of the New Testament; Lücke, the theologian; Ernst
Schulze, the poet, and others, — Bunsen felt the influence of the great events that brought about the regeneration of Germany; nor was he the man to stand aloof,
absorbed in literary work, while others were busy
doing mischief difficult to remedy. The princes of
Germany and their friends, though grateful to the people for having at last shaken off with fearful sacrifices

the foreign yoke of Napoleon, were most anxious to maintain for their own benefit that convenient system of police government which for so long had kept the whole of Germany under French control. "It is but too certain," Bunsen writes, "that either for want of good-will or of intelligence our sovereigns will not grant us freedom such as we deserve. . . . And I fear that, as before, the much-enduring German will become an object of contempt to all nations who know how to value national spirit." His first political essays belong to that period. Up to August, 1814, Bunsen continued to act as private tutor to Mr. Astor, though we see him at the same time, with his insatiable thirst after knowledge, attending courses of lectures on astronomy, mineralogy, and other subjects apparently so foreign to the main current of his mind. When Mr. Astor left him to return to America, Bunsen went to Holland to see a sister to whom he was deeply attached, and who seems to have shared with him the same religious convictions which in youth, manhood, and old age formed the foundation of Bunsen's life. Some of Bunsen's detractors have accused him of professing Christian piety in circles where such professions were sure to be well received. Let them read now the annals of his early life, and they will find to their shame how boldly the same Bunsen professed his religious convictions among the students and professors of Göttingen, who either scoffed at Christianity or only tolerated it as a kind of harmless superstition. We shall only quote one instance : —

"Bunsen, when a young student at Göttingen, once suddenly quitted a lecture in indignation at the unworthy manner in which the most sacred subjects were treated by one of the professors. The professor paused at the interruption, and hazarded the remark that 'some one belonging to the Old Testament had possibly slipped in unrecognized.' That called forth a burst of laughter from the entire audience, all being as well aware as the lecturer himself who it was that had mortified him."

During his stay in Holland, Bunsen not only studied the language and literature of that country, but his mind was also much occupied in observing the national and religious character of this small but interesting branch of the Teutonic race. He writes:—

"In all things the German, or, if you will, the Teutonic character is worked out into form in a manner more decidedly national than anywhere else.... This journey has yet more confirmed my decision to become acquainted with the entire Germanic race, and then to proceed with the development of my governing ideas (i. e. the study of Eastern languages in elucidation of Western thought). For this purpose I am about to travel with Brandis to Copenhagen to learn Danish, and, above all, Icelandic."

And so he did. The young student, as yet without any prospects in life, threw up his position at Göttingen, declined to waste his energies as a schoolmaster, and started, we hardly know how, on his journey to Denmark. There, in company with Brandis, he lived and worked hard at Danish, and then attacked the study of the ancient Icelandic language and literature with a fervor and with a purpose that shrank from no difficulty. He writes (p. 79):—

"The object of my research requires the acquisition of the whole treasures of language, in order to complete my favorite linguistic theories, and to inquire into the poetry and religious conceptions of German-Scandinavian heathenism, and their historical connection with the East."

When his work in Denmark was finished, and when he had collected materials, some of which, as his copy taken of the "Vŏluspa," a poem of the Edda, were not published till forty years later, he started with Brandis for Berlin. "Prussia," he writes on the

10th of October, 1815, "is *the true* Germany." Thither he felt drawn, as well as Brandis, and thither he invited his friends, though, it must be confessed, without suggesting to them any settled plan of how to earn their daily bread. He writes as if he was even then at the head of affairs in Berlin, though he was only the friend of a friend of Niebuhr's, Niebuhr himself being by no means all powerful in Prussia, even in 1815. This hopefulness was a trait in Bunsen's character that remained through life. A plan was no sooner suggested to him and approved by him than he took it for granted that all obstacles must vanish, and many a time did all obstacles vanish, before the joyous confidence of that magician, a fact that should be remembered by those who used to blame him as sanguine and visionary. One of his friends, Lücke, writes to Ernst Schulze, the poet, whom Bunsen had invited to Denmark, and afterwards to Berlin: —

"In the inclosed richly filled letter you will recognize Bunsen's power and splendor of mind, and you will also not fail to perceive his thoughtlessness in making projects. He and Brandis are a pair of most amiable speculators, full of affection; but one must meet them with the *ne quid nimis*."

However, Bunsen in his flight was not to be scared by any warning or checked by calculating the chances of success or failure. With Brandis he went to Berlin, spent the glorious winter from 1815 to 1816 in the society of men like Niebuhr and Schleiermacher, and became more and more determined in his own plan of life, which was to study Oriental languages in Paris, London, or Calcutta, and then to settle at Berlin as Professor of Universal History. A full statement of his literary labors, both for the past and for the future, was drawn up by him, to be submitted to Niebuhr, and it will be read even now with interest by those who knew Bunsen when he tried to take up after forty years the threads that had slipped from his hand at the age of four-and-twenty.

Instead of being sent to study at Paris and London by the Prussian government, as he seems to have wished, he was suddenly called to Paris by his old pupil, Mr. Astor, who, after two years' absence, had returned to Europe, and was anxious to renew his relations with Bunsen. Bunsen's object in accepting Astor's invitation to Paris was to study Persian; and great was his disappointment when, on arriving there, Mr. Astor wished him at once to start for Italy. This was too much for Bunsen, to be turned back just as he was going to quench his thirst for Oriental literature in the lectures of Sylvestre de Sacy. A compromise was effected. Bunsen remained for three months in Paris, and promised then to join his friend and pupil in Italy. How he worked at Persian and Arabic during the interval must be read in his own letters:—

"I write from six in the morning till four in the afternoon, only in the course of that time having a walk in the garden of the Luxembourg, where I also often study; from four to six I dine and walk; from six to seven sleep; from seven to eleven work again. I have overtaken in study some of the French students who had begun a year ago. God be thanked for this help! Before I go to bed I read a chapter in the New Testament, in the morning on rising one in the Old Testament; yesterday I began the Psalms from the first."

As soon as he felt that he could continue his study of Persian without the aid of a master, he left Paris. Though immersed in work, he had made several acquaintances, among others that of Alexander von Humboldt, "who intends in a few years to visit Asia, where I may hope to meet him. He has been beyond measure kind to me, and from him I shall receive the best recommendations for Italy and England, as well as from his brother, now Prussian Minister in London. Lastly, the winter in Rome may become to me, by the presence of Niebuhr, more instructive and fruitful than in any other place. Thus has God ordained all things for me for the best, according to His will, not mine, and far better than I deserve."

These were the feelings with which the young scholar, then twenty-four years of age, started for Italy, as yet without any position, without having published a single work, without knowing, as we may suppose, where to rest his head. And yet he was full, not only of hope, but of gratitude, and he little dreamt that before seven years had passed he would be in Niebuhr's place; and before twenty-five years had passed in the place of William von Humboldt, the Prussian Ambassador at the Court of St. James.

The immediate future, in fact, had some severe disappointments in store for him. When he arrived at Florence to meet Mr. Astor, the young American had received peremptory orders to return to New York; and as Bunsen declined to follow him, he found himself really stranded at Florence, and all his plans thoroughly upset. Yet, though at that very time full of care and anxiety about his nearest relations, who looked to him for support when he could hardly support himself, his God-trusting spirit did not break down. He remained at Florence, continuing his Persian studies, and making a living by private tuition. A Mr. Cathcart seems to have been his favorite pupil, and through him new prospects of eventually proceeding to India seemed to open. But, at the same time, Bunsen began to feel that the circumstances of his life became critical. "I feel," he says, "that I am on the point of securing or losing the fruit of my labors for life." Rome and Niebuhr seemed the only haven in sight, and thither Bunsen now began to steer his frail bark. He arrived in Rome on the 14th of November, 1816. Niebuhr, who was Prussian Minister, received him with great kindness, and entered heartily into the literary plans of his young friend. Brandis, Niebuhr's secretary, renewed in common with his old friend his study of Greek philosophy. A native teacher of Arabic was engaged to help Bunsen in his Oriental studies. The necessary supplies seem to have come partly from Mr. Astor, partly from private lessons for which Bunsen had to make time in the midst of his varied occupations. Plato, Firdusi, the Koran, Dante, Isaiah, the Edda, are mentioned by himself as his daily study.

From an English point of view that young man at Rome, without a status, without a settled prospect in life, would have seemed an amiable dreamer, destined to wake suddenly, and not very pleasantly, to the stern realities of life. If anything seemed unlikely, it was that an English gentleman, a man of good birth and of independent fortune, should give his daughter to this poor young German at Rome. Yet this was the very thing which a kind Providence, that Providence in which Bunsen trusted amid all his troubles and difficulties, brought to pass. Bunsen became acquainted with Mr. Waddington, and was allowed to read German with his daughters. In the most honorable manner he broke off his visits when he became aware of his feelings for Miss Waddington. He writes to his sister: —

"Having, at first, believed myself quite safe (the more so as

I cannot think of marrying without impairing my whole scheme of mental development, and, least of all, could I think of pretending to a girl of fortune), I thought there was no danger."

A little later he writes to Mrs. Waddington to explain to her the reason for his discontinuing his visits. But the mother — and, to judge from her letters, a high-minded mother she must have been — accepted Bunsen on trust; he was allowed to return to the house, and on the 1st of July, 1817, the young German student, then twenty-five years of age, was married at Rome to Miss Waddington. What a truly important event this was for Bunsen, even those who had not the privilege of knowing the partner of his life may learn from the work before us. Though little is said in these memoirs of his wife, the mother of his children, the partner of his joys and sorrows, it is easy to see how Bunsen's whole mode of life became possible only by the unceasing devotion of an ardent soul and a clear head consecrated to one object, — to love and to cherish, for better for worse, for richer for poorer, in sickness and in health, till death us do part, — aye, and even after death! With such a wife, the soul of Bunsen could soar on its wings, the small cares of life were removed, an independence was secured, and, though the Indian plans had to be surrendered, the highest ambition of Bunsen's life, a professorship in a German university, seemed now easy of attainment. We should have liked a few more pages describing the joyous life of the young couple in the heyday of their life; we could have wished that he had not declined the wish of his mother-in-law, to have his bust made by Thorwaldsen, at a time when he must have been a model of manly beauty. But if we know less than we could wish of what Bunsen then was in the eyes of the world, we are allowed an insight into that heavenly life which underlay all the outward happiness of that time, and which shows him to us as but one eye could then have seen him. A few weeks after his marriage he writes in his journal:—

"Eternal, omnipresent God! enlighten me with thy Holy Spirit, and fill me with thy heavenly light! What in childhood I felt and yearned after, what throughout the years of youth grew clearer and clearer before my soul, I will now venture to hold fast, to examine, to represent the revelation of Thee in man's energies and efforts: thy firm path through the stream of ages I long to trace and recognize, as far as may be permitted to me even in this body of earth. The song of praise to Thee from the whole of humanity, in times far and near, — the pains and lamentations of men, and their consolations in Thee, — I wish to take in, clear and unhindered. Do Thou send me thy Spirit of Truth, that I may behold things earthly as they are, without veil and without mask, without human trappings and empty adornment, and that in the silent peace of truth I may feel and recognize Thee. Let me not falter, nor slide away from the great end of knowing Thee. Let not the joys, or honors, or vanities of the world enfeeble and darken my spirit; let me ever feel that I can only perceive and know Thee in so far as mine is a living soul, and lives, and moves, and has its being in Thee."

Here we see Bunsen as the world did not see him, and we may observe how then, as ever, his literary work was to him hallowed by the objects for which it was intended. "The firm path of God through the stream of ages" is but another title for one of his last works, "God in History," planned with such youthful ardor, and finished under the lengthening shadow of death.

The happiness of Bunsen's life at Rome may easily be imagined. Though anxious to begin his work at a German university, he stipulated for three more years of freedom and preparation. Who could have made the sacrifice of the bright spring of life, of the unclouded days of happiness at Rome with wife and children, and with such friends as Niebuhr and Brandis? Yet this stay at Rome was fraught with fatal consequences. It led the straight current of Bunsen's life, which lay so clear before him, into a new bed, at first very tempting, for a time smooth and sunny, but alas! ending in waste of energy for which no outward splendor could atone. The first false step seemed very natural and harmless. When Brandis went to Germany to begin his professorial work, Bunsen took his place as Niebuhr's secretary at Rome. He was determined, then, that nothing should induce him to remain in the diplomatic career (p. 130), but the current of that mill-stream was too strong even for Bunsen. How he remained as Secretary of Legation, 1818; how the King of Prussia, Frederick William III., came to visit Rome, and took a fancy to the young diplomatist, who could speak to him with a modesty and frankness little known at courts; how, when Niebuhr exchanged his embassy for a professorial chair at Bonn, Bunsen remained as Chargé d'Affaires; how he went to Berlin, 1827-28, and gained the hearts of the old King and of everybody else; how he returned to Rome and was fascinated by the young Crown Prince of Prussia, afterwards Frederick William IV., whom he had to conduct through the antiquities and the modern life of the world city; how he became Prussian Minister, the friend of popes and cardinals, the centre of the best and most brilliant society; how, when the difficulties began between Prussia and the Papal government, chiefly with regard to mixed marriages, Bunsen tried to mediate, and was at last disowned by both parties in 1838, — all this may now be read in the open memoirs of his life. His letters during these twenty years are numerous and full, particularly those addressed to his sister, to whom he was deeply attached. They are the most touching and elevating record of a life spent in important official business, in interesting social intercourse, in literary and antiquarian researches, in the enjoyment of art and nature, and in the blessedness of a prosperous family life, and throughout in an unbroken communion with God. There is hardly a letter without an expression of that religion in common life, that constant consciousness of a Divine Presence, which made his life a life in God. To many readers this free outpouring of a God-loving soul will seem to approach too near to that abuse of religious phraseology which is a sign of superficial rather than of deep-seated piety. But, though through life a sworn enemy of every kind of cant, Bunsen never would surrender the privilege of speaking the language of a Christian, because that language had been profaned by the thoughtless repetition of shallow pietists.

Bunsen has frequently been accused of pietism, particularly in Germany, by men who could not distinguish between pietism and piety, just as in England he was attacked as a freethinker by men who never knew the freedom of the children of God. "Christianity is ours, not theirs," he would frequently say of those who made religion a mere profession, and imagined they knew Christ because they held a crosier and wore a mitre. We can now watch the deep emotions and firm convictions of that true-hearted man, in letters of undoubted sincerity, addressed to his sister and his friends, and we can only wonder with what feelings they have been perused by those who in England questioned his Christianity or who in Germany suspected his honesty.

From the time of his first meeting with the King of Prussia at Rome, and still more, after his stay at Berlin in 1827, Bunsen's chief interest with regard to Prussia centred in ecclesiastical matters. The King, after effecting the union of the Lutheran and Calvinistic branches of the Protestant Church, was deeply interested in drawing up a new Liturgy for his own national, or, as it was called, Evangelical Church. The introduction of his Liturgy, or *Agenda*, particularly as it was carried out, like everything else in Prussia, by royal decree, met with considerable resistance. Bunsen, who had been led independently to the study of ancient liturgies, and who had devoted much of his time at Rome to the collection of ancient hymns and hymn tunes, could speak to the King on these favorite topics from the fullness of his heart. The King listened to him, even when Bunsen ventured to express his dissent from some of the royal proposals, and when he, the young attaché, deprecated any authoritative interference with the freedom of the Church. In Prussia the whole movement was unpopular, and Bunsen, though he worked hard to render it less so, was held responsible for much which he himself had disapproved. Of all these turbulent transactions there remains but one bright and precious relic, Bunsen's "Hymn and Prayer Book."

The Prussian Legation on the Capitol was during Bunsen's day not only the meeting-place of all distinguished Germans, but, in the absence of an English embassy, it also became the recognized centre of the most interesting portion of English society at Rome. Among the Germans, whose presence told on Bunsen's life, either by a continued friendship or by common interests and pursuits, we meet the names of Ludwig,

King of Bavaria; Baron von Stein, the great Prussian
statesman; Radowitz, the less fortunate predecessor of
Bismarck; Schnorr, Overbeck, and Mendelssohn.
Among Englishmen, whose friendship with Bunsen
dates from the Capitol, we find Thirlwall, Philip Pusey,
Arnold, and Julius Hare. The names of Thorwaldsen,
too, of Leopardi, Lord Hastings, Champollion, Sir
Walter Scott, Chateaubriand, occur again and again in
the memoirs of that Roman life which teems with interesting events and anecdotes. The only literary
productions of that eventful period are Bunsen's part in
Platner's "Description of Rome," and the "Hymn
and Prayer Book." But much material for later
publications had been amassed in the mean time. The
study of the Old Testament had been prosecuted at all
times, and in 1824 the first beginning was made by
Bunsen in the study of hieroglyphics, afterwards continued with Champollion, and later with Lepsius. The
Archæological Institute and the German Hospital, both
on the Capitol, were the two permanent bequests that
Bunsen left behind when he shook off the dust of his
feet, and left Rome on the 29th of April, 1838, in
search of a new Capitol.

At Berlin, Bunsen was then in disgrace. He had
not actually been dismissed the service, but he was prohibited from going to Berlin to justify himself, and he
was ordered to proceed to England on leave of absence.
To England, therefore, Bunsen now directed his steps
with his wife and children, and there, at least, he was
certain of a warm welcome, both from his wife's relations and from his own very numerous friends.
When we read through the letters of that period, we
hardly miss the name of a single man illustrious at that
time in England. As if to make up for the injustice

done to him in Italy, and for the ingratitude of his
country, people of all classes and of the most opposite
views vied in doing him honor. Rest he certainly
found none, while travelling about from one town to
another, and staying at friends' houses, attending meetings, making speeches, writing articles, and, as usual,
amassing new information wherever he could find it.
He worked at Egyptian with Lepsius; at Welsh while
staying with Lady Hall; at Ethnology with Dr. Prichard. He had to draw up two state papers, — one on
the Papal aggression, the other on the law of divorce.
He plunged, of course, at once into all the ecclesiastical
and theological questions that were then agitating
people's minds in England, and devoted his few really
quiet hours to the preparation of his own "Life of
Christ." With Lord Ashley he attended Bible meetings, with Mrs. Fry he explored the prisons, with
Philip Pusey he attended agricultural assemblies, and
he spent night after night as an admiring listener in the
House of Commons. He was presented to the Queen
and the Duke of Wellington, was made a D. C. L. at
Oxford, discussed the future with J. H. Newman, the
past with Buckland, Sedgwick, and Whewell. Lord
Palmerston and Lord John Russell invited him to
political conferences; Maurice and Keble listened to
his fervent addresses; Dr. Arnold consulted the friend
of Niebuhr on his own "History of Rome," and tried
to convert him to more liberal opinions with regard to
Church reform. Dr. Holland, Mrs. Austin, Ruskin,
Carlyle, Macaulay, Gaisford, Dr. Hawkins, and many
more, all greeted him, all tried to do him honor, and
many of them became attached to him for life. The
architectural monuments of England, its castles, parks,
and ruins, passed quickly through his field of vision

during that short stay. But he soon calls out: "I care not now for all the ruins of England; it is her life that I like."

Most touching is his admiration, his real love of Gladstone. Thirty years have since passed, and the world at large has found out by this time what England possesses in him. But it was not so in 1838, and few men at that early time could have read Gladstone's heart and mind so truly as Bunsen. Here are a few of his remarks: —

"Last night, when I came home from the Duke, Gladstone's book was on my table, the second edition having come out at seven o'clock. It is the book of the time, a great event, — the first book since Burke that goes to the bottom of the vital question; far above his party and his time. I sat up till after midnight; and this morning I continued until I had read the whole, and almost every sheet bears my marginal glosses, destined for the Prince, to whom I have sent the book with all dispatch. Gladstone is the first man in England as to intellectual powers, and he has heard higher tones than any one else in this island."

And again (p. 493): —

"Gladstone is by far the first living intellectual power on that side. He has left his schoolmasters far behind him, but we must not wonder if he still walks in their trammels; his genius will soon free itself entirely, and fly towards heaven with its own wings. . . . I wonder Gladstone should not have the feeling of moving on an *inclined plane*, or that of sitting down among ruins, as if he were settled in a well-stored house."

Of Newman, whom he had met at Oxford, Bunsen says: —

"This morning I have had two hours at breakfast with Newman. O! It is sad, — he and his friends are truly intellectual people, but they have lost their ground, going exactly my way, but stopping short in the middle. It is too late. There has been an amicable change of ideas and a Christian understanding. Yesterday he preached a beautiful sermon. A new period of life begins for me; may God's blessing be upon it!"

Oxford made a deep impression on Bunsen's mind. He writes: —

"I am luxuriating in the delights of Oxford. There has never been enough said of this queen of all cities."

But what as a German he admired and envied most was, after all, the House of Commons: —

"I wish you could form an idea of what I felt. I saw for the first time *man*, the member of a true Germanic State, in his highest, his proper place, defending the highest interests of humanity with the wonderful power of speech-wrestling, but with the arm of the spirit, boldly grasping at or tenaciously holding fast power, in the presence of his fellow-citizens, submitting to the public conscience the judgment of his cause and of his own uprightness. I saw before me the empire of the world governed, and the rest of the world controlled and judged, by this assembly. I had the feeling that, had I been born in England, I would rather be dead than not sit among and speak among them. I thought of my own country, and was thankful that I *could* thank God for being a German and being myself. But I felt, also, that we are all children on this field in comparison with the English; how much they, with their discipline of mind, body, and heart, can effect even with but moderate genius, and even with talent alone! I drank in every word from the lips of the speakers, even those I disliked."

More than a year was thus spent in England in the very fullness of life. "My stay in England in 1838–39," he writes at a later time, the 22d of September, 1841, "was the poetry of my existence as a man; this is the prose of it. There was a dew upon those fifteen months, which the sun has dried up, and which nothing can restore." Yet even then Bunsen could not have been free from anxieties for the future. He had a large family growing up, and he was now again, at the age of forty-seven, without any definite prospects in life. In spite, however, of the intrigues of his enemies, the personal feelings of the King and the Crown Prince prevailed at last; and he was appointed in July, 1839, as Prussian Minister in Switzerland, his secret and confidential instructions being "to do nothing." These instructions were carefully observed by Bunsen, as far as politics were concerned. He passed two years of rest at the Hubel, near Berne, with his family, devoted to his books, receiving visits from his friends, and watching from a distance the coming events in Prussia.

In 1840 the old King died, and it was generally expected that Bunsen would at once receive an influential position at Berlin. Not till April, 1841, however, was he summoned to the court, although, to judge from the correspondence between him and the new King, Frederick William IV., few men could have enjoyed a larger share of royal confidence and love than Bunsen. The King was hungering and thirsting after Bunsen, yet Bunsen was not invited to Berlin. The fact is that the young King had many friends, and those friends were not the friends of Bunsen. They were satisfied with his honorary exile in Switzerland, and thought him best employed at a distance in doing nothing. The King too, who knew Bunsen's character from former years, must have known that Berlin was not large enough for him; and he therefore left him in his Swiss retirement till an employment worthy of him could be found. This was to go on a special mission to England with a view of establishing, in common with the Church of England, a Protestant bishopric at Jerusalem. In Jerusalem the King hoped that the two principal Protestant churches of Europe would, across the grave of the Redeemer, reach to each other the right hand of fellowship. Bunsen entered into this plan with all the energy of his mind and heart. It was a work thoroughly con-

genial to himself; and if it required diplomatic skill,
certainly no one could have achieved it more expeditiously and successfully than Bunsen. He was then a
persona grata with bishops and archbishops, and Lord
Ashley — not yet Lord Shaftesbury — gave him all
the support his party could command. English influence was then so powerful at Constantinople that all
difficulties due to Turkish bigotry were quickly removed. At the end of June, 1841, he arrived in
London; on the 6th of August he wrote, "All is settled;" and on the 7th of November the new Bishop of
Jerusalem was consecrated. Seldom was a more important and more complicated transaction settled in so
short a time. Had the discussions been prolonged,
had time been given to the leaders of the Romanizing
party to recover from their surprise, the bill that had
to be passed through both houses would certainly have
been defeated. People have hardly yet understood
the real bearing of that measure, nor appreciated the
germ which it may still contain for the future of the
Reformed Church. One man only seems to have seen
clearly what a blow this first attempt at a union between the Protestant churches of England and Germany was to his own plans, and to the plans of his
friends; and we know now, from Newman's "Apologia," that the bishopric of Jerusalem drove him to
the Church of Rome. This may have been for the
time a great loss to the Church of England; it
marked, at all events, a great crisis in her history.

In spite, however, of his great and unexpected success, there are traces of weariness in Bunsen's letters
of that time, which show that he was longing for
more congenial work. "O, how I hate and detest
diplomatic life!" he wrote to his wife; "and how

little true intellectuality is there in the high society here as soon as you cease to speak of English national subjects and interests; and the eternal hurricanes, whirling, urging, rushing, in this monster of a town! Even with you and the children life would become oppressive under the diplomatic burden. I can pray for our country life, but I cannot pray for a London life, although I dare not pray against it, *if it must be.*"

Bunsen's observations of character amidst the distractions of his London season are very interesting and striking, particularly at this distance of time. He writes:—

"Mr. Gladstone has been invited to become one of the trustees of the Jerusalem Fund. He is beset with scruples; his heart is with us, but his mind is entangled in a narrow system. He awaits salvation from another code, and by wholly different ways from myself. Yesterday morning I had a letter from him of twenty-four pages, to which I replied early this morning by eight.

"The Bishop of London constantly rises in my estimation. He has replied admirably to Mr. Gladstone, closing with the words, 'My dear sir, my intention is not to limit and restrict the Church of Christ, but to enlarge it.'"

A letter from Sir Robert Peel, too, must here be quoted in full:—

"WHITEHALL, *October* 10, 1841.

"MY DEAR MR. BUNSEN,—My note merely conveyed a request that you would be good enough to meet Mr. Cornelius at dinner on Friday last.

"I assure you that I have been amply repaid for any attention I may have shown to that distinguished artist, in the personal satisfaction I have had in the opportunity of making his acquaintance. He is one of a noble people distinguished in every art of war and peace. The union and patriotism of that people, spread over the centre of Europe, will contribute the surest guarantee for the peace of the world, and the most powerful check upon the spread of all pernicious doctrines injurious to the cause of religion and order, and that liberty which respects the rights of others.

"My earnest hope is that every member of this illustrious race, while he may cherish the particular country of his birth as he does his home, will extend his devotion beyond its narrow limits, and exult in the name of a German, and recognise the claim of Germany to the love and affection and patriotic exertions of all her sons.

"I hope I judge the feelings of every German by those which were excited in my own breast (in the breast of a foreigner and a stranger) by a simple ballad, that seemed, however, to concentrate the will of a mighty people, and said emphatically, —

'They shall not have the Rhine.'

"*They* will not have it: and the Rhine will be protected by a song, if the sentiments which that song embodies pervade, as I hope and trust they do, every German heart.

"You will begin to think that I am a good German myself, and so I am, if hearty wishes for the union and welfare of the German race can constitute one.

"Believe me, most faithfully yours,
"ROBERT PEEL."

When Bunsen was on the point of leaving London, he received the unexpected and unsolicited appointment of Prussian Envoy in England, an appointment which he could not bring himself to decline, and which again postponed for twelve years his cherished plans of an *otium cum dignitate*. What the world at large would have called the most fortunate event in Bunsen's life proved indeed a real misfortune. It deprived Bunsen of the last chance of fully realizing the literary plans of his youth, and it deprived the world of services that no one could have rendered so well in the cause of freedom of thought, of practical religion, and in teaching the weighty lessons of antiquity to the youth of the future. It made him waste his precious hours in work that any Prussian baron could have done as well, if not better, and did not set him free until his bodily strength was undermined, and the joyful temper of his mind saddened by sad experiences.

Nothing could have been more brilliant than the beginning of Bunsen's diplomatic career in England. First came the visit of the King of Prussia, whom the Queen had invited to be godfather to the Prince of Wales. Soon after the Prince of Prussia came to England under the guidance of Bunsen. Then followed the return visit of the Queen at Stolzenfels, on the Rhine. All this, no doubt, took up much of Bunsen's time, but it gave him also the pleasantest introduction to the highest society of England; for as Baroness Bunsen shrewdly remarks, "there is nothing like standing within the Bude-light of royalty to make one conspicuous, and sharpen perceptions and recollections." (II. p. 8.) Bunsen complained, no doubt, now and then, about excessive official work, yet he seemed on the whole reconciled to his position, and up to the year 1847 we hear of no attempts to escape from diplomatic bondage. In a letter to Mrs. Fry he says:—

"I can assure you I never passed a more quiet and truly satisfactory evening in London than the last, in the Queen's house, in the midst of the excitement of the season. I think this is a circumstance for which one ought to be thankful; and it has much reminded me of hours that I have spent at Berlin and Sans Souci with the King and the Queen and the Princess William, and, I am thankful to add, with the Princess of Prussia, mother of the future King. It is a striking and consoling and instructive proof that what is called the world, the great world, is not necessarily worldly in itself, but only by that inward worldliness which, as rebellion against the spirit, creeps into the cottage as well as into the palace, and against which no outward form is any protection. Forms and rules may prevent the outbreak of wrong, but cannot regenerate right, and may quench the spirit and poison inward truth. The Queen gives hours daily to the labor of examining into the claims of the numberless petitions addressed to her, among other duties to which her time of privacy is devoted."

The Queen's name and that of Prince Albert occur often in these memoirs, and a few of Bunsen's remarks and observations may be of interest, though they contain little that can now be new to the readers of the "Life of the Prince Consort" and of the "Queen's Journal."

First, a graphic description, from the hand of Baroness Bunsen, of the Queen opening Parliament in 1842:—

"Last, the procession of the Queen's entry, and herself, looking worthy and fit to be the converging point of so many rays of grandeur. It is self-evident that she is not tall; but were she ever so tall, she could not have more grace and dignity, a head better set, a throat more royally and classically arching; and one advantage there is in her not being taller, that when she casts a glance, it is of necessity upwards and not downwards, and thus the effect of the eyes is not thrown away,—the beam and effluence not lost. The composure with which she filled the throne, while awaiting the Commons, was a test of character,—no fidget and no apathy. Then her voice and enunciation could not be more perfect. In short, it could not be said that *she did well*, but she *was* the Queen,—she was, and felt herself to be, the acknowledged chief among grand and national realities." (Vol. II. p. 10.)

The next is an account of the Queen at Windsor Castle on receiving the Princess of Prussia, in 1842:—

"The Queen looked well and *rayonnante*, with that expression that she always has when thoroughly pleased with all that occupies her mind, which you know I always observe with delight, as fraught with that truth and reality which so essentially belong to her character, and so strongly distinguish her countenance, in all its changes, from the *fixed mask* only too common in the royal rank of society." (Vol. II. p. 115.)

After having spent some days at Windsor Castle, Bunsen writes in 1846:—

"The Queen often spoke with me about education, and in particular of religious instruction. Her views are very serious, but at the same time liberal and comprehensive. She (as well as Prince Albert) hates all formalism. The Queen reads a great deal, and has done my book on 'The Church of the Future' the honor to read it so attentively, that the other day, when at Cashiobury, seeing the book on the table, she looked out passages which she had approved in order to read them aloud to the Queen-Dowager." (Vol. II. p. 121.)

And once more : —

"The Queen is a wife and a mother as happy as the happiest in her dominions, and no one can be more careful of her charges. She often speaks to me of the great task before her and the Prince in the education of the royal children, and particularly of the Prince of Wales and the Princess Royal."

Before the troubles of 1847 and 1848, Bunsen was enabled to spend part of his time in the country, away from the turmoil of London, and much of his literary work dates from that time. After his "Church of the Future," the discovery of the genuine Epistles of Ignatius by the late Dr. Cureton led Bunsen back to the study of the earliest literature of the Christian Church, and the results of these researches were published in his "Ignatius." Lepsius' stay in England and his expedition to Egypt induced Bunsen to put his own materials in order, and to give to the world his long-matured views on "The Place of Egypt in Universal History." The later volumes of this work led him into philological studies of a more general character, and at the meeting of the British Association at Oxford, in 1847, he read before the brilliantly attended ethnological section his paper "On the Results of the recent Egyptian Researches in reference to Asiatic and African Ethnology, and the Classification of Languages," published in the "Transactions" of the Association, and separately under the title, "Three Linguistic Dissertations, by Chevalier Bunsen, Dr. Charles Meyer, and Dr. Max Müller." "Those three days at Oxford," he writes, "were a time of great distinction to me, both in my public and private capacity." Everything important in literature and art attracted not only his notice, but his warmest interest; and no one who wanted encouragement, advice, or help in literary or historical researches, knocked in vain at Bunsen's door. His table at breakfast and dinner was filled by ambassadors and professors, by bishops and missionaries, by dukes and poor scholars, and his evening parties offered a kind of neutral ground, where people could meet who could have met nowhere else, and where English prejudices had no jurisdiction. That Bunsen, holding the position which he held in society, but still more being what he was apart from his social position, should have made his presence felt in England, was not to be wondered at. He would speak out whenever he felt strongly, but he was the last man to meddle or to intrigue. He had no time even if he had had taste for it. But there were men in England who could never forgive him for the Jerusalem bishopric, and who resorted to the usual tactics for making a man unpopular. A cry was soon raised against his supposed influence at court, and doubts were thrown out as to his orthodoxy. Every Liberal bishop that was appointed was said to have been appointed through Bunsen. Dr. Hampden was declared to have been his nominee, — the fact being that Bunsen did not even know of him before he had been made a bishop. As his practical Christianity could not well be questioned, he was accused of holding heretical opinions, because his chronology differed from that of Jewish Rabbis and Bishop Usher. It is extraordinary how little Bunsen himself cared about these attacks, though they caused acute suffering to his family. He was not surprised that he should be hated by those whose theological opinions he considered unsound, and whose ecclesiastical politics he had openly declared to be fraught with danger to the most sacred interests of the Church. Besides, he was the personal friend of such men as Arnold, Hare, Thirlwall, Maurice, Stanley, and Jowett. He had even a kind word to say for Froude's "Nemesis of Faith." He could sympathize, no doubt, with all that was good and honest, whether among the High Church or Low Church party, and many of his personal friends belonged to the one as well as to the other; but he could also thunder forth with no uncertain sound against everything that seemed to him hypocritical, pharisaical, unchristian. Thus he writes (II. p. 81):—

"I apprehend having given the ill-disposed a pretext for considering me a semi-Pelagian, a contemner of the Sacraments, or denier of the Son, a perverter of the doctrine of justification, and therefore a crypto-Catholic theosophist, heretic, and enthusiast, deserving of all condemnation. I have written it because I felt compelled in conscience to do so."

Again (II. p. 87):—

"In my letter to Mr. Gladstone, I have maintained the lawfulness and the apostolic character of the German Protestant Church. You will find the style changed in this work, bolder and more free."

Attacks, indeed, became frequent, and more and more bitter, but Bunsen seldom took any notice of them. He writes:—

"Hare is full of wrath at an attack made upon me in the 'Christian Remembrancer'—in a very Jesuitical way insinuating that I ought not to have so much influence allowed me. Another article execrates the bishopric of Jerusalem as an abomination. This zeal savors more of hatred than of charity."

But though Bunsen felt far too firmly grounded in

his own Christian faith to be shaken by such attacks upon himself, he too could be roused to wrath and indignation when the poisoned arrows of theological Fijians were shot against his friends. When speaking of the attacks on Arnold, he writes: —

"Truth is nothing in this generation except a means, in the best case, to something good; but never, like virtue, considered as good, as the good,— the object in itself. X dreams away in twilight. Y is sliding into Puseyism. Z (the Evangelicals) go on thrashing the old straw. I wish it were otherwise; but I love England, with all her faults. I write to you, now only to you, all I think. All the errors and blunders which make the Puseyites a stumbling-block to so many, — the rock on which they split is no other than what Rome split upon, self-righteousness, out of want of understanding justification by faith, and hovering about the unholy and blasphemous idea of atoning for our sins, because they feel not, understand not, indeed, believe not, *the Atonement*, and therefore enjoy not the glorious privileges of the children of God, — the blessed duty of the sacrifice of thanksgiving through Him who atoned for them. Therefore no sacrifice, — therefore no Christian priesthood, — no Church. By our fathers these ideas were fundamentally acknowledged; they were in abeyance in the worship of the Church, but not on the domestic altar and in the hymns of the spirit. With the Puseyites, as with the Romanists, these ideas are cut off at the roots. O when will the Word of God be brought up against them? What a state this country is in! The land of liberty rushing into the worst slavery, the veriest thralldom!"

To many people it might have seemed as if Bunsen during all this time was too much absorbed in English interests, political, theological, and social, that he had ceased to care for what was passing in his own country. His letters, however, tell a different tale. His voluminous correspondence with the King of Prussia, though not yet published, will one day bear witness to Bunsen's devotion to his country, and his enthusiastic attachment to the house of Hohenzollern. From year to year he was urging on the King and his advisers the wisdom of liberal concessions, and the absolute necessity of action. He was working at plans for constitutional reforms; he went to Berlin to rouse the King, to shame his ministers, to insist in season and out of season on the duty of acting before it was too late. His faith in the King is most touching. When he goes to Berlin in 1844, he sees everywhere how unpopular the King is, how even his best intentions are misunderstood and misrepresented. Yet he goes on working and hoping, and he sacrifices his own popularity rather than oppose openly the suicidal policy that might have ruined Prussia, if Prussia could have been ruined. Thus he writes in August, 1845:—

"To act as a statesman at the helm, in the Fatherland, I consider not to be in the least my calling: what I believe to be my calling is to be mounted high before the mast, to observe what land, what breakers, what signs of coming storm there may be, and then to announce them to the wise and practical steersman. It is the same to me whether my own nation shall know in my life-time or after my death how faithfully I have taken to heart its weal and woe, be it in Church or State, and borne it on my heart as my nearest interest, as long as life lasted. I give up the point of making myself understood in the present generation. Here (in London) I consider myself to be upon the right spot. I seek to preserve peace and unity, and to remove dissatisfaction, wherever it is possible."

Nothing, however, was done. Year after year was thrown away, like a Sibylline leaf, and the penalty for the opportunities that had been lost became heavier and heavier. The King, particularly when he was under the influences of Bunsen's good genius, was ready for any sacrifice. "The commotion," he exclaimed, in 1845, "can only be met and overcome by freedom, absolute freedom." But when Bunsen wanted measures, not words, the King himself seemed powerless. Surrounded as he was by men of the most opposite characters and interests, and quite capable of gauging them all, — for his intellect was of no common stamp, — he could agree with all of them to a certain point, but could never bring himself to go the whole length with any one of them. Bunsen writes from Berlin: "My stay will certainly not be a long one; the King's heart is like that of a brother toward me, but our ways diverge. The die is cast, and he reads in my countenance that I deplore the throw. He too fulfills his fate, and we with him."

When, at last, in 1847, a Constitution was granted by the King, it was too late. Sir Robert Peel seems to have been hopeful, and in a letter of twenty-two pages to Bunsen he expressed an opinion that the Prussian government might still be able to maintain the Constitution if only sincere in desiring its due development, and prepared in mind for that development. To the King, however, and to the party at court, the Constitution, if not actually hateful, was a mere plaything, and the idea of surrendering one particle of his independence never entered the King's mind. Besides, 1848 was at the door, and Bunsen certainly saw the coming storm from a distance, though he could not succeed in opening the eyes of those who stood at the helm in Prussia. Shortly before the hurricane broke loose, Bunsen had once more determined to throw up his official position, and retire to Bonn. But with 1848 all these hopes and plans were scattered to the winds. Bunsen's life became more restless than ever, and his body was gradually giving way under the constant tension of his mind. "I feel," he writes in 1848 to Archdeacon Hare, "that I have entered into a new period of life.

I have given up all private concerns, all studies and researches of my own, and live entirely for the present political emergencies of my country, to stand or to fall by and with it."

With his love for England he deeply felt the want of sympathy on the part of England for Prussia in her struggle to unite and regenerate the whole of Germany. "It is quite entertaining," he writes, with a touch of irony very unusual in his letters, "to see the stiff unbelief of the English in the future of Germany. Lord John is merely uninformed. Peel has somewhat staggered the mind of the excellent Prince by his unbelief; yet he has a statesmanlike good-will towards the *Germanic* nations, and even for the *German* nation. Aberdeen is the greatest sinner. He believes in God and the Emperor Nicholas!" The Schleswig-Holstein question embittered his feelings still more; and in absence of all determined convictions at Berlin, the want of moral courage and political faith among those in whose hands the destinies of Germany had been placed, roused him to wrath and fury, though he could never be driven to despair of the future of Prussia. For a time, indeed, he seemed to hesitate between Frankfort, then the seat of the German Parliament, and Berlin; and he would have accepted the Premiership at Frankfort if his friend Baron Stockmar had accepted the Ministry of Foreign Affairs. But very soon he perceived that, however paralyzed for the moment, Prussia was the only possible centre of life for a regeneration of Germany; that Prussia could not be merged in Germany, but that Germany had to be resuscitated and reinvigorated through Prussia. His patriotic nominalism, if we may so call his youthful dreams of a united Germany, had to yield to the force of that political realism which sacrifices names to things, poetry to prose, the ideal to the possible. What made his decision easier than it would otherwise have been to a heart so full of enthusiasm was his personal attachment to the King and to the Prince of Prussia. For a time, indeed, though for a short time only, Bunsen, after his interview with the King in January, 1849, believed that his hopes might still be realized, and he seems actually to have had the King's promise that he would accept the crown of a United Germany, without Austria. But as soon as Bunsen had left Berlin, new influences began to work on the King's brain; and when Bunsen returned, full of hope, he was told by the King himself that he had never repented in such a degree of any step as that which Bunsen had advised him to take; that the course entered upon was a wrong to Austria; that he would have nothing to do with such an abominable line of politics, but would leave that to the Ministry at Frankfort. Whenever the personal question should be addressed to him, then would he reply as one of the Hohenzollern, and thus live and die as an honest man. Bunsen, though mourning over the disappointed hopes that had once centred in Frederick William IV., and freely expressing the divergence of opinion that separated him from his sovereign, remained throughout a faithful servant and a loyal friend. His buoyant spirit, confident that nothing could ruin Prussia, was looking forward to the future, undismayed by the unbroken succession of blunders and failures of Prussian statesmen, — nay, enjoying with a prophetic fervor, at the time of the deepest degradation of Prussia at Olmütz, the final and inevitable triumph of that cause which counted among its heroes and martyrs such names as Stein, Gneisenau, Niebuhr, Arndt, and, we may now add, Bunsen.

After the reaction of 1849 Bunsen's political influence ceased altogether, and as Minister in England he had almost always to carry out instructions of which he disapproved. More and more he longed for rest and freedom, for "leisure for reflection on the Divine which subsists in things human, and for writing, if God enables me to do so. I live as one lamed; the pinions that might have furthered my progress are bound, — yet not broken." Yet he would not give up his place as long as his enemies at Berlin did all they could to oust him. He would not be beaten by them, nor did he altogether despair of better days. His opinion of the Prince of Prussia (the present King) had been raised very high since he had come to know him more intimately, and he expected much in the hour of need from his soldier-like decision and sense of honor. The negotiations about the Schleswig-Holstein question soon roused again all his German sympathies, and he exerted himself to the utmost to defend the just cause of the Schleswig-Holsteiners, which had been so shamefully misrepresented by unscrupulous partisans. The history of these negotiations cannot yet be written, but it will some day surprise the student of history when he finds out in what way public opinion in England was dosed and stupefied on that simple question. He found himself isolated and opposed by nearly all his English friends. One statesman only, but the greatest of English statesmen, saw clearly where the right and where the wrong was, but even he could only dare to be silent. On the 31st of July, 1850, Bunsen writes: —

"Palmerston had yielded, when in a scrape, first to Russia, then to France; the prize has been the protocol; the victim, Germany. They shall never have my signature to such a piece of iniquity and folly."

However, on the 8th of May, 1852, Bunsen had to sign that very piece of iniquity. It was done, machine like, at the King's command; yet, if Bunsen had followed his own better judgment, he would not have signed, but sent in his resignation. "The first cannon-shot in Europe," he used to say, "will tear this Pragmatic Sanction to tatters;" and so it was; but alas! he did not live to see the Nemesis of that iniquity. One thing, however, is certain, that the humiliation inflicted on Prussia by that protocol was never forgotten by one brave soldier, who, though not allowed at that time to draw his royal sword, has ever since been working at the reform of Prussia's army, till on the field of Sadowa the disgrace of the London protocol and the disgrace of Olmütz were wiped out together, and German questions can no longer be settled by the Great Powers of Europe, "with or without the consent of Prussia."

Bunsen remained in England two years longer, full of literary work, delighted by the success of Prince Albert's Great Exhibition, entering heartily into all that interested and agitated English society, but nevertheless carrying in his breast a heavy heart. Prussia and Germany were not what he wished them to be. At last the complications that led to the Crimean War held out to his mind a last prospect of rescuing Prussia from her Russian thralldom. If Prussia could have been brought over to join England and France, the unity of Northern Germany might have been her reward, as the unity of Italy was the reward of Cavour's alliance with the Western Powers. Bunsen used all his influence to bring this about, but he used it in vain, and in April, 1854, he succumbed, and his resignation was accepted.

Now, at last, Bunsen was free. He writes to a son:—

"You know how I struggled, almost desperately, to retire from public employment in 1850. Now the cord is broken, and the bird is free. The Lord be praised!"

But sixty-two years of his life were gone. The foundations of literary work which he had laid as a young man were difficult to recover; and if anything was to be finished, it had to be finished in haste. Bunsen retired to Heidelberg, hoping there to realize the ideal of his life, and realizing it, too, in a certain degree, — *i. e.* as long as he was able to forget his sixty-two years, his shaken health, and his blasted hopes. His new edition of "Hippolytus," under the title of "Christianity and Mankind," had been finished in seven volumes before he left England. At Heidelberg his principal work was the new translation of the Bible, and his "Life of Christ," an enormous undertaking, enough to fill a man's life, yet with Bunsen by no means the only work to which he devoted his remaining powers. Egyptian studies continued to interest him while superintending the English translation of his "Egypt." His anger at the machinations of the Jesuits in Church and State would rouse him suddenly to address the German nation in his "Signs of the Times." And the prayer of his early youth, "to be allowed to recognize and trace the firm path of God through the stream of ages," was fulfilled in his last work, "God in History." There were many blessings in his life at Heidelberg, and no one could have acknowledged them more gratefully than Bunsen. "Yet," he writes,—

"I miss John Bull, the sea, "The Times" in the morning, and, besides, some dozens of fellow-creatures. The learned class has greatly sunk in Germany, more than I supposed; all behindhand. . . . Nothing appears of any importance; the most wretched trifles are cried up."

Though he had bid adieu to politics, yet he could not keep entirely aloof. The Prince of Prussia and the noble Princess of Prussia consulted him frequently, and even from Berlin baits were held out from time to time to catch the escaped eagle. Indeed, once again was Bunsen enticed by the voice of the charmer, and a pressing invitation of the King brought him to Berlin to preside at the meeting of the Evangelical Alliance in September, 1857. His hopes revived once more, and his plans of a liberal policy in Church and State were once more pressed on the King,—in vain, as every one knew beforehand, except Bunsen alone, with his loving, trusting heart. However, Bunsen's hopes, too, were soon to be destroyed, and he parted from the King, the broken idol of all his youthful dreams,—not in anger, but in love, "as I wish and pray to depart from this earth, as on the calm, still evening of a long, beautiful summer's day." This was written on the 1st of October; on the 3d the King's mind gave way, though his bodily suffering lasted longer than that of Bunsen. Little more is to be said of the last years of Bunsen's life. The difficulty of breathing, from which he suffered, became often very distressing, and he was obliged to seek relief by travel in Switzerland, or by spending the winter at Cannes. He recovered from time to time, so as to be able to work hard at the "Biblework," and even to make short excursions to

Paris or Berlin. In the last year of his life he executed the plan that had passed before his mind as the fairest dream of his youth: he took a house at Bonn, and he was not without hope that he might still, like Niebuhr, lecture in the university, and give to the young men the fruits of his studies and the advice founded on the experience of his life. This, however, was not to be, and all who watched him with loving eyes knew but too well that it could not be. The last chapter of his life is painful beyond expression as a chronicle of his bodily sufferings, but it is cheerful also beyond expression as the record of a triumph over death in hope, in faith, — nay, one might almost say, in sight, — such as has seldom been witnessed by human eyes. He died on the 28th of November, 1860, and was buried on the 1st of December in the same churchyard at Bonn where rests the body of his friend and teacher, Niebuhr.

Thoughts crowd in thick upon us when we gaze at that monument, and feel again the presence of that spirit as we so often felt it in the hours of sweet counsel. When we think of the literary works in which, later in life and almost in the presence of death, he hurriedly gathered up the results of his studies and meditations, we feel, as he felt himself when only twenty-two years of age, that "learning annihilates itself, and the most perfect is the first submerged, for the next age scales with ease the height which cost the preceding the full vigor of life." It has been so, and always will be so. Bunsen's work, particularly in Egyptian philology and in the philosophy of language, was to a great extent the work of a pioneer, and it will be easy for others to advance on the roads which he has opened, and to approach nearer to the goal which he has pointed out. Some of his works, however, will hold their place in the history of scholarship, and particularly of theological scholarship. The question of the genuineness of the original Epistles of Ignatius can hardly be opened again after Bunsen's treatise; and his discovery that the book on "All the Heresies," ascribed to Origen, could not be the work of that writer, and that most probably it was the work of Hippolytus, will always mark an epoch in the study of early Christian literature. Either of those works would have been enough to make the reputation of a German professor, or to found the fortune of an English bishop. Let it be remembered that they were the outcome of the leisure hours of a hard-worked Prussian diplomatist, who, during the London season, could get up at five in the morning, light his own fire, and thus secure four hours of undisturbed work before breakfast.

Another reason why some of Bunsen's works will prove more mortal than others is their comprehensive character. Bunsen never worked for work's sake, but always for some higher purpose. Special researches with him were a means, a ladder to be thrown away as soon as he had reached his point. The thought of exhibiting his ladders never entered his mind. Occasionally, however, Bunsen would take a jump, and being bent on general results, he would sometimes neglect the objections that were urged against him. It has been easy, even during his life-time, to point out weak points in his arguments, and scholars who have spent the whole of their lives on one Greek classic have found no difficulty in showing to the world that they know more of that particular author than Bunsen. But even those who fully appreciate the real importance of Bunsen's labors — labors that were more like a shower of rain fertilizing large acres than like the artificial irrigation which supports one greenhouse plant — will be first to mourn over the precious time that was lost to the world by Bunsen's official avocations. If he could do what he did in his few hours of rest, what would he have achieved if he had carried out the original plan of his life! It is almost incredible that a man with his clear perception of his calling in life, so fully expressed in his earliest letters, should have allowed himself to be drawn away by the siren voice of diplomatic life. His success, no doubt, was great at first, and the kindness shown him by men like Niebuhr, the King, and the Crown Prince of Prussia was enough to turn a head that sat on the strongest shoulders. It should be remembered, too, that in Germany the diplomatic service has always had far greater charms than in England, and that the higher members of that service enjoy often the same political influence as members of the Cabinet. If we read of the brilliant reception accorded to the young diplomatist during his first stay at Berlin, the favors showered upon him by the old King, the friendship offered him by the Crown Prince, his future King, the hopes of usefulness in his own heart, and the encouragement given him by all his friends, we shall be less surprised at his preferring, in the days of his youth, the brilliant career of a diplomatist to the obscure lot of a professor. And yet what would Bunsen have given later in life if he had remained true to his first love! Again and again his better self bursts forth in complaints about a wasted life, and again and again he is carried along against his will. During his first stay in England he writes (November 18, 1838): —

"I care no more about my external position than about the mountains in the moon; I know God's will will be done, in spite of them all, and to my greatest benefit. What that is He alone knows. Only one thing I think I see clearly. My whole life is without sense and lasting use, if I squander it in affairs of the day, brilliant and important as they may be."

The longer he remained in that enchanted garden, the more difficult it became to find a way out, even after he had discovered by sad experience how little he was fitted for court life or even for public life in Prussia. When he first appeared at the court of Berlin, he carried everything by storm; but that very triumph was never forgiven him, and his enemies were bent on "showing this young doctor his proper place." Bunsen had no idea how he was envied, for the lesson that success breeds envy is one that men of real modesty seldom learn until it is too late. And he was hated not only by chamberlains, but, as he discovered with deepest grief, even by those whom he considered his truest friends, who had been working in secret conclave to undermine his influence with his royal friend and master. Whenever he returned to Berlin, later in life, he could not breathe freely in the vitiated air of the court, and the wings of his soul hung down lamed, if not broken. Bunsen was not a courtier. Away from Berlin, among the ruins of Rome, and in the fresh air of English life, he could speak to kings and princes as few men have spoken to them, and pour out his inmost convictions before those whom he revered and loved. But at Berlin, though he might have learnt to bow and to smile and to use Byzantine phraseology, his voice faltered and was drowned by noisy declaimers; the diamond was buried in a heap of beads, and his rays could not shine forth where there was no heavenly sunlight to call them out.

King Frederick William IV. was no ordinary King: that one can see even from the scanty extracts from his letters given in "Bunsen's Memoirs." Nor was his love of Bunsen a mere passing whim. He loved the man, and those who knew the refreshing and satisfying influence of Bunsen's society will easily understand what the King meant when he said, "I am hungry and thirsty for Bunsen." But what constitution can resist the daily doses of hyperbolical flattery that are poured into the ears of royalty, and how can we wonder that at last a modest expression of genuine respect does sound like rudeness to royal ears, and to speak the truth becomes synonymous with insolence? In the trickeries and mimicries of court life Bunsen was no adept, and nothing was easier than to outbid him in the price that is paid for royal favors. But if much has thus been lost of a life far too precious to be squandered among royal servants and messengers, this prophet among the Sauls has taught the world some lessons which he could not have taught in the lecture-room of a German university. People who would scarcely have listened to the arguments of a German professor sat humbly at the feet of an ambassador and of a man of the world. That a professor should be learned, and that a bishop should be orthodox, was a matter of course; but that an ambassador should hold forth on hieroglyphics and the antiquity of man rather than on the *chronique scandaleuse* of Paris; that a Prussian statesman should spend his mornings on the Ignatian Epistles rather than in writing gossiping letters to ladies in waiting at Berlin and Potsdam; that this learned man "who ought to know," should profess the simple faith of a child and the boldest freedom of a philosopher, was enough to startle society, both high and low. How Bunsen inspired those who knew him with confidence, how he was consulted, and how he was loved, may be seen from some of the letters addressed to him, though few only of such letters have been published in his "Memoirs." That his influence was great in England we know from the concurrent testimony both of his enemies and his friends, and the seed that he has sown in the minds and hearts of men have borne fruit, and will still bear richer fruit, both in England and in Germany. Nor should it be forgotten how excellent a use he made of his personal influence in helping young men who wanted advice and encouragement. His sympathy, his condescension, his faith when brought in contact with men of promise, were extraordinary: they were not shaken, though they have been abused more than once. In all who loved Bunsen his spirit will live on, imperceptibly, it may be, to themselves, imperceptibly to the world, but not the less really. It is not the chief duty of friends to honor the departed by idle grief, but to remember their designs, and to carry out their mandates. (Tac. Ann. II. 71.)

LETTERS

FROM BUNSEN TO MAX MÜLLER

IN THE YEARS 1848 TO 1859.

LETTERS

FROM BUNSEN TO MAX MÜLLER

IN THE YEARS 1848-1859.

AFTER hesitating for a long time, and after consulting both those who had a right to be consulted, and those whose independent judgment I could trust, I have at last decided on publishing the following letters of Baron Bunsen, as an appendix to my article on the Memoirs of his Life. They will, I believe, show to the world one side of his character which in the Memoirs could appear but incidentally, — his ardent love of the higher studies from which his official duties were constantly tearing him away, and his kindness, his sympathy, his condescension in his intercourse with younger scholars who were pursuing different branches of that work to which he himself would gladly have dedicated the whole energy of his mind. Bunsen was by nature a scholar, though not exactly what in England is meant by a German scholar. Scholarship with him was always a means, never in itself an object; and the study of the languages, the laws, the philosophies and religions of antiquity, was in his eyes but a necessary preparation before approaching the problem of all problems, Is there a Providence in the world, or is there not? "To trace the firm path of God through the stream of ages," this was the dream of his youth, and the toil of his old age; and during all his life, whether he was studying the laws of Rome or the hieroglyphic inscriptions of Egypt, the hymns of the Veda or the Psalms of the Old Testament, he was always collecting materials for that great temple which in his mind towered high above all other temples, the temple of God in history. He was an architect, but he wanted builders; his plans were settled, but there was no time to carry them out. He therefore naturally looked out for younger men who were to take some share of his work. He encouraged them, he helped them, he left them no rest till the work which he wanted was done; and he thus exercised the most salutary influence on a number of young scholars, both in Rome, in London, and in Heidelberg.

When I first came to know Bunsen, he was fifty-six, I twenty-four years of age; he was Prussian ambassador, I was nobody. But from the very beginning of our intercourse, he was to me like a friend and fellow-student; and when standing by his side at the desk in his library, I never saw the ambassador, but only the hard-working scholar, ready to guide, willing to follow, but always pressing forward to a definite goal. He would patiently listen to every objection, and enter readily into the most complicated questions of minute critical scholarship; but he always wanted to see daylight; he could not bear mere groping for groping's sake. When he suspected any scholar of shallowness, pettiness, or professorial conceit, he would sometimes burst forth into rage, and use language the severity of which he was himself the first to regret. But he would never presume on his age, his position, or his authority. In that respect few men remained so young, remained so entirely themselves through life as Bunsen. It is one of the saddest experiences in life to see men lose themselves when they become ministers or judges or bishops or professors. Bunsen never became ambassador, he always remained Bunsen. It has been my good fortune in life to have known many men whom the world calls great, — philosophers, statesmen, scholars, artists, poets; but take it all in all, take the full humanity of the man, I have never seen, and I shall never see his like again.

The rule followed in editing these letters has been a very simple one. I have given them as they were, even though I felt that many could be of interest to scholars only or to Bunsen's personal friends; but I have left out whatever could be supposed to wound the feelings of any one. Unless this rule is most carefully observed, the publication of letters after the death of their writers seems to me simply dishonorable. When Bunsen speaks of public measures and public men, of parties in Church and State, whether in England or in Germany, there was no necessity for suppressing his remarks, for he had spoken his mind as freely on them elsewhere as in these letters. But any personal reflections written on the spur of the moment, in confidence or in jest, have been struck out, however strong the temptation sometimes of leaving them. Many expressions, too, of his kind feelings towards me have been omitted. If some have been left, I hope I may be forgiven for a pride not altogether illegitimate.

LETTERS.[1]

[1.]   LONDON, *Thursday, December* 7, 1848,
                                     9 o'clock.

MY DEAR M.,—I have this moment received your affectionate note of yesterday, and feel as if I must respond to it directly, as one would respond to a friend's shake of the hand. The information was quite new to me, and the success wholly unexpected. You have given a home to a friend who was homeless in the world; may you also have inspired him with that energy and stability, the want of which so evidently depresses him. The idea about Pauli is excellent, but he must decide quickly and send me word, that I may gain over William Hamilton, and his son (the President). The place is much sought after; Pauli would certainly be the man for it. He would not become a *Philister* here, as most do.

And now, my very dear M., I congratulate you on the courageous frame of mind which this event causes you to evince. It is exactly that which, as a friend, I wish for you for the whole of life, and which I perceived and loved in you from the very first moment. It delights me especially at this time, when your contemporaries are even more dark and confused than mine are sluggish and old-fashioned. The reality of life, as we enter the period of full manhood, destroys the first dream of youth; but with moral earnestness, and genuine faith in eternal providence, and in the sacredness of human destiny in that government of the world which exists for all human souls that honestly seek after good,—with these feelings, the dream of youth is more than realized.

You have undertaken a great work, and have been rescued from the whirlpool and landed on this peaceful island that you might carry it on undisturbed, which you could not have done in the Fatherland. This is the first consideration; but not less highly do I rate the circumstances which have kept you here,

---

[1] Translated by G. A. M.

and have given you an opportunity of seeing English life in its real strength, with the consistency and stability, and with all the energy and simplicity, that are its distinguishing features. I have known what it is to receive this complement of German life in the years of my training and apprenticeship. When rightly estimated, this knowledge and love of the English element only strengthens the love of the German Fatherland, the home of genius and poetry.

I will only add that I am longing to see you amongst us: you must come to us before long. Meanwhile think of me with as much affection as I shall always think of you. Lepsius has sent me his splendid work "On the Foundations of Egyptian Chronology," with astounding investigations.

As to Germany, my greatest hopes are based on this, — that the King and Henry von Gagern have met and become real friends.

[2.] *Sunday Morning, February 18, 1849.*

MY DEAR M., — Having returned home last night, I should like to see you quietly to-day, before the turmoil begins again to-morrow. Can you and Mr. Trithen come to me to-day at five o'clock? I will ask Elze to dinner, but I should first like to read to you two my treatise "On the Classification of Languages," which is entirely rewritten, and has become my fifth book *in nuce*.

I will at once tell you that I am convinced that the Lycians were the *true* Pelasgians, and I shall not give you any rest till you have discovered the Pelasgic language from the monuments existing here. It is a sure discovery. It must be an older form of Greek, much as the Oscan or the Carmen Saliare were of Latin, or even perhaps more so.

[3.] TOTTERIDGE PARK, *Monday Morning, February 19, 1849.*

I landed yesterday, and took refuge here till this afternoon; and my first employment is to thank you for your affectionate and faithful letter, and to tell you that I am not only to be here as hitherto, but that, with the permission of the King, I am to fill the post of confidential accredited minister of the *Reichsverweser*, formerly held by Baron Andrian. During my stay here, be it long or short, it will always be a pleasure and refreshment to me to see you as often as you can come to us. You know our way of living, which will remain the same, except now and then, when Palmerston may fix his conferences for a Sunday.

Pertz is quite ready to agree to the proposal of a regular completion of the Chambers collection: the best thing would be for you to offer to make the catalogue. He is waiting your proposal. The dark clouds of civil war are lowering over our dear and mighty Fatherland. Prussia will go on its own way quietly as a mediating power.

[4.]   CARLTON TERRACE, *April 22, 1849.*

Yesterday evening, and night, and this morning early, I have been reading Froude's "Nemesis of Faith," and am so moved by it that I must write you a few lines. I cannot describe the power of attraction exercised upon me by this deeply searching, noble spirit: I feel the tragic nature of his position, and long have I foreseen that such tragical combinations await the souls of men in this island-world. Arnold and Carlyle, each in his own way, had seen this long before me. In the general world, no one can understand such a state of mind, except so far as to be enabled to misconstrue it.

In the shortcoming of the English mind in judging of this book, its great alienation from the philosophy of Art is revealed. This book is not comprehended as a work of Art, claiming as such due proportions and relative significance of parts; otherwise many individuals would at least have been moved to a more sparing judgment upon it, and in the first place they would take in the import of the title.

This book shows the fatal result of the renunciation of the Church system of belief. The subject of the tale simply experiences moral annihilation; but the object of his affection, whose mind he had been the means of unsettling in her faith, burst through the boundaries which humanity has placed, and the moral order of the world imposes: they perish both, — each at odds with self, with God, and with human society: only for him there yet remains room for further development. Then the curtain falls, — that is right, according to artistic rule of composition; true and necessary according to the views of those who hold the faith of the Church of England; and from a theological point of view, no other solution could be expected from the book than that which it has given.

But here the author has disclosed the inward disease, the fearful hollowness, the spiritual death, of the nation's philosophical and theological forms, with resistless eloquence; and like the Jews of old, they will exclaim, "That man is a criminal! stone him!"

I wish you could let him know how deeply I feel for him, without ever having seen him; and how I desire to admonish him to accept and endure this fatality, as, in the nature of things, he must surely have anticipated it; and as he has pointed out and defended the freedom of the spirit, so must he now (and I believe he will) show in himself, and make manifest to the world, the courage, active in deed, cheerful in power, of that free spirit.

It is presumptuous to intrude into the fate and mystery of life in the case of any man, and more especially of a man so remarkable; but the consciousness of community of spirits, of knowing, and endeavoring after what is morally good, and true, and perfect, and of the yearning after every real disciple of the inner religion of Christians, impels me to suggest to you to tell him from me, that I believe the spasm of his spiritual efforts would sooner be calmed, and the solution of the great problem would sooner be found, if he were to live for a time among us; I mean, if he resided for a time in one of the German universities. We Germans have been for seventy years working as thinkers, inquirers, poets, seers, also as men of action, to pull down the old and to erect the new Zion; each great man with us has contributed his materials towards the sanctuary, invisible, but firmly fixed in German hearts; the whole nation has neglected and sacrificed political, individual existence and common freedom — to pursue in faith the search after truth. From us something may be learnt, by every spirit of this age. He will experience how truly the divine Plato spoke, when he said, "Seven years of silent inquiry were needful for a man to learn the truth, but fourteen in order to learn how to make it known to his fellow-men."

Froude must know Schleiermacher's "Discourses on Religion," and perhaps also his "Dogmatica." In this series of developments this is perhaps, as far as the form is concerned, the most satisfactory work which immediately concerns religion and its reconciliation with philosophy on the basis of more liberal Christian investigation. But at all events we have not striven and suffered in vain: our philosophy, research, and poetry show

this. But men, not books, are needed by such a mind, in order
to become conscious of the truth, which (to quote Spinoza)
"remoto errore nuda remanet." He has still much to learn, and
he should learn it as a man from man. I should like to propose
to him first to go to Bonn. He would there find that most
deeply thoughtful and most original of speculative minds among
our living theologians, the Hamann of this century, my dear
friend R. Rothe; also a noble philosopher and teacher of ethics,
Brandis; an honest master of exegesis, Bleek; and young
minds would soon attach themselves to him. In Halle he would
find Erdmann, almost the only distinguished speculative follower
of Hegel, and Tholuck, who has advanced much farther in the
philosophical treatment of Christianity than is generally thought.
I will gladly give him introductions to all of these. They would
all willingly admit him into their world of thought, and enter
with sympathy into his. It would be sure to suit him. . . .
The free atmosphere of thought would do him good, as formerly
the atmosphere of free England was good for Germans still
struggling for political liberty. He certainly needs physical
change and invigorating. For this the lovely Rhine is decidedly
to be recommended. With £100 he could live there as a prince.
Why go off to Van Diemen's Land? I should always be glad
to be of the least service to him, still more to make his personal
acquaintance. And now, my dear M., you can, if you wish, read
out to him what I have written, but do not give the letter out
of your own hands.

[5.] 9 CARLTON TERRACE, *Monday,*
May 21, 1849.

I thank you for two letters. I cannot tell how the first delighted and rejoiced me. The state of things in England is
really as you describe it. As to what concerns the second, you
will by this time know that I have seen Froude twice. With
M., too, personal acquaintance has been made, and the point as
to money is touched on. I must see him again alone before I
give my opinion. At all events, he is a man of genius, and
Germany (especially Bonn) the country for him.

I can well imagine the terrible scenes your dear mother has
witnessed in Dresden. However, I believe we have, in the very
midst of the storm, reached the harbor. Even in Frankfort
every one believes in the complete success of Prussia's negotiations with the four Courts. We shall have the whole constitu-

tion of the empire, and now with all necessary improvements. As to matters of form, they must be arranged as between equals. Gagern and his friends are ready for this. The constitution is to be declared at Berlin on the 25th. The disturbances will then be quieted as by magic. George is *aux anges* over this unexpected turn of affairs. At all events I hope soon to see you.

[6.]   LONDON, *Wednesday, July 14, 1849.*

"Hurrah for Müller!" — so writes George, and as an answer I send you his note from Frankfort. Hekscher's proposal is quite reasonable. I have since then broken off all negotiations with the Danes. You will soon read the documents in the newspapers.

If the proposal of the parliamentary committee on the directory of the Bund passes, which admits of little doubt, the question of to be or not to be must be immediately decided.

I do not intend going to Frankfort for this, so pray come here; I am alone here with Charles.

[7.]   9 CARLTON TERRACE, *Friday Morning*.[1]

MY DEAR M., — I did not thank you immediately for your delightful and instructive letter, because there were many points on which I wished to write fully. The last decisive crisis of the German-European business has at length arrived, and I have had the opportunity of doing my duty in the matter. But I have been doing nothing else since last Saturday, nothing Chinese even. I recommend the inclosed to you. The young man is a good and highly informed German bookseller. He has of course written just what I did not tell him, and omitted what he ought to have said, "that he had been here for five years with the first booksellers, and before that was trained under his father in Bonn; that he understands English, German, French, Italian, and Spanish." I have only heard what is good of him. How grateful I feel to you for having begun the Index of Egyptian words at once! We wanted one here for a special purpose, so our trouble has not been thrown away. I now perceive how impossible it is to understand the Egyptian language and history thoroughly without Chinese. In the chronology there is still much to be done.

[1] No date, but about December, 1849.

We have as yet held our own in London and Warsaw as against Vienna. But in the Schleswig-Holstein question we have the whole world, and unfortunately our own peace of July 2d, against us. Radowitz has worked most devotedly and honestly. When shall we see you again?

[8.]   PRUSSIAN LEGATION, *May 15, 1850.*

By return of post thanks and greetings to my dear M. Your proposal as to Schütz is excellent. Let me know if I am to write to Humboldt. I draw a totally different lesson from your news of the loss of the Veda MS. Wait till a good copy arrives, and in the mean time pursue your philological studies in some other direction, and get on with your Introduction. You can work more in one day in Europe than in a week in India, unless you wish to kill yourself, which I could not allow. So come with bag and baggage here, to 9 Carlton Terrace, to one who longs to see you.

F. must have gone mad, or have been far more so politically than I imagined. The "Leader," edited by him and N., is (as Mills says) *red and raw!* and, in addition, badly written. It is a pity for prophets and poets to meddle with realities, instead of devoting themselves to futurity and poetry. George is happy in the intellectual wealth of Paris life, and quite perplexed at the perverseness and follies of the political cliques. He promises to write about the acquaintance of Lamenais and George Sand. I am well, but fully use the right of a convalescent, and hardly go anywhere.

Friend Stockmar sends a report from Erfurt, where the Parliament meets on the 26th to receive the oaths of the Directory and the Ministers of the Union. Usedom, Pertz, and Co. are quite mad in their enthusiasm for the Black and White, as I have openly written to them.

[9.]   CARLTON TERRACE, *July 10, 1850.*

Mr. Eastwick, the translator of Bopp's Grammar, tells me that he and Murray wish for an article on this work in the "Quarterly Review" for January, 1851; so it must be sent in in November. Wilson refuses, as he is too busy. I believe you could best write such a review, of about sixteen pages

(£16). If you agree to this, write a line to me or direct to Eastwick, who would then get a letter from Lockhart with the commission for you. God help Schleswig-Holstein!

[10.]   LONDON, *October* 10, 1850.

You have given me the greatest pleasure, my dear M., by your beautiful present. Already, last night, I read the new "Greek Songs," and others that were new to me, with the greatest delight. We have, at all events, derived one benefit from the great storm,—that the setters have been taken off the press. It is a very charming edition, and a beautiful memorial.

As to F——, it seems to me *contra rei naturam* to arrange anything with the "Quarterly Review." The channel for such things is now really the "Edinburgh;" in the "Quarterly" everything not English must be run down, at all events in appearance, if it is to be appreciated. And now "Modern German Poetry and F——," and Liberal politics! I cannot understand how F—— could think of such a thing. I will willingly take charge of it for the "Edinburgh Review." The editor is my political, theological, personal friend, and sympathises with me in such things as I consider F——'s beautiful review will be. I have for years wished for such a one; epic-lyric poetry has made much greater advances since Goethe's time than people in Germany (with the one exception of Platen) seem to perceive. It seems to me, though, that one should begin with the flowers of the Romantic school of poetry, with Schenkendorf and Körner,—that is, with the whole romantic German national epoch, which found Goethe already a retired philosopher. The whole development, from that time till now, appears to me as one intimately united whole, even including the present day. Even 1848 to 1850 have furnished their contribution (Arndt's two inspired songs, for instance); and in 1843–44, Geibel shines as a star of the first magnitude. Heine is difficult to treat. In fact, I do not think that F—— has read enough of these poets. He spoke to me lately of an historical work that he had in view, and which he wished to talk over with me; he meant to come up to me from the country, but has not yet appeared. He is always welcome, for he is decidedly a man of genius, and I would willingly help him.

Now to something different. My Chinese work is tolerably

far advanced. I have arranged the 214 keys alphabetically, and have examined about 100 of them historically — that is, I have separated the oldest (entirely hieroglyphic and ideographic) signs, and as far as possible fixed the relationship of identical or similarly sounding roots. Then I laid aside the work, and first began a complete list of all those pronominal, adverbial, and particle stems, arranged first alphabetically and then according to matter, in which I found the recognisable corpses of the oldest Chinese words. The result repays me even far more than I expected. I hope to have finished both works before Christmas; and at last, too, the alphabetical examination of the 450 words (of which about 150 are hidden in the 214 keys; the 64 others are similarly sounding roots). Naturally all this is only in reference to ancient Chinese, which is at least as different (grammatically) from modern Chinese as Egyptian is from Coptic.

At the same time, I am reading the translation of the three "Kings," and transliterate some passages. And now I must ask you to examine the inclosed system of transliteration. I have devised it according to my best powers after yours and Lepsius' system. Secondly, I want you to tell me whether I ought to buy the Leipzig translation of Eichhoff's "Parallèle des Langues Sanscrites." My own copy of the French edition has disappeared. Pauli works at an Index of the Egyptian hieroglyphics and words, which I can send you by and by.

"The days and times are hard," says an old song.

[11.]   TOTTERIDGE PARK, *Tuesday Morning,*
          October 16, 1850.

MY DEAR FRIEND, — So it seems that I am really not to see you this time. I am truly sorry, and count all the more on your calling on your return, if I am still in England. I should like to have thanked you at once for your affectionate letter for my birthday. But you know, if you altogether trust me, that a lifelong love for you lies deep in my heart.

I had expected more from the great programme of New Oxford. It is not, however, much more unsatisfactory than the article on Plato, the writer of which now avows himself. It is only possible to excuse the milk-and-watery treatment of the subject through the general mental cowardice and ignorance in intellectual matters which is so predominant in this country. I find

a comfort in the hope that this article is the prologue to able
exegetical works, combined with a concrete statement of the
absurdity, the untruth, and untenableness of the present English
conception of inspiration. Do not call me to account too
sharply for this hope, or it is likely to evaporate simply in
pious wishes. Moral earnestness is the only thing that pleases
me in this matter; the important thing now is to prove it, in
opposition to invincible prejudices. Your plan of publishing
your Introduction after you have talked it over with Lassen and
Burnouf, and drawn in fresh breath, and just in January too,
pleases me very much. If I may, all in the dark, give you some
good advice, try to make yourself clear on two points. First,
as to the proper limits of language for the investigation of past
and prehistoric times. As yet, no one has known how to handle these gigantic materials; what Jacob Grimm has lately attempted with them is child's play. It is no longer of any use,
as a Titan in intention, but confused as to aim, and uncertain
in method, — it is no longer of any use to put down dazzling
examples which demonstrate nothing, or at most only that something ought to be there to be demonstrated. What you have
told me entitles one to the highest hopes; and these will be
realised, if you in the French, not the Teutonic manner, arrive
at full understanding of what is at present a mere instinctive intuition, and thus arrive at the right method. You can do it.
Only I have some anxiety as to the second point, the historical
proofs of the beginnings of nations. That is the weak side, first
of all etymologists and word-masters, and then especially of all
" Indologues," and of the whole Indian past itself. There is an
enormous difference between what *can* have been, nay, according to certain abstract theoretic views *must* have been, and what
has been. That, however, is the distinctive problem for historical investigation. And here, above all, much depends on philological knowledge and sagacity; but still more on that historical tact which understands how inferences should be drawn.
This demands much acquaintance with what is real, and with
purely historical material; much practice, and, as regards character, much self-denial. In this *judicium subactum* of the historian lies the difference between Niebuhr and O. Müller. To
satisfy these demands, it is only necessary, with your gifts and
your character, that you should wish to do so earnestly, and
perseveringly wish it. Of course you will not separate the inquiry as to the oldest seat of the Sanskrit language from the

surrounding problems. I am perhaps too strongly prejudiced
against the idea that the family of which we are speaking must
have wandered from the banks of the Upper Indus towards Bactria, and from thence founded Media and Persia. But I have
for the present good grounds for this, and views which have
long been tested by me. I can well imagine a migration of this
family to and fro from the northern to the southern slopes of
the Hindu-Kush and back again; in Egypt one sees most plainly
how the Semitic, or the family which inclines towards Semitism,
migrated frequently from the Mediterranean and the Euphrates
to the Red Sea and *back again*. But this alters nothing in the
theory, on the one hand, that it is one and the same family historically, and, on the other hand, that it is not originally African,
but Asiatic. You will certainly not adopt Niebuhr's autoch-
thonic theory, where such facts lie before you. But enough.
Only receive these remarks as a proof of my lively interest in
your researches, and in yourself; and may Minerva be your
guide. I rejoice in the prize you have gained at the French
Academy in Paris, both for you and the Fatherland.

The King *has* subscribed for twenty copies of your Veda, and
you have received 500 thalers of it beforehand. The rest you
will receive, according to the agreement then made, and which
was communicated to you, as certainly *after* the revolution and
constitution as *before*. I cannot have said a word with any other
meaning. I may have recommended you not to demand future
prepayment: there might have been difficulties. Examine, then,
the communication made to you, take twenty copies of your first
volume in your pocket, or rather in the ship, and hand them in,
writing in any case to Humboldt, and beside him to the minister
concerned, therefore to the Minister of Public Instruction. As
to what concerns the King personally, ask Humboldt what you
have to do. The thing itself is as clear and settled a matter
of business as anything can well be; on this very account I
have completely forgotten the particulars.

And now, God bless you, my dear friend. Greet all friendly
minds and souls, and first, "though I have not the pleasure of
her acquaintance," your mother; and then Humboldt and Lepsius before any one else.

[12.]   LONDON, *November 4, 1850.*

I must tell you by return of post that your letter has frightened me by what you tell me respecting your strong impulse to

go to Benares or to Bonn. This is the very worst moment for
Bonn, and the very best for your publication of the Introduction
to the Vedas. The crisis in our country disturbs everything;
it will soon be over, and, as I have good reason to believe,
without dishonor or bloodshed. They would do everything to
make your stay in Bonn pleasant, as soon as they have recovered breath. Still, you must print that English book in England; and I should add, before you settle across the Channel. Or do you only intend to pay Lassen a visit? You
knew that some time ago Lassen longed to see you, more than
any other man. It would be a good idea if you settle to make
an excursion to Germany. You are one of those who always
arrange things best personally. At all events, you must come
to us the day after to-morrow, and stay till the 9th. We shall
have a house full of visitors that day (evening), but till then be
quite alone. On the 7th you will give your presence to George
as a birthday gift, a proof of great affection. Of Froude I
have heard and seen nothing.

Empson has been here twice, without leaving his address. I
have advanced as far in the astronomy and chronology of the
Chinese as I can without an astronomer. *They have begun with
the beginning of the Chaldeans.* With the language, too, I have
reached firm soil and ground, through the 120 words which become particles. More by word of mouth.

The struggle is over. Open conferences will be held at
Vienna, where Prussia will represent and securely maintain the
principle of free opinion.

The 8,000 Bavarians will return home again. The new constitution of the Bund will include all Austria (except Italy), and
will have a diet which has no legislative power in internal
German affairs. Will Radowitz stay? Send a line in answer.

[12.] LONDON, *December* 11, 1850.

In spite of the courier, who goes to-day, I must write a few
words in answer to your friendly inquiries.

I am more and more convinced that you stake *everything* if
you begin the important affair in Bonn without going there
yourself; and on the other hand, that the business *cannot* fail *if*
you go there; *lastly,* that you should go there at once, that Lassen and the government may not hit on something else. Once
begun, the thing will, I hope, go exactly as you wish. But I

should be *very* sorry if you were to leave Oxford before finishing the printing of the Introduction. That is your farewell to England, your greeting to the professoriate in Germany, both worthy and suited to you.

The Lectures at Oxford appear, by the side of this, as a secondary consideration. I cannot, however, restrain the wish that you should not refuse the thing. It is not expected that a deputy-professor should spend more time than is necessary on the charge committed to him. I should think you could arrange such a course very pleasantly, and feel certain of success, if you only bear in mind Lockhart's advice, to write as for ladies, — "Spartam quam nactus es orna," as Niebuhr always told me, and I have always found it a good maxim. I await the sending in of your article for the "Edinburgh," in order to make all preparations at once. I hope you will be back from Bonn by Christmas Eve, or else wait till after Christmas before you go.

As a friend of many years' standing, you will forgive me if I say that if the journey to Bonn is not financially convenient to you just now, I *depend* upon your thinking of *me*.

[14.]   9 CARLTON TERRACE, *January* 2, 1851.

Most heartily do I wish you success and happiness in the new year. Stanley will have told you of our negotiations as to your beautiful article. He will have laid before you the sketch of a genuine English prologue and epilogue promised by him, and for which I gave him a few ideas. You can then choose between the "Quarterly" and "Edinburgh Review."

Pertz has authorized me to pay you £20 on the 1st of January, as you wished. So send your receipt, that I may at once send you the £20 (in four bank-notes), unless you will fetch them yourself. If you can be here on Monday, you are invited to dinner with Macaulay, Mahon, and General Radowitz, otherwise any other day.

P. S. (Wednesday). No, my dear M., I will not send your article, but take it myself. Let me have it soon.

[15.]   LONDON, *March* 12, 1851.

It is such a delight to be able at last to write to you, to tell you that few events this year have given me such great pleasure as your noble success in Oxford. The English have shown how gladly they will listen to something good and new, if any one will lay it before them in their own halls and in their "gown." Morier has faithfully reported everything, and my whole family sympathise in your triumph, as if it concerned ourselves.

I have heard from Empson that he will let your article appear in the third quarter (1st July). All space for the 1st of April had been promised since December. He will have it printed very early, that we may have time to read it comfortably, and see if it really wants a "head and tail." He seems to think it is *not* wanted. So much the better, I answered him.

George writes diligently, *De Nili fontibus*, and revels in the scientific life of Bonn. He is coming at Easter for four weeks, and intends immediately after Whitsuntide to take his degree *cum honore*.

You have seen that Lachmann was obliged to have his foot amputated, as it was mortifying. The operation was very well performed; but the question is, whether the evil may not still spread. Haupt writes in great anxiety; he hurried off to his friend, to nurse him.

Theodore comes as early as the 7th of April, and goes to the University after Easter.

We have all had something of influenza, but not so that we were obliged to give up our *Tuesday evenings*, which are very well attended, as many as 300 people, who amuse themselves and us well. When are you coming to us?

I have come to the end of the third volume, in working over "Egypt," and have already besides a third of the fourth volume ready for press. By the 1st of May the fourth volume must be sent to Gotha.

(16.)   CARLTON TERRACE, *Tuesday Morning*,
May 13, 1851, 7 o'clock.
(*Olymp.* I. t. 1.) according to new German
Chronology. See tables for "Egypt."

I must at last take my early morning hour to write to you, instead of writing, or rather preparing, a chapter of my fifth volume. For I find the flood of business which begins with breakfast subsides now only after midnight, and I have many things I must say to you. First, my thanks and good wishes for the sketch of your lectures. You have rightly understood the importance of epic poetry in its historical bearing, and for *the first time* connected it with the earliest times of the epic nations, namely, the primitive period of their community of language.

This has given me indescribable pleasure, and daily roused a longing to see you again very soon, and to read to you some chapters out of my 5th volume, the writing of which has continued to be an excessive delight to me. I have attempted the restoration of the times of the patriarchs, in the full belief in their real existence and in my own method, and have been surprised at the great results. After I had finished this section I felt inspirited to add the Introduction to the Preface, written at Easter, "The History and Method of the Philosophy of History," and then, as by a stroke of magic, I found myself again in the lost Paradise of the deepest philosophical and historical convictions of all my life, on the strength of which I consecrated my dim anticipations to definite vows in the holy vigils of 1810-13, and wrote them down in the last weeks of my German life (January, 1816) in Berlin in order to explain myself to Niebuhr. The little book which I then wrote comes back again, after the lapse of quite thirty-five years, into my thoughts. The journey to India has turned out a journey to Egypt, and the journey of life hastens towards its close. But though I, since 1816, never found the means and opportunity to fix my eyes on the first youthful ideal, after I had dedicated my life to investigate, to think, and to live for it; and though all the grand and elevated views had been hidden from me in the narrow valleys of life and of special research, except some blessed moments of intuition, I am now again raised by the flood of Egyptian research, after a quarter of a century, on to the heights of the same Ararat from whence, in the battle of life, I had to descend. I only wished to give an introductory survey of the manner of treating the world's history, and to my astonishment something else appears, to which I yield myself with fear as well as delight, with the old youthful ardor. I believe I owe something of my good fortune this time also to my enemies and enviers. For it is quite true, as the newspaper said, that my removal or recall was demanded from the King, not only by our Camarilla and its tool, the ministry, but by more than "flesh and blood," that high demoniacal power, which would willingly crush Prussia and Germany in its unholy embrace. It has come to an avowed struggle. As yet the King has held fast to me as king and friend. Such attacks always fill me with courageous indignation and indignant courage, and God has graciously filled my heart with this courage ever since I, on the day of the news of our complete defeat (November 10), determined to finish "Egypt." Never, since I projected the five books on Egypt, when besieged on the Capitol by the Pope and his followers, and abandoned by the ministry at Berlin, from January 6th till Easter Sunday, 1838, — never have I worked with such success. Even the Great Exhibition and the visit of the Prince and Princess of Prussia have not hindered me. Volume IV. was finished on Sunday evening, April 27; and Tuesday morning, the 29th, I wrote at Dover the first chapter of the "Traditions of Prehistoric Times," after Easter Sunday had presented me with the above-mentioned Preface. On the 27th of May all that is entailed by the Prince's visit ceases again on the beach at Dover, and on the 1st June I hope to be able to begin with the "Methodology." I have now arrived at Leibnitz in the historical survey, which is to close with Schelling and Hegel, Goethe and Schiller, and which began with Abraham. Don't be frightened, it will please you.

But now, if Oxford and the gods of the Veda allow it, you should come here. George will, before he returns to Bonn, sail up the waters of the Nile with me; he has written the first sketch of the dissertation, and can get through everything in Bonn in six weeks; I believe he returns at the end of the first week.

Think this over. I do so wish for him to see you before he leaves. Meanwhile I may tell you, *sub rosa*, that on Saturday morning he, with Colonel Fischer and the charming Prince Friedrich Wilhelm, will go to Oxford from Birmingham (12 o'clock), and, in strictest *incognito*, show the Benares of Europe to the future King of Prussia, who is enthusiastic about England. He will write to you beforehand; he is now asleep, resting himself, after running about all day yesterday with the Prince, and staying at a ball till morning.

But enough of the outpourings of my heart. I hasten to business.

First, Empson has sent me the proof-sheets of your article. I mean your article for the "Edinburgh Review." Early this morning I read it through at last, and joyfully and heartily utter my *Macte virtute*. You have worked up the article since I first read it in MS. far more than I expected; and certainly with good and practical results. Your examples, and particularly your notes, will help and please the English reader very much. The introduction is as excellent (*ad hominem* and yet dignified) as the end. Many thanks for it. God will bless it. To-night I shall read out the article to my wife, children, and Neukomm, as I long ago promised, and to-morrow I will send it to the printer (with a few corrected misprints), and will write to Empson "what I think about it." So far, so good.

Secondly, I find I cannot with honor shrink from some sort of comparison of my Egyptian forms and roots with the Semitic and Iranian forms and roots. The facts are so enormously great, that it does not in the least matter whether the proof can be *thoroughly* given in all its details. I have therefore in my need thought of Rödiger, and have sent a letter to him, of which I inclose a copy. You will see from it that I hold fast to your friendly promise, to stand by me in the matter of Iran. What I said on the certainty and satisfactory completeness of the tools contained in my English edition, is, I am firmly convinced, not too strong. Still, I do not mean to say that a comparison with rich results might not be instituted between such Coptic *roots* (I do not admit it of the grammatical *forms*) as have not yet been rediscovered among the hieroglyphics and the ancient Asiatic: some of them may be found again in ancient Egyptian, almost unformed and not yet ground down; but that is mere pedantry in most cases. We have enough in what lies before us in the oldest form in attested documents, to show us the right formula for the equation.

And now for a few words about my family, which is so truly attached to you, and watches your success with real affection. But no, I have something else to say first on the Niebelungen. Your delightful letter awoke a thought which has often crossed my mind, namely, that it does not appear to me that the historical and early national element, which is but thinly veiled under the poetical matter, has ever been sufficiently searched out and distinguished. Grimm hates the historical elements which lie beyond his "Beginnings of Nations," and my late dear friend Lachmann occupied himself with them most unwillingly. When, in 1825, I wrote that little treatise in French for Chateaubriand, which he printed in his "Mélanges," I went over what had been said on this point, as far as it concerned me, and I was surprised to see how little had been done in it. Since that time I have heard of no investigations of the kind. But who can now believe that the mention of Gunther and the Burgundians is the one isolated historical fact in the poem? Is it not evident, for instance, that the myth of the contemporary of Attila, a certain great

Theodoric of the Ostrogoths has its historical root in the fact that *Theodoric, King of the Visigoths*, fell in the great battle of Chalons, 451, fighting against Attila; but his son Thorismund, to revenge his father's death, defeated the barbarians in a last assault, and gained the victory, on which the Franks pursued the Huns even across the Rhine. From this arose the connection of Attila with *Theodoric, the great King of the Ostrogoths*, who lived forty years later, and was intimately connected with the royal family of the Visigoths, and with the kingdom of the Visigoths, but of course could never have had any dealings with Attila.

If one neglects such intimations, one arrives at last at the Görres and Grimm clairvoyance, where not only everything is everything, but also everything again is nothing. Etzel, though, is not really Attila to Grimm, but the fairy nature of the legend allows of no certain conclusions. But I find that everywhere, where the tools are not wanting, the fermentation and decomposition process of the historical element can be proved; from which organically and by a process exactly analogous to that of the formation of languages in the first ages of the world, the epic legend arises, which the genius of the epic poet lays hold of when the time comes, with a consciousness of an historical destiny; as the tragic poet does in later times.

If you have time, follow up this idea. This is the weak side of your generation and guild. The whole national element has been kept too much in the background in the conceit and highstiltedness, not to say woodenness, of our critical researches. Instead of saying with the humorists of the eighteenth century, "Since Herman's death nothing new has happened in Germany," one ought to say "since Siegfried's death." The genius of the nation which mourned over Herman's fall and murder was the same that in its sorrow gave shape to the legend of Sigurd. Must not the hearts of our ancestors, whose blood flows in our veins, have felt as we do in like circumstances? The princes and their relatives have betrayed and sold and murdered the true prince of the German people, even to this day. And yet were there now but a Siegfried-Herman! "Exsurget aliquando Istis ex ossibus ultor."

I take this opportunity of calling your attention to a pamphlet by Bethman-Hollweg, which has just appeared, "The Ancient Germans before the Migration of Nations." I send it to you to-day, and you must bring it back when you come. Send me word by George when you can and will come.

TO MAX MÜLLER.   413

The Exhibition is, and will continue to be, the poetical and historical event of the period. "Les Anglais ont fait de la poésie sans s'en douter," as that excellent Jourdain said of his prose. Come and see it and to as soon as you can.

[17.]   *Thursday, May 15, 1851, 7 A. M.*

George, in the hurry of his journey, begs you, through me, to be so kind as to be at the Oxford station when the Birmingham train arrives, Saturday (the day after to-morrow) at 12 o'clock, and then kindly to help him in showing Oxford to the *princeps juventutis*. They leave again at 8 o'clock in the evening. The party will of course want some rooms in the best hotel, to rest themselves. So it might be well to bespeak some rooms for the travellers as a *pied à terre*. The party travel under the name of Colonel Fischer or George Bunsen.

I talked over the whole plan of the forms and roots with that good Steinschneider yesterday, and requested him to ask you further about it. He willingly undertook to do the work in the course of the summer. Thus we have certainly got one, perhaps two, for the Semitic work. I have given him a copy of my "Egypt." He seems to be getting *tame*.

[18.]   LONDON, *February 3, 1852.*

I have exactly a quarter of an hour before I must make myself grand for the opening of Parliament, and I will spend it in chatting with you.

I will write to Pocoke notwithstanding. I cannot help believing that the German method of etymology, as applied to history by Schlegel, Lassen, and Humboldt, and of which I have endeavored to sketch the outline, *is the only safe one.*

You have opened my eyes to the danger of their laying such dry and cheap ravings to our account, unless we, " as Germans," protest against it.

I am rejoiced at your delight with the "Church Poetry." But Pauli never sent you what I intended; I wanted to send you the first edition of my Hymn Book (no longer to be had at the booksellers'), because it has historical and biographical notices about the composers, and contains in the Preface and Introduction the first attempt to res------- ----ures of continuity and the epochs more conspic·   ·ly copy.

please for this reason take great care of it.) Also I wish to draw your attention to *two translations* from my collection. First by Miss Cox (daughter of the Bedell in Oxford), c. 1840, small 8vo. Second by Arnold (Rugby), not Dr. Arnold. This last I can send you. It contains *one* translation by the great Arnold, first part. You will observe, among other points, that the most animated hymns of praise and thanksgiving were composed amid the sufferings of the Thirty Years' War. My attention has been directed to Hillebrand's "History of German Literature," three volumes, as the *best* work, and to Vilmar's ditto, one volume, as the *most popular*. I myself only possess Gelzer's thoughtful "Lectures" (from Lessing to Goethe), a book which I prefer to Gervinus, as far as a just appreciation of the national character and sentiment is concerned. (With many extracts.) I rejoice at your cheerful spirit. But now be satisfied, and make more use of the Romance languages. *Tutius ibis.* You have already sufficient materials. We can and will benefit this hospitable land, even without their desiring it; but *cautiously!* You will laugh at this, and forgive me; but I know what I am about. Next Saturday Volume II., ready bound, will lie on my table. The plan of the doctrine of the Trinity, critical and reconstructive, is a bold undertaking: the restoration of the genuine substance of the Apostolical constitutions and canons (in the second half of Volume II.) will probably have at present more success. But Volume III., The Reconstruction and the Reform! "The two text-books of the Early Church, The Church and House-Book and The Law-Book," in biblical phraseology and orthography, chiefly derived from documents never yet made known, is my *pièce de résistance*; the sauce for it, in the Introduction, contains three chapters (The Picture, The Mirror, The Practical Reconstruction) for each section (Baptism, School, Constitution, Worship, Life).

So far I had written everything in English, *tant bien que mal*, without hesitating a moment for thoughts or words. But here the Muse refused, — not a single idea would flow into my pen. After three days I discovered that the spirit *would* and *could* speak German. So I then hastily added the first half of the Introduction; and I hope that the first cast of the whole will be ready this week; and a week later Cottrell will have it for translation, whilst the text-book (about 140 pages) is being printed in slips. I am afraid the English edition will not appear before the end of March; of the second I have already re-

ceived Volume II. I think you will approve of the offspring. May
Apollo and the Muses enlighten people about Bernays. I might
then hope that he would again come here to me in the summer.
George has not yet announced his dissertation as "sent in to
the faculty :" till then he is wisely silent. He appears to me to
be too much there in the fashion and in society. May the devil
carry off all fashionable women !

John calls. God bless you.

Wednesday. — *Vivat Müller !* I am just writing my congratulations to Bernays. *Vivat Dean !*

Pauli's book appears in English without his doing anything to it.

You may recommend in Oxford, even to the most refined ladies and most Christian evangelicals, "Spiritual Words" from Goethe, by Lancizolle, 120 pages, 12mo (3s. beautifully bound). That is a German Bible.

You know Wackernagel's "Anthology"? It is useful, but gives too much of second rate. I will make my daughters copy out Arndt's German song for his eighty-third birthday for you. Adieu.

[19.] *Saturday, March 13, 1852.*

What in all the world is this undertaking to which Vaux asks my aid, the new edition of Herbelot's "Bibliothéque Orientale"? It might be made a good work, although I hate the form, but *everything depends on the management.* It is otherwise a mere bookseller's speculation or Jesuit's trick. I have answered provisionally that in case biblical literature is to be taken up (which is highly necessary), Ewald, Freytag, Bernays, Rödiger, Hengstenberg, and Bernstein should be summoned to help. I don't quite trust the thing; but if it is possible to introduce the people to good ideas, I am ready to aid.

When are you coming? I have sent the last MS. to-day to the press, or rather to the translator. I have only now reached the point on which I can really speak in a practical tone. Volume III. will contain 600 pages.

[20.] LONDON, *November 13, 1852.*

Though late, I send you my hearty greetings on your return to England. I heard from Wilson that you were well, and that you had left your mother well for the winter.

Hippolytus lies here *ready* for you, on purpose that you may fetch it. I hope you will do so on the 18th, for which you have already received the invitation. You will find Morier also here. Is not that furious and ridiculous article in the "Morning Chronicle" on the second volume (the first article, as yet without a continuation) by the same man (of Jesus College?) on whose article in the "Ecclesiastic" on Hippolytus' book I have thrown some degree of light? The leading thought is exactly the same in both; the account of Calixtus' knavery is interpolated (by Novatianus), says the writer in the "Chronicle." This is a proof that nothing can be said against my argument requiring a serious answer. Gladstone felt ashamed of the review. It has helped the book; but it would be read even without this and the recommendation of the "Guardian" — so Longman says. *One* circulating library here has taken twenty-five copies, and wants more. So the book cannot be ignored; and that is all I first of all wished for, *aculeum reliqui*. As the people of this country, with a few exceptions that one can count upon one's fingers, do not understand the book, not even the title, and have never had a conception of what it means, to reproduce the spirit of a century of which men as yet, with the exception of Irenæus, Tertullian, Clemens Alexandrinus, and Origen, know only the names and enigmas (of which latter Hippolytus was one), their fault-finding with the composition of the book does not affect me at all. In spite of the timidity of nearly *all* English theologians, *inter muros academicos et extra*, I have received very many hearty and manly letters from numerous and distinguished people. The King has, on my recommendation, sent Dr. Boetticher to spend two years here and in Paris in order to bring to light the Syriac treasures which have not been laid claim to by Cureton. I see that I have not been mistaken in him in spite of his sporadic many-sidedness. I am free from the 2d of December. There is a letter of mine just printing to Miss Winkworth, "On Niebuhr's Political Character," with extracts from letters.

[91.]   PRUSSIAN LEGATION, *Tuesday, November 30, 1852.*

General von Scharnhorst, the worthy and highly educated son of his great father, intends going to Oxford the day after to-morrow, Thursday, by the morning express, perhaps to stay over the night. I will give him a line for you, begging you to set him a little on his way. As to the collections, geographical charts will be the most interesting to him; he himself possesses the largest known collection (40,000).

As soon as this infernal game is played out in Paris, I hope to have a little leisure again. I have written a warning to Bernays; he is very much out of spirits, and still far behindhand; says he only received the proper appointment (from Gaisford) in February, and without mention of any fixed time. He will write to you, and inclose what is done as a specimen. I am delighted to hear from Lassen that Aufrecht is coming to England. Tell him to call on me. *Cura ut valeas.* Rawlinson has been preferred to Luynes and Wilson by the Berlin Academy.

[92.] *Wednesday, December* 15, 1852.

Tell Aufrecht I will try and arrange the affair for him without his paying any duty; and so at all events there will be a reduction. I was excessively pleased with Aufrecht. Your parcels for Pertz will go safely and quickly if they are here on the 1st or 15th of the month.

P. S. Aufrecht must be courageous, and keep in good spirits. Haupt is called to Berlin, which rather surprises me. Read the "Journal des Débats," Sunday, December 12, on Hippolytus. Do you know Laboulaye?

[93.] PRUSSIAN LEGATION, *February* 19, 1853.

Please tell me at leisure how Amestris (Herod. ix. 109) is to be explained as the wife of Xerxes? I am convinced that *Esther* is hidden here, which name, according to the testimony of the Book of Esther, was her *Persian* name, as she was first called *Myrtle*, as her Jewish maiden name. Therefore *Am* must mean "queen," "mistress," "lady," or what you may discover. I find that the idea had occurred to one and the other even about 100 years ago; but was given up, partly on account of its "godlessness;" partly on account of the uncertainty whether Ahasuerus was really Xerxes, as Scaliger declared. The Suabian simpletons (for they are so in historical matters) are the only people who now doubt this, and that the book is historical, — a book with a history on which depends the only great Jewish feast established since the days of Moses (till the Purification of the Temple, after the fall of Epiphanes). So, my dear

M., send it to me. There can have been at that same time, in Persia, but one woman so vindictive and clever as Esther is. The first volume of my Prophets (from Abraham to Goethe) is ready, with a popular explanation of the age of the so-called "Great Unknown" (Isaiah) of Daniel, and *all the Psalms*, etc. I write *only German* for this, but only *for the English*, and yet without any reserve.

The most remarkable of the thirteen articles which I have seen on Hippolytus, is by Taylor (a Unitarian in Manchester), in the "Prospective Review" (February). He confesses that I have made the principle of the Trinity, and the national blessing of the Episcopacy and the Liturgy, clear to him. I have never seen him, but he seems to me a deep thinker. I am again in correspondence with Bernays, who promises to work at Lucretius with all diligence. I think he has more leisure, and his health is better.

To-morrow the new African expedition sets sail, — Dr. Vogel, the botanical astronomer, and his army, two volunteers from the sappers and miners. I am fully occupied with this; and but for my curiosity about Esther, you would not have had a line from me before Monday.

[34.] PRUSSIAN LEGATION, *Monday.*

My best thanks. All hail to the "Great Esther." She was really called Myrtle, for Hadascha is in Hebrew the myrtle — a name analogous to Susannah (the lily). That Esther is *dorṣp* has long been generally admitted, also that Xerxes is Ahasverus. The analogy of Achasverosh and Kshayarsha has also been proved. Finally, the chronology is equally decisive. The only thing still wanting is *Amestris*. What it is still important to know, is, whether *Ama*, "great," was a common designation of exalted personages, or specially of *queens* (in opposition to the *Pallakai*), or whether the name is to be considered as an adjective to *star, magna stella.* The first interpretation would make the Jewish statement more clear. I think decidedly it is the most natural. It is conceivable that Uncle Otanes, like l'oncle de Madame l'Impératrice, should have taken a distinguished name, just as the Hebrew *myrtle* had been changed into a Persian *star*. But there is not the least hurry about all this.

I rejoice extremely over your extemporary lectures. You are now on the open sea, and "will go on swimmingly." Always

keep the *young men* well in mind, and arrange your lectures
entirely for them. I should think that the history of Greek literature (with glances backwards and forwards) after O. Müller's "History of Greek Literature," would be a fine subject.
Mure's book gives many an impulse for further thought. In
what concerns the Latin inscriptions, you must rely on *Gruter's*
"Thesaurus," after him on Morelli; of the more recent, only
on Borghese and Sarti, and on the little done by my dear Kellermann. There is nothing more rare than the power of copying accurately.

Be patient with ——, if he has an honest mind. I can fancy
that such a mind, having been torn, wronged, and bothered, has
become very cross-grained. Only patience and love can overcome this.

Overweg has fallen a victim to his noble zeal; he lies buried
in the Lake of Tsad. Vogel is happily already on the way to
Malta and Tripoli.

[25.]   PRUSSIAN LEGATION, *March* 21, 1853.

Mrs. Malcolm and Longman are as delighted as I am that
Dr. Thomson will have the great kindness to write a preface to
the "Theologia Germanica," and to look through the last proof-sheets. Longman has informed me this morning that he makes
over *half the net profits* to Mrs. Malcolm, and leaves to her the
future arrangements with Dr. Thomson. Mrs. Malcolm wishes
for nothing for herself, but will hand over the profits to some religious institution. Will you arrange the matter with Dr. Thomson? Longman wishes to begin on the 15th of May, or even
earlier, if everything is ready for press. Of course Dr. Thomson knows the beautiful (though not exhaustive, for it is unfinished) treatment of the history of this school, in the last
volume of Neander's "Church History," published after his
death; in which that delightful little book by Dr. C. Schmidt,
"Johannes Tauler" (Heidelberg, 1841), is made use of. You
know that the author has proved that the famous story of the
conversion of Tauler by a layman is *real history*. The man was
called Nicholas of Basle, and was in secret one of the Waldenses, and was afterwards burnt as such in France. I can lend
this little book to your excellent friend, as well as Martensen's
"Master Eckhardt" (1842), and the authentic copy of the rediscovered South-German MS. of the "Theologia Germanica."

Master Eckhardt was the deepest thinker of his school. Does Dr. Thomson ever come to London? God bless you.

[26.] *April 8, 1853.*

——'s attempt on " St. Hippolytus " is a new proof that he no longer even understands Greek. The critical conjecture about the spuriousness of the tenth book is worthy of the champion of the false Ignatius as against Cureton. Many thanks for your news about Dr. Thomson, which I have imparted to Mrs. Malcolm.

[27.] *London, May 13, 1853.*

I am going to-day to 77 Marina, St. Leonard's-on-Sea (near Hastings), till the 21st or 23d, and do not see why you cannot pay me a visit there. Our hosts, the Wagners, would be delighted to give you a room, and — the sea a bath.

I take refuge there in order to write a new half-volume for the so-called second edition of Hippolytus. The whole will, however, really be a new work in three separate works and six volumes.

I hear that —— has lost his father. In future, when you send such a shy Englishman to me, let me know beforehand that he comes to talk over something with me. I had the greatest wish, and leisure too, to do all he wanted, but discovered only after he was gone that he came to ask me something.

A young friend, Dr. Arnold's son, has translated Wiese's book on schools, and wishes to know whether the translation about which you have written to Wiese, has been or will be really printed; otherwise he will publish his. Or has any other already appeared ? I have been turning tables with Brewster. It is purely mechanical, the involuntary motion of the muscles of the hand to right or left, just like the ring on a thread with which one can strike the hour. Every one is mad about it here. *Che razza di gente*

Now comes an urgent private request. Bekker wishes to publish a grand work, through the Clarendon Press, in return for a proper honorarium, — a definitive edition of Homer, with every possible commentary that could be wished. This is a great work, worthy of the University and of Bekker. I should like to learn through you what would be the Dean's opinion, who is, I think, favorably inclined to Bekker. It appears to me to be especially needful to guard against the work appearing as a *rechauffé* of Wolf, a party-work, for which the sanction of the University is desired. The proposal is "To publish a definitive edition of Homer, with Scholia and Commentary, making it as complete and *absolutum* as is wished." Please take the first good opportunity. I wanted to speak to the excellent man myself when he was in London, but came too late. Hearty greetings to Aufrecht. Böttcher works famously.

[23.] St. Leonard's, *Saturday, May 22*, 1852.

I think incessantly of you, though I cannot fancy that you are in any danger. I have written to my brotherly friend Philip Pusey to help you, if needful. If you wish for good advice about the different parties, combined with perfect acquaintance with the place and people, go to him. I know few men so able to give good advice. Besides, he is very much attached to you.

The inclosed has just reached me through George. I will write to Bekker according to your advice. That your intercourse with A. has become so delightful and comfortable fulfills a hope I have cherished ever since I first saw him. I think that you have given him, in all respects, a delightful position. The German cannot easily get over the idea that God's providence shows itself far less in the eternal government of the world, and in the care taken of every soul, than in an appointment to the civil service. There are few such places in England for men of genius. But he cannot fail with us in Germany, if he distinguishes himself in England; only he should in time undertake some important and great work.

The Cologne choir sing here from the 7th to the 21st of June. Eighty voices. It will be a great treat. Arrange so as to hear something of it. Carl is Secretary of Legation and Chargé d'Affaires at Turin. George tills the ground, but not yet his own; but that will come some day, like the kingdom of heaven. Henry is preparing to collate the "Codex Claromontanus," and has already worked well on the imperfect text. Ernst arranges his garden and house, and has made a bowling-green for me. I am now translating my Hippolytus into historical language, in what I call a second edition. Write soon, as to how it is arranged about your professorship.

[29.]   CARLTON TERRACE, *Derby Day.*

I received your letter here yesterday, from St. Leonard's, and wrote at once to Pusey. I think it will all go right. In your place, I would go at once to Pusey, after announcing myself the previous day.

Tell me why cannot you help that good A. to the £250 for the best treatise on the Sankhya philosophy? I believe he has the right stuff in him for opposing Pantheism, which is what is desired.

Now for a request. I am writing the second of my five works, which have been called into existence by Hippolytus.

Sketches on the Philosophy of the History of Mankind:—
    A. On the Philosophy of Language.
    B. On the Philosophy of Religion.

A. is a reproduction and improved arrangement of the lecture in Oxford, which now lies buried in the "Transactions." In working over the historical part, I have put aside a chapter, "The Primitive Languages in India;" but find out, just as I intended to make you the *heros eponymus*, that you only dealt in your lecture with Bengali, the Sanskrit affinity of which requires to be demonstrated only to such wrong-headed men as the Buddhists are. Could you not write a little article on this for my book? The original language in India *must* have been Turanian, not Semitic; but we are bound in honor to prove it.

Monday, May 30.—My letter has been left unsent. I have just received yours. Let me repeat what I wrote and underlined on the first page. It is a great trial of patience, but *be patient, that is, wise.* One must never allow the toilsome labor of years of quiet reflection and of utmost exertion for the attainment of one's aim to be destroyed by an unpropitious event. It is most probable, and also the best for you, that the affair should not now be hurried through. Your claims are stronger every quarter, and will certainly become more so in the eyes of the English through good temper and patience under trying circumstances. I don't *for a moment doubt* that you will be elected. Germany would suit you now as little as it would me; and we both should not suit Germany. *Spartam quam nactus es orna,* your good genius cries to you. So patience, my dear friend, and *with a good will.*

Böttcher is on the eve of bringing to a successful issue his thesis, "That the triliteral roots have become biliteral, according to an organic law." He has advanced very much in critical research. I shall write a *reductio ad absurdum* review on the Rev. —— ——. It is really a book written *invita Minerva*.

Write soon again to me. With hearty sympathy and true friendship.

Can you do anything for the good man in Naumburg?

[30.]   LONDON, *July* 1, 1852.

Good morning, my dear M. You were so good as to promise me *a chapter* for my "Sketch of the History of the Philosophy of Language;" namely, the results of the latest investigations concerning the unity and Turanian character of the non-Sanskrit languages of India. The printing of my three volumes goes on so fast that I am already revising the Celtic portion, of which Meyer is the Heros.

If, in your researches on the relationship of the Vedic language with Zend, you have hit on new formulas, please gather these results together into a separate chapter. Only one request, — without any delay, for the printing *presses*. I hope you are satisfied about your future in Oxford. Greet your friend and companion, whom we all liked very much. Again four new men from Dessau among the arrivals! One is a famous actor from Berlin, and has brought a letter from Lepsius. Lucien Bonaparte (brother of Canino) is now writing a book here, " Sur l'Origine des Langues." *No war!*

[31.]   *Monday, July* 5, 1852.

A word of explanation, with my best thanks. I do not want the Egyptian-Iranian work before September. I am just printing the treatise on the " Origin of Languages" as a part of my philosophical work, and in it I would gladly have something *on you*, and *from you*, on the non-Sanskritic languages. Both chapters can be quite short, only definite. You must help me over these two chapters. I shall soon send you as a reminder the proof-sheets of what goes before, that you may see how I am driven for it. So write away, regardless of consequences. You are by instinct far too cautious for me to feel the least hesitation about saying this.

I am going on rapidly with the printing of my four volumes, and write *con amore* at the eighth (Hippolytus I.) The court goes on the 12th for a week to Dublin. All right. No war, only uplifted fists!

[32.] LONDON, *Friday Evening, July 9*, 1853.

Here follow the sheets, which I have just looked through, and where I wish to have two short chapters interpolated. We have one page for each, as the last leaf remains blank. Besides this, there is room for many additions to the other chapters, which I commend to your critical and sympathizing attention. Your Breslau friend has never called on me. He may have been at the office whilst I was out. He would be welcome. Your opinion about Sidney Pusey has set me at ease. Go soon to Pusey's, to see the old man himself.

[33.] LONDON, *Tuesday Morning, July* 12, 1853.

"What one desired in youth one obtains in old age." I felt this as I read your chapter yesterday evening. It is exactly what I first wished to know myself, in order to tell it to my readers. You have done it after my own heart, — only a little too briefly, for a concluding sentence on the connection of the language of the Achæmenian Inscriptions with Zend is wanting. Pray write for me at once just such a Turanian chapter. I have introduced that chapter this morning as coming from you, and have placed your name in the list of Investigators mentioned in the title, where it belongs. For the Turanian part, however, you must yourself write me such an Introduction as I shall only need to preface by a line. I mean, you should give what you send me as the result of a portion of the investigations with which you have busied yourself in your Oxford Lectures, and which you intend to publish in your "Vestiges." Never mind space; it will all fit in. You have just hit the right tone and measure, and have written the little chapter just after my own heart, though I first learnt the matter from what you told me. Do you wish to see the list of examples to " Grimm's Law " again, which you made out for my lecture, and which I shall give in my Appendix in order to make any additions? I have as much space as you wish, even for new Appendices, if you will only give me some. This will be a pet book of mine, and a forerunner of my "Philosophy of History." I do not doubt but that it will be read in England, and indeed before all my other works on Hippolytus; for I give it as a philosophical key to Hippolytus. I find that though at first despised, it has in the last few months become the favorite part of my Hippolytus. Write me a line to say how you are, and what you are about. Again, my dear M., my best thanks.

P. S. Is there anything to be said in the text, or Appendix, or in both, about the real results of Aufrecht's investigations on the Italian languages? I should like to take the opportunity of bringing his name before the English public.

[34.] *Wednesday, July 14, 1853.*

This will do, my dear M. To-morrow early I will send you the fifth chapter, printed, for correction, and expect your other chapter. Concerning A., it is clear *you* must write that chapter, for A. can do it as little as I. So let me have that too. In the Catalogue of the examples for "Grimm's Law," get everything ready, and I will then send you the sheet, that you may enter the additions and corrections, — or, better still, you can send me the additions and corrections first, and I will have them inserted at once. Please do this.

[35.] *London, July 15, 1853.*

Your MS., my dear friend, is just dispatched to the printer, with the order to send the proof of the whole chapter direct to you at Oxford. Send the Mongolian chapter as soon as you conveniently can, but not sooner; therefore, when your head is more free. The printing goes on, and it cannot be paged till your chapters are ready, and also I hope the Italian one from Aufrecht, to whom I am writing about it to-day. He can send it to me in German. You must give him some help as to the length and form. It is best for him, if I *personally* introduce him to the English public, amidst which he now lives, and to which he must look for the present. So I hope to receive a real masterpiece from the Oxford Mission of German Science.

Vale. Cura ut valeas. Totus tuus.

[36.] *Tuesday, July 21, 1853.*
10 o'clock.

"As to the language of the Achæmenians, represented to us by the Persian texts of the Cuneiform inscriptions"—so I began this morning, determined to interpolate a paragraph which is wanting in your beautiful chapter, namely, the relationship of the language of the Inscriptions to that of the Zend books, including the history of the deciphering with Grotefend in the background, at the same time avoiding the sunken rocks of personal quarrels (Burnouf contra Lassen). My young house-pundit gives the credit to Burnouf (as he first informed Lassen of the idea about the satrapies). However, it seems to me only natural that you should write the conclusion of this chapter yourself. I shall also write a short chapter on Babylon, for which I have still to read Hincks only, an uncomfortable author, as he has no method or clearness, probably also therefore no principles.

Now let us make this little book as attractive and useful to the English as we can; for that is really our mission.

Bötticher asks if you do not wish to say something on the two dialects of Zend, discovered by Spiegel,—an inquiry which delights me, as Bötticher and Spiegel are at war, and in German fashion have abused each other.

[37.] CARLTON TERRACE, *Friday Morning,*
July 23, 1853.

Anything so important, so new, and so excellent, as what you send me can never be too long. Your table is already gone to the printer. With regard to the general arrangement, I would ask you to keep the plan in mind.

1. That *all references* (as for instance the table of the forty-eight languages) belong to the Appendix or Appendices.

2. The arrangement of the leading ideas and facts to the text (Chapter X.).

3. Nothing must be wanting that is necessary for the establishing a new opinion.

Your *tact* will in all cases show you what is right. The justification of those principles you will assuredly find with me in the arrangement of all the other chapters, and of the whole work, as also in the aim in view, namely, to attract all educated

Englishmen to these inquiries, and show them what empty straw they have hitherto been threshing.

Greet Aufrecht, and thank him for his parcel. I cannot arrange Chapter IV. till I have his whole MS. before me. I can give him till Tuesday morning.

The separate chapters (twelve) I have arranged according to the chronology of the founders of the schools. What is still in embryo comes as a supplement; as Koelle's sixty-seven African Languages, and Dietrich and Bötticher's Investigation of Semitic Roots. If your treatise is not so much a statement of Schott, Castrén, and Co. as your own new work, you shall have the last chapter for yourself.

And now, *last but not least*, pray send me a transliteration table, *in usum Delphini*. I will have it printed at the end of the Preface, that everybody may find his way, and I shall turn in future to it, and see that all transliterations in the book accord with it. I must ask for it therefore by return. You understand what we want. "A transliteration alphabet, for explaining the signs employed," would be a good precursor to yours and Lepsius' scientific work. We shall do well to employ in the text as few technical letters as possible.

To-day I am going to see the "Bride of Messina" for the first time in my life. I have no idea that the piece can possibly produce any effect; and I am afraid that it may fail. But Devrient is of good courage.

[38.]   CARLTON TERRACE, *July* 29, 1853.

"What is long delayed must be good when it comes." So I would be patient till you had really caught your Tartar, did I not fear that my dear friend was suffering again from his wretched headaches. Meanwhile I worked up the Italics, and the summary of the sixty-seven African languages is getting into shape, and the printer's devils are run off their legs. It would be delightful if my dear M. were to send me soon the chapter on the Mongols; only he must not work up a headache. You will have received my Schott last week by book post.

I have not been well. Theodora has had gastric fever, but is quite on the mend since this morning.

At last I have received Lassen III. (2) with the map.

[39.] CARLTON TERRACE, *Tuesday, August 2, 1853.*
Half-past eleven o'clock.

My courier occupied me till nine. Since then I have read through your letter with intense delight; and now in a quarter of an hour I must go to the railway for a country party with Grote. I hasten to thank you for this beautiful gem for my Introduction and for my whole book. You shall have the last word. Your treatise is the only one in the collection which extends beyond isolated types of speech and families, although it preserves throughout the scientific method of Indo-Germanic philology. It was a double refreshment to me, as out of conscientiousness I had looked at and skimmed through L.'s perverse books. What determined impudence there is in that man!

Whilst I am looking over my materials, among which Aufrecht's contribution looks very well, I feel very strongly the want of a report of the last results of the Caucasian languages. My two lines on Rosen look too miserable; also new works have appeared on the subject. Samiel help!

I am entirely of your opinion concerning the transliteration, but I maintain that you must send me a table (key) to *your own* transliteration. For your table of the forty-eight is otherwise not easy for my good English readers, or even for me; and to most it is unintelligible. With the others I shall soon find my way.

I intend to insert a chapter on definite terminology. I think it must be settled from the only tenable hypothesis, namely, the spreading abroad from one central point in mid-Asia, — that is, from the great district which (originally) was bounded towards the north by the open Polar Sea, with the Ural Island or Peninsula; to the west by the Caucasus and Ararat; east by the Altai and Altan Mountains; and south by the continuation of the Taurus Mountains, which stretch in the interior from west east, as far as the Hindu-Kûsh.

Therefore, for Turanian = Ural-Altaic, or the northeastern branch.

For Semitic = Aramean, from Aram, the Mesopotamian highland.

For Japhetic = Eastern highland, or southeastern branch.

What do you think of this? I must get free from Semitic,

etc., because *Chamitic* appears to be primitive Semitic, just as Turanian leans towards Iranian.

The carriage is there. Best thanks to Aufrecht.

You are indulging in a beautiful dream if you imagine that I have Dietrich here. I have studied his two volumes. I wish I could summon him to help me. He was most anxious to come to England. I am afraid of a young scholar whom I do not know personally.

[40.] *August 4, 1853.*

Only a word, my dear friend, to express to you my delight and admiration at your Turanian article. I was so carried away by it that I was occupied with it till far into the night. It is exhaustive, convincing, and succinct.

What do you feel about the present state of the investigations on the Basque? I have convinced myself by my extracts from the grammar and dictionary that Basque is Turanian, but I have nothing fit for printing. I have never seen Rask's work. Do you know it, and can you make anything out of it?

There is only one point on which I do not agree with you. You say there is no purely monosyllabic language. But even that wretched modern Chinese has no disyllabic word, as that would entail a loss of the accent. Or do you deny this? I have covered the baldness of our German vulgarism, "thief," "liar," in Böhtlingk versus Schott, and said, "With an animosity more German than Attic." Does that please you? Greetings to Aufrecht.

[41.] *Abbey Lodge, August 22, 1853.*

(Continuation of our conversation.) Before anything else, finish the Iranian Chapter III. for me, a copy of which I gave you; that is to be printed at once, as the Italic Chapter II. is printed, and needs only revising. You will shake this at once out of your conjuring bag, won't you?

[42.] *Highwood, Friday, August 26, 1853.*

It strikes me, my dearest M., that we should be more correct in christening your essay *Arian*, instead of *Iranian*. I have always used *Iranian* as synonymous with *Indo-Germanic* (which expresses too much and too little) or (which is really a senseless name) Indo-European: Arian for the languages of Aria in the wider sense, for which Bactria may well have been the starting-point. Don't you think we may use Arian, when you confine yourself to Sanskrit, Zend, and Parsi?

I get more and more angry at L.'s perverseness in doubting that the Persians are Aryans. One cannot trace foreign words in Persian, and just these it must have carried off as a stigma, if there were any truth in the thing. One sees it in Pehlevi. But then, what Semitic *forms* has Persian? The curious position of the words in the *status constructus* is very striking. Yet you have explained that. Where, then, are the *Aramaïsms* in the Achæmenian Inscriptions, which surely are Persian in the strictest sense? Earlier the Persians may have been tormented by the Turanians, and even subjugated; but the Babylonian rule of Shemites over Persia cannot be of old date. About 2200 B. C., on the contrary, the Bactrians conquered Babylon, and kept it for a long time. But would not totally different corruptions have appeared in Persian, if they had allowed their language to be so entirely ruined? A corruption, and then a later purification through the Medes, sounds Quixotic. Will you not prove this point?

If you can give some chronological landmarks for the epoch of the Veda dialect, pray do so. There is so much in Lassen, that one learns nothing. I fancied the age of the Mahâbhârata and Râmâyana epoch was tolerably settled, and that thus a firm footing had been gained, as the language is that of the same people and the same religion. If you can say anything in the language-chapter about the genealogy of the mythological ideas it would be delightful for you to take possession of it, without encroaching on your own future explanations. And so good luck to you!

[43.]   HIGHWOOD, *Friday Morning,*
August 26, 1853.

Your hearty and affectionate words for my birthday added to the happiness of the day, which I spent here in the quiet of the country, with my family. I have long looked on you as one of us; and when I look forward into the future, I see your form as one of the bright points which there present themselves to me. You groan now under the burden of a very heavy mountain, which you have taken on your shoulders as others would take a block; only the further you advance, the more will you be satisfied that it is a part of the edifice which you will yet find time to finish; and at the same time it will stand by itself as a κτῆμα ἐς ἀεί.

George is well, and will be with us to-morrow week: Theodora a week later.

Place your essay where you will. I find the connection with the Gothic by means of "Grimm's Law" most natural. The foundation of my arrangement was the purely external idea of progression from the nearer to the more remote, — from the known to the unknown. I hope that next time Aufrecht's muse will give us an intermediate chapter on the Hellenes, Pelasgians, Thracians, Æolians, Dorians, and Ionians; it is curious enough that these are entirely passed over. I do not know, though, what positive facts have resulted up to now from comparative philology as regards the Hellenic element. An historical insight is needed here, such as Ottfried Müller had just begun to acquire when death robbed us of his noble mind. But Müller really understood *nothing* of comparative philology, as the Introduction to his Etruscans proves. The Pelasgians must have been a nearly connected people; the Thracians were certainly so. But from the north comes Hellas, and from Hellas the Ionian Asia Minor. However, the history of the language falls infinitely earlier than the present narrow chronologists fancy. The Trojan War, that is the struggle of the Æolian settlers with the Pelasgians, on and around the sea-coast, lies nearer 2000 than 1000 B. C. The synchronisms require it. It is just the same with Crete and Minos, where the early Phœnician period is out of all proportion older than people imagine. Had we but monuments of Greek, like the Fratres Arvales in Latin! Homer is so modern; even though he certainly belongs to the tenth or eleventh century. That was a time in which the Hellenic mind sang the history of the creation in the deep myth of Prometheus, the son of Iapetos, with his three brothers, the emblem of humanity; a poem which Homer no longer understood.

Now cheer up, my dearest friend. The book must come out. Truly and cheerfully yours.

My wife sends her hearty greetings.

[44.]   LONDON, *September 2, 1853.*

My good wishes follow you to Wales, without knowing your address; so for my letter I must apply to Aufrecht. I hope you will speedily send me the linguistic proof that the noble Vedic hymn you sent us belongs to at least 1,000 years — not B. C., but before the language of the epic poets. Still this cannot really be the oldest; for it already contains a perfect reflection of the old poetic age.

Hare thinks the translation excellent, as I do; only one expression, "Poets in their hearts discerned," we can understand only if we make it "have discerned" (or seen) — for otherwise it is only a continuation of the narrative, which cannot be the meaning. Send it to me in German, for Schelling.

It is cold and rainy here; so don't find fault with Wales, if you are having bad weather there.. *Cura ut valeas.* All the Muses be with you.

[45.]   LONDON, *Friday Morning,*
September 24, 1853.

You have sent me the most beautiful thing you have yet written. I read your Veda essay yesterday, first to myself, and then to my family circle (including Lady Raffles, your great friend *in petto*), and we were all enchanted with both matter and form. I then packed up the treasure at once; at nine it goes to the printers. I think that the translation of the hymn is really improved; it is not yet quite clear to me whether instead of "poets discerned," it should not be "poets discern," or "have discerned," which is at all events the meaning. And now, I hope the same father of the Muses, with their mother, Mnemosyne, will accompany you into the Turanian wilderness, and give you courage to adopt the poor Malays; that in the next separate edition of this sketch, as Mithridates, we may already have the links for joining on Australia and East Africa. We go on printing valiantly. Dietrich has at once accepted my proposal with true German good-nature, although he has only been married for seven months to a young and charming wife. His good mother-in-law tried to shorten the six months, which he at first offered; but that would neither suit me nor him: so have written to him to come away at once — to arrive here e 16th of October, instead of in November, that I may dismiss m with my blessing early in April.

J. Mohl is here, and Rosen. Both go on Monday. I give them on Saturday (to-morrow) an evening party of *literati*, to which I have invited Wilson, Norris, Loftus, Birch, etc., etc. Mohl, as well as Rosen, would like to see you. Could not you by a stroke of genius fly here, rest yourself Sunday, and think on Monday if you really need go back again? Theodore is here, and George is expected. My household all share my wish to see you. Greetings to Aufrecht.

Bötticher has discovered a fragment of Livy (palimpsest), and the Greek translation of Diocles, who, 120 B. C., wrote the "Founding of Rome" (fragment).

Another idea has just struck me. Could one not perhaps make the original unity of Aryans and Europeans clear, if one furnished the hymn written in Latin letters, with an interlinear translation, just as you once gave me an intuition of the first lines, which I have never forgotten. The translation would be best in Latin, with references to the other languages, according as the one or the other of them contains certain radicals with the same meaning as in Sanskrit. If you do not like this, you must prepare for me a Vedic Paternoster, just as Lepsius devised for me a pyramido-Pharaonic, and now prepares a Nubian.

I have announced you as a member of the Assyrian Society, and so saved you three guineas. It is arranged that whoever pays two guineas should receive all reports, transactions, etc. I have therefore inserted your name, with two guineas, and paid it.

Lord Clarendon has, on my recommendation, attached Loftus to the embassy at Constantinople, so that he has a position at Bagdad and Mosul. He leaves on the 1st of October, and we give him a parting entertainment on the 28th of this month. The plan is a secret, but we hope great things from it. I hope to secure the best duplicates for the Berlin Museum.

A Cheruscan countryman, personally unknown to me, Schütz from Bielefeld, the Sanskritist, has asked, with antique confidence, for a bed for his young daughter, on her way to Liverpool as a governess, which we have promised him with real pleasure. This has again shown me how full Germany is of men of research and mind. O! my poor and yet wealthy Fatherland, sacrificed to the Gogym (heathen)!

[46.] CARLTON TERRACE, *Monday, October* 17, 1853,
10 o'clock.

I have already admonished the printer most seriously. You have revised the tables *once*, but they had to be fresh printed on account of the innumerable alterations. But that is no reason why you should not get them. You would have had them long ago, had I had an idea of it. I am impatiently awaiting yours and Aufrecht's revision of Chapters II., III., and IV., which I sent you myself last week. This *presses* very much. You have not much to do to them. I will look after the correct English here with Cottrell; but all the rest Aufrecht can shake out of his bag. In your letter you say nothing of having received them. They were taken to the book-post on Monday evening, the 16th, a week ago, and sent off.

Mi raccomanda, Signor Dottore, per il manuscritto. I will arrange the printing as much as possible according to your wishes. Much depends on the manner in which you organise the whole. With short chapters, easily looked through, the whole can be brought forward as a treatise intended for *all* readers. I have not, however, been so fortunate with my Semitic essay; I have printed a good deal of it in small print, partly to save space (for the volume on the " Philosophy of Religion " must really not be even half as thick as the first), partly on account of the legibility.

I am so sorry to hear from Pertz that you have been suffering from headache. I hope you are quite well and brisk again.

[47.] CARLTON TERRACE, *Saturday Morning*,
October 22, 1853, 10 o'clock.

All right, my dear friend. I have already sent everything off to the printer. It is certainly better so. Where practicable you should have *two* chapters instead of *one*.

Ffoulkes' book shall be taken care of, either on the 1st or 15th. The same with the " Bampton Lectures," if it is wished. I shall receive Mr. Thomson *summo cum honore*.

But now, my dear friend, where does the great Turanian essay hide itself? Pray let me soon receive something, not later than Monday or Tuesday; send it as a parcel by parcels' delivery, or, which is the cheapest and quickest, by book-post, which takes MS. (not letters) as well as printed matter, and forwards both for 6*d*. the lb.

I have sent my most difficult task to the printers, "Origin of
the Three Gospels as part of the Second Age, 66–100." I am
longing for the promised addenda from Aufrecht on the Harus-
pex. The printing is stopped for it, also for the answer about
a hieroglyphic which is unintelligible in London, instead of the
honest *amā* = mother, which is not good enough for him.

[48.] CARLTON TERRACE. *Monday Evening,*
October 24, 1853.
"It has lightened — on the Danube!"

It is of too much importance to me to have my dear Turanian's thoughts according to his own best way and form, for me
not to be ready to wait till the end of November. The entire
work, in seven volumes, must come out together, and I can keep
back till then the first part of the "Philosophy," which is entirely printed in slips up to your chapter, and go on with the
second. Just look once at that book by the Scotch missionary,
"The Karens, or Memoir of Ko-tha-bya," by Kincaid, on the
Karens in Pegu. He maintains the unity of the Karens and
Kakhyans, another form of the same, and of all the scattered
branches of the same race, starting from Thibet (five millions
altogether) as the remnant of a once very powerful people. To
judge from the representations the race must be *very handsome*.
Frau von Helfer told me the same, and she knows them. There
are extracts given in the "Church Missionary Intelligence," October, 1853. Prichard says little about it, and has no specimens of the language. I have not got Latham at hand. Ha-
ruspex is printing; it waits for the conclusion. I have received
Thomson's "Bampton Lectures." Where does *rife* come from
— Anglo-Saxon *ryfe*? It means prevalent, abundant.

[49.] *Friday Morning, October 28, 1853.*
Here is the printer's excuse. It is useless to think of printing at Oxford. You had better now keep the tables, in case
you make more alterations, till you have quite finished your
work, that nothing more may require alteration, but what you
change during your work. I will send you Kincaid, if it is in
London. Perhaps by a smile from the Muses you can get the
first part ready in November. Is the Dean back? Good-by.

[50.] CARLTON TERRACE, *Monday, November 1, 1853.*

Please send me the letter for Humboldt. I will inclose it. Write him (and me) word in English what are the name and object of the Taylor Institution, and the name of the office. You will receive Kincaid from me. I will see after the tables. So courage.

[51.] CARLTON TERRACE, *Tuesday Evening, November 2, 1853.*

I have written to Humboldt to announce your letter and request, so write at once direct to him. I have told Pertz to send me the treatise of Schott by the courier on the 15th. So you will receive it on the 20th of this month. I have again admonished the printer. God bless you.

[52.] LONDON, *Wednesday, February 8, 1854.*

My heartiest congratulations on your well-earned success (Taylorian Professorship). Your position in life now rests on a firm foundation, and a fine sphere of work lies before you; and that in this heaven-blest, secure, free island, and at a moment when it is hard to say whether the thrones of princes or the freedom of nations is in greatest danger. I send you the papers as they are. There is hope that the war may yet be rendered impossible.

With true affection yours.

Thanks for your Schleswig communication.

[53.] CARLTON TERRACE, *April 14, 1854.*

DEAREST FRIEND, — So it is. My father has not up to this moment received a recall, and probably will not, in spite of the efforts of the Russians, within and without Berlin. On the other hand, we expect to-morrow the reply to an answer sent by my father in opposition to a renewed and very impetuous offer of leave of absence. In this answer (of the 4th of this month) my father made his accepting leave of absence dependent on the fulfillment of certain conditions guaranteeing his political honor. If the reply expected to-morrow from Berlin does not contain those conditions, nothing remains but for my father to send in his resignation and leave the Prussian mock negotiations to be fought through by another Prussian ambassador. If they are accorded to him, he will go on long leave of absence. But in either case he will certainly remain provisionally in England. More I cannot tell, but this is enough to give you information *confidentially*.

Dietrich is gone, and begged me to tell you, that in spite of constant work at it here, he could not finish your commission. He will have leisure in Marburg to make it all clear for you, and will send the packet here by the next courier. I will send you a line to-morrow as to the events of the day. My father does not go into the country before Tuesday.

GEORGE BUNSEN.

[54.]   CARLTON TERRACE, *Maundy Thursday, April*, 1854.

MY DEAR FRIEND, — The bearer, Herr von Fennenberg from Marburg, has brought me greetings and a little book from Thiersch, and wishes to be introduced to you. He is a philologist, in particular a Sanskritist. He wishes to have a place or employment that would make it possible for him to stay in England. I know no one who could better advise him than you. Before you receive these lines you will hear from George about me. I am determined to fight through the crisis, and am quite calm.

[55.]   CARLTON TERRACE, *Wednesday, May* 10, 1854.

DEAR FRIEND, — Of course Dietrich has sent nothing. The affair presses. My summary of the Semitic alphabet (lithographed) gives the summary of the system of transliteration used in this work, and is also in the press. Set aside then what is still wanting, and hurry on the matter for me. My journey to Heidelberg with my family, who at all events go on the 20th, depends on the work being finished. To-day I take refuge at St. Leonard's-on-Sea, 77 Marina, till the telegraph calls me to London to receive my letters of recall. I depend, therefore, on your friendly help in one of the most important parts of the book. All right here; the house is deserted, but the heart rejoices and the soul already spreads its wings. Truly yours.

Just starting. Dear M., pray send the MS. Spottiswoode lays everything on you.

[56.]   77 MARINA, ST. LEONARD'S, *Monday Morning,*
                        May 15, 1854.

Your despairing letter of Thursday has alarmed me very much. You had offered me the alternative of leaving out the Semitic tables, if Dietrich does not send them by the courier. I did *not* write to him, as the omission of that list really did not seem to me a great misfortune. But now you say something quite new to me, and most dreadful, that you cannot make the *corrections* without having what I am unable to procure for you. I must own I cannot make this out. Trusting to your goodwill to do the *utmost*, I wrote to Petermann to send you at once an impression of the Semitic paraphrase put together by me and Bötticher. The courier comes on Friday, only I have given up all dependence on Dietrich, since he could take away the lists with him. He never said a word to me about it.

I *must* go to Germany on the 16th of June. Yesterday I sent *all the rest* to Spottiswoode, and at the same time complained about Watts. Only what can they, and what can I do, if you do not enable us to finish the most important book of the three works? I hope you have not worked yourself to death for Trevelyan, and that you will reserve a free hour for London to say good-by. Since last night I am at work at my German "Egypt," to my inexpressible delight. *Friday* I return to town, and stay probably (at Ernest's) till my things are sold. *Cura ut valeas.*

What is the original meaning of *glauben*, to believe?

[57.]   ST. LEONARD'S, *Wednesday, May* 24, 1854.

You have done wonders; and I hope you will rest yourself. A thousand thanks. I have at once sounded an alarm. I go to-day to town; Fanny and her two daughters will embark on Sunday morning: we have taken a house from the 1st of July, on the Neckar. I hope you will soon make your appearance there. George goes into the country to-morrow on business. I stay with Ernest till Hippolytus is out.

The snare is broken, and the bird is free; for which let us bless the Lord. As they once let me out of my cage, they shall not catch me again. My fifth book is ready for printing, down to the general philosophical article. Johannes Brandis, the Assyrian chronologist, arranges for me the synchronistic tables from Menes to Alexander.

Greetings to Aufrecht. I have not yet received the impression of the text, which he restored from the Codex.

[58.]   ABBEY LODGE, REGENT'S PARK,
                    Friday, June 9, 1854.

Your letter came just when wanted, my dearest friend. My wife and children leave the house to-morrow; and I follow them a week later, on account of Spottiswoode. Come here then to-morrow morning, and stay at least till Monday: so my daughter-in-law Elizabeth begs, who herself goes to Upton. George, Brandis, and I help Ernest to keep house this week.

I have *to-day* sent to press the "Resolutions and Statements on the Alphabet" which you wrote, with Lepsius's not "amendments" but certain explanations on his part, and my now English "recapitulations." I shall receive the first impression to-morrow evening. Lepsius has sent a long Essay, of which I only print the "Exposition of the System," with some "specimens of application."

You should rejoice, as I do, over "Hippolytus VII., Christianity and Mankind, their Beginnings and Prospects," in seven volumes (also as three separate works).

I shall easily finish it. Also "Egypt II." is publishing; I have written a new Preface to it. The "Theologia Germanica" is waiting for you; one copy for my dear M., and one for Dr. Thomson, whose address I don't know. Spottiswoode has vowed to have *all* ready next week. If you could stay here, and revise your sheets at once, I might believe the vow.

We have secured a beautiful house in Heidelberg (Heidtweiler), on the right bank, opposite the Castle.

[59.]   *Thursday Morning, June 15, 1854, 9 o'clock.*

Immediately saw about Venn: wrote urgently to him to send the order direct to Spottiswoode, and marked this on the sheet. I cannot send Lepsius, because the sheets are being printed; refer the printer to it. You deceiver! the hymn is without the interlineal version for the non-Iranians. Just as if you were a German professor! I personally beg earnestly for it, for myself and for those who are equally benighted. I have everything now at press, except some Latin abuse for M. Your visit refreshed me very much. Fanny had an exceedingly good journey, and will be to-morrow in Heidelberg.

[60.]   *Thursday, June 15, 1854.*

DEAREST FRIEND, — All ready for the journey. Your slips come in. Thirty-two men are day and night printing, composing, correcting, etc. I am ready. Venn will print nothing of yours, and will not even send Lepsius' Essay to the missionaries, that they may not be driven mad.

I do not know what books you have of mine: if I can have them by Saturday morning, 9 o'clock, good — if not, you must bring them yourself. George goes with me, instead of Ernest.

[61.]   HEIDELBERG, *June 23, 1854.*

DEAR MAX M., — Allow me, through this note, to recommend to you, in my own name, as well as in the name of the Duke of Coburg and Baron Stockmar, the bearer of this, Dr. Wilhelm Pertsch, who is going to England on Sanskrit business, and needs kind advice and a little assistance in his undertaking. Bunsen, who sends you his heartiest greetings, had at first offered to give him a letter to Wilson, but thought afterwards a word from you was worth more with Wilson than a letter from any one else.

The Bunsens have quite decided now to settle at Heidelberg for at least a year, and are already hoping for a speedy visit from you, by which I hope also to profit. He is studying upstairs with great delight your official and scientific *vade mecum* on the Turanian languages. Yesterday, by means of a breakfast, I introduced him to most of the scientific and literary celebrities here — such as H. Gagern, Mohl, Dusch, Harper, Jolly, etc., etc. George came with them, and helped in arranging things, but returns to-morrow.

A thousand good wishes. And always keep in friendly remembrance
                                                Your true friend,
                                                        K. MEYER.

[62.]   HEIDELBERG, CHARLOTTENBERG,
                                                June 29, 1854.

I cannot let George, who took care of me here, return without a token for you of my being alive. I read your book for the English officers partly on the road, and partly here, with real delight and sincere admiration. What an advance from a " Guide Interprète," or a " Tableau Statistique," to such an introduction to languages and nationalities. The map, too, is excellent. The excellent Petermann must make us several, just of this kind, for our unborn Mithridates.

I should like to scold your English reviser for several Gallicisms, for which I feel certain you are not to blame. Rawlinson's barbaric *débris* instead of "ruins," and *fauteuil* instead of "chair," which in French as well as in English is the right expression for a professor's chair; whilst *fauteuil* is only used in French to denote the "President's chair" (for instance, in the Institute), and is quite inadmissible in English, even by the "Upholsterer." The third I have forgotten, but not forgiven.

I cannot *even now* give up my habit of using Iranian in opposition to Turanian, in deference to you. He who uses Turanian must use Iranian. Arian is to me something belonging to the land of Aria, therefore Median, part of Bactria and Persia. It is decidedly a great step in advance to separate the Indian from this. That the Indians acknowledge themselves to be Arians, suits me as it does you. But Iranian is a less localized name, and one wants such a name in contradistinction to Turanian and Semitic. It is only despised by the German "Brahmans and Indomaniacs."

There you have my opinions and criticisms.

I have already written 67 of the 150 pages belonging to the fifth book, and cannot go on till I have my books. I am now occupied with the principles of the method for the historical treatment of mythology, with especial reference to three points in the Egyptian:—

1. Age and relation of the Osiris-worship to the θεοὶ νοητοί and the astronomical gods (Ra, Horus, etc.).
2. History of Seth in Asia and in Egypt, *ad vocem Adam*.
3. Position and signification of animal worship.

Book IV. goes to press on the 15th of July. Book V. must be ready (D. V.) on the 24th of August.

Both the people and the country here please me. The land is enchantingly beautiful, nay, fairy-like, and our house is in the best situation of all. Fanny is almost more at home in Germany than I am, and the girls revel in the German enjoyment of life. I count on your paying us a visit. Say a good word for us to your mother, and persuade her to come with you to visit us in Heidelberg. We should much like to make her acquaintance, and tell her how dear you are to us all. Meyer is *proxenus Anglorum* and *Anglaram*, and does nothing. I hope to form here a little Academia Nicorina. Shall I ever leave Heidelberg? God bless you. *Cura ut valeas.* Ever yours.

P. S. I have worked through Steinschneider's sheet on the Semitic Roots in Egyptian with great advantage, and have sent it to Dietrich. The analogy of the consonants is unmistakable. Dietrich will certainly be able to fix this. And now you must shake that small specimen Aricum out of your Dessau conjuring sleeve. You need only skim the surface, it is not necessary to dig deep where the gold lies in sight. But we must rub the German nose in Veda butter, that they may find the right track.

We shall have a hard battle to fight at first in the Universities. Were Egypt but firmly established as the primitive Asiatic settlement of the as yet undivided Arian and Semitic families, we should have won the game for the recognition of historical truth.

I hope the "Outlines" and "Egypt" will come over next week. Longman will send them both to you; and also the copy of the Outlines for Aufrecht (to whom I have written an ostensible letter such as he wished for). I wish something could be found in Oxford for that delightful and clever man Johannes Brandis. He would exert an excellent influence, and England would be a good school for him. Will the Universities admit Dissenters to take a degree?

[63.]   CHARLOTTENBERG, *December* 12, 1854.

MY DEAR VANISHED FRIEND, — Where thou art and where thou hast turned since thy fleeting shadow disappeared, I have asked in vain on all sides during my journey through Germany. No one whom I met had seen you, which Ewald particularly deplored very much. At all events you are now in the sanctuary on the Isis, and I have long desired to communicate one thing and another to you. But first I will tell you what at this moment lies heavy on my heart — "Galignani" brought me the news yesterday: my dear friend Pusey lies seriously ill at his brother's house in Oxford; "his life is despaired of." Unfortunately there is nothing improbable in this sad intelligence. I had already been anxious before this, for ten days, as I had written to him, to Pusey, nearly three weeks ago, on the news of the death of his wife, entreating him most pressingly, for his own and his family's sake, to spend the winter here, and to live as much as possible with us, his old friends. I know he would have answered the letter, were he not ill. Perhaps he was not even able to read it.

Dr. Acland is our mutual friend, and without doubt attends the dear invalid. At all events, he has daily access to him. My request therefore is, if he is not already taken from us, that you will let Acland tell you how it really is with him, and let me hear by return of post, via Paris: if possible also, whether Pusey did receive my letter, and then how Sidney and the two daughters are; who is with them, whether Lady Carnarvon or only the sisters of charity.

Now to other things.

1. Dietrich gave me the inclosed, of course *post festum*. I have marked at the back what he still wants in your Tables.

2. Greet Dr. Aufrecht, and tell him I am very sorry that Dietrich has found fault with his Paternoster. I was obliged in the hurry to leave the printing of this section to him. I will let A.'s metacritic go to him.

3. I have a letter from Hodgson of Darjeling as an answer to the letter written here by you, very friendly and "in spirits," otherwise but slightly intelligible. He refers me to a letter forty pages long which he has sent to Mohl in Paris, an improved edition of the one he sent to Wilson. He supposes that I received both; if not, I should ask for the one to Mohl.

Of course I have received neither. But I have sent to Mohl through his niece, to beg he would send the said letter to *you*, and you would inform me of the particulars. I hope you have already received it. If not, see about it, for we must not lose sight of the man.

The copy of the "Outlines" must now be in his hands. These "Outlines," the child of our common toil, begin now to be known in Germany. Ewald has already taken a delight in them; he will review them. Meyer is quite enchanted with your Turanians, but would gladly, like many others, know something more of the Basques. For me it is a great event, having made a *friendship for life* and an alliance with Ewald, over Isaiah's

"No peace with the wicked;"

and on still higher grounds. Those were delightful days which I spent in Göttingen and Bonn, as also with Bethman-Hollweg, Camphausen, and others. I see and feel the misery of our people far more deeply than I expected, only I find more comfort than I hoped in the sympathy of my contemporaries, who willingly give me a place among themselves.

A proposal to enter the Upper House (of which, however, I do not care to speak) I could of course only refuse, with many thanks. I have finished my "Egypt," Volume IV., with Bötticher, and sent it for press for the 1st January.

As an intermezzo, I have begun a specimen for a work suggested to me in a wonderful manner from England, America, and Germany (particularly by Ewald and Lücke), — a real Bible for the people, that is, a sensible and sensibly printed text, with a popular statement of the results of the investigations of historical criticism, and whatever the spirit may inspire besides.

I am now working from Isaiah, Jeremiah, and Baruch, where, beyond all expectation, I found new light on the road I was treading.

We live in the happiest retirement. Your visit, and that of your mother, of whom we all became very fond, was a great delight to us, though a short one. Fanny and I have a plan to greet her at Christmas by a short letter. Now write me word how it fares with you.

[84.]   CHARLOTTENBERG, BADEN, January 11, 1855.

MY DEAR FRIEND, — I think you will not have misunderstood my silence since your last letter. Your heart will have told you that no news could be pleasanter to me than that you would undertake to bring the last sevenfold child of my English love into public notice. This can of course only be during the Parliamentary recess. You know better than any one what is the unity of the seven volumes, and what is the aim and result. Your own is a certainly not unimportant, and an independent part of it. But you have with old affection worked yourself and thought yourself into the whole, even where the particulars were of less interest to you. Lastly, as you have told me to my delight, Jowett has begun to interest himself in the work, and you have therefore one near at hand who, from one point of view, can help you as reflecting English opinion. Ewald told me that I had wished to give a Cosmos of the mind in that work. At all events, this idea has floated before me for many years, and is expressed in the Preface to the "God Consciousness." Only it is not more than a *study* for that which floats before me. My two next volumes will give more of it. If I only knew what to do with the work for Germany! My task was arranged for England. It seemed to me important, under the guidance of the rediscovered Hippolytus, whose form first rose clearly before me during the first work, to show the organic development of the leading ideas of Christendom in the teachers and heroes, beginning from the first Pentecostal feast; in order to sift the ground, and show to my readers —

a. That the old system of inspiration and the Theodicee of the Middle Ages, that is to say, that of the seventeenth century, has no *support* in ancient Christianity, but just the *contrary.* That is now a fact.

b. That we have something infinitely more reassuring to put in its place. Truth instead of delusion; reality instead of child's play and pictures.

c. That it is high time to be in earnest about this.

d. That for this, *clear insight* and practical purpose, also reasoning and moral earnestness, will be required on the part of the spiritual guides.

e. But that before all things Christianity must be introduced into the reality of the present; and that the corporation of the Church, the life of the community in its worship as in its mutually supporting work, must become the centre whence springs the consciousness of communion, — *not* a system of theology. Christianity is nothing to me but the restoration of the ideal of humanity, and this will become especially clear through the antecedent forms (præformations) of the development in language and religion. (See " Outlines.") There is a natural history of both, which rests on laws as sure as those of the visible Cosmos. The rest is professional, philological, — *legitimatio ad causam.*

How much of this idea can be presented to the English public, and in what manner, you know much better than I. Therefore you know the one as well, and the other better than I do. This is the reason why I believe you would not wait for my answer. Still I should have sent to you, if during this time two passions had not filled my heart. For once the dreadful distress of our condition forced me to try, from the midst of my blessed Patmos, to help by letters as far and wherever I could, through advice and cry of distress and summons to help. Now there is nothing more to be done but to wait the result. *Alea jacta esse.* Ernest is in Berlin.

My second passion is the carrying out of an idea by means of a Christian philosophical People's Bible, from the historical point of view, to get the lever which the development of the present time in Europe has denied me. That I should begin this greatest of all undertakings in the sixty-fifth year of my age, is, I hope, no sign of my speedy death. But I have felt since as if a magic wall had been broken down between me and reality, and long flowing springs of life stream towards me, giving me the discernment and the prolific germ of that which I desired and still strive after. The Popular Bible will contain in two volumes (of equal thickness), 1st, the corrected and reasonably divided text; and 2d, the key to it. For that purpose I must see whether I shall succeed in executing the most difficult part, Isaiah and Jeremiah. And I have advanced so far with this since yesterday evening, that I see the child can move, it can walk. The outward practicability depends on many things, but I have thoroughly worked through the plan of it.

By the end of 1856 all must be ready. My first letter is to you. Thanks for your affection: It is so exactly like you, breaking away at once from London and going to Oxford, to talk over everything with Acland.

Meyer has once more descended from Pegasus, to our prosaic sphere. I believe he is working at a review of our work for the Munich Literary Journal of the Academy. Laboulaye (Vice-President of the Academy) says I have given him so much that is new to read, that he cannot be ready with his articles before the end of February. We shall appear in the "Débats" the beginning of March.

Holzmann is working at the proofs that the Celts were *Germans*. Humboldt finds the unity of the Turanians not proved. (Never mind!) Osborn's "Egypt" runs on in one absurdity (the Hyksos period *never* existed), which the "Athenæum" censures sharply.

What is Aufrecht about? But above all, how are you yourself? God preserve you. My family greet you. Heartily yours in old affection.

[66.]   HEIDELBERG, *February* 28, 1855.

It was, my dear friend, in expectation of the inclosed that I did not sooner return an answer and my thanks for your affectionate and detailed letter. I wish you would take advantage of my communication to put yourself in correspondence with Benfey. He is well disposed towards you, and has openly spoken of you as "the apostle of German science in England."

And then he stands *infinitely* higher than the present learned men of his department. He would also be very glad if you would offer yourself to him for communications suitable for his Oriental Journal from England, to which he always has an eye. (Keep this copy, perhaps Jowett may read it.) Humboldt's letter says in reality two things: —

1. He does not approve of the sharply defined difference between nomadic and agricultural languages; the occupations may change, yet the language remains the same as before. That is against *you*. The good old man does not consider that the language will or can become another without perishing in the root.

2. He does not agree in opposing one language to all others as *inorganic*. This is against *me*. But *first*, this one language is still almost the half of the human race, and *secondly*, I have said nothing which his brother has not said as strongly. It is only said as a sign of life, and that "my praise and my admiration may appear honest."

In the fifth volume of my "Egypt" I call the languages sentence-languages and word-languages; that is without metaphor, and cannot be misunderstood. The distinction itself is *right*. For *organic* is (as Kant has already defined it) an unity in parts. A granite mountain is not more thoroughly granite than a square inch of granite, but a man without hands or head is no man.

I am delighted to hear that your Veda gets on. If you would only not allow yourself to be frightened from the attempt to let others work for you in mere handicraft. Even young men have not time for everything. You have now fixed your impress on the work, and any one with the *will* and with the necessary knowledge of the tools, could not go far wrong under your eye. I should so like to see you free for other work. *Only do not leave Oxford. Spartam quam noctus es orna.* You would not like Germany, and Germany could offer you no sphere of activity that could be compared ever so distantly with your present position. I have often said to you, "Nature and England will not allow themselves to be changed from *without*, and therein consists exactly their worth in the divine plan of development; but they often alter themselves rapidly from within. Besides, the reform is gone too far to be smothered. Just now the Dons and other Philisters can do what they like, for the *people* has its eyes on other things. But the war makes the classes who are pressing forwards more powerful than ever.

The old method of government is bankrupt forever. So do not be low-spirited, my dear M⸺ impatient. It is not so much the fault of England, as of yourself, that you do not feel settled and at home. You have now as good a position as a young man of intellect, and with a future before him, could possibly have anywhere, either in England or in Germany. Make a home for yourself. Since I saw your remarkable mother, I have been convinced that unlike most mothers, she would not stand in the way of your domestic happiness, even were it contrary to her own views, but that she must be the best addition to your household for any wife who was worthy of you. Oxford is London, and better than London; and London is the world, and is *German*. How gladly would Pauli, that honest, noble German soul, stay, if he had but an occupation. The subjection of the mind by the government here becomes more vexatious, more apparent, more diabolical. *One form of tyranny is that of Augustus*, the more thorough, because so sly. They will not succeed in the end, but meanwhile it is horrible to witness. More firmly than ever I settle myself down here in Heidelberg, and will take the whole house, and say, "You must leave me my cottage standing, and my hearth, whose glow you envy me." *We are now on the point of binding ourselves, without binding ourselves; and the prudent man in P(aris) pretends not to observe it*—just like the devil, when a soul is making some additional conditions.

Still, it is possible that the desire to aid in the councils of Vienna at any price may carry us so far that we may join in the march against Poland and Finland. After all, the rivers flow according to the laws of gravitation.

I have definitely arranged my "Biblework' in two works:—

A. The Bible (People's Bible), corrected translation, with very short and purely historical notes below the text. One volume, large Bible-octavo.

B. The Key, in three equally large volumes (each like the Bible). I. Introduction; II. The restored documents in the historical books of the Old Testament, and restoration of the prophets Jeremiah and Isaiah, and of some of the smaller prophets; III. The New Testament. (The life of Christ is a part of this.)

The work looks well. I have now not only perfectly defined the Exodus and time of the Judges, but have put it so clearly and authentically before the public, that as long as the world

of Europe and America lasts, ... theologians cannot make the
faithful crazy, nor the scoffers .   them astray. It can be finished in three years. I can depend on *Ewald* and *Rothe.*

We have got through the winter. I, for the first time for
twenty years, without cold or anything of that sort. The delicious air of Spring begins to blow, the almond-trees promise to
be in blossom in a week. With true love, yours.

[66.]   CHARLOTTENBERG, *Tuesday Morning,*
April 17, 1855.
(The day when peace or war will be decided.)

MY DEAR M.,—I cannot delay any longer to tell you that
your first article announced to us by George, has reached me,
and excited the delight and admiration of us all. It is pleasant,
as Cicero says, "laudari a viro laudato;" but still sweeter
"laudari a viro amato." And you have so thoroughly adopted
the English disguise, that it will not be easy for any one to suspect you of having written this "curious article." It especially
delights me to see how ingeniously you contrive to say what you
announce you do not wish to discuss, namely, the purport of the
theology. In short, we are all of opinion that your aunt or
cousin was right when she said in Paris, to Neukomm, of you,
that you ought to be in the diplomatic service. From former
experience I have never really believed that the second article
would be printed; it would have appeared by last Saturday at
the latest, and would then have been already in my hands.
But the article as it is has given me great pleasure, and all the
greater because it is yours. I only wish you might soon give
me the power of shaking your dear old hand, which I so often
feel the want of.

Meanwhile I will tell you that Brockhaus writes in a very
friendly way, in transmitting Ernst Schulze's biography (the unfortunate poet's journal, with very pleasant affectionate descriptions of his friends, of me especially), to ask if I would not make
something out of the new Hippolytus for Germany. This letter
reached me just as I had blended my past and future together
for a large double work, the finished parts of which are now
standing before me in seven large portfolios, with completed
Contents, Preface, and Introduction.

"The Bible of the Faithful," four volumes, large Bible-octavo; Volume I. the Bible; Volumes II.-IV. (separated) Key.

"The Faithful of the Bible." (A.) The *government* and the *worship* of the faithful. Two books, one volume. (B.) The congregational and family book (remodeling of the earlier devotional books for the faithful of the Bible), two volumes.

At the same time "Egypt" was at last ready for press as two volumes; and so I took courage to take up again that old idea, especially that which we had so often discussed. But first I can and will make a pretty little volume from the historical portraits in Hippolytus: "The first seven generations of Christians." A translation (by Pauli) of the exact text of the first English volume, preceded by the restoration of the line and the chronology of the Roman bishops down to Cornelius, since revised and much approved of by Röstell (quite clearly written out; about ten printed sheets with the documents).

This gives me hardly any trouble, and costs me very little thought. But secondly, to use Ewald's expression: "The Kosmos of Language" (in four volumes). This is *your* book, if it is to exist. It appears to me before anything else to be necessary to draw proper limits, with a wisdom worthy of Goethe.

I do not think that the time has come for publishing in the German way a complete or uniformly treated book; I think it is much more important to fortify our view of language from within, and launch it forth armed with stings upon these inert and confused times. *Therefore* method, and satisfactory discussion of that on which everything depends; with a general setting forth of *the* points which it concerns us now to investigate. I could most easily make you perceive what I mean, by an abstract of the prospectus, which I have written off, in order to discuss it thoroughly with you as soon as you can come here. As you would have to undertake three fourths of the whole, you have only to consider all this as a proposal open to correction, or rather a handle for discussion.

FIRST VOLUME. (Bunsen.)
General Division.

Introduction. The Science of Language and its Epochs (according to Outlines, 35–60).

1. The Phenomena of Language (according to Outlines, ii. 1–72).

2. The Metaphysics of Language (according to Outlines, ii. 73–122) — manuscript attempt to carry out Kant's Categories, not according to Hegel's method.

3. The Historical Development (Outlines, ii. 123–140; and Outlines of Metaphysics, second volume, in MS.). Müller *ad libitum*. (With this an ethnographical atlas, colored according to the colors of the three families.)

SECOND VOLUME. (Müller.)

First Division. The *sentence-languages* of Eastern Asia (Chinese).

Second Division. The *Turanian* word-languages in Asia and Europe.

THIRD VOLUME. (Müller and Bunsen.)

First Division. The *Hamitic-Semitic* languages in Asia and Africa. (Bunsen.)

Second Division. The *Iranian* languages in Asia and Europe.

FOURTH VOLUME. (Müller.)

The branching off of the Turanians and Hamites in Africa, America, and Polynesia.

a. The colony of East Asiatic Turanians in South Africa (great Kaffir branch).

b. The colony of North Asiatic Turanians (Mongolians) in North America.

c. The Turanian colonies in South America.

d. The older colonies of the East Asiatic Turanians in Polynesia (Papuas).

e. The newer ditto (light-colored Malay branch).

Petermann or Kiepert would make the ethnographical atlas *beautifully*. I have in the last few months discovered that the three Noachic families were originally named according to the three colors.

1. Ham is clear; it means *black*.

2. Shem is an honorary name (the glorious, the famous), but the old name is Adam, that is, Edom, which means *red*, reddish $=\phi o \tilde{\iota} \nu \iota \xi$: this has given me great light. The Canaanites were formerly called Edomi, and migrated about 2850, after the volcanic disturbance at the Dead Sea (Stagnum Assyrium, Justin. xviii. 3), towards the coast of Phœnicia, where Sidon is the most ancient settlement, the first begotten of Canaan; and the era of Tyre begins as early as 2760 (Herodotus, ii. 44).

3. Japhet is still explained in an incredible way by Ewald according to the national pun of Genesis x. as derived from Patah, "he who opens or spreads." It is really from Yaphat, "to be shining" $=$ the light, *white*.

It would certainly be the wisest plan for us to fall back on this for the ethnographical atlas, at least for the choice of the colors; and I believe it could easily be managed. For the *Semitic* nations *red* is naturally the prevailing color, of a very deep shade in Abyssinia and Yemen; black in negro Khamites, and a light shade in Palestine and Northern Arabia. For the *Turanians*, *green* might be thought of as the prevailing color. For the *Iranians* there remains *white*, rising into a bluish tint. But that could be arranged for us by my genial cousin Bunsen, the chemist.

That would be a work, my dearest M.! The genealogy of man, and the first parable, rising out of the Infinite. Were you not half Anglicized, as I am, I should not venture to propose anything so "imperfect"—that is, anything to be carried out in such unequal proportions. But this is the only way in which it is possible to us, and, as I think, only thus really useful for our Language-propaganda, whose apostles we must be "in hoc temporis momento." And now further, I think we should talk this over together. I give you the choice of Heidelberg or Nice. We have resolved (D. V.) to emigrate about the 1st of October, by way of Switzerland and Turin, to the lovely home of the palm-tree, and encamp there till March: then I should like very much to see *Sicily*, but at all events to run through *Naples and Rome in April;* and then return here in the end of April by Venice. It is *indescribably lovely* here now; more enjoyable than I have ever seen it. We shall take a house there, where I could get into the open air four or five times every day. I fancy in the five working months I could do more than in the eight dreary winter months here. Much is already done, the *completion* is certain. Were not Emma (who has become inexpressibly dear to us) expecting her confinement about the 21st of September we should already at this time break up from here, in order to reach the heavenly Corniche Road (from Genoa to Nice) in the finest weather. Theodore goes in ten days for a year to Paris. Of course Emilia and the other girls go with us. They all help me in a most remarkable way in my work. I thought of inviting Brockhaus here in the summer to discuss with him the edition of the "Biblework." Now we know what we have in view. Now write soon, how you are and what *you* have in view. All here send most friendly greetings. Ever yours.

[67.] BURG RHEINDORF, NEAR BONN, *December* 2, 1855.

MY DEAR FRIEND,—I think you must now be sitting quietly again in Oxford, behind the Vedas. I send you these lines from George's small but lovely place, where we have christened his child, to stop, if possible, your wrath against Renan. He confesses in his letter that "ma plume m'a trahi;" he has partly not said what he thinks, and partly said what he does not think. But his note is not that of an enemy. He considers his book an homage offered to German science, and had hoped that it would be estimated and acknowledged in the present position of French science, and that it would be received in a friendly way. Though brought up by the Jesuits, he is entirely free from the priestly spirit, and in fact his remarkable essay in the "Revue des Deux Mondes" of the 15th of November on Ewald's "History of the People of Israel" deserves all our thanks in a theological, national, and scientific point of view. We cannot afford to quarrel unnecessarily with such a man. You must deal gently with him. You will do it, will you not, for my sake? I am persuaded it is best.

Brockhaus will bring out the third unaltered edition of my "Signs of the Times," as the 2,500 and the 1,000 copies are all sent out, and more are constantly asked for. I have, whilst here, got the first half of the "World-Consciousness" (Weltbewusstsein) ready to send off. The whole will appear in May, 1856, as the herald and forerunner of my work on the Bible. I have gone through this with H. Brockhaus, and reduced it to fifteen delightful little volumes in common octavo, six of the People's Bible, with a full Introduction, and nine of the Key with higher criticism. I am now expecting three printed sheets of the Bible, Volume I., the Key, Volumes I. and VII. The fourth and fifth volumes of "Egypt" are being rapidly printed at the same time for May. The chronological tables appear in September. And now be appeased, and write again soon. George sends hearty greetings. Thursday I shall be in Charlottenberg again. Heartily yours.

[68.] CHARLOTTENBERG, *March* 10, 1856.

I should long ago have told you, my dearest friend, how much your letter of last September delighted me, had I not been so plunged in the vortex caused by the collision of old and new work, that I have had to deny myself all correspondence. Since then I have heard from you, and of you from Ernst and some travelling friends, and can therefore hope that you continue well. As to what concerns me, I yesterday sent to press the MS. of the last of the *three* volumes which are to come out almost together. Volumes III. and IV. (thirty-six sheets are printed) on the 1st of May; Volume V. on the 15th of July. I have taken the bold resolution of acquitting myself of this duty before anything else, that I may then live for nothing but the "Biblework," and the contest with knaves and hypocrites in the interest of the faithful.

In thus concluding "Egypt," I found it indispensable to give *all* the investigations on the beginnings of the human race in a compressed form. Therefore SET = YAHVEH and all discoveries connected with this down to Abraham. Also the Bactrian and Indian traditions. I have read on both subjects all that is to be found here; above all Burnouf (for the second time), and Lassen's "Indian Antiquities," with *Diis minorum gentium.* I find then in Lassen much which can be well explained by my discoveries in the Egyptian, Babylonian, and Phœnician, but a huge chasm opens out for everything concerning the Vedas. I find in particular nothing analogous to the history of the Deluge, of which you most certainly told me. I therefore throw myself on your friendship, with the request that you will write out for me the most necessary points, so far as they do not exist in Colebrooke and Wilson, which I can order from Berlin. (1.) On the Deluge tradition; (2.) On the Creation of Man, if there is any; (3.) On the Fall of Man; (4.) On recollections of the *Primitive Homes* on the other side of Meru and Bactria, if such are to be found. I know of course what Lassen says. I do not expect much, as you know, from these enthusiastic emigrants; but all is welcome.

One must oppose with all one's power, and in solemn earnest, such pitiful nihilism and stupid jokes as Schwenk has made of the Persian mythology. I have done this in the "Doctrine of Zoroaster;" I am to-day applying to Haug about some *hard nuts* in this subject. The number seven predominates here also, of course, and in the symbolism depends on the time of each phase of the moon; but the Amshaspands have as little to do with it as with the moon itself. The Gahanbar resemble the six days of creation, if the Sanskrit translation by Neriosengh (which I don't understand) is more to be trusted than the Vispered. But at all events there is an ideal element here, which has been fitted in with the old nature worship.

The sanctity of the Hom (havam?) must also be ideal, the plant can only be a symbol to Zoroaster. Can it be connected with Om? As to the *date*, Zoroaster the prophet *cannot* have lived later than 3000 B.C. (250 years before Abraham therefore), but 6000 or 5000 before Plato may more likely be correct, according to the statements of Aristotle and Eudoxus. Bactria (for that surely is Bakhdi) was the first settlement of the Aryans who escaped from the ice regions towards Sogd. The immigration, therefore, can hardly fall later than 10,000 or 9000 before Christ. Zoroaster himself must be considered as *after* the migration of the Aryans towards the Punjab, for his demons are your gods.

Now will you please let me have, at latest at Easter, what you can give me, for on the 25th the continuation of the MS. must go off, and of this the Indians form a part.

I do not find the account by Megasthenes of Indian beginnings (Plinius and Arrianus) at all amiss: the Kaliyuga computation of 3102 B.C. is purely humbug, just like the statement about the beginning of the Chinese times, to which Lassen gives credit. How can Herodotus have arrived at a female Mithra, Mylitta? Everything feminine is incompatible with the sun, yet nowhere, as far as I can see, does any deity corresponding to *Mater* appear among the Persians or Indians. Altogether *Mithra* is a knotty point in the system of Zoroaster, into which it fits like the fist into the eye.

And now I come to the subject of the inclosed. Kuno Fischer has given a most successful lecture in Berlin on Bacon, which has grown into a book, a companion to Spinoza and Leibnitz, but much more attractive through the references to the modern English philosophy and Macaulay's conception of Bacon. The book is admirably written. Brockhaus is printing it, and will let it appear in May or at latest in June, about twenty-five sheets. He reserves the right of translation. And now I must appeal to your friendship and your influence, in order to find, 1st, the right translator, and 2d, the right publisher, who would give the author £50 or £100, for Fischer is dependent on his own resources. The *clique* opposes his appearance: Raumer has declared to the faculty that "a Privat-docent suspended in any state of the Bund because of his philosophical opinions which were irreconcilable with Christianity, ought not to teach in Berlin." The faculty defends itself. I have written public and private letters to Humboldt, but what good does that do? Therefore it is now a matter of consequence to enable this very distinguished thinker and writer, and remarkably captivating teacher (he had here 300 pupils in metaphysics), to secure the means of subsistence. Miss Winkworth's publisher offered her £150 when she sent him the first chapter of my "Signs;" Longmans half profits, that is — nothing! I only wish to have the matter set going. The proof-sheets can be sent.

Who wrote the foolish article in the "Quarterly" against Jowett? The book will live and bear fruit. We are well, except that George has had scarlet fever. Frances is nursing him at Rheindorf. Heartily yours.

I have myself undertaken the comparison of the Aryan with the Semitic, on Lassen's plan. Two thirds of the stems can be authenticated. What a scandal is Roth's deciphering of the Cyprian inscriptions. Renan mourns over the "Monthly Review," but is otherwise very grateful. I have made use of your Alphabet in my "Egypt."

[89.]   CHARLOTTENBERG, *March* 12, 1854.

MY DEAREST M., — You receive at once a postscript. I have since read W.'s essay on the Deluge of the Hindūs, in the second volume of the "Indian Studies;" and can really say now that I understand a little Sanskrit, for the essay is written in a Brahmanic jargon, thickly strewn with very many German and French foreign terms. O, what a style! I am still to-day reading *Roth* (Münchener Gelehrte Anzeigen). I know therefore what is in it; that is, a child's tale which came to India from the Persian Gulf, or at least from Babylonia, about Oannes, the man in the shape of a fish, who gives them their revelation and saves them. Have you really nothing better? It is just like the fable of Deucalion, from the backward-thrown λᾶς, that is, stones! Or was it ἀπὸ δρυὸς ἢ ἀπὸ πέτρας?

Faith in the old beliefs sits very lightly on all the emigrant children of Japhet. Yet many historical events are clearly buried in the myths before the Pāndavas. Wilson's statement (Lassen, i. 479 n.) of the contents of a Purāna, shows still a consciousness of those epochs. There *must* be (1) a dwelling in the primitive country (bordering on the Ideal), quite obscure, historically; (2) expulsion, through a change of climate; (3)

life in the land of the Aryans (Iran.); (4) migration to and life in the Punjab.

For the western Aryans and *for southern Europe*, there is another epoch, between 6000 and 5000 B. C. at latest, namely, the march of the Cushite (Turanian) Nimrud (Memnon?) by Susiana, and then across Northern Africa to Spain. The discovery of Curtius, of the Ionians being Asiatics that had migrated from Phrygia, who disputed with the Phœnicians for the world's commerce long before the colonies started from Europe, is *very* important.

Write me word what you think of Weber's Indian-Semitic Alphabet.

I have to-day written to Miss Winkworth, to speak to the publisher. If he will undertake it and pay Fischer well, both editions would appear at the same time; and she must then come here in April, to make the translation from the proof-sheets. The printing begins at Easter.

[70.]   CHARLOTTENBERG, *April 22,* 1856.
                            (*Palilia anni urbis* 2610.)

So there you are, my worthy Don, sitting as a Member of Committees, etc.; and writing reports, and agitating and canvassing *in Academicis!* This delights me: for you have it in you, and feel the same longing, which seized me at your age — to *act* and to exert an influence on the God-given realities of life. It inspirits me; for you, like me, will remain what you are — a German, and will not become a "Philister."

I have missed you here very much, even more than your answers to my questions. No one escapes his fate: so I cannot escape the temptation to try my method and my insight on indirect chronology. I confess that such confusion I have not seen as that of these investigations hitherto beyond Colebrooke and Wilson, Lassen and Duncker. Something can already be made of Megasthenes' accounts in connection with the Brahmanic traditions, in the way cleared up by Lassen (in the "Journal"). I believe in the 153 kings before Sandrokottus and the 6402 years. The older tradition does not dream of ages of the world, the historical traditions begin with the Tretâage, and point back to the life on the Indus; the first period is like the divine dynasties of the Egyptians. The Kaliyuga is 1354 B.C., or 1400 if you like, *but not a day older.* The so called cataclysms "after the universe had thrice attained to freedom" (what nonsense!) are nothing but the short interregnums of freedom obtained by the poor Indian Aryans between the monarchies. They are 200 + 300 + 120. And I propose to you, master of the Vedas, the riddle, how do I know that the first republican interregnum (anarchy, to the barbarians) was 200 years long? The Indian traditions begin therefore with 7000, and that is the time of Zaradushta. I find *many* reasons for adopting *your* opinion on the origin of the Zend books. The Zoroastrians came out of India; but tell me, do you not consider this as a *return migration?* The schism broke out on the Indus, or on the movement towards the Jumna and lands of the Ganges. The dull, intolerable Zend books may be as late as they will, but they contain in the Vendidad, Fargard I., an (interpolated) record of the oldest movements of our cousins, which reach back further than anything Semitic.

About Uttara-Kuru and the like, you also leave me in the lurch; and so I was obliged to see what Ptolemy and Co., and the books know and mention about them. It seems then to me impossible to deny that the Ὀττοροκόρροι is the same, and points out the most eastern land of the old north, now in or near Shensi, the first home of the Chinese; to me the *eastern* boundary of *Paradise.* But how remarkable, not so much that the Aryans, faithful people, have not forgotten their original home, but that the name should be *Sanskrit!* Therefore Sanskrit in Paradise! in 10,000 or 9000. Explain this to me, my dear friend. But first send me, within half an hour of receiving these lines, in case you have them, as they assume here, Lassen's maps of India (mounted), belonging to my copy of the book, and just now very necessary to me. You can have them again in July on the Right. Madame Schwabe is gone to console that highminded afflicted Cobden, or rather his wife, on the death of his *only* son, whom we have buried here. She passes next Sunday through London, on her return to her children, and will call at Ernst's. Send the maps to him with a couple of lines. If you have anything else new, send it also. I have read with great interest your clever and attractive chapter on the history of the Indian Hellenic mind, called mythology. Does John Bull take it in? With not less pleasure your instructive essay on "Burning and other Funereal Ceremonies." How noble is all that is really old among the Aryans! Weber sent me the "Málavikâ," a miserable thing, harem stories, — I hope by a dissolute fellow of the tenth century, and surely not by the author of "Sakuntala." For your just, but sharply expressed and *nobly* suppressed essay against ——, a thousand thanks. I have to-day received the last sheet of "Egypt," Book IV., and the last but one of Book V. (a), and the second of Book V. (b). These three volumes will appear on the 1st of June. The second half of Book V. (b) (Illustrations, Chronological Tables, and Index) I furnish subsequently for Easter, 1857, in order to have the last word against my critics.

Meanwhile farewell.

[71.]   CHARLOTTENBURG, *Wednesday, April 23*, 1856.

It would be a great pleasure to you, my dear friend, if you could see the enthusiasm of my reawakened love for India, which possessed me in the years 1811-14, and which now daily overpowers me. But it is well that you are not here, for I dare not follow the notes of the siren till I have finished the "Signs of the Times," and have the first volume of my five books of the "Bible" before me. I see clearly, from my point of view, that when one has the right frame, the *real facts* of the Indian life can be dug out from the exuberant wealth of poetry as surely as your Eros and the Charites, and the deepest thoughts from their ritual and mythology. True Germans and Anglo-Saxons are these Indian worthies. How grateful I am to Lassen for his conscientious investigations; also to Duncker for his representation of the history, made with the insight of a true historian. But all this can aid me but little. I can nowhere find the materials for *filling up my frame-work*; or, in case this frame-work should not itself be accurate, for destroying it and my whole chapter. Naturally all are ignorant of the time which precedes the great fable, — namely, the time of the Vedas.

And so I turn to you, with a request and adjurntion which you cannot set aside. I give you my frame-work, *the chronological canon*, as it has been shaped by me. It is clear that we cannot depend on anything that stands in the noble Mahábhárata and the sentimental Rámáyana, as to kings and lines of kings, unless it is confirmed by the Vedas; but they generally say the very opposite. All corruptions of history by our school men and priests are but as child's play compared to the system alic falsifying and destruction of all history by the Brahmans. Three things are possible; (1) you may find my frame-work *wrong* because facts are against it; (2) you may find it *useless* because facts are missing; or (3) you may find the plan correct, and discover facts to support and further it. I hope for the last; but *every* truth is a gain. My scheme is this: The poets of the Veda have no chronological reckoning, the epic poets a false one. There remain the Greeks. To understand the narrative of Megasthenes, one must first restore the corrupted passages, which Lassen unfortunately has so entirely misunderstood.

Arr. Ind. ix., in Didot's "Geographi," i. p. 320: Ἀπὸ μὲν δὴ Διονύσου (Svayambhû) βασιλέας ἠρίθμεον Ἰνδοὶ ἐς Σανδράκοττον τρεῖς καὶ πεντήκοντα καὶ ἑκατὸν, ἔτεα δὲ δύο καὶ τεσσαρακόσια (instead of πεντήκοντα) καὶ ἑξακισχίλια (6402, according to Pliny's text, confirmed by all MSS., and by Solinus Polyhist. 59; of Arrian we have but copies of one *codex*, and the *lacuna* is the same in all).

Ἐν δὲ τούτοισι τρὶς ICTANAI (instead of τὸ πᾶν εἰς, Arr. writes only ἐς) ἐλευθερίην (ἱστάναι is Herodotean for καθιστάναι, as every rational prose writer would have put).

ΤΗΝ ΜΕΝ ΕΣ ΔΙΑΚΟCΙΑ.
τὴν δὲ καὶ ἐς τριακόσια,
τὴν δὲ εἴκοσί τε ἐτέων καὶ ἑκατόν.

The restoration is certain, because the omission is explained through the ὁμοιοτέλευτον, and gives a meaning to the καί. The sense is made indubitable by Diodorus' rhetorical rendering of the same text of Megasthenes, ii. 38: τὸ δὲ τελευταῖον, πολλαῖς γενεαῖς ὕστερον καταλυθείσης τῆς ἡγεμονίας δημοκρατηθῆναι τὰς πόλεις; cf. 39, ὕστερον δὲ πολλοῖς ἔτεσι τὰς πόλεις δημοκρατηθῆναι.

From this it follows that the monarchy was thrice interrupted by democratic governments, and that there were *four* periods. This is the Indian tradition. But the whole was conceived as one history, doubtless with a prehistoric ideal beginning, like our Manus and Tuiskon. Therefore, no cosmic *periods* (Brahmanical imposture), but four *generations* of Aryan history in India.

The Kaliyuga is a new world, just as much as Teutonic Christendom, but no more. The Indians will probably have commenced it A. D. 410, as friend Kingsley too (in his " Hypatia"). Where is the starting-point? I hold to as the chronological computation up to the time of the Nandas. ... 1015 years.

For the Nandas, I hold to the 22 years.

If they say that Kâlâśoka and his ten sons reigned 22 years; and Nanda, nine brothers in succession, 22 years; the 22 years is not wrong, either here or there, but the 22 is correct and the ten kingly personages also, for aught I care: but the *names* are altered (and really to do away with the plebeian Nanda), therefore it is neither 44, nor 88, nor 100 (which is nothing), but . . . . 22 "

From Parikshit to the year before Sandrakottus . . . . 1037 "

Sandrak.'s first year 312 (?), 317 (?), 320 (?). I have no opinion on the point, therefore take the middle number *about* . . . . 317 "

Beginning of the fourth period . . 1354 B. C.
Interregnum, popular government . 120 "

                                                        1474 "

End of the third period . . . . 1475 "

Nakshatra era 1476? (Weber, "Indian Studies," li. 240.)

This fourth period is that of the supremacy of the Brahmans in the beginning, with its recoil in Buddha towards the end.

In the year 1250 B. C., about the one hundredth year of the era, Semiramis invaded India (Dâvpara).

Third period of the royal dynasties, the great empire on the Jumna, not far from the immortal Aliwal. Beginning with the *Dynasty of the Kurus*. (Here the names of the kings and their works, as canals, etc. *Seat of the empire*, the Duâb; Hastinapura, Ayodhyâ; or still on the Sarasvatî) . . . . 0 years.

Interregnum between III. and II. (Must have left its traces. A pasted up break is surely there.) . . . . 300 "

Second period of royal dynasties (Treta) . 0 years.
(Is this the historical life in the Punjab, with already existing kingdoms?) N. B. What is the third of the pure flames? Is it the people? Atria, latria, patria?

Interregnum between II. and I. . . . 200 "

First period. Beginning of the history after first *x* years, with an ideally filled up unmeasured period.

Beginning: Manu . . 6402
317

6719 B. C. 6719

Deduct from this a mythical beginning: a cycle of $5 \times 12 = 60$, or 600: at most $60 \times 60 = 3600$, at least $12 \times 60 = 720$. Or about 6 kings of 400 years each. } mean time 2160

─────
4559

(There remain, deducting 6 from 154 kings (with Dionysos), about 148.)

Length of time: $4559 - 1354 = 3205 \div 148 = 21\frac{1}{2}$ mean number of years for each historical government; which is very appropriate.

Zoroaster lived, according to Eudoxus and Aristotle (compared with Hermippos) 6350 or 6300 B. C. This points to a time of Zoroastrians migrating towards India, or *having migrated, returning* again. Accept the latter, and the beginning of the 6402 years lies very near the first period, and the Indianizing of the Aryans. Those accounts about Zoroaster are (as Eudoxus already proves) *pre*-Alexandrian, therefore not Indian, but Aryan. Do not the hymns of the Rig-veda, of which several are attributed to the kings of the Treta period, contain hints on that schism? If it really occurred in the Punjab some reminiscence would have been left there of it. The Zend books (wretched things) only give negative evidence.

The Brahmans of the most sinful period have of course smothered all that is historical in prodigies, and *this* wretched taste long appeared to the Germans as *wisdom;* whilst they despised the (certainly superficial) but still sensible English researches of Sir W. Jones and Co., as philistering! One must oppose this more inflexibly than even that admirable Lassen does. (N. B. Has Colbrooke anything on this? or Wilson?)

There may have been *two* points of contact between the Aryans and the kingdoms on the Euphrates *before* the expedition of Semiramis.

a. By means of the Zoroastrian Medo-Babylonian kingdom, which had its capital in Babylon from 2234 B. C. (1903 before Alexander) for about two centuries.

b. In the oldest primitive times, by the Turanian-Cushite or North African kingdom of Nimrod, which cannot be placed later than in the seventh chiliad. The Egyptians had a tradition of this, as is proved according to my interpretation by the historical germ in the story in the Timæos of the great combat of Europe and Asia against the so-called Atlantides: but these are uncertain matters.

That is a general sketch of my frame-work. If you are able to do anything with it, I make you the following proposition: You will send me an *open letter* in German (only without *your Excellency*, and as I beg you will always write to me, as friend to friend), in which you will answer my communication. Send me beforehand a few reflections and doubts for my text, which I must send away by the 15th of May. Your open letter must be sent in in June, if possible before the 15th, in order to appear before the 15th of July as an Appendix to my text of Book V. b. (fourth division) first half. *I* can do nothing in the matter; everything here is wanting. I cannot even find German books here. Therefore keep Lassen's maps, if you have them. I have in the mean time helped myself by means of Ritter and Kiepert to find the old kingdoms and the sacred Sarasvati. That satisfies me for the present.

Soon a sign of life and love to your sorely tormented but faithful B.

[72.]   CHARLOTTENBERG, *Sunday Morning, April*, 27, 1850.

I have laid before you my restoration of the text of Megasthenes, and added a few preliminary thoughts on the possibility of the restoration of his traditions, and something of my restoring criticism. I have not however been able to rest since that time, without going to the very ground of the matter, to see if I am on a side-path, or on the right road. I now send you the summary of the two chapters which I have written since

I. The restoration of the list of Megasthenes. (153 kings in 6402 years.)

1. The list begins, like the Sanskrit tradition, with the first generation; three interregnums presuppose four periods.

2. The whole fourfold divided chronology is *one*: three sections of *historical recollections* lie before the Kali age. Lassen is therefore wrong in saying that Megasthenes began with the Tretâ age. The progress of the gradual extension of the kingdom is organic.

3. The foundation of the whole tradition of the four periods of time are the *genealogical registers of the old royal families*, which must if possible be *localized*; of course with special reference to Magadha, which however begins late. As in Egypt, every branch tried somewhere to find its place; we must therefore throw away or mark all names not supported by the legend (that is, the Vedic traditions). The contemporary dynasties must be separated from those that follow each other.

4. Each period was divided from the preceding by an *historical fact*, — a dissolution followed by a subjugation or a popular government. The first is divided from the second by Herakles — Krishna. The third from the second by Râma, the extirpator of the heroes and royal races (great rising of the people). The fourth from the third by purely historical revolutions, caused or fostered by the Assyrian invasion.

5. The mythical expression for these periods is *one thousand years*.

6. The historical interregnums are 200, 300, 120.

7. As both are the same, therefore 3 × 1000 years vanish, and there remain but the 620.

8. Therefore Megasthenes' list . . 6402
3000

Kings from the first patriarch to Sandrakottus . . . . . . 3402 years.
Interregnums 620
———
4022

FIRST PERIOD.

A. Aryan recollections. Megasthenes' list unites the traditions of the Moon-race (Budha) with that of the Sun-race (direct from Manu).

(1.) Questions. First question. What do the names Ayus and Yayâti mean? Is Nahusha = man?

(2.) I know king Ikshvâku, i. e., the gourd. Who are the Asuras, conquered by Prithu?

(3.) Anu, one of the four sons of Yayâti, is the North, not the Iranian, nor the Turanian, which is Turvasa, but the Semitic, i. e., Assur. Anu is the chief national god of the Assyrians, according to the cuneiform inscriptions. The cradle of the old dynasty was therefore called Telanu = hill of Anu. Salmanassar is called Salem-anu, i. e., face of Anu.

B. Indian primitive times.
   1. Manu (primitive time) . . . 1000
   2–14. Thirteen human kings in the Punjab, each reigns on an average thirty-six years 468
   15. Krishna, destruction . . . 1000

2468 years, representing really only 268 + 200 years, with an unknown quantity representing Aryan migrations and settlements in the Punjab.

   (4.) Question. Is Jones' statement correct in his chronology (Works, i. 299), that the fourth Avatâr must be placed between the first and second periods?

SECOND PERIOD.

The kingdom of the Puru, and the Bharata kings. Royal residence, province of the Sarasvatî. Epos, the Râmâyana.

A. *Period from Puru to Dushyanta.*
Conquests from the Sarasvatî on the north, and to Kalinga (Bengal) on the south. Conquerors: Tansu, Ilina, Bharata, Suhôtra (all Vedic names).

B. *Period of destruction through the Pañkâlas.* — *Agamîdha* (Suhôtra's son, according to the unfalsified tradition) is the human *Râma*, the instrument of destruction.

   (5.) Question. Why is he called in Lassen, i. 590, the son of *Rikshu*? (This is another thousand years.)

Riksha is called in M. Bh. (Lassen, xxiii. note 17) son of Agamîdha, and in another place, *wife* of Agamîdha, or both times *wife!*

THIRD PERIOD.

The Kurus; the Pañkâlas; the Pândavas. Seats in Middle Hindostan. Advance to the Vindhya (Epos, the Mahâbhârata of the third period, as the Râmâyana of the second).

A. Kingdoms of the Kurus.

B. Kingdom of the Pañkâlas. Contemporary lists; but the Pañkâlas outlast the Kurus. Both are followed by —
C. Kingdom of the Pândavas.
Ad. A. From Kuru to Devâpi who retires (that is, is driven away), Sântanu, Bahlika, the Bactrian (?), there are eleven reigns. Then the three generations to Duryodhana and Arguna.

Parikshit represents the beginning of the Interregnum.

The list in the Vishnu-purâna of twenty-nine kings, from Parikshit to Kshemaka, with whom the race becomes extinct in the Kali age, does not concern us.

They are the lines of the pretenders, who did not again acquire the throne. The oldest list is probably only of six reigns; for the son of Satânika, the third V. P. king of this list, is also called Udayana (Lassen, xxvi. note 23), and the same is the name of the twenty-fifth king, the son of Satânika II. Therefore Brihadratha, Vasudâna, and Sudâsa (21, 22, 23) are likewise the last of a Parikshit line. But they do not count chronologically.

Fourth Period.

The kingdom of Magadha. Chronological clews for Megasthenes. The first part of the Magadha list preserved to us (Lassen, xxxi.) from Kuru to Sahadeva is an unchronological list of collateral lines of the third period, therefore of no value for the computation of time. The Kali list of Magadha begins with Somâpi to Ripungaya, 20 kings. The numbers are cooked in so stupid a way that they neither agree with each other nor are possible. One can only find the right number from lower down.

Restoration of the Chronology.

Kali II. *Pradyota*, five kings with	. . .	138 years.
" III. *Saisunâga*, ten kings with	. .	360 "
" IV. *Nanda*, father with eight or nine sons .		22 "
		520
" V. *Kandragupta* king		. 317 B. C.
		837 "

If one deducts these 837 years from 1182, the first year of the Kali age, there remain 345 years for the twenty kings from Somâpi to Ripungaya (First Dynasty), averaging 17½ years. (That will do!) I adopt 1182 years, because 1354 is *impossible*,

but 1181 is the historical chronological beginning of a kingdom
in Kashmir. Semiramis invaded India under a *Sthavirapati*
(probably only a title), about 1250. This time must therefore
fall in the interregnum (120 years, after Megasthenes). The
history of the war with Assyria (Asura?) is smothered by pushing forward the Abhira, that is, the Naval War on the Indus
(Diodorus).

I pass over the approximate restoration of the first three
periods. I have given you a scanty abstract of my treatise,
which I naturally only look upon as a *frame-work*. But if the
frame-work be right, and of this I feel convinced, if I have
discovered the true grooves and the system — then the unfalsified remains of traditions in the Vedas must afford further
confirmation. The Kali can be fixed for about —— 1150 / 1190 —— by powerful synchronisms. The three earlier ages can be approximately restored. One thus arrives, by adding 200 + 300 +
120 (= 620) to each of the earlier and thus separated periods, to the beginning of the Tretâ (foundation of the *Bharata
kingdom* beginning with Puru). This leads to the following
computation.

I. Anarchy before Puru	.	200 years.
II. From Puru to Bharata's father, 10 reigns of 20 years	.	200 "
From Bharata to Agamidha's son, 6 reigns		120 "
End of II.	.	300 "
III. From Kuru to Bahlika (migration towards Bactria?) 10 reigns	.	200 "
(Parikshit) apparently 6–7 reigns	.	120 "
End of the oldest Indian kingdom, before Kali		1340 years.
		1182 "
Beginning of Tretâ =		2522 B. C.
(2234 Zoroaster invaded Babylon from Media)		
Second dynasties in Babylon	.	1100 "
		3622 "

We have still to account for the time of the *settlement in the
Punjab* and formation of kingdoms there. This gives as the beginning approximately = 4339 B. C.

And now I am very anxious to hear what you have made out, or whether you have let the whole matter rest as it is. I have postponed everything, in order to clear up the way as far as I can. I shall try to induce Weber to visit me in the Whitsun holidays, to look into the details for me, that I may not lay myself open to attack. Before that I shall have received Haug's *entirely new translation of the first Fargard*, which I shall print as an Appendix, with his annotations. My *Chinese* restoration has turned out *most* satisfactory.

I may now look forward to telling them: (1.) The rabbinical chronology is false, it is impossible; it has every tradition opposed to it, most of all so the biblical — therefore away with it! (2.) Science has not to *turn back*, but now first to press really forward, and to restore: the question is not the fixing of abstract speculative formulas, but the employing of speculation and philology for the *reconstruction of the history of humanity*, of which revelation is only a portion, though certainly the centre if we believe in our moral consciousness of God.

This is about what I shall say, as my last word, in the Preface to the sixth volume of "Egypt." Volumes IV. and V. *are* printed. *Deo soli gloria.*

[73.] CHARLOTTENBERG, *May 22, 1856.*

MY DEAR FRIEND, — H. R. H. the Prince Regent, who starts for England to-morrow, wishes to see Oxford, and *quietly* and *instructively*. I therefore give these lines to his private secretary, Herr Ullmann, that he may by letter, or (if the time allows) by word of mouth, apply to you, to fix *a day*. Herr Ullmann is the son of the famous Dr. U., the present prelate and chief church-councilor, and a man of good intentions.

I have at last gone in for Vedic and Bactrian chronology, after having had Dr. Haug of Bonn with me for eight days. He translated and read to me many hymns from your two quartos (which he does very fluently), and a little of Sâyana's commentary. By this and by Lassen and Roth, and yours and Weber's communications, I believe I have saved myself from the breakers, and I hold my proofs as established : —

That the oldest Vedas were composed 3000-2500 B. C., and that everything else is written in a learned dead Brahmanical language, a precipitate of the Veda language, and certainly *very late*: scarcely anything before 800 B. C.

Manu takes his place after Buddha.

The ages of the world are the miserable system of the book of Manu, and nothing more than evaporated historical periods. These epochs can be restored not by the aid, but in spite of the two epics and their chronology.

Petermann sends me a beautiful map. The routes and settlements of the Aryans from their primitive home to the land of the five rivers (or rather seven).

Haug has worked out all the fourteen names. Kabul and Kandahar are hidden amongst them. I hope he will settle in the autumn with me, and for the next few years.

In haste, with hearty thanks for your affectionate and instructive answers. God bless you.

P. S. I shall take the liberty of sending you, about the 1st of July, the first five sheets of my *Aryans*, before they are printed off, and ten days later the remaining three or four, and beg for your instructive remarks on them.

[76.] CHARLOTTENBERG, *July* 17, 1856.

MY DEARLY LOVED FRIEND,—Yesterday evening at half-past seven o'clock I wrote off my *last chapter* of " Egypt's Place " for press, and so the work is finished, the first sheets of which were sent to Gotha from London in 1843, the chief part of which however was written in 1838–39. You will receive the two new volumes (Books IV., V. a) in a fortnight; they will be published to-day. Of the third volume (the sixth of the German editions), or V. (b), twelve sheets are printed, and the other eighteen are ready, except a few sheets already at Gotha, including the Index to I. to V. (a). I am in the main satisfied with the work.

You are the first with whom I begin paying off my debts of correspondence; and I rejoice that I can take this opportunity to thank you for all the delightful news which your last dear letter (sent by that most amiable Muir) conveyed to me; especially for the completion of the *third big volume of the Rigveda*, and for the happy arrival of your mother and cousin, which has doubtless already taken place. You know it was a letter from the *latter*, which first told me *of you*, and made me wish to see you. And then you came *yourself;* and all that I prophesied of you after the first conversation in London and your first visit in the country, has been richly fulfilled — yes, beyond my boldest hopes. You have won an honorable position in the first English university, not only for yourself but for the Fatherland, and you have richly returned the love which I felt for you from the first moment, and have faithfully reciprocated a friendship which constitutes an essential portion of my happiness. I therefore thank you all the more for all the love and friendship of your last letters. I can only excuse myself *by my book* for not having sooner thanked you. I soon perceived that *you were quite right*, that the chronological researches on Indian antiquity have led to nothing more sure than the conviction that the earlier views, with few exceptions, were wrong or without foundation. As soon as I acquired this conviction, through reading the last works on the subject (Lassen and Roth), I grew furious, as it happens to me from time to time, and at the same time reawoke the longing after the researches which I had to lay aside in 1816, and which I now determined to approach again, in the course of my work, which is chronological in the widest sense. After I had read all that is written, I let Haug come to me in the Whitsun holidays. He brought with him the translation I wished for of the *First Fargard of the Vendidad*; and you can imagine my delight, when in Books XII. and XIII. he discovered for me (purely linguistically) the two countries, the non-appearance of which was the *only* tenable counter-reason which opposed itself to the intuition to which I had held fast since 1814 — namely, that this document, so ancient in its primitive elements, contained nothing less than the history of the gradual invasion, founding of states, and peopling of Asia by the Aryans. How could Kandahar and Kabul be missing if this were true? Without the least *suspicion* of this historical opinion, Haug proved to me that they are not wanting. Petermann will make the whole clear in a little map, such as I showed him. You will find it in the sixth volume. Then he rejoiced my heart by translating some *single hymns of the Rig-veda*, especially in Book VII., which I found threw great light on the God-Consciousness, the faith in the moral government of the world. *He comes to me*: from the 1st of August he is free in Bonn, and goes for the Zend affairs to Paris, marries his bride in Ofterdingen, and comes here to me on the 1st of October for *Mithridates* and the Old Testament, the printing of which begins in January, 1857, with the *Pentateuch*. With him (in default of your personal presence) I have now gone through everything at which I arrived with regard to the period of the entry of the Aryans (4000 B.C.) in the Indus country (to which Saraswati does not belong — one can as easily count seven as five rivers from the eastern branch of the upper Indus to the west of the Satadru), and with regard to the difficult questions of the connection of these migrations with Zoroaster. That is, I *must* place Zoroaster *before* the emigration; on the march (from 5000–4000) the emigrants gradually break off. Three heresies, one after another, are mentioned in the record itself. The not exterminated germs of the nature-worship (with the adoration of fire) spring up again, but the moral life remained. (1.) Therefore the Veda language is to me the precipitate of the Old Bactrian (as the Edda language of the Old Norse). (2.) The *Zend language* is the second step from the Northern Old Bactrian. (3.) The Sanskrit is one still further advanced from the Southern Old Bactrian, or from the Veda language. (4.) All *Indian literature*, except the Vedas, is in the New South Bactrian, already become a learned language, which has been named the perfect or Sanskrit language. The *epochs of the language* are the three *great historical catastrophes*.

A. *Kingdom in the region of the Indus.* — 4000–3000. The Veda language as a living popular language.

B. *Second Period.* — On the Saraswati and in the Duáb. The Veda tongue becomes the learned language. Sanskrit is the *popular* language, 3000–2000.

C. *Third Period.* — Sanskrit *begins* to be the learned language, at least at the end.

D. Kali = 1150 B.C. Sanskrit merely the learned language.

Therefore the oldest Vedas, the purely popular, cannot be younger than 3000; the *collection* was made in the third period, the tenth book is already in chief part written in a *dead language*. You see all depends on whether I can authenticate the four periods with their three catastrophes; for a new form of language presupposes a political change. Forms such as Haraqaiti I can explain just as that the Norwegian names of places are younger than the corresponding Icelandic forms; in the colony the old remains as a fixed form, in the mother country the language progresses.

For what concerns now seriously the *Mythology*, your spirited essay opening the way was a real godsend, for I had just arrived at the conviction which you will find expressed in the Introduction to Book V. (a) : That the so-called nature-religion can be nothing but the *symbol* of the primitive consciousness of

God, which only gradually became independent (through misunderstanding) and which already lies prefigured in organic speech. P——, K—— and Co., are on this point in great darkness, or rather in utter error. You have kept yourself perfectly free from this mistake. I however felt that I must proclaim what is positively true far more sharply, and have drawn the outlines of a method which is to me the more convincing, as it has stood the test of the whole history of old religion. For in taking up the Aryan investigations, I closed the circle of my historical mythological inquiry. What will you say to this? For I have written the whole especially for you, to come to an understanding with you. I arrive at the same point which you aim at, but without your roundabout way, which is but a makeshift. But in the fundamental conception of nature-religion, we do certainly agree altogether. If you come to Germany, you will find here with me the proof-sheets of Book V. (b) (about pages 1–200) which treat of this section, as well as the analysis of the table of the Hebrew patriarchs. They will be looked through before Haug's journey to Paris and mine to Geneva (August 1), and will be therefore all struck off when I return here on the 23d August.

Your essay holds a beautiful place in the history of the subject. The work on that section gave me inexpressible delight, and a despaired-of gap in my life is filled up, as far as is necessary for my own knowledge; and I believe too not without advantage to the faithful.

How disgraceful it is that we do not instinctively understand the Veda language, when we read it in respectable Roman letters, with a little previous grammatical practice! Your Veda Grammar will be a closed book to me, as you print in the later Devanagari goose-foot character. Haug shall transliterate for me the grammatical forms into *your* alphabet. He is a noble Suabian, and much attached to me; also a great admirer of yours.

My "God-Consciousness" is printed (thirty-two sheets), twenty are corrected (and fought through with Bernays). This work, too, will be carried through the second revise before my journey. I wonder myself what will come of the work. Its extent remains unaltered (three volumes in six books), but its contents are ever swelling. I hope it *will take*. I shall strike the old system *dead forever*, if we do not go to ruin; of this I am sure; therefore I must all the more lay the foundations of the new structure in the heart, the conscience, and the reason.

"O! what a hideous time! God be praised, who made us
both free. So also is Carl now, through his official efficiency
and his happy marriage. The wedding will take place in Paris
between the 8th and 15th October. We shall go there.

I take daily rides, and was never better. Please God I shall
finish the "God-Consciousness" (II. and III.) between the 25th
August and the end of October (the third volume is nearly
ready), and then I shall take up the "Biblework," the proof-
sheets of which lie before me, with *undivided* energy. The contract with Brockhaus is concluded and exchanged. I shall perhaps come to England in October, 1857; that is to say *with* the
first volume of the Bible, but *not without* it.

Neukomm and Joachim have been with us for six weeks,
which gave us the greatest enjoyment. Neukomm returns here
at the end of August.

My children promise me (without saying it) to meet here for
the 25th August, to introduce the amiable bride to me. I am
rejoicing over it like a child.

Why do you not make a journey to the Neckar valley with
your mother and cousin? My people send hearty greetings.
With true love, yours.

I am purposely not reading your Anti-Renan all at once, that
I may often read it over again before I finish it. I think it is
admirably written. Perhaps a distinguished philologist, Dr.
Fliedner (nephew of the head of the Deaconesses), may call on
you. He has been highly recommended to me, and is worthy
of encouragement. What is Aufrecht about? I cannot cease
to feel interested about him.

[75.]   CHARLOTTENBERG, *October* 7, 1856.

Yesterday, my dearest friend, I sent off the close of the last
volume of "Egypt," together with the printed sheets 13–19, and
at the same time to Brockhaus the last two revised sheets of the
"God in History," Volume I.; and to-day I have again taken up
the translation of the Bible (Exodus), with Haug and Camphausen — that is, Haug arrived the day before yesterday. (Between ourselves, I hope Bernays is coming to me for three years.)
How I should have liked to show you these sheets, 13–19 (the
Bactrians and Indians and their chronology). You will find
in them a thorough discussion of your beautiful essay (which
has been admired everywhere as a perfect masterpiece), not with-

out some shakings of the head at K—— and B——. In fact I
have gone in for it, and by New Year's Day you shall have it
before you. This, with the journey to Switzerland and three
weeks of indisposition afterwards, are an excuse for my silence.

It always gives me great and inexpressible pleasure when
you *talk* to me by letter and *think aloud*. And this time I have
been deeply touched by it. I am convinced you have since
then yourself examined the considerations which oppose themselves to your bold and noble wish with regard to the Punjab.
What would become of your great work? I will not here say
what shall we in Europe do without you? Also; do you mean
to go *alone* to Hapta Hendu, or as a married man? There you
will never find a wife. And would your intended go with you?
And the *children?* All Englishmen tell me it is just as unbear-
ably hot in Lahore as in Delhi; in *Umritsir* there is no fresh air.
No Sirg goes to Cashmir because he who reigns there would
soon dispatch him out of the world at the time of the fever.

By the by, what has become of your convert? Does he still
smoke without any scruple?

Your gorgeous Rig-veda at Brockhaus' frightens people here
because of its extent (they would have given up the Sanhita,
satisfied with various readings) and the exorbitant price.
Others would willingly have had your own Veda Grammar besides the Indian grammatical treatise, especially on account of
the Vedic forms. In fact you are admired, but criticised. You
must not allow this to annoy you. I find that Haug thinks
about the mythology nearly as I do.

Everything in Germany resolves itself more and more into
pettinesses and cliques, and the pitiful question of subsistence.
"The many princes are our good fortune, but poverty is our
crime." Had not *Brunn* offered himself to take Braun's place,
giving up his private tutorship, we must have given up the Archæological Institute at Rome! With difficulty Gerhard has
found *one* man in Germany who could undertake the Italian
printing of the "Annali" (appearing, as you know, in Gotha).
" Resta a vedere se lo pub!" All who can, leave Prussia —
and only blockheads or hypocrites are let in, with the exception of physical science; whoever can do so turns engineer, or
goes into a house of business, or emigrates. My decided advice on this account therefore is, reserve yourself for better
times, and stay at present in England, where you have really
won a delightful position for yourself.

Now for various things about myself. Every possible thing is done to draw me away from here (my third capitol, the first of my own). The King quite recently (which I could not in the least expect) received me here at the railway station, in the most affectionate way, and demanded a promise from me that I would pay him a visit within a year and a day. But I have once for all declared myself as the "hermit of Charlottenburg," and hermits and prophets should stay at home. I do not even go to Carlsruhe and Coblentz. *Cui bono?* What avails good words, without good deeds? But the nation is not dead. Don't imagine that. Before this month is out you will see what I have said on this subject in the Preface to the "God in History." Within six to ten years the nation will again be fit to act. Palmerston will cut his throat if nothing comes of the Neapolitan business, and just the same if he cannot make "a good case;" the principle of intervention even against Bomba is self-destruction for England, and disgraceful in the highest degree. The *fox* cannot begin war in Italy at *the present moment* from want of money, and his accomplices are afraid of losing their stolen booty. So he tries to gain time. He will still live a few years.

I have seen ——: he knows a great deal more than he allows to appear, but is the driest, and most despairing Englishman I have ever seen. He has suffered shipwreck of everything on the Tübingen sand bank. The poor wretches! Religion and theology without philosophy is bad; philosophy without philosophy is a monster! So Comte is a trump-card with many in Oxford! He is so in London. What a fall of intellect! what a decay of life! what an abyss of ignorance! Jowett is a living shoot, and will continue so; but John Bull is my chief comfort, even for my "God in History." America is my greatest misery after my misery for Germany; but the North *will* prove itself in the right.

With hearty greetings of truest attachment and love to your mother, truly yours.

We expect George on the 18th. Ernst is here.

[76.]   CHARLOTTENBERG. *January* 29, 1857.

You have really inflicted it on me! For though I have but one leg to stand upon (I cannot *sit* at all), as the other has been suffering for four days from sciatica (let Dr. Acland explain that to you, whilst you at the same time thank him heartily for his excellent book on the cholera), still I am obliged to place myself at the desk, to answer my dear friend's letter, received yesterday evening in bed. The last fortnight I have daily thought of you incessantly, and wished to write you a dunning letter, at the same time thanking you for the third volume of the Veda, which already contains some hymns of the seventh book, as the admiring Haug read it out to me. Out of this especially he promises me a great treasure for my Vedic God-Consciousness, without prejudice to what the muse may perhaps prompt you to send me in your beautiful poetical translation; for my young assistant will have nothing to do with that. You will certainly agree with him, after you have read my first volume, that much is to be found in that Veda for the centre of my inquiries; the consciousness in the Indian Iranians of the reality of the divine in human life. I find in all that has yet come before me, almost the same that echoes through the Edda, and that appears in Homer as popular belief; the godhead interferes in human affairs, when crime becomes too wanton, and thus evil is overcome and the good gains more and more the upper hand. Of course that is kept in the background, when despair in realities becomes the keynote of the God-Consciousness, as with the Brahmans, and then with the much-praised apostles of annihilation, the Buddhists. You are quite right; it is a pity that I could not let the work appear all at once, for even you misunderstand me. When I say " we cannot pray with the Vedas and Homer and their heroes, not even with Pindar," I mean, we as worshippers, as a community; and that you will surely allow. Of course the thoughtful philosopher can well say with Goethe, "worship and liturgy in the name of St. Homer, not to forget Æschylus and Shakespeare." But that matter is nevertheless true in history without any limitation. I have only tried it with Confucius, but it is more difficult; it is as if an antediluvian armadillo tried to dance.

But what will my Old Testament readers say when I lead them into the glory of the Hellenic God-Consciousness? Crossing and blessing themselves won't help! My expressions therefore in the second volume are carefully considered and cautiously used. But the tragedy of my life will be the fourth book. Yet I write it, I have written it!

You are quite right about the English translation; all the 'ree volumes at once, and the address at the beginning. But you must read the second book for me. It is no good saying you don't understand anything about it. I have made it easy enough for you. I have asserted nothing simply, without making it easy for every educated person to form his own opinion, if he will only reflect seriously about the Bible. The *presuppositions* are either as good as granted, or where anything peculiar to me comes in, I have in the notes justified everything thoroughly, although apparently very simply. Take the Lent Sundays for this, and you will keep Easter with me, and also your amiable mother (from whom you never send me even a word of greeting).

But now, how does it fare with "Egypt?" The closing volume, which, as you know, I wrote partly out of despair, because you would not help me, and in which I most especially thought of you, and reckoned on your guiding friendship, must surely now be in your hands (the two preceding volumes, of course, some time ago). Why don't you read them?

I am not at all easy at what you tell me about yourself and your feelings; even though I feel deeply that you do not quite withdraw your inmost thoughts from me. But why are you unhappy? You have gained for yourself a delightful position in life. You are getting on with your gigantic work. You (like me) have won a fatherland in England, without losing your German home, the ever excellent. You have a beautiful future before you. You can at any moment give yourself a comfortable and soul-satisfying family circle. If many around you are Philisters, you knew that already; still they are worth something in *their* own line. Only step boldly forward into life. Then Heidelberg would come again into your itinerary.

One thing more this time. I have not received Wilson's translation. I possess both the first and second volumes. Has he not continued his useful work? What can I do to remind him of the missing part? The third volume, too, must contain much that is interesting for me.

I cannot forget Aufrecht. Is he free from care and contented? The family greet you and your dear mother. We expect Charles and his young wife next week. Ernst is, as you will know, back at Abbey Lodge. With unaltered affection.

[77.]   CHARLOTTENBERG, *April* 27, 1857.

The month is nearly over, my dear friend, before the close of which I must, according to agreement, deliver up my revised copy of the amendments and additions to the English edition of my "Egypt." (They are already there.) I hoped that in this interval you would have found a little leisure (as Lepsius and Bernays have done, who sent me the fruits of their reading already at the beginning of the month, in the most friendly way) to communicate to me your criticisms or doubts or thoughts or corrections on that which I have touched on in your own especial territory, as I had expressly and earnestly begged you to do. I have improved the arrangement very much. As you have not done this, I can only entertain one of two disagreeable suppositions, namely, that you are either ill or out of spirits, or that you have only what is disagreeable to say of my book, and would rather spare yourself and me from this. But as from what I know of you, and you know of me, I do not find in either the one or the other supposition a sufficient explanation of your obstinate silence, I should have forced myself to wait patiently, had I not to beg from you alone a small but indispensable gift for my "God in History."

I have again in this interregnum taken up the interrupted studies of last year on the Aryan God-Consciousness in the Asiatic world, and thanks to Burnouf's, yours, Wilson's, Roth's and Fausböll's books, and Haug's assistance and translations, I have made the way easy to myself for understanding the two great Aryan prophets Zaradushtra and Sâkya, and (so far as that is possible to one of us now) the Veda; and this not without success and with inexpressible delight. My expectations are far exceeded. The Vedic songs are by far the most glorious, which in first going through that fearful translation of Wilson's, seemed to wish to hide themselves entirely from me. The difficulties of making them intelligible, even of a bare translation, are immense; the utter perverseness of Sâyana is only exceeded by that of Wilson, to whom however one can never be grateful enough for his communications. I now first perceive what a difficult but also noble work you have undertaken, and how much still remains doubtful; even after one has got beyond the collectors and near to the original poets. It is as if of the Hebrew traditions we only had the Psalms, and that without an individual personality like David, without, in fact, any one; on the contrary, allusions to Abraham's possible poems and the cos-

mical dreams of the Aramæans. But yet how strong is the feeling
of immediate relation to God and nature, how truly human, and
how closely related to our own! What a curious similarity to the
Edda, Homer, and Pindar, Hesiod, and the Hellenic primitive
times! Nothing however gave me greater delight than the dignity and solemnity of the funeral ceremonies, which you have
made so really clear and easy to be understood. This is as yet
the only piece of *real life* of our blood relations in the land of
the five rivers. I have naturally taken possession of this treasure with the greatest delight, and perfected the description for
my problem by the explanation of Yama (following on the whole
Roth, who however overlooks the demiurgic character), of the
Ribhus (departing entirely, not only from Nève's mistaken
views, but also from what I have read elsewhere, representing
them as the three powers which divide and form matter,
namely, Air, Water, and Earth, to whom the fourth, Agni, was
joined under the guidance of Tvashvar), and of the funeral ceremonies as the condition of the laws of inheritance; where I return to my own beginning. And here it strikes me at once that
in the Vedas, so far as they are accessible to me, there is not a
trace to be found of the *joining together of the three generations*
(the departed and his father and grandfather), and making them
the unity of the race through the sacrificial oblations. And yet
the *idea* must be older than the Vedas, as this precise, though
certainly not accidental limitation is found with Solon and the
Twelve Tables, just as clearly as with Manu and all the books
of laws, and the commentaries collected by Colebrooke. You
would of course have mentioned this in your account if anything
of the sort had existed in the tenth book. But even the Pitris,
the fathers, are not mentioned, but it passes on straight to Yama
the first ancestor. Haug, too, has discovered nothing; if you
know anything about it, communicate it to me in the course of
May, for my second volume goes to press on the 1st June. I
shall read it aloud to George and Miss Wynn here, between the
25th and 31st.

But my real desire is that you should send me one of your
melodious and graceful metrical translations of your hymn,
"Nor ought nor nought existed." I must of course give it (it
belongs with me to the period of transition, therefore, comparatively speaking, late); and how can I venture to translate it?
I have, to be sure, done so with about five poems, which Haug
chose for me out of the first nine books, and translated literally

and then explained them to me; as well as with those which I
worked out of Wilson's two first volumes by the help of Roth
and Haug. But that is your hymn, and I have already written
my thanks for your communication in my MS. and then left a
space. That good Rowland Williams thinks it theistic, or at
all events lets one of the speakers say so.

Rowland Williams' "Christ and Hinduism" has been a real
refreshment to me, in this investigation of the Indian consciousness of God in the world. The mastery of the Socratic-Platonic
dialogue, the delicacy and freedom of the investigation, and the
deep Christian and human spirit of this man, have attracted me
more than all other new English books, and even filled me with
astonishment. Muir, that good man, sent it me through Williams and Norgate, and I have not only thanked him, but Williams himself, in a full letter, and have pressingly invited him
for his holidays to our little philosophers' room. It is an especial pleasure to me that Mary and John, whose neighbor he is
in summer, have appreciated him, and loved and prized him,
and Henry also.

Henry will bring me "Rational Godliness." This book,
English as it is, should be introduced into India, in order to
convert the followers of Brahma and the English Christians!
One sees what hidden energy lies in the English mind, as soon
as it is turned to a worthy object, but for this of course the
fructifying influences of the German spirit are required. I
have, on the contrary, been much disappointed by G——'s communication contained in Burnouf's classical works, on that most
difficult but yet perfectly soluble point of the teaching of Buddha, the twelve points "beginning with ignorance and ending
with death." G—— leaves the rational way even at the first
step, and perceives his error himself at the ninth, but so far he
finds Buddha's (that is his own) proofs unanswerable. How
totally different is Burnouf. He is fresh, self-possessed, and
clear. I can better explain why William von Humboldt went
astray on this subject. But I have already gossiped too much
of my own thoughts to you. Therefore to Anglicis.

What are you about in Oxford? According to Haug's account you have abused me well, or allowed me to be well abused
in your "Saturday Review," which passes as yours and Kingsley's mouthpiece. If it were criticism, however mistaken, but
why personal aspersions? Pattison's article on the "Theologia Germanica" in the April number of the "Westminster

Review" is very brave, and deserves all thanks. He has learnt
to prize Bleek: in all respects he has opened himself more to
me in the last few weeks, and I like him. But the man who
now writes the survey of foreign literature in the "Westminster
Review" might have just *read* my book: this he cannot have
done, or else he is a thorough bungler; for he (1) understands
me only as representing the personal God (apparently the one
in the clouds, as you once expressed it, *a-struddle*, riding) and
leaving out everything besides; (2) that the last twenty-seven
chapters of the book of Isaiah are not, as one has hitherto conceived, written by one man, but by Jeremiah, although he is already the glorified saint of the 53d chapter, *and* by Baruch.
Now thank God that the sheet is finished, and think occasionally in a friendly way of your true friend.

I shall to-day finish the ante-Solonic God-Consciousness of the
Hellenes. That does one good.

---

[78] CHARLOTTENBERG, *Friday, May 8,* 1857.

I must at least begin a letter to you to-day, because I feel I
must thank you, and express my delight at the letter and article. The *letter* confirms my fears in the highest degree, namely,
that you *are not well*, not to say that you begin to be a hypo-
chondriacal old bachelor. But that is such a natural consequence of your retired sulky Don's life, and of your spleen, that
I can only wonder how you can fight so bravely against it. But
both letter and article show me how vigorous are both your
mind and heart. It is quite right in you to defend Froude,
though no one better knows that the general opinion is (as is
even acknowledged by members of the German romantic school)
that Shakespeare intentionally counteracted the corrupt instinct
and depraved taste of his nation in the matter of Oldcastle.
Whatever strange saints there have been in all countries, yet
the Wycliffites, true to their great and noble master, were martyrs, and Milman has insisted on this most nobly. To misap-
prehend Wycliffe himself, that is, not to recognize him as the
first and purest reformer, the man between the Waldenses,
Tauler, and Luther, is, however, a heresy more worthy of condemnation than the ignoring of Germany in the Reformation,
and doubly deplorable when one sees such blind faith in the
bloody sentences of that most miserable court of judgment of
Henry VIII. I must therefore invert your formula thus,

"L'histoire romanique (romantique) ne vaut pas le Roman historique." (I am not speaking of "Two Years Ago," for I only began to read the book yesterday.) *But* I am very glad that you think so highly of Froude personally, and therefore this matter does not disturb me. On the other hand, I rejoice without any *but*, that you have taken up Buddha so lovingly and courageously. (Do you know that extracts from the article have found their way into the papers, through "Galignani" as "Signs of the Times." You will soon see how nearly we agree together, although I cannot say so much of the humanizing influence of Buddhism: it makes of the Turanians what the Jesuits make of the people of Paraguay, "praying machines." In *China* the Buddhists are not generally respected; in *India* they could not maintain their position, and would with difficulty convert the people, if they tried to regain their lost ground. But Buddha, *personally*, was a saint, a man who felt for mankind, a profound man. I have said in my section, "Buddha has not only found more millions of followers than Jesus, but is also even more misunderstood than the Son of Mary." Have you read *Dhammapadam*? What is the authority for Buddha's "Ten Commandments?" I have always considered this as an invention of Klaproth's, confirmed by Prinsep. I do not find them on Asoka's pillars, nor in that didactic poem; on the contrary, four or five *ad libitum*. I shall, however, now read the sermons of the (really worthless) convert Asoka at the fountain head, from Sprenger's library.

· You have represented the whole as with a magic wand. We really *edified* ourselves yesterday evening with it. Frances read aloud, and we listened; and this morning early my wife has made it into a beautiful little book in quarto, with which I this afternoon made *Trübner* very happy for some hours. He is a remarkable man, and is *much* devoted to you, and I have entered into business relations with him about my "Biblework," the first volume of which goes to press on the 1st of January; the other six stand before me as far finished as they can be, till I have the printed text of "The People's Bible" in three volumes before me, on which the "Biblical Documents," three volumes, and the "Life of Jesus and the Eternal Kingdom of God," one volume, are founded. He appears to me to be the right negotiator between America, England, and Germany. He will before long call on you some Saturday. (Write me word how you think of him as a bookseller.) The duty you pay for your place, by putting together a Chrestomathy, is very fair; whether you are obliged to print your Lectures I cannot decide. I shall curse them both if they prevent you from tearing yourself away from the Donnish atmosphere and bachelor life of Oxford, and from throwing yourself into the fresh mental atmosphere of Germany and of German mind and life. You must take other journeys besides lake excursions and Highland courses. Why don't you go to Switzerland, with an excursion (by Berlin) to Breslau, to the German Oriental Congress? There is nothing like the German spirit, in spite of all its one-sidedness. What a *læta paupertas!* What a recognition of the sacerdocy of science! And then the strengthening air, free from fog, of our mountains and valleys! You bad fellow, to tell me nothing of your mother's leaving you, for you ought to know that I am *tenderly* devoted to her; and it vexes me all the more, as I should long ago have sent her my " God in History," had I known that she was in Germany. (Query where? Address?) Therefore fetch her, instead of luring her away to the walks under the lime-trees. *George* is going too at the end of June from here to the Alps; we expect him in a fortnight. He is a great delight to me.

Now something more about Yama. I think you are *perfectly* right with regard to the origin. It is exactly the same with *Osiris*, the husband of Isis, the earth, and then the judge of the dead and first man. Only we do not on this account explain *Anubis* as a *symbol of the sun*, but as the watchful Dog of Justice, the accuser. So there are features in Yama (and Yima) which are not to be easily explained from the cosmogonic conception, although they can be from the idea of the divine, the first natural representation of which is the astral one. I think, however, that Yama is Geminus, that is "the upper and lower sun," to speak as an Egyptian. *The two dogs* must originally have been what their mother the old bitch Sarama is; but with the God of Death they are something different, and the lord of the dead is to be as little explained by the so-called nature-religion *without returning to the eternal factor*, as this first phase itself could have arisen without it as cosmical — *therefore,* as first symbol. How I long for your two translations! The hymn which you give in the article is *sublime:* the search after the God of the human heart is expressed with indescribable pathos; and how much more will this be the case in your hands in a new Indian translation! For we are most surely now the Indians of the West. I am delighted that you so value Rowland Williams. We must never forget that he has undertaken (as he himself most pointedly wrote to me) the difficult task "to teach Anglican theology (and that to Anglican Cymri)." He has not yet quite promised to pay me a visit, — he is evidently afraid of me as a German and freethinker, and is afraid "to be catechised." He, like all Englishmen, is wanting in *faith*. He seems to occupy himself profoundly with the criticism of the Old Testament. Poor fellow! But he will take to Daniel.

The Harfords are determined to keep him there, in which Henry has already encouraged them. I, however, think he *ought* to go to Cambridge if they offer him a professorship. Muir has written to me again, — an honest man; but he has again taken a useless step, a prize, for which Hoffmann (superintendent-in-general) is to be the arbiter; and the three judges will be named by him, Lehnert as theologian (Neander's unknown successor), H. Ritter as the historian of philosophy (very good). — and who as *Orientalist!* No magister will touch his pen, *his ducibus* and *tali auspicio*. You should perform the Bonares vow by a catechism drawn up for the poor young Brahmans in the style of Rowland Williams, and yet quite different, that is, in your own manner, telling and short. At all events, no one in Germany will write half as good a book for the Brahmans as Williams has done. The Platonic dialogue requires a certain breadth, unless one is able and willing to imitate the Parmenides. At the same time the ordinary missionaries may convert the lower classes through the Gospel and through Christian-English-German life, in which alone they prove their faith. By the by, it seems that Williams hopes for an article from you in the "North British Review." That you intend to read my "Egypt" is delightful; only not in the Long Vacation, when you ought to travel about. Have you read the friendly article on "God in History" in the "National Review" (April), which however certainly shows an ignorance bordering on impudence. Even tho man in the "Westminster Review" pleases me better, although he looked through my book fast asleep, and puts into my mouth the most unbelievable discoveries of his own ignorance, — Isaiah chapters xlix.-lxvi. are written by *Jeremiah* and *Baruch*, and similar horrors! When will people learn something? But in four years I hope, with God's help, to state this, in spite of them, and force them at last to learn something through "the help of their masters and mine." With true love, yours.

[79.]   CHARLOTTENBERG, *Friday Morning.*
            August 28, 1857.

See there he remains in the centre of Germany for a month, and lets one hear and see nothing of him! Had I not soon after the receipt of your dear and instructive letter gone to Wildbad, and there fallen into indescribable idleness, I should long ago have written to Oxford; for the letter was a great delight to me. The snail had there crept out of his shell and spoke to me as the friend, but now " Your Excellency" appears again; so the snail has drawn his head in again.

Now, my dear friend, you ought to be thanked for the friendly thought of paying me a visit, and writing to me. Therefore you must know that I returned here on the 19th, in order to greet, in his father's native country, Astor, my now sixty-three years old pupil, who proposed himself for the 20th to the 25th, and who for my sake has left his money-bags in order to see me once again. And now Astor is really in Europe, and has called at Ablwy Lodge; but his wife and granddaughter have stayed on in Paris or Brussels, and Astor is *not* yet here. This, however, has no effect on my movements, for I do not accompany him to Switzerland, where, I know, Brockhaus would send a hue and cry after me.

That the Oxford Don should ask him if I would afford him a "few hours," shows again the English leaven. For you well know that my hermit's life is dear to me for this reason,—that it leaves me at liberty to receive here the Muses and my friends. And what have we not to talk over? The "hours" belong to the Don's gown; for you know very well that we could in a "few hours" only figure to ourselves *what* we have to discuss by turns. So come as soon as you can, and stay at least a week here. You will find my house to be sure rather lonely, as Henry has robbed me of the womankind, and Sternberg of Theodora; and that excellent princess keeps Emilia from me, who is faithfully nursing her benefactress in an illness that I hope is passing away. We two old people are, however, here and full of old life. Perhaps you will also still find Theodore, who, however, soon after Astor's departure will be hurrying off to Falmouth for sea-bathing, in acceptance of his brother Ernst's invitation. Laboulaye has announced himself for the 8th; Gerhard and his wife for the first or second week in September; therefore, if you do find any one, they will be friends. Besides

Meyer, there is Dr. Sprenger, the Arabic scholar, as house
friend, whose library I have at last secured for us, — a delightful
man, who is my guide in the Arabian desert, so that I may be
certain of bringing the children of Israel in thirty months
to the Jabbok, namely, in the fifth of the eight volumes.

I can give you no better proof of my longing to see you than
by saying that you shall *even* be welcome without your mother,
who is so dear and unforgotten to us all, although we by no
means give up the hope that you will bring her with you here.
For I *must* see her again in this life. I ought to have thanked
her before this for a charming letter, but I did not know *where*
she had gone from Carlsbad; her son never sent me the address. Should she *not* come with you, you must pay toll for
the delay, which, however, must not be longer than one year,
with a photograph, for I *must* soon see her.

So you have looked at my Genesis! I am pleased at this.
But I hope you will look at the chapters once again, when they
are set *in pages*, after my last amendments; also at my discussions on Genesis i. 1–4, ii. 4–7, as i. and ii. of the thirty thorns
(in the Appendix, p. cxxxv.) which I have run into the weak
side of the Bible dragon, though less than one thirtieth of its
heaviest sins. I feel as if I had got over three quarters of the
work since I sent the eleven chapters and the thirty thorns into
the world. My holidays last till the 21st of October. Haug is
in the India House, over Minokhired and Parsi Bundehesh. If
you have a moment's time, look at my quiet polemic against you
and Burnouf in favor of Buddha, in reference to the Nirvâna.
Koeppen has given me much new material, although he is of
your opinion. I am quite convinced that Buddha thought on
this point like Tauler and the author of the "German Theology;" but he was an Indian and lived in desperate times. A
thousand thanks for the dove which you sent me out of the ark of
the Rig-Veda. I had sinned against the same hymn by translating
it according to Haug, as I had not courage enough to ask you
for more. And that leads me to tell you with what deep sympathy and melancholy pleasure your touching idyl has filled me.
You will easily believe me that after the first five minutes I saw
you vividly behind the mask. I thank you *very much* for having ordered it to be sent to me. I am very glad that you *have*
written it, for I would far rather see you mixing in the life of
the present and future, with your innate freshness and energy.
I must end. All love from me and Fanny to your incomparable
mother. So to our speedy meeting. Truly yours.

George will have arrived in London yesterday with wife and child; his darling Ella has a serious nervous affection, and they are to try sea air. He is much depressed.

[80.] CHARLOTTENBERG, *February* 17, 1858.

Your affectionate letter, my dear friend, has touched me deeply. First your unaltered love and attachment, and that you have perfectly understood me and my conduct in this affair. Naturally my fate will be very much influenced by it. I must be *every year* in Berlin: this year I shall satisfy myself with the last three weeks after Easter. In 1859 (as I shall spend the winter in Nice) I shall take my seat, when I return in April across the Alps. But later (and perhaps from 1859) I must not only live in Prussia, which is prescribed by good feeling and by the constitution, but I must stay for some time in Berlin. They all wish to have me there. God knows how little effort it costs me not to seek the place of Minister of Instruction, to say nothing of declining it, for everything is daily going more to *ruin*. But it could only be for a short time, and Bethmann-Hollweg, Usedom, and others can do the right thing just as well, and have time and youth to drag away the heavy cart of a Chinese order of business, which now consumes nine tenths of the time of a Prussian minister (who works twelve hours a day).

What I wish and am doing with my "Biblework," *you* will see between the lines of my first volume; other people, twelve months later, when my first volume of the Bible documents "comes out:" and even then they will not see where the concluding volume tends, — the world's history in the Bible, and the Bible in the world's history. Already in the end of 1857 I finished all of the first volume: the stereotyping goes on fearfully slow. You will receive one of the first copies which goes across the Channel; and you will read it at once, will you not? I am delighted that you are absorbed in *Eckart*: he is the key to Tauler, and there is nothing better, *except the Gospel of St. John*. For there stands still more clearly than in the other gospel writings, that the object of life in this world is to *found the Kingdom of God on earth* (as my friends the Taipings understand it also). Of this, Eckart and his scholars had despaired, just as much as Dante and his parody, Reineke Fuchs. You will find already many pious ejaculations of this kind in my two volumes of "God in History;" but I have deferred the closing

word till the sixth book, where *our* tragedy will be revealed, in
order to begin boldly with a new epos. I send you to-day four
sheets by book-post, "The Aryans in Asia;" for I cannot finish
it without your personal help. You will find that you have
already furnished a great portion of the matter. The same hymn
which I translated with difficulty and trouble from Haug's literal translation (in strophes which you however do not recognize?) (Ps. li.), you have translated for me, in your own
graceful manner, on a fly-sheet, and sent to me from Leipzig.
Of course I shall use this translation in place of my own. I
therefore venture to request that you will do the same with regard to the other examples which I have given. If you wish
to add anything *new*, it will suit perfectly, for everything fits in
at the end of the chapter: the number of the pages does not
come into consideration in the present stage. You will receive
the leaves on Saturday; it would be delightful if you could
finish them in the course of the following week, and send them
back to me. (We have a contract here with France, which
gives us a sort of book-post.) I expect next week the continuation of the Brahmanism and Buddha. I should like to send
both to you. The notes and *excursus* will only be printed at the
close of the volume, therefore not before May. The rest (Books
V., VI.) will be printed during the summer, to appear before
I cross the Alps. In this I develop the tragedy of the Romano-
Germanic world, and shall both gain many and lose many
friends by it. I have read your brilliant article on Welcker
with great delight. I possess it. Have you sent it (if
only anonymously) to the noble old man? He has deserved it.
The article makes a great noise, and will please him very much.
In fact, everything would give me undisturbed pleasure, did I
not see (even without your telling me, which, however, you have
done, as is the sacred duty between friends) that you are not
happy in yourself. Of *one* thing I am convinced, — you would
be just as little so, *even less*, in Germany, and least of all
among the sons of the Brahmans. If you continue to live as
you do now, you would everywhere miss England, — perhaps
also Oxford, if you went to London. Of this I am not clear:
in general a German lives far more freely in the World-city than
in the Don-city, where every English idiosyncrasy strengthens
itself, and buries itself in coteries. Unfortunately I have neither
read "Indophilus" nor "Philindus:" please tell me the numbers
of the "Times." I can get a copy of the "Times" here from

the library from month to month. Trevelyan is an excellent
man, occasionally unpractical and mistaken, always meaning
well and accessible to reason. But does any one *study* in London? *Dubito!* But I don't understand the plan of an Oriental College. Perhaps it is possible to undertake London without giving up Oxford entirely. The power of influencing the
young men, who after ten or twenty years will govern the
land, is far greater in Oxford or Cambridge than in London. I
am curious about your " German Reading Book."

I maintain one thing, — you are not happy ; and that comes
from your bachelor life. The progress of your Vedic work delights me : but how much in it is still a riddle ! Thus, for instance, the long hymn (2 Ashṭaka, third Adhyâya, Sûkta viii.
CLXIV.) p. 125. The hymn is first of all, as can be proved,
beyond verse 41 *not genuine ;* but even this older portion is late,
surely already composed on the Sarasvatî. The Veda is already
a finished book (verse 39), Brahma and Vishnu are gods (35, 86).
The whole is really wearisome, because it wishes to be mysterious without an idea. (See 4 Ashṭaka, seventh Adhyâya, vol. iii.
p. 463.) Is not Brahma there a god like Indra?

I depend on your marking all egregious blunders with a red
pencil. Many such must still have remained, leaving out of
view all differences of opinion. Tell me as much as you can
on this point in a letter, for on the Continent only notes for
press are allowed to go as a packet. (But of these you can
bring in as much as you wish : the copy is a duplicate.) At the
end I should much like to write something about the present
impossibility of enjoying the Rig-Veda, and of the necessity of a
spiritual key. But I do not quite know, first of all, whether one
can really enter upon the whole : there is much that is conventional and mortal by the side of what is imperishable. An
anthology in about two or three volumes would find a rapid
sale, and would only benefit a more learned and perfect edition.
If you have arrived at the same conclusion, *I will blow the
trumpet.*

George greets you heartily, as do his mother and sisters.
Perhaps I shall move in April, 1859, to Bonn ; *here* I shall *not*
stay. *Deus providebit.* With truest affection, yours.

Best remembrance to your mother. Have you read my preface to " Debit and Credit ? " I have poured out my heart
about Kingsley in the Introduction to the German " Hypatia,"
and told him that everybody must say to himself, sooner or
late, " Let the dead bury the dead."

[81.] CHARLOTTENBERG, *July* 31, 1858.

With threefold joy, my loved friend, have I heard the news through your great admirer Mme. Schwabe, of your charming intention of delighting us in August with a visit. *First*, on account of the plan itself: *then* because I can now compress into a few lines the endless letter I have so long had in my thoughts, to develop it in conversation according to my heart's desire; *thirdly*, because really since yesterday the day has come when the one half of the concluding volume (iii.) of "God in History" has gone to press, so that its appearing is secured. A letter to you, and a like debt to Lepsius, therefore open the list. And now before anything else receive my hearty *thanks* for your friendly and instructive letter, and what accompanied it *in Vedicis*. It came just at the right time, and you will see what use I made of it in the work.

And now here first come my *congratulations*. Nothing could be more agreeable and suitable; it is personally and nationally an honor, and an unique acknowledgment. I can only add the wish that you may enjoy the dignity itself as short a time as possible, and take leave as soon as possible of the Fellow-celibates of All Souls'. Your career in England wants nothing but this crowning-point. How prosperous and full of results has it been! Without ceasing to be a German, you have appropriated all that is excellent and superior in English life, and of that there is much, and it will last for life. I imagine you will bring your historical *Chrestomathy* with you, and propose to you, as you most probably give something out of the Heliand and Ulphilas, to reserve my Woluspa for the next edition, as I have just established the first tenable text of this divine poem, on which the brothers Grimm would never venture. I have had this advantage, of working on the good foundation of my studies (with a Danish translation) of 1815 from Copenhagen. Neither Magnusson, nor Munch, nor Bergmann has given the text of the only MS. (Cod. Regius); one has disfigured it with the latest interpolations, another with unauthorized transpositions. I have at last worked out the unity of the Helgi and the Sigurd songs with each other, and the oldest purely mythological stratum (the solar tragedy) of both, as an important link in the

in of evidence, for the reality of the God-Consciousness of kind and its organic laws. What people will say to the ults" (Book VI.) which fall into one's hands, I do not

I have been obliged to postpone the journey to Italy from September to November. October (the 23d) is the great crisis for Prussia, and I ought not to forsake the Fatherland then, and have willingly agreed not to do so. A brighter, better day is approaching. May God give his blessing. Every one must help; it is the highest time.

But nothing disturbs me from the work of my life. The fourth volume of the "Biblework" goes to press the day after to-morrow; on the 1st of September, the fifth (Documents I. a). I have now finished my preliminary work for the old Testament in the main points, and only reserved the last word before the stereotyping; so I begin at once on the New Testament and Life of Jesus. The friendly and clever notice of the first volume of the "Biblework" in the "Continental Review" gave me and my whole family *great pleasure;* and Bernays is here since yesterday (for August and September), which helps the printing of the Pentateuch very much, as I always sent him a last revise, and now all can be worked off here. I finish with Haug in the beginning of September; he will go probably to Poonah with his very sensible bride. Charles and Theodore are well. I expect George this week with Emilia for a visit. My family greet you. Bernays sighs. He has again made some *beautiful discoveries;* that of Aristotle (about the tragedies) I have carried further philosophically. Suggest to that good Arthur Stanley (to whom I have sent my "Biblework") to send me his "Palestine." I cannot get it here, and should like to say something about it.

With most true love, yours.

[82.]   CHARLOTTENBERG, *July 22, 1859.*

My sons know too well what delight they would give me through their confidential communication, which has already given us all a foretaste of the delight of your visit with your bride, and meanwhile has brought me your expected and affectionate letter.

I have felt all these years what was the matter with you, and I sympathize with your happiness as if it concerned one of my own children. I therefore now, my loved friend, wish you all the more happiness and blessing in the acquisition of the highest of life's prizes, because your love has already shown the right effect and strength, in that you have acquired courage for finishing at *this present time* your difficult and great work on the Vedas. The work will also give you further refreshment for the future, whilst the editing of the Veda still hangs on your hands.

Therefore let us all wish you joy most heartily (my wife has received the joyful news in Wildbad), and accept our united thanks beforehand for your kind intention of visiting us shortly with your young wife. By that time we shall all be again united here. Your remarkable mother will alone be wanting. Beg your bride beforehand to feel friendly towards me and towards us all. You know how highly I esteem her two aunts, though without personal acquaintance with them, and how dear to me is the cultivated, noble, Christian circle in which the whole family moves. I have as yet carried out my favorite plan with a good hope of success; six months in Charlottenberg on the true spiritually historical interpretation of the Old Testament, in the first volumes of the second division of the work (the so-called documents); six months of the winter on the "Life of Jesus," and what in my view immediately joins on to that. The first volume of the Bible documents is printed, *the Pentateuch.* You will see that I have handled Abraham and Moses as freely here as I did Zoroaster and Buddha in my last work; the explanation of the books and the history from Joram to Zedekiah is as good as finished.

We shall keep peace; Napoleon and Palmerston understand each other, and Palmerston is the *only* statesman in England and Europe who conceives rightly the Italian question. Russia follows him. I still hope by the autumn to be able to bless the God of free Italy beside Dante's and Machiavelli's graves. With us (Prussia) matters move fairly forwards; here they have been fools, and begin to feel ashamed of themselves. So a speedy and happy meeting.

Your heartily affectionate friend,
BUNSEN.

www.ingramcontent.com/pod-product-compliance
Lightning Source LLC
Chambersburg PA
CBHW021421300426
44114CB00010B/583